T0257622

IET COMPUTING SERIES 28

Security and Privacy for Big Data, Cloud Computing and Applications

IET Book Series on Big Data—Call for authors

Editor-in-Chief: Professor Albert Y. Zomaya, University of Sydney, Australia

The topic of Big Data has emerged as a revolutionary theme that cuts across many technologies and application domains. This new Book Series brings together topics within the myriad research activities in many areas that analyze, compute, store, manage and transport massive amounts of data, such as algorithm design, data mining and search, processor architectures, databases, infrastructure development, service and data discovery, networking and mobile computing, cloud computing, high-performance computing, privacy and security, storage and visualization.

Topics considered include (but not restricted to) IoT and Internet computing; cloud computing; peer-to-peer computing; autonomic computing; data center computing; multi-core and many core computing; parallel, distributed and high performance computing; scalable databases; mobile computing and sensor networking; green computing; service computing; networking infrastructures; cyber infrastructures; e-Science; smart cities; analytics and data mining; Big Data applications and more.

Proposals for coherently integrated International co-edited or co-authored handbooks and research monographs will be considered for this Book Series. Each proposal will be reviewed by the editor-in-chief and some board members, with additional external reviews from independent reviewers. Please email your book proposal for the IET Book Series on Big Data to: Professor Albert Y. Zomaya at albert.zomaya@sydney.edu.au or to the IET at author_support@theiet.org.

Security and Privacy for Big Data, Cloud Computing and Applications

Edited by
Wei Ren, Lizhe Wang, Kim-Kwang Raymond Choo
and Fatos Xhafa

The Institution of Engineering and Technology

Published by The Institution of Engineering and Technology, London, United Kingdom

The Institution of Engineering and Technology is registered as a Charity in England & Wales (no. 211014) and Scotland (no. SC038698).

© The Institution of Engineering and Technology 2019

First published 2019

The Institution of Engineering and Technology
Michael Faraday House
Six Hills Way, Stevenage
Herts, SG1 2AY, United Kingdom

www.theiet.org

British Library Cataloguing in Publication Data
A catalogue record for this product is available from the British Library

ISBN 978-1-78561-747-8 (hardback)
ISBN 978-1-78561-748-5 (PDF)

Typeset in India by MPS Limited

Contents

6 Security of marine-information system   **121**

Lin Mu and Jun Song

12   Privacy verification of PhotoDNA based on machine learning   **263**
Muhammad Shahroz Nadeem, Virginia N.L. Franqueira,
and Xiaojun Zhai

13   Chaos-based communication systems   **281**
Xiaojing Gao

About the editors

Wei Ren is a full professor at the School of Computer Science, China University of Geosciences (Wuhan), China. He has held positions as Department of Electrical and Computer Engineering, Illinois Institute of Technology, USA; the School of Computer Science, University of Nevada Las Vegas, USA and the Department of Computer Science, Hong Kong University of Science and Technology, Hong Kong. He has published more than 80 refereed papers as corresponding author, 1 monograph and 4 textbooks, and is a senior member of China Computer Federation.

Lizhe Wang is a "ChuTian" chair professor at the School of Computer Science, China University of Geosciences (CUG), China. He received B.E. and M.E from Tsinghua University and Doctor of Engineering from University of Karlsruhe (Magna Cum Laude), Germany. He is a fellow of IET, fellow of British Computer Society, and a series board member of the IET Book Series on Big Data. He serves as an associate editor of IJDE, Remote Sensing, IEEE TPDS, TCC and TSUSC. His main research interests include HPC, e-Science and remote sensing image processing.

Kim-Kwang Raymond Choo holds the Cloud Technology Endowed Professorship at the University of Texas, San Antonio, USA. His research interests include data analytics, cyber security and digital forensics. He is a Fellow of the Australian Computer Society and an IEEE Senior Member.

Fatos Xhafa holds a permanent position of Professor Titular d'Universitat (Hab. Full Professor) at the Departament de Ciències de la Computació, Universitat Politècnica de Catalunya, Barcelona, Spain. His research interests include parallel and distributed computing, combinatorial optimization, cloud, Grid and P2P computing, trustworthy computing.

Preface

This book is a collection of intellectual contributions on a broad range of security and privacy challenges and potential solutions, faced in big data, cloud computing and related applications.

The first chapter by Mengmeng Yang and Tianqing Zhu introduces the mathematical definitions, metrics and models relating to Big Data privacy preservation. This chapter also surveys various attacks related to different types of dataset and distinct application scenarios. Chapter 2, by Rui Xu, reviews the privacy preserving approaches for big data in cloud computing and outsourcing computation. The author also describes the multiple approaches that can be used to achieve privacy preserving data analysis, based on cryptographic tools (i.e., property-preserving encryption, searchable symmetric encryption and secure computation).

Following those two chapters, a range of security challenges is studied. Yongjun Zheng, Haider Ali and Umair Ullah Tariq provide an overview of security and privacy challenges relating to Big Data in an Internet of Things (IoT) environment, in Chapter 3. They also discuss the associated privacy and security approaches, with reference to the underpinning infrastructure, application and data, including Hadoop security, cloud security, monitoring, auditing, key management and anonymization. Liangli Ma, Jinyi Guo, Wei Ren and Yi Ren explore the security of image Big Data in Chapter 4, and they propose a watermark-based access control scheme to provide persistent fain-grained control by differentiating multiple layers or areas in a single image during data sharing. In Chapter 5, Rongyue Zheng, Jianlin Jiang, Xiaohan Hao and Wei Ren study the Building Information Model (BIM) Big Data in the construction automation industry. They also propose a blockchain-based method to provide provenance and audit for BIM data modification. They further propose a context-aware access control scheme for manipulating BIM Big Data in mobile cloud computing scenario. Lin Mu and Jun Song focus on Big Data in ocean information system in Chapter 6, where they discuss corresponding security requirements, security techniques and security systems.

In Chapter 7, Pooneh Nikkhah Bahrami, Ali Dehghantanha, Tooska Dargahi, Reza Parizi, Kim-Kwang Raymond Choo and Hamid H.S. Javadi propose a layered security architecture based on Cyber Kill Chain against Advanced Persistent Threats (APT). Their work can be used to inform defensive and mitigation strategy and policy formulation against prospective APT actors. Privacy-Aware Digital Forensics is studied in Chapter 8 by Ana Nieto, Ruben Rios and Javier Lopez. They seek to determine how to strike a balance between achieving privacy protection and performing digital forensics. They review existing privacy and digital forensic principles, prior to presenting a way to perform privacy-aware computer and network forensic investigation. Fatos Xhafa surveys the issues related to trust, trustworthiness and trustworthy computing in Chapter 9, where trust models for collaboration in virtual campuses, social networking, IoTs, MANETs, VANETs are reviewed and evaluated, and limitations in the trust models are explained. In Chapter 10, Yongfeng Qian and Min Chen study software-defined mobile networks security. Specifically, they discuss relevant security threats and their corresponding countermeasures with respect to the data layer, control layer, application layer and communication protocols. Chapter 11 by Shuaishuai Zhu, Xu An Wang and Yiliang Han presents dynamic public opinion evolvement modeling and supervision in social networks. They design and evaluate a model to supervise and optimize the public-opinion express in social networks. Muhammad Shahroz Nadeem, Virginia N.L. Franqueira and Xiaojun Zhai explain how one can perform a privacy verification of PhotoDNA based on machine learning in Chapter 12. As PhotoDNA is widely used to detect child exploitation/abuse materials, they attempt to evaluate the privacy protection capability of PhotoDNA. In Chapter 13, Xiaojing Gao investigates chaos-based secure communication systems that can be applied in applications such as mobile communications and cloud computing.

While we have taken efforts to minimize the errors in this book, it is inevitable that errors (e.g., typographical and/or grammatical errors) will be present. Hence, we invite you, the readers, to send us your valuable feedback at weirencs@cug.edu.cn, lizhe.wang@gmail.com, raymond.choo@fulbrightmail.org and fatos@lsi.upc.edu.

Chapter 1

Privacy preserving in big data

Mengmeng Yang[1] and Tianqing Zhu[2]

Due to the rapid growth of computers and the technology that is capable of capturing data, the data is increasing exponentially; they are collected from the everyday interactions with digital products or services, including mobile devices, information sensing, social media and so on. Big data gives us unprecedented insights and opportunities, but the collected big data contains a large amount of personal or sensitive information, which raises big privacy concerns. This chapter provides an extensive literature review on privacy attack models, privacy-preserving technologies and privacy metrics. We systematically analysis how the data privacy can be disclosed, what kind of privacy technology has been developed and how to evaluate the privacy provided by the proposed privacy-preserving method.

1.1 Privacy attacks

We classify the privacy attack models according to the type of the data set. Specifically, we survey the privacy attacks for tabular data set, graph data set, location data set and other applications.

1.1.1 Tabular data attack

The tabular data set is an arrangement of data in rows and columns; each row represents a record of an individual and each column is an attribute of the person. The form of the table is

$$D(Explicit - identifier, Quasi - identifier,$$
$$Sensitive - attributes, Non - sensitive\ attributes)$$

Explicit-identifier is a set of attributes that can identify the person's identity directly, such as the name. *Quasi-identifier* is a set of attributes that can potentially identify

[1]The Strategic Centre for Research in Privacy-Preserving Technologies and Systems (SCRIPTS), Nanyang Technological University, Singapore
[2] School of Software, University of Technology Sydney, Sydney, Australia

Job	Sex	Age	Disease
Engineer	Male	35	Hepatitis
Engineer	Male	38	Hepatitis
Lawyer	Male	38	HIV
Writer	Female	30	Flu
Writer	Female	30	Flu
Dancer	Female	30	HIV
Dancer	Female	30	HIV

(a)

Name	Job	Sex	Age
Alice	Writer	Female	30
Bob	Engineer	Male	35
Cathy	Writer	Female	30
Doug	Lawyer	Male	38
Emily	Dancer	Female	30
Fred	Engineer	Male	38
Gladys	Dancer	Female	30
Henry	Lawyer	Male	39
Irene	Dancer	Female	30

(b)

Figure 1.1   A degree attack [1]: (a) patient table and (b) external table

the person's identity. *Sensitive attributes* is a set of sensitive attributes such as disease and salary. *Non-sensitive attributes* is a set of attributes outside of previous scopes.

Normally, the data set is published without the *explicit-identifier*; however, it is not enough to protect the individual's privacy. Various attack models can be used to identify the person's identity or the sensitive information. We summaries the typical attack models as given next.

1.1.1.1   Record linkage attack

Record linkage attack identifies the victim's record in one table by linking the record to a record in another public table.

For example, a hospital published the patient records, as shown in Figure 1.1(a), assume the attacker has access to an external table shown in Figure 1.1(b), and the person who has the record in Figure 1.1(a) has the record in Figure 1.1(b). Joining the tables in the common attributes will link the victim's identity to his disease. For example, Bob is identified as a hepatitis patient by linking attributes < *Engineer*, *Male*, 35 > after the join. Minkus *et al.* [2] successfully identified the Facebook user who resides in the city by linking the Facebook user's social ties to the city's voter registration records.

1.1.1.2   Attributes linkage attack

Attributes linkage attack may not identify the record of the victim but can infer the victim's sensitive value by observing the sensitive values belong to the same group. For example, from Figure 1.1(a), the attacker can confidently infer that all the female writers at age 30 have Flu, and all the female dancers at age 30 have HIV.

Both record and attribute linkage attack assume that the attacker already knows that the victim's record already exists in the released table.

1.1.1.3   Table linkage attack

Table linkage attack identifies whether the victim's record exist in the released table. As in some cases, the presence or absence of the victim's record already reveals his sensitive information.

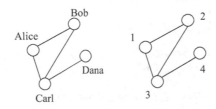

Figure 1.2   A degree attack

For example, assume Figure 1.1(a) ⊆ (b). There are three records in Figure 1.1(b) with attributes < *Dancer*, *Female*, 30 >, and two records in Figure 1.1(a) with same attributes. Therefore, the attacker can infer that Emily's record has 2/3 probability presents in Figure 1.1(a). The presence of her records reveals that she is an HIV patient.

1.1.2   Graph data attack [3]

The social network is a very popular platform where people make new friends and share their interests. More and more social network data are published for many applications, such as social network analysis and data mining. Unlike the case in traditional relational data sets, all identities in the social network are connected with each other by edges, which allow the attackers to launch the structural-based attacks.

Background knowledge plays an important role in modelling privacy attacks. This section summaries that the background knowledge can be used by the attacker to launch structure attack.

1.1.2.1   Vertices degree

Vertices degree represents the number of direct connections between a node and its neighbours. Once the degree of the user is different from others in the graph, the vertex is re-identified. For example, in Figure 1.2, nodes 3 and 4 can be identified directly if the adversary knows that Carl has three friends and Danna has only one friend.

Tai *et al.* [4] identified a new attack called friendship attack, which is based on degree pair of an edge. They launched both degree and friendship attacks on the 20Top-Conf data set and proved that the friendship attack causes a much more privacy disclosure than the degree attack.

1.1.2.2   Neighbourhood

Neighbourhood refers to the neighbours of an individual who have connections with each other. Attackers make use of this kind of structural information to identify individuals [5]. For example, in Figure 1.3, if attackers know Bob has three friends and two neighbours and they connected with each other, Bob can be recognized in the anonymized graph.

Ninggal *et al.* [6] proposed another kind of attack called neighbourhood-pair attack, which uses a pair of neighbourhood structural information as background

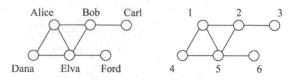

Figure 1.3   A neighbourhood attack

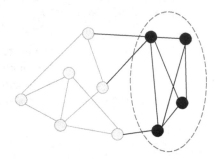

Figure 1.4   An embedded sub-graph attack

knowledge to identify victims. Such attacks assume that attackers know more information than neighbourhood attacks do, so attackers have a higher chance to distinguish users in a data set.

1.1.2.3   Embedded sub-graph

Sub-graph refers to a subset of the whole graph. Some adversaries create few fake nodes and build links using a specific way before the data is published and then match the target graph with reference graph based on the sub-graph which has been planted. In Figure 1.4, the grey part is the original graph and the black part is the sub-graph embedded by the adversary. Normally, the embedded sub-graph is unique and easy for attackers to identify after the data set is released.

1.1.2.4   Link relationship

The relationship between two vertices also can be acquired by an adversary. Wang *et al.* [7] considered that the public users' identities are public and not sensitive. They utilized the connection between victims and public users to perform attack. For example, in Figure 1.5, A, B and C are public users, such as BBC and Michael Jackson. Their identities are publicity, and if attackers know vertex d has one hop to A and C and two hops to B, d can be identified.

Sun *et al.* [8] committed a mutual friend attack. Their algorithm identifies a pair of users who connect to each other based on the number of mutual friends. For example, in Figure 1.6, the numbers on the edge represent the number of mutual friends between two nodes. If the adversary knows Alice and Ford have two mutual friends, then she/he can identify a and c combined with other reference information (e.g. degree).

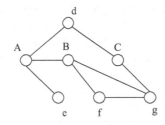

Figure 1.5   A fingerprint attack

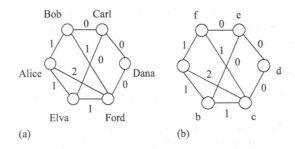

Figure 1.6   A mutual friends attack: (a) A and (b) B

1.1.2.5   Attributes of vertices

Attributes of individuals in a social network are represented as labels to vertices. Attackers may get the attributes of victims, such as age, sex and occupation. Such information can be helpful for adversaries to compromise users' privacy. For example, in Figure 1.6, if the attacker knows that Alice is a girl and Ford is a boy, he can identify them specifically by checking labelled sex information.

1.1.3   Location privacy attack

Location privacy disclosure happens when the location information leaves the user's sensing device. To hide the user's exact location information, privacy-preserving technologies performs on it. However, the user location information still can be inferred. We surveyed the location attack models in this section as follows.

1.1.3.1   Context linking attack

In the context linking attack, the attacker utilizes the context information of the victim to decrease the privacy. For example, Gruteser and Grunwald [9] proposed a *personal context linking attack*, which is based on personal context information, such as personal preferences and habits. For example, if the attacker knows the victim would like to visit the club at a certain time, and the victim simply protects his location by cloaking region, the attacker can increase the infer accuracy simply by decreasing the cloaking region to the club within the region. Krumm [10] proposed a *map matching attack* that decrease the obfuscated area by removing the irrelevant areas, such as lakes. Shokri *et al.* [11] proposed a *probability distribution attack*, which utilize the victim's distribution context information to infer the victim's location. Specifically, the attacker gets a probability distribution function of the user position in the obfuscated area. Then, the attacker can identify the area where the victim located at with high probability.

1.1.3.2   Region intersection attack

Region intersection attack [12] increases the precision of the obfuscated location by calculating the intersections between the user's multiply imprecise position updates or queries. The intersection can be used to infer the user's sensitive region. For example, to protect the user's trajectory information, a series of obfuscated regions are generated when the user reaches a spot. However, the intersection between the obfuscated regions reduces the user's privacy significantly.

1.1.3.3   Machine-learning-based attack

Li *et al.* [13] proposed a machine-learning-based attack method to infer users' demographics from the disclosed locations. To infer a specific attribute of a user, they identify a group of users who has similar location traces with each other and check the attributes of the users in the same group who set their attributes as public. Murakami and Watanabe [14] proposed a learning method, which uses matrix factorization to accurately estimate personalized transition matrices from a small amount of training data. They applied the proposed learning method to the localization attack, which identifies the real location of a user at a given time instant from an obfuscated trace.

1.1.4   Attacks for other applications

Various attack models are designed according to different application scenario. Except for the aforementioned attacks for tabular data, graph data and location privacy, privacy attacks happen in other applications as well.

For example, smart meters have been wildly used in more and more households. It brings convenience while raising privacy concern. The purpose of attacks in the smart meter is to infer the user's behaviour and habits by observing the power usage data. Dinesh *et al.* [15] utilized the uncorrelated spectral information of active power signals with low sampling rate to identify the turned-on residential appliances and estimate their energy consumption, which further discloses the user's behaviour. Greveler *et al.* [16] showed that the personal TV watching habits can be inferred by simply analysing the electricity usage profile. And in many cases, the view content also can by identified based on the smart meter power consumption data. Fan *et al.* [17] proposed a reactive power-based attack, which extracts reactive power-based appliance signatures, and identifies the turned-on events of the appliance based on each appliance's unique signature.

Privacy attack also happens in the recommendation system. The most popular one is the k nearest neighbour attack. Suppose the attacker knows m ratings of the items of an intended victim, the attacker can then compromise the victim's privacy by creating $k - 1$ fake users with the same ratings to replicate their recommendation list. In addition, van Moorsel [18] proposed an attack on contactless payments. Liu and Li [19] identified a collusion privacy attack against online friend search engine.

1.2 Privacy technologies

Various privacy technologies have been proposed in the past few decades. This section mainly surveys three categories: the encryption-based methods, anonymization methods and differential privacy-related methods. We also discussed other new developed privacy technologies in the last section.

1.2.1 Encryption

Encryption is a direct method to protect the user's data. Nobody can know the other user's data without description. Therefore, the user's data can be stored safely in the application server or the cloud. However, the encrypted data cannot contribute to the various services and is meaningless to the researchers.

One class of approaches is access control that the data owner grants the specific person access to these encrypted data. For example, Qian *et al.* [20] proposed that the personal health record (PHR) should be encrypted before outsourcing it to the cloud, and the patent should be able to decide who can access what kind of PHR. Only the users with the corresponding secret keys can access the corresponding encrypted PHRs. Ruj *et al.* [21] proposed a decentralized access control scheme for secure data storage in the cloud, and the proposed scheme supports anonymous authentication that the cloud verifies the authenticity of the user without knowing his identity.

Another class of methods is utilizing some encryption technologies that allows performance over encrypted data. There are mainly two technologies: secure multiparty computing and homomorphic encryption.

1.2.1.1 Secure multiparty computing

Secure multiparty computing was originally introduced by Yao [22], and it allows different parties to jointly collaborate to compute a specific function on their private data, while preserving the data privacy of each party. The secure multiparty computing ensures the independence of the input and the correctness of the calculation without disclosing the input value to other participants in the calculation. Secure multiparty computation has many applications in the area where people need to operate numbers which are sensitive and private.

Tso *et al.* [23] introduced a method to prevent data disclosure from inside attack in wireless medical sensor networks. The proposed method is based on the secure multiparty computation protocol and has been implemented in the FairplayMp framework. Also, the proposed approach supports private-preserving data mining for medical data stored in the distributed hospitals or institutions. Wang *et al.* [24] proposed a privacy-preserving protocol to estimate the edit distance between two genome sequence. The secure multiparty computation technology is used to compute the set intersection. Secure multiparty is also used in point of interest recommendation [25] that provides the users accurate PoIs without disclosing their real-location information.

Secure multiparty computing is designed for few sides security calculations, and it is not easy to expand to a collaborative environment that has many users, because the cost of calculation increases exponentially. Therefore, secure multiparty computing is not widely used for deep-learning techniques.

1.2.1.2   Homomorphic encryption

Homomorphic encryption was proposed by Rivest *et al.* [26] in 1987. It is a way of encryption method that allows the computation over ciphertexts. The calculation result over ciphertexts, when decrypted, matches the result of the operation performed on the plaintext. The purpose of homomorphic encryption is to allow certain operations to perform on the encrypted data without disclosing the original data information.

Homomorphic encryption is widely used in various areas. For example, Alabdulatif *et al.* [27] applied it to the data-clustering tasks. They introduced a distributed data-processing framework, which is based on a fully homomorphic. The proposed framework utilizes MapReduce to perform distributed computations on a large number of cloud virtual machines. Abdallah and Shen [28] proposed a lightweight lattice-based homomorphic privacy-preserving data-aggregation scheme for the residential electricity consumers in the smart grid. Kim *et al.* [29] studied the privacy problem in matrix factorization-based recommendation system and proposed the first privacy-preserving matrix factorization using fully homomorphic encryption. Homomorphic encryption is also used for privacy-preserving anomaly detection [27], outsourced calculation of rational numbers [30] and location-based services [31]. However, due to the large computational overhead, most of them are still far from being ready to use in practical applications.

1.2.2   Anonymization

Data anonymization is a very important method for preserving data. It is a type of information sanitization that removes the personal identifiable information, so that the person cannot be identified from the data or the sensitive attributes cannot be matched to the specific person.

1.2.2.1   *k*-Anonymity

k-Anonymity [32] is the most popular anonymity technology, which was first introduced by Sweeney and Samarati in 1998. We say the release data satisfy *k*-anonymity if the information for each person cannot be distinguished from at least $k - 1$ other individuals in the same data set. That is, the personal information is hidden in a group that each individual in the group has the same information with each other and cannot be distinguished. The group is referred to the equivalence class.

k-Anonymity can be used in various application domains, including location-based service [33,34], clustering [35], Internet of Things [36] and so on. For location-based services, multiple ways can be used to achieve *k*-anonymity. For example, Niu *et al.* [33] proposed a dummy-location selection algorithm to protect user's location privacy against adversaries with side information. In the dummy locations methods, $k - 1$ false locations are reported together with the user's real location to guarantee *k*-anonymity. Song *et al.* [37] protected the private location by applying cloaking region technology that satisfies k-anonymity by including at k users' locations in the cloaked region.

k-Anonymity is easy to achieve and widely used; however, it only considers the identity without considering the sensitive attributes. If all the sensitive values in the equivalence class are the same, the user's sensitive information will be disclosed.

1.2.2.2 *l*-Diversity

l-Diversity solves the weakness of the k-anonymity by requiring the equivalence class has at least l different sensitive values. That is, l-diversity protects the user's sensitive information by increasing the diversity of the sensitivity value in the equivalence class.

A stronger notation of l-diverse is the definition of *entropy l-diversity*, which is defined as follows:

Definition 1.1 (entropy *l*-diverse). *An equivalence class is entropy l-diverse if the entropy of the distribution of the sensitive value is at least* $\log(l)$:

$$- \sum_{s \in S} P(QID, s)\log(P(QID, s)) \geq \log(l) \tag{1.1}$$

s indicates the sensitive value and the $P(QID, s)$ indicates the proportion of s in equivalence class.

Though the l-diversity considers the diversity of sensitive values in the equivalence class, it does not consider the distribution of the sensitive values. Though the released data satisfy the l-diversity, if one sensitive value accounts for a large proportion in the equivalence class, the user's information will be easily disclosed by skewness attack.

1.2.2.3 *t*-Closeness

t-Closeness [38] improves the l-diversity by requiring the distribution of the sensitive value in the equivalence class close to the corresponding distribution in the original data set. That is, the distance between the distribution of the sensitive value in the original data set and equivalence class is bounded by t.

Many other extensions are also be proposed, for example (α, k)-anonymity [39], (k, e)-anonymity [40] and m-invariance [41]. Most of these methods add the different constraint on the sensitive values in the equivalence class, which enhanced the privacy protection. However, the anonymization method does not consider the attacker's background knowledge. User's sensitive information and even the identity can easily be disclosed once the attacker holds the corresponding background knowledge.

1.2.3 Differential privacy

Differential privacy, a powerful privacy model, is widely accepted for providing rigorous privacy guarantees for aggregate data analysis. In this section, we study the details of the differential privacy technology and its extensions.

1.2.3.1   Differential privacy

Differential privacy is a provable privacy notation, developed by Dwork *et al.* [42] that has emerged as an essential standard for preserving privacy in a variety of areas. It was originally introduced for statistical databases, requiring that changes to a single data record should result in no statistical differences to a query's output. The formal definition of differential privacy is stated next.

Definition 1.2 (ε-differential privacy). *A randomized algorithm $\mathcal{M}$ gives ε-differential privacy for any pair of neighbouring data sets D and D' where, for every set of outcomes Ω, $\mathcal{M}$ satisfies:*

$$Pr[\mathcal{M}(D) \in \Omega] \leq \exp(\varepsilon) \cdot Pr[\mathcal{M}(D') \in \Omega] \tag{1.2}$$

Data sets D and D' are neighbouring data sets, which only differ in one individual record. This definition ensures that the presence or absence of an individual will not significantly affect the output of the query.

Normally, the differential privacy can be achieved by adding random noise to the results of the query. *Laplace* mechanism and *exponential* mechanism are the two mechanisms that are usually used. The definitions are shown as follows:

Definition 1.3 (*Laplace* mechanism). *Given a function $f : D \rightarrow \mathbb{R}$ over a data set D, Definition 1.3 provides ε-differential privacy:*

$$\widehat{f}(D) = f(D) + Laplace\left(\frac{s}{\varepsilon}\right) \tag{1.3}$$

Definition 1.4 (*exponential* mechanism). *Let $q(D, r)$ be a score function of the data set D that measures the score of outputting r. Then the exponential mechanism $\mathcal{M}$ satisfy ε-differential privacy if:*

$$\mathcal{M}(D) = return \propto exp\left(\frac{\varepsilon q(D, r)}{2\Delta q}\right) \tag{1.4}$$

$\Delta q = \max \|q(D, r) - q(D', r)\|$, *which is the sensitivity of q.*

A *Laplace* mechanism is used for numeric output, and an *exponential* mechanism is used for non-numeric output. Both mechanisms are associated with the sensitivity, which determines how much perturbation is needed. Two types of sensitivity are usually used in differential privacy: the global sensitivity [43], which measures the maximal change over all the neighbour data sets, and the local sensitivity [44], which measures the change over the records related to the query. The details are shown as follows:

Definition 1.5 (global sensitivity). *For a query $Q : D \rightarrow \mathbb{R}$, the global sensitivity of Q is defined as follows:*

$$GS = \max_{D,D'} \|Q(D) - Q(D')\|_1 \tag{1.5}$$

Definition 1.6 (local sensitivity). *For a query $Q : D \rightarrow \mathbb{R}$, the global sensitivity of Q is defined as follows:*

$$LS = \max_{D'} \|Q(D) - Q(D')\|_1 \tag{1.6}$$

Observe that the global sensitivity from Definition 1.5 is $GS = \max_x LS$. The global sensitivity is widely used, but it only considers the worst case that induces much redundant noise to the output. Local sensitivity avoids the unnecessary noise by only considering the query-related records.

Two privacy budget compositions [45] are widely used in the design of mechanisms [63]: the sequential composition and the parallel composition, as defined in Definition 1.7 and Definition 1.8, respectively.

Definition 1.7. Sequential composition: *Suppose a method* $\mathcal{M} = \{\mathcal{M}_1, \ldots, \mathcal{M}_m\}$ *has m steps, and each step* $\mathcal{M}_i$ *provides* ε *privacy guarantee, the sequence of* $\mathcal{M}$ *will provide* $(m \times \varepsilon)$-differential privacy.

Definition 1.8. Parallel composition: *Suppose a method* $\mathcal{M} = \{\mathcal{M}_1, \ldots, \mathcal{M}_m\}$ *has m steps, and each step* $\mathcal{M}_i$ *provides* ε *privacy guarantee on a disjointed subset of the entire data set, the parallel of* $\mathcal{M}$ *will provide* $\max \varepsilon_1, \ldots, \varepsilon_m$-differential privacy.

The *sequential composition* measures the privacy level for a sequence of differentially private computations. When a series of randomized mechanisms have been performed sequentially on a same data set, the total privacy guarantee proposed will be calculated by adding up the privacy budgets for each step. The *parallel composition* applies to the situation where each $\mathcal{M}_i$ is applied on disjointed subsets of the data set. The ultimate level of privacy guarantee only depends on the largest privacy budget.

1.2.3.2 Extensions of differential privacy

With the application of the traditional differential privacy, many extensions are proposed to solve more complex problems. We review the proposed new differential privacy mechanisms in this section.

Approximate differential privacy [46]

For a given metric on the input space, differential privacy requires that the distance between two neighbouring inputs is at most 1 and the probability that the outputs of performing the random algorithm differs at most $\exp(\varepsilon)$. Approximate differential privacy relaxes this requirement by additionally allowing for an additive slack δ. Specifically,

Definition 1.9 ((ε, δ)-differential privacy). *A randomized algorithm* $\mathcal{M}$ *gives* (ε, δ)-*differential privacy for any pair of neighbouring data sets D and D$'$ where, for every set of outcomes* Ω, $\mathcal{M}$ *satisfies:*

$$Pr[\mathcal{M}(D) \in \Omega] \leq \exp(\varepsilon) \cdot Pr[\mathcal{M}(D') \in \Omega] + \delta \tag{1.7}$$

Approximate differential privacy weakens the privacy guarantee but allows data release results more accurate. Many privacy-preserving methods are based on approximate differential privacy, for example Du *et al.* [47] proposed a differential privacy-based query model for sustainable fog-computing supported data centre. Lin *et al.* [48] designed two frameworks for privacy-preserving auction-based incentive mechanisms that achieve approximate social cost minimization.

Distributed differential privacy [46]

Traditional differential privacy considers a trusted aggregator who can access the participants' real data and release the perturbed statistics. However, the aggregator might be untrusted. To solve this problem, Emura [49] proposed the concept of distributed differential privacy, which extended the approximate differential privacy to a setting that the distributed entities contribute the perturbed data to the control aggregator. The aggregator can be untrusted and possibly colludes with a subset of the participants.

Definition 1.10 ((ε, δ)-distributed differential privacy). *Suppose $\varepsilon > 0, 0 \le \delta \le 1$ and $0 < \gamma \le 1$. We day that the data-randomization procedure, given by the joint distribution $r := (r_1, \ldots, r_n)$ and the randomization mechanism $\mathcal{M}$, achieves (ε, δ)-distributed differential privacy with respect to the mechanism $\mathcal{M}$ and under γ fraction of uncompromised participants if the following condition holds:*

$$Pr[\mathcal{M}(D) \in \Omega] \le \exp(\varepsilon) \cdot Pr[\mathcal{M}(D') \in \Omega] + \delta \tag{1.8}$$

Joy [50] believed that the released aggregate information under distributed privacy protection only reveals the underlying ground truth distribution and nothing else, and they proposed a sampling mechanism, which achieves differential privacy in the distributed setting. Distributed differential privacy is also widely used in the situation that answering queries about the privacy data that is spread across multiple different databases. Narayan and Haeberlen [51] introduced two new primitives, BN-PSI-CA and DCR, that can be used to answer queries over distributed databases with differential privacy guarantees. Zhang *et al.* [52] addressed the problem of distributed knowledge extraction with differential privacy guarantee in the data mining.

Joint differential privacy [46]

Private matching and allocation problems have not been considered in the differential privacy literature. While Kearns *et al.* [53] introduced a variant which they call joint differential privacy, which requires that simultaneously for every player i, the joint distribution on the suggested actions to all players $j \ne i$ be differentially private in the type of agent i.

Definition 1.11 (joint differential privacy). *A mechanism $\mathcal{M}$ satisfies (ε, δ)-joint differential privacy if for every i, any pair of i-neighbours D, D', and for every subset of outputs $\Omega \subseteq \mathscr{R}^{n-1}$:*

$$Pr[\mathcal{M}(D)_{-i} \in \Omega] \le \exp(\varepsilon) \cdot Pr[\mathcal{M}(D'_{-i}) \in \Omega] + \delta \tag{1.9}$$

Later, Hsu *et al.* [54] gave algorithms to accurately solve the private allocation problem when bidders have gross substitute valuations using joint differential privacy. Tong *et al.* [55] studied the location privacy problem in the scheduling of ridesharing services. They proposed a jointly differentially private scheduling protocol for protecting riders' location information and minimizing the total additional vehicle mileage in the ridesharing system.

Geo-indistinguishability

Andrés *et al.* [56] proposed the concept of geo-indistinguishability, which extended the traditional differential privacy to the location privacy scenarios. The main idea behind this notion is that, for any radius $r > 0$, the user enjoys εr- privacy within r. The level of privacy is proportional to the radius r. The details of definition is shown as follows.

Definition 1.12 (geo-indistinguishability). *A mechanism K satisfies ε-geo-indistinguishability if for all x, x':*

$$d_p(K(x), K(x')) \leq \varepsilon d(x, x') \tag{1.10}$$

For all points x' within a radius r from x, the definition forces the corresponding distributions to be at most εr distant.

Geo-indistinguishability is widely used for protecting the location privacy [57–60]. For example, Wang *et al.* [60] solved the location privacy problem in mobile crowdsensing application. The uploaded locations for optimal task allocation are protected under geo-indistinguishability guarantee. Mao *et al.* [61] presented a scheme for aggregating the installation ratio for applications with privacy-preserving on mobile devices. Hua *et al.* [62] proposed an improved geo-indistinguishability location-perturbation mechanism for location-based services, which significantly reduced the privacy cost and can support multiple queries.

1.2.4 Other technologies

Except the aforementioned privacy-preserving technologies, more new technologies are being proposed. For example, caching and game theory.

1.2.4.1 Caching

Caching system has been proposed to enhance the privacy in various application scenario by prefetching the data on a device before it is actually needed [63]. The data can be accessed locally when it is needed, which reduces the interaction between the user and the service providers and reduces the risk of privacy information exposure. Caching method is widely used in location-based services.

Peng *et al.* [64] proposed a collaborative trajectory privacy preserving scheme for continuous queries in which trajectory privacy is ensured by caching-aware collaboration between users, and no need for any fully trusted parties. The main idea behind the proposed algorithm is that it allows the mobile user to communicate with multi-hop neighbours and share the valid information between each other. Users' collaborative caching reduces the number of queries sent to the server, thereby reducing the amount of private information exposed to the server. Zhang *et al.* [65] proposed a caching-based method to protect location privacy in continuous location-based services. The proposed scheme adopts a two-level caching mechanism to cache the users' result data at both the client and the anonymizer sides. Liu *et al.* [66] proposed a framework which enhances the privacy of location-based services by actively caching in the wireless vehicular network scenario. Niu *et al.* [67] proposed a privacy metric to model the effect of caching. In addition, they proposed a caching-aware dummy selection algorithm, which is combined with multiple privacy technologies and side information to achieve a higher privacy degree.

1.2.4.2   Game theory

Game theory is the study of mathematical models of strategic interaction between rational decision-makers [68]. Game theory answers the question of how the defender react to the attacker. The strategic interaction between them is captured by a two-player game where each player tries to maximize his or her own interests. The effectiveness of a defence mechanism relies on both of the defender's and attacker's strategic behaviours.

Recent years, game theory has been applied in privacy-preserving area. For example, Wu *et al.* [69] studied the privacy problem in correlated data publishing. They modelled the trade-off problem between privacy and utility as a game problem, and analysed the utility efficiency of the proposed method from the point of game theory. Khaledi *et al.* [70] investigated attacks where a person's location can be inferred using the radio characteristics of wireless links and modelled the radio network leakage attack using a Stackelberg game. They used a greedy method to obtain the optimal strategy for the defender. The experimental results showed that the proposed game theoretic solution significantly reduces the chance of an attacker to infer the user's location.

1.3   Privacy metrics

The privacy metrics are used to evaluate the privacy level in a system or the privacy protection level provided by the proposed privacy protection method. A large number of metrics have been proposed in the literature. We categorize the existing privacy metrics according to the output of the algorithms.

1.3.1   Uncertainty

Uncertainty means the situation in which something is not known or not certain. The uncertainty metrics in the privacy area evaluate how far the attacker's estimation is to the certain correct value. Most uncertainty metrics are built on anonymity parameter and entropy. We review the related matrices in the following section.

1.3.1.1   Anonymity parameter

Some literature protect the user's privacy by hiding an individual or the sensitive attribute in an anonymity set in which the attacker cannot identify the correct one. The most popular one is the *k-anonymity*. The size of the anonymity set is k, the user's information cannot be identified to the other $k - 1$ users. Therefore, the privacy level can be measured by the size of the anonymity set as

$$PM = k \tag{1.11}$$

Similar to k-anonymity, the extensions of k-anonymity try to protect the sensitive attributes by adding some qualifications. The qualification can be used to evaluate the privacy-preserving level.

For example, (α, k)-*anonymity* [39] requires the frequency of the single sensitive value in the equivalence class has to be less than α. Therefore, the privacy level can be evaluated by

$$PM = (\alpha, k) \tag{1.12}$$

Smaller α indicate higher privacy protection, as the probability of inferring the victim's sensitive attributes becomes lower.

(k, e)-*Anonymity* [40] additionally requires the range of the attributes in the equivalence class must be greater than e. Bigger e and k indicate higher privacy level. Therefore,

$$PM = (k, e) \tag{1.13}$$

l-Diversity bounds the diversity of sensitive information. Similar with (k, e)-anonymity, l-diversity requires l distinct values in each equivalence class. Therefore, the privacy level can be evaluated by

$$PM = l \tag{1.14}$$

The main weakness of this metric is that it only counts the number of records in the anonymity set and does not consider the attacker's background knowledge. If the attacker holds some background knowledge, it cannot provide the corresponding level of privacy protected measured by the anonymity set size.

1.3.1.2 Entropy

The entropy in the information theory refers to disorder or uncertainty. When a lower probability event occurs, the event carries more information than the higher probability event happens. As a privacy metric, the entropy measures the uncertainty associated with inferring the sensitive value of an individual.

Shannon entropy [71] is the basis for many other metrics. The Shannon entropy is defined as follows:

$$H(X) = -\sum_{x_i \in X} p(x_i)\log_2 p(x_i) \tag{1.15}$$

x_i is the value in the set of all possible values, $p(x_i)$ is the probability of the value $p(x_i)$ to be the target.

Max-entropy [72] is the upper bound of the Shannon entropy. It is a conservative measure of how certain the adversary is of his estimate. Specifically:

$$H_{\max} = \log_2 |X| \tag{1.16}$$

The max-entropy only depends on the size of the variable values set, which represents the ideal privacy situation for the user.

Min-entropy is the lower bound of Shannon entropy, which is the worst case scenario because it only depends on the user for whom the adversary has the highest probability regardless of whether this is also the true outcome [73]. Specifically:

$$H_{\min} = -\log_2 \max p_{x \in X}(x) \tag{1.17}$$

Puglisi *et al.* [74] used Shannon's entropy as the measure of user privacy in social tagging systems. Parra-Arnau *et al.* [75] investigated mathematically the privacy utility trade-off posed by the suppression of tags, measuring privacy as Shannon's entropy of the perturbed profile. Peters and Maxemchuk [76] used Shannon entropy to compare the performance of the distributed application to a centralized one regarding storing and processing electronic health records. In [77] and [11], min-entropy is considered rather than the usual Shannon entropy.

Rényi [78] introduced *Rényi entropy*, which is a more general metric that based on Shannon entropy. The formula is shown as follows:

$$H_\alpha(X) = \frac{1}{1-\alpha}\log_2 \sum_{x\in X} p(x)^\alpha \qquad (1.18)$$

The Shannon entropy is the special case when $\alpha \to 1$. Also, the more α grows, the more Rényi entropy approaches to min-entropy, and the more α reduces to zero, the more Rényi entropy approaches to max-entropy.

Conditional entropy is used to measure the attacker's uncertainty about the user's real sensitive information when the prior knowledge is known. The uncertainty of the attacker regarding the value of x given z can be measured as the entropy of the posterior as follows:

$$H(x|z) = -\sum_{x\in X} p(x|z)\log(p(x|z)) \qquad (1.19)$$

Oya *et al.* [79] utilized the conditional entropy to justify the defences created by the proposed strategies for location privacy-preserving. Wang and Jia [80] used it to quantify the degree of disclosure risk in a medical data publishing. Osia *et al.* [81] verified and evaluated the privacy of the features extracted by the private feature extractor using conditional entropy.

There are also many other entropy-based metrics, such as *unreliability*, that measures the attacker's uncertainty about which items are related; *cross-entropy* that measures the uncertainty in predicting the original data set from the clustered model and *Kullback–Leibler divergence* [82] evaluates the distance between two distribution. Readers can refer to paper [83] for more entropy-based metrics.

Although entropy has an intuitive interpretation of the information that the attacker needs, the value of entropy does not convey many meaning [77]. The entropy indicates the attacker's uncertainty but does not state how accurate the attacker's estimation is [11]. In addition, many literatures argue that the entropy is strongly influenced by outlier values as the privacy metric (i.e. if some element of the probability distribution is very unlikely, the entropy of the source increases very much [73]).

1.3.2 Error/Accuracy

1.3.2.1 Error

The error metrics quantify the error the attacker makes to infer the user the real information. This type of metrics is applicable to all domains and widely used in recommendation system and location privacy.

Mean square error (MSE) describes the error between observations x by the attacker and the true output x' of the query:

$$MAE = \frac{1}{|X|} \sum_{x \in X} \|x - x'\|^2 \tag{1.20}$$

Meng *et al.* [84] used MSE to evaluate the privacy protection level by conducting reconstruction attack on the rating data set. MSE is also used in reconstructing user data in participatory sensing [85]. In addition, the MSE is widely used as the utility metric in the literature as well. For example, Tan *et al.* [86] used it to evaluate the image quality, and Wang *et al.* [87] used MSE to measure the utility loss in anonymized mobile-context streams.

Similar metrics, such as root MSE (RMSE) [88] and mean absolute error (MAE) [88], are also used to measure the accuracy. For example, Polatidis *et al.* [89] used both RMSE and MAE to measure the accuracy of generated recommendations of the proposed protection method.

Expected estimation error [11] measures the expected distance between the real value and estimated value. The estimation is computed over the posterior probability of the attacker's estimation x on his or her observation y. Specifically:

$$Error = \sum_{x \in X} p(x|y)d(x, x') \tag{1.21}$$

$d(\cdot)$ is the distance metric. In location privacy, $d(\cdot)$ measures the distance between the estimated location and the true location, $p(x|y)$ means the probability that the attacker infers the location is x based on the observed location y. The bigger the value error, the stronger the protection of the user's location.

Hoh and Gruteser [90] proposed a similar distance error, called *expectation of distance error*, which captures how accurate the attacker can estimate the user's position. The metric is defined as follows:

$$Error = \frac{1}{nT} \sum_{t \in T} \sum_{h \in \mathcal{H}} p_{h,t}(x)d_{h,t}(x, x') \tag{1.22}$$

n is the number of users and T is the total observation time. $d_{h,t}(x, x')$ indicates the distance error between the real location and the location in hypothesis space $\mathcal{H}$ at time step t.

These distance-based privacy metrics can also be used in other application scenarios if an appropriate distance metric is available. For example, the distance metric used in paper [91] depends on how the values of genetic variations are encoded.

Percentage incorrectly classified measures the percentage of incorrectly classified users or events. This metric is wildly used in machine-learning area for classification application:

$$Error = \frac{|I'|}{|I|} \tag{1.23}$$

I' indicates the incorrect classification. $|I|$ is the size of the instance set.

Kathwadia and Patel [92] studies the privacy-preserving data-mining problem and evaluate the performance of the proposed method by analysing the incorrectly classified instance. Narayanan and Shmatikov [93] used it to measure how often the highest probability in the attacker's estimate does not correspond to true genotype.

1.3.2.2 Accuracy

Accuracy metrics quantify the accuracy of the attacker's estimation. The inaccurate estimate indicates higher privacy protection. Most metrics in this category are used to measure the geographic precision in location-based services.

Size of uncertainty region [94] represents the minimum region that the attacker can narrow down to locate the target user's location. This metric is used for the cloaking-region-based location privacy-preserving method. The user's location is hiding in a cloaking region, the bigger the size of the final region for the attacker, the higher is the level of protection provided:

$$PM = Area(R) \tag{1.24}$$

where R refers to the cloaking region.

Coverage of sensitive region is another expression form, which is shown as follows:

$$PM = Area\left(\frac{R_s \cap R}{R}\right) \tag{1.25}$$

R_s is the sensitive region for a user and R is the attacker's uncertainty region. Equation (1.25) indicates the proportion that the attacker can link the user's location to his sensitive region.

Confidence interval width [95] is a type of interval estimate, computed from the statistics of the observed data, that might contain the true value of an unknown variable. The privacy at confidence coefficient γ is given by the width of confidence region $[u(X), v(X)]$ for the attacker's estimation:

$$PM = |u(X) - v(X)|, p(u(X) \le x \le v(X)) = \frac{\gamma}{100} \tag{1.26}$$

The confidence level is designated prior to examining the data. Most commonly, the 95% confidence level is used.

1.3.3 Indistinguishability

Indistinguishability metrics indicate whether the attacker can distinguish the real sensitive value of the user from the other values. Most of these metrics are associated with differential privacy mechanism.

Differential privacy states that the outputs of the random mechanism performed on the two neighbour data sets differ by at most e^ε. That is, today the value of a variable to be protected cannot be distinguished with other values under differential privacy protection. The ε measures the biggest difference between the true value and the other values. The smaller value of ε indicates higher privacy protection.

Most extensions of differential privacy are based on the approximate differential privacy that introduces a slack parameter δ relaxes the requirement of traditional differential privacy. For example, distributed differential privacy and joint differential privacy. The smaller ε and δ, the more difficult for the attacker to identify the real value of the variable. When $\delta = 0$, the method satisfies pure differential privacy.

Geo-indistinguishability is also an extension of the traditional differential privacy, and it is applied to the location privacy scenarios. The privacy level depends on the privacy budget ε and the radius r. The user's location is protected under geo-indistinguishability guarantee, which meaning that the user's true location cannot be distinguished with other locations in the region with radius r by the attacker.

1.4 Summary

Big data has great potential to revolutionize our lives through its predictive power and provide insights far beyond what we know about ourselves. It has become a necessity in today's world. It is expected to grow exponentially in the coming years. Big data has brought us great benefits; however, it can also cause great privacy issues. This chapter surveys various attacks that happened on different types of data set and different application scenarios, the privacy technologies and privacy metrics that how to evaluate the privacy level based on different privacy-preserving methods. Most privacy-preserving methods can only deal with single type of privacy attack, while new attack models keep coming up. Therefore, it is a very big challenge to design the privacy-preserving methods that can deal with multiple types of attack and defend the new developed attack.

References

[1]   Wang K, Chen R, Fung B, *et al.* Privacy-preserving data publishing: A survey on recent developments. ACM Computing Surveys. ACM; 2010. p. 1–53.

[2]   Minkus T, Ding Y, Dey R, *et al.* The city privacy attack: Combining social media and public records for detailed profiles of adults and children. In: Proceedings of the 2015 ACM on Conference on Online Social Networks. ACM; 2015. p. 71–81.

[3]   Yang M, Zhu T, Zhou W, *et al.* Attacks and countermeasures in social network data publishing. ZTE Communications. 2016;2:1.

[4]   Tai CH, Yu PS, Yang DN, *et al.* Privacy-preserving social network publication against friendship attacks. In: Proceedings of the 17th ACM SIGKDD International Conference on Knowledge Discovery and Data Mining. ACM; 2011. p. 1262–1270.

[5]   Zhou B, and Pei J. The k-anonymity and l-diversity approaches for privacy preservation in social networks against neighborhood attacks. Knowledge and Information Systems. 2011;28(1):47–77.

[6]   Ninggal MIH, and Abawajy JH. Neighbourhood-pair attack in social network data publishing. In: International Conference on Mobile and Ubiquitous Systems: Computing, Networking, and Services. Springer; 2013. p. 726–731.

[7]   Wang Y, and Zheng B. Preserving privacy in social networks against connection fingerprint attacks. In: Data Engineering (ICDE), 2015 IEEE 31st International Conference on. IEEE; 2015. p. 54–65.

[8]   Sun C, Philip SY, Kong X, *et al.* Privacy preserving social network publication against mutual friend attacks. In: Data Mining Workshops (ICDMW), 2013 IEEE 13th International Conference on. IEEE; 2013. p. 883–890.

[9]   Gruteser M, and Grunwald D. Anonymous usage of location-based services through spatial and temporal cloaking. In: Proceedings of the 1st International Conference on Mobile Systems, Applications and Services. ACM; 2003. p. 31–42.

[10] Krumm J. Inference attacks on location tracks. In: International Conference on Pervasive Computing. Springer; 2007. p. 127–143.

[11] Shokri R, Theodorakopoulos G, Le Boudec JY, *et al.* Quantifying location privacy. In: Security and Privacy (sp), 2011 IEEE Symposium on. IEEE; 2011. p. 247–262.

[12] Talukder N, and Ahamed SI. Preventing multi-query attack in location-based services. In: Proceedings of the Third ACM Conference on Wireless Network Security. ACM; 2010. p. 25–36.

[13] Li H, Zhu H, Du S, *et al.* Privacy leakage of location sharing in mobile social networks: Attacks and defense. IEEE Transactions on Dependable and Secure Computing. 2016;15(4):646–660.

[14] Murakami T, and Watanabe H. Localization attacks using matrix and tensor factorization. IEEE Transactions on Information Forensics and Security. 2016;11(8):1647–1660.

[15] Dinesh C, Nettasinghe BW, Godaliyadda RI, *et al.* Residential appliance identification based on spectral information of low frequency smart meter measurements. IEEE Transactions on Smart Grid. 2016;7(6):2781–2792.

[16] Greveler U, Justus B, and Loehr D. Multimedia content identification through smart meter power usage profiles. Computers, Privacy and Data Protection. 2012;1:10.

[17] Fan J, Li Q, and Cao G. Privacy disclosure through smart meters: Reactive power based attack and defense. In: Dependable Systems and Networks (DSN), 2017 47th Annual IEEE/IFIP International Conference on. IEEE; 2017. p. 13–24.

[18] van Moorsel A. NFC Payment spy: A privacy attack on contactless payments. In: Security Standardisation Research: Third International Conference, SSR 2016, Gaithersburg, MD, USA, December 5–6, 2016, Proceedings. vol. 10074. Springer; 2016. p. 92.

[19] Liu Y, and Li N. Retrieving hidden friends: A collusion privacy attack against online friend search engine. IEEE Transactions on Information Forensics and Security. 2018;14(4):833–847.

[20] Qian H, Li J, Zhang Y, *et al.* Privacy-preserving personal health record using multi-authority attribute-based encryption with revocation. International Journal of Information Security. 2015;14(6):487–497.

[21] Ruj S, Stojmenovic M, and Nayak A. Decentralized access control with anonymous authentication of data stored in clouds. IEEE Transactions on Parallel and Distributed Systems. 2014;25(2):384–394.

[22]   Yao AC. Protocols for secure computations. In: Foundations of Computer Science, 1982. SFCS'08. 23rd Annual Symposium on. IEEE; 1982. p. 160–164.

[23]   Tso R, Alelaiwi A, Rahman SMM, *et al.* Privacy-preserving data communication through secure multi-party computation in healthcare sensor cloud. Journal of Signal Processing Systems. 2017;89(1):51–59.

[24]   Wang XS, Huang Y, Zhao Y, *et al.* Efficient genome-wide, privacy-preserving similar patient query based on private edit distance. In: Proceedings of the 22nd ACM SIGSAC Conference on Computer and Communications Security. ACM; 2015. p. 492–503.

[25]   Wang W, Liu A, Li Z, *et al.* Protecting multi-party privacy in location-aware social point-of-interest recommendation. World Wide Web. 2019;22(2): 863–883.

[26]   Rivest RL, Adleman L, and Dertouzos ML. On data banks and privacy homomorphisms. Foundations of Secure Computation. 1978;4(11):169–180.

[27]   Alabdulatif A, Kumarage H, Khalil I, *et al.* Privacy-preserving anomaly detection in cloud with lightweight homomorphic encryption. Journal of Computer and System Sciences. 2017;90:28–45.

[28]   Abdallah A, and Shen XS. A lightweight lattice-based homomorphic privacy-preserving data aggregation scheme for smart grid. IEEE Transactions on Smart Grid. 2018;9(1):396–405.

[29]   Kim S, Kim J, Koo D, *et al.* Efficient privacy-preserving matrix factorization via fully homomorphic encryption. In: Proceedings of the 11th ACM on Asia Conference on Computer and Communications Security. ACM; 2016. p. 617–628.

[30]   Liu X, Choo KKR, Deng RH, *et al.* Efficient and privacy-preserving outsourced calculation of rational numbers. IEEE Transactions on Dependable and Secure Computing. 2018;15(1):27–39.

[31]   Eryonucu C, Ayday E, and Zeydan E. A demonstration of privacy-preserving aggregate queries for optimal location selection. In: 2018 IEEE 19th International Symposium on "A World of Wireless, Mobile and Multimedia Networks" (WoWMoM). IEEE; 2018. p. 1–3.

[32]   Samarati P, and Sweeney L. Protecting privacy when disclosing information: k-anonymity and its enforcement through generalization and suppression. Technical Report, SRI International; 1998.

[33]   Niu B, Li Q, Zhu X, *et al.* Achieving k-anonymity in privacy-aware location-based services. In: INFOCOM, 2014 Proceedings IEEE. IEEE; 2014. p. 754–762.

[34]   Li X, Miao M, Liu H, *et al.* An incentive mechanism for K-anonymity in LBS privacy protection based on credit mechanism. Soft Computing. 2017; 21(14):3907–3917.

[35]   Liu J, Yin SL, Li H, *et al.* A density-based clustering method for K-anonymity privacy protection. Journal of Information Hiding and Multimedia Signal Processing. 2017;8(1):12–18.

[36]   Belsis P, and Pantziou G. A k-anonymity privacy-preserving approach in wireless medical monitoring environments. Personal and Ubiquitous Computing. 2014;18(1):61–74.

[37]   Song D, Sim J, Park K, *et al.* A privacy-preserving continuous location monitoring system for location-based services. International Journal of Distributed Sensor Networks. 2015;11(8):815613.

[38]   Li N, Li T, and Venkatasubramanian S. t-Closeness: Privacy beyond k-anonymity and l-diversity. In: Data Engineering, 2007. ICDE 2007. IEEE 23rd International Conference on. IEEE; 2007. p. 106–115.

[39]   Wang K, Fung BC, and Philip SY. Handicapping attacker's confidence: An alternative to k-anonymization. Knowledge and Information Systems. 2007; 11(3):345–368.

[40]   Zhang Q, Koudas N, Srivastava D, *et al.* Aggregate query answering on anonymized tables. In: Data Engineering, 2007. ICDE 2007. IEEE 23rd International Conference on. IEEE; 2007. p. 116–125.

[41]   Xiao X, and Tao Y. M-invariance: Towards privacy preserving re-publication of dynamic datasets. In: Proceedings of the 2007 ACM SIGMOD international conference on Management of data. ACM; 2007. p. 689–700.

[42]   Dwork C, McSherry F, Nissim K, *et al.* Calibrating noise to sensitivity in private data analysis. In: Theory of Cryptography Conference. Springer; 2006. p. 265–284.

[43]   Sweeney L. Privacy-enhanced linking. ACM SIGKDD Explorations Newsletter. 2005;7(2):72–75.

[44]   Nissim K, Raskhodnikova S, and Smith A. Smooth sensitivity and sampling in private data analysis. In: Proceedings of the Thirty-ninth Annual ACM Symposium on Theory of Computing. ACM; 2007. p. 75–84.

[45]   McSherry F, and Talwar K. Mechanism design via differential privacy. In: Foundations of Computer Science, 2007. FOCS'07. 48th Annual IEEE Symposium on. IEEE; 2007. p. 94–103.

[46]   Dwork C, Kenthapadi K, McSherry F, *et al.* Our data, ourselves: Privacy via distributed noise generation. In: Annual International Conference on the Theory and Applications of Cryptographic Techniques. Springer; 2006. p. 486–503.

[47]   Du M, Wang K, Liu X, *et al.* A differential privacy-based query model for sustainable fog data centers. IEEE Transactions on Sustainable Computing. 2019;4(2):145–155.

[48]   Lin J, Yang D, Li M, *et al.* Frameworks for privacy-preserving mobile crowd-sensing incentive mechanisms. IEEE Transactions on Mobile Computing. 2018;17(8):1851–1864.

[49]   Emura K. Privacy-preserving aggregation of time-series data with public verifiability from simple assumptions. In: Australasian Conference on Information Security and Privacy. Springer; 2017. p. 193–213.

[50]   Joy J. Distributed differential privacy by sampling. Clinical Orthopaedics and Related Research. arXiv preprint arXiv:1706.04890. 2017.

[51]   Narayan A, and Haeberlen A. DJoin: Differentially private join queries over distributed databases. In: OSDI; 2012. p. 149–162.

[52]   Zhang N, Li M, and Lou W. Distributed data mining with differential privacy. In: Communications (ICC), 2011 IEEE International Conference on. IEEE; 2011. p. 1–5.

[53] Kearns M, Pai M, Roth A, *et al.* Mechanism design in large games: Incentives and privacy. In: Proceedings of the 5th Conference on Innovations in Theoretical Computer Science. ACM; 2014. p. 403–410.

[54] Hsu J, Huang Z, Roth A, *et al.* Private matchings and allocations. SIAM Journal on Computing. 2016;45(6):1953–1984.

[55] Tong W, Hua J, and Zhong S. A jointly differentially private scheduling protocol for ridesharing services. IEEE Transactions on Information Forensics and Security. 2017;12(10):2444–2456.

[56] Andrés ME, Bordenabe NE, Chatzikokolakis K, *et al.* Geo-indistinguishability: Differential privacy for location-based systems. In: Proceedings of the 2013 ACM SIGSAC Conference on Computer & Communications Security. ACM; 2013. p. 901–914.

[57] Zhang JD, and Chow CY. Enabling probabilistic differential privacy protection for location recommendations. IEEE Transactions on Services Computing. 2018;(1):1.

[58] Shokri R, Theodorakopoulos G, and Troncoso C. Privacy games along location traces: A game-theoretic framework for optimizing location privacy. ACM Transactions on Privacy and Security (TOPS). 2017;19(4):11.

[59] Xiao Z, Yang JJ, Huang M, *et al.* QLDS: A novel design scheme for trajectory privacy protection with utility guarantee in participatory sensing. IEEE Transactions on Mobile Computing. 2018;17(6):1397–1410.

[60] Wang Z, Hu J, Lv R, *et al.* Personalized privacy-preserving task allocation for mobile crowdsensing. IEEE Transactions on Mobile Computing. 2019;18(6):1330–1341.

[61] Mao T, Cao C, Peng X, *et al.* A privacy preserving data aggregation scheme to investigate apps installment in massive mobile devices. Procedia Computer Science. 2018;129:331–340.

[62] Hua J, Tong W, Xu F, *et al.* A geo-indistinguishable location perturbation mechanism for location-based services supporting frequent queries. IEEE Transactions on Information Forensics and Security. 2018;13(5):1155–1168.

[63] Amini S, Lindqvist J, Hong J, *et al.* Caché: Caching location-enhanced content to improve user privacy. In: Proceedings of the 9th International Conference on Mobile Systems, Applications, and Services. ACM; 2011. p. 197–210.

[64] Peng T, Liu Q, Meng D, *et al.* Collaborative trajectory privacy preserving scheme in location-based services. Information Sciences. 2017;387:165–179.

[65] Zhang S, Liu Q, and Wang G. A caching-based privacy-preserving scheme for continuous location-based services. In: International Conference on Security, Privacy and Anonymity in Computation, Communication and Storage. Springer; 2016. p. 73–82.

[66] Liu B, Zhou W, Zhu T, *et al.* Silence is golden: Enhancing privacy of location-based services by content broadcasting and active caching in wireless vehicular networks. IEEE Transactions on Vehicular Technology. 2016; 65(12):9942–9953.

[67] Niu B, Li Q, Zhu X, *et al.* Enhancing privacy through caching in location-based services. In: Computer Communications (INFOCOM), 2015 IEEE Conference on. IEEE; 2015. p. 1017–1025.

[68] Myerson R. Game theory: Analysis of conflict. Harvard Univ. Press, Cambridge; 1991.

[69] Wu X, Dou W, and Ni Q. Game theory based privacy preserving analysis in correlated data publication. In: Proceedings of the Australasian Computer Science Week Multiconference. ACM; 2017. p. 73.

[70] Khaledi M, Khaledi M, Kasera SK, *et al.* Preserving location privacy in radio networks using a Stackelberg game framework. In: Proceedings of the 12th ACM Symposium on QoS and Security for Wireless and Mobile Networks. ACM; 2016. p. 29–37.

[71] Shannon CE. A mathematical theory of communication. ACM SIGMOBILE Mobile Computing and Communications Review. 2001;5(1):3–55.

[72] Clauß S, and Schiffner S. Structuring anonymity metrics. In: Proceedings of the 2006 Workshop on Digital Identity Management, Alexandria, VA, USA, November 3, 2006; 2006. p. 55–62.

[73] Clauß S, and Schiffner S. Structuring anonymity metrics. In: Proceedings of the Second ACM Workshop on Digital Identity Management. ACM; 2006. p. 55–62.

[74] Puglisi S, Parra-Arnau J, Forné J, *et al.* On content-based recommendation and user privacy in social-tagging systems. Computer Standards & Interfaces. 2015;41:17–27.

[75] Parra-Arnau J, Rebollo-Monedero D, Forné J, *et al.* Optimal tag suppression for privacy protection in the semantic web. Data & Knowledge Engineering. 2012;81:46–66.

[76] Peters E, and Maxemchuk N. A privacy-preserving distributed medical insurance claim clearinghouse & EHR application. In: Connected Health: Applications, Systems and Engineering Technologies (CHASE), 2017 IEEE/ACM International Conference on. IEEE; 2017. p. 70–76.

[77] Hamel A, Grégoire JC, and Goldberg I. The misanthropists: New approaches to measures in TOR. Centre for Applied Cryptographic Research (CACR); 2011.

[78] Rényi A. On measures of entropy and information. Hungarian Academy of Sciences, Budapest, Hungary; 1961.

[79] Oya S, Troncoso C, and Pérez-González F. Back to the drawing board: Revisiting the design of optimal location privacy-preserving mechanisms. In: Proceedings of the 2017 ACM SIGSAC Conference on Computer and Communications Security. ACM; 2017. p. 1959–1972.

[80] Wang EK, Jia B, and Ke N. Modeling background knowledge for privacy preserving medical data publishing. In: 2017 International Conference on Computer Systems, Electronics and Control (ICCSEC). IEEE; 2017. p. 136–141.

[81] Osia SA, Shamsabadi AS, Taheri A, *et al.* A hybrid deep learning architecture for privacy-preserving mobile analytics. arXiv preprint arXiv:170302952. 2017.

[82] Qu Y, Yu S, Gao L, *et al.* Big data set privacy preserving through sensitive attribute-based grouping. In: Communications (ICC), 2017 IEEE International Conference on. IEEE; 2017. p. 1–6.

[83] Wagner I, and Eckhoff D. Technical privacy metrics: A systematic survey. ACM Computing Surveys (CSUR). 2018;51(3):57.

[84] Meng X, Wang S, Shu K, *et al.* Personalized privacy-preserving social recommendation. In: Proc. AAAI Conf. Artif. Intell.; 2018.

[85] Ganti RK, Pham N, Tsai YE, *et al.* PoolView: Stream privacy for grassroots participatory sensing. In: Proceedings of the 6th ACM Conference on Embedded Network Sensor Systems. ACM; 2008. p. 281–294.

[86] Tan HL, Li Z, Tan YH, *et al.* A perceptually relevant MSE-based image quality metric. IEEE Transactions on Image Processing. 2013;22(11):4447–4459.

[87] Wang SL, Hsiu MJ, Tsai YC, *et al.* Analysis of privacy and utility tradeoffs in anonymized mobile context streams. Intelligent Data Analysis. 2017; 21(S1):S21–S39.

[88] Chai T, and Draxler RR. Root mean square error (RMSE) or mean absolute error (MAE)? Geoscientific Model Development Discussions. 2014;7:1525–1534.

[89] Polatidis N, Georgiadis CK, Pimenidis E, *et al.* Privacy-preserving collaborative recommendations based on random perturbations. Expert Systems with Applications. 2017;71:18–25.

[90] Hoh B, and Gruteser M. Protecting location privacy through path confusion. In: Security and Privacy for Emerging Areas in Communications Networks, 2005. SecureComm 2005. First International Conference on. IEEE; 2005. p. 194–205.

[91] Humbert M, Ayday E, Hubaux JP, *et al.* Addressing the concerns of the lacks family: Quantification of kin genomic privacy. In: Proceedings of the 2013 ACM SIGSAC Conference on Computer & Communications Security. ACM; 2013. p. 1141–1152.

[92] Kathwadia K, and Patel A. Rotation perturbation technique for privacy preserving in data stream mining. International Journal of Scientific Research in Science, engineering and Technology. 2018;4(8):217–223.

[93] Narayanan A, and Shmatikov V. De-anonymizing social networks. In: 30th IEEE Symposium on Security and Privacy (S&P 2009), Oakland, California, USA, 17–20 May 2009; 2009. p. 173–187.

[94] Cheng R, Zhang Y, Bertino E, *et al.* Preserving user location privacy in mobile data management infrastructures. In: Privacy Enhancing Technologies, 6th International Workshop, PET 2006, Cambridge, UK, 28–30 June 2006, Revised Selected Papers; 2006. p. 393–412.

[95] Agrawal R, and Srikant R. Privacy-preserving data mining. ACM SIGMOD Record. 2000;29(2):439–450.

Chapter 2

Privacy-preserving analysis for big data using cryptographic tools

Rui Xu[1]

In this chapter, we review the efforts to protect data privacy in the scenario of cloud computing and outsourcing computation. We pay special interest in the efficiency boost which is dedicated to properly handle the challenge of large data volume coming from the trend of big data. Differently from the previous chapter focusing on the technique of differential privacy, we discuss here the approaches for privacy-preserving data analysis using cryptographic tools.

The popularization of cloud computing and the recent trend of big data brought a new stirring of interest in research of privacy-preserving techniques. Cloud computing has brought a shift from traditional client-server model of computation to the new DataBase as a Service (DBaaS) model. The DBaaS model enables a data owner to outsource her database to a public cloud in order to get economic and administrative benefits from the highly developing cloud-computing technology. Although DBaaS can relieve data owner from the burden of storing the data locally, a significant concern of data privacy remains. Data are almost always treated as the biggest asset of a company, so any service provider cannot be confident enough to just outsource its data to the public cloud server. Thus, both academic community and industrial participants are highly interested in the domain of privacy-preserving data analysis. Nowadays, the impact of big data further enhanced the motivation of efficient solutions for privacy-preserving data analysis for at least two reasons: (1) First, the big amount of data available makes DBaaS a must choice for most data service providers and (2) second, traditional solutions cannot scale well with the gross of data amount. New solutions with high efficiency are at the highest demand.

In the following sections, we will review different approaches for privacy-preserving data analysis. We first outline the basic model of privacy-preserving data analysis in the cloud-computing framework. Then we organize our introduction based on different cryptographic tools used; in each category, we pay special interest to the efforts being made to improve the scalability of each technique so as to embrace the coming feature of big data. We also mention the limitations within each category. Finally, we share some of our opinions on existing challenges and point out possible further-research directions.

[1]School of Computer Science, China University of Geosciences, Wuhan, China

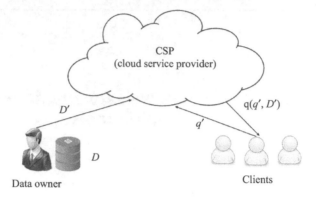

Figure 2.1   Privacy-preserving data analysis

2.1   Privacy-preserving data analysis

We consider the following scenario. A data owner who holds a database D and wants to provide certain data service **q** to its client. Instead of providing the service itself, which requires the data owner to store its large amount of data locally and to compute the response of a query locally, the data owner outsource its whole database as well as the computing tasks to a public cloud service provider (CSP). Certainly, the data owner encrypts its database before outsourcing it to the cloud server. When a authenticated client wants to use the data service to get a response of the query **q**, she resorts to the CSP. It is possible that the client and the data owner distrust each other. In that case, the client encrypts her query q and uses the encrypted query q' to interact with the CSP. We model the data service as a function $\mathbf{q} = \mathbf{q}(D', q')$ which takes as inputs the encrypted database D' and the encrypted query q'. Thus, a cloud server must be able to correctly execute the possibly encrypted query on the encrypted database. The core research problem here is how to enable correct and efficient queries on encrypted database without breaching the data privacy of the data owner and the query privacy of the clients. Figure 2.1 illustrates the model of privacy-preserving data analysis we consider in this chapter.

2.1.1   Security model of privacy-preserving data analysis

There are many different security models of privacy-preserving data analysis in the literature. Here, we briefly discuss security model from several aspects.

1. **Trusting model of the participants.** In the above privacy-preserving data-analysis model, there are three participants, the data owner, the CSP and the query client, respectively. Usually the CSP is modeled as an untrusted third party. Neither the data owner nor the query client fully trusts it. Regarding the data owner and query client, some work treat the query client and data owner as the same entity or the client and data owner fully trust each other. For example, in most works on symmetric searchable encryption schemes, the data owner first

encrypts her database and creates some encrypted index. Later on, when the data owner wants to retrieve some of the records in the database, she encrypts some token and uses the token to search the encrypted database from the CSP. In some of the works, the data owner and query client distrust each other. In such cases, the designed protocols for privacy-preserving data-analysis tasks should guarantee that the data owner learns nothing about the query and query result of the client and that the query client get only the result of her query but nothing beyond it.

2. **Behavior of the CSP.** There are two frames of work which consider different behavior of the untrusted CSP. One is called semi-honest CSP and the other is called malicious CSP. The semi-honest CSP is also called honest-but-curious. Semi-honest CSP is honest in the sense that it faithfully follows the protocol design, but it is curious about the private data from its clients, including the database of the data owner and the query content of the query client. The semi-honest CSP will try to learn information about others' inputs from whatever it sees during the protocol execution. The malicious CSP, however, may deviate arbitrarily from the designed protocol. Normally designing protocols secure in the semi-honest setting is a start point, and there are generic constructions which can transfer protocols secure in the semi-honest setting to protocols secure in the malicious setting.

3. **Power of the adversary.** Another dimension of security modeling is the power of the adversary. First, the adversary can be passive or active. A passive adversary only observes the communication between parties during the protocol execution, e.g., she can only see encrypted messages. An active adversary however has access to an encryption oracle and a query oracle. The encryption oracle allows the adversary to ask for encryption of any message of her choice. The query oracle allows the adversary to launch any queries and to get the results of these queries. A more meticulous active adversary differentiates static adversary from active adversary. A static adversary chooses her queries to the oracles (encryption oracle or query oracle) statically before getting the response from the oracles. On the other hand, an adaptive adversary can adapt her queries to the oracles based on the results of her previous queries.

4. **Collusion between corrupted parties.** We use corrupted party to mean a dishonest participant in the privacy-preserving data-analysis setting. The security model should also take into consideration the collusion between several corrupted parties. For example, the CSP and the query client might collude together and try to deduce useful information about the data owner's database. Clearly, a scheme secure against collusion is harder to design than one without such property.

5. **Level of security.** The privacy of data owner refers to the property that the CSP and the query client cannot derive any useful information of the database. But this description is rather informal. Usually, there are several different levels in the definition of security. The most basic requirement of security is that the CSP cannot learn the exact records of the database. One can pursue further to require that an adversary cannot distinguish two databases of her choice under the encryption of the underlying scheme. But even the above definition (corresponding to the

standard indistinguishability under chosen plaintext attack (IND-CPA) security definition of normal encryption schemes) is sometimes insufficient. Researchers realize that it is also important to hide the access pattern of each query. In other words, the privacy-preserving data-analysis protocol cannot leak the information that which records correspond to the query to the CSP.

In this chapter, we are going to review some of the existing solutions in the broad area of privacy-preserving data analysis. Since different works use different security models, we do not give a formal definition of security here. We listed above the various considerations when defining the security model. Next we begin the review of the literature based on different approaches used to tackle the problem.

2.2   Encryption schemes with special properties

Various encryption schemes with special properties have been proposed to realize different applications of privacy-preserving data analysis.

2.2.1   *Deterministic encryption and keyword search*

The very basic application of privacy-preserving data analysis is keyword search over encrypted database. The data owner outsources her encrypted database to the public cloud server and later uses encrypted keyword to retrieve needed records from the encrypted database. This problem was first studied by Song *et al.* [1] in 2000.

The general idea of deterministic encryption for keyword search over encrypted database is the following: assume we have an encryption scheme which is IND-CPA secure called ENC^d and a deterministic encryption scheme called ENC^i. Further, we denote the database as $D = \{d_1, d_2, \ldots, d_n\}$ and assume each data record d_i is identified by an identifier id_i. The data owner first encrypts each data record as $d_i' = ENC^d(d_i)$ and then encrypts the corresponding identifier as $id_i' = ENC^i(id_i)$. The cloud server will hold an encrypted version of the database as $D' = \{t_1, \ldots, t_n\}$, where $t_i = (id_i', d_i)$. At a later time, when the data owner wants to retrieve a record identified by an identifier id, she encrypts the id using the deterministic encryption scheme ENC^i and gets a token $tk = ENC^i(id)$. By receiving the token tk from data owner, the CSP can simply compare the token tk with the encrypted identifiers $(id_1', \ldots, id_n')$ and return the matching records accordingly. The above overly simplified description shows a secure search scheme with time complexity $O(n)$. But since the deterministic encryption makes it possible to search the encrypted identifier as if it were plaintext, some property data structure can be used to index the encrypted record identifier to make the search procedure sublinear and in fact logarithmic in the number of records of the database.

Using deterministic encryption for secure keyword search can be as efficient as search in the plaintext setting. But this solution is limited by its security drawbacks. First of all, deterministic encryption encrypt the same keyword to the same ciphertext which already leaks a large amount of information to the CSP. Second, deterministic encryption does not provide query privacy since every time when the client searches the same keyword, the CSP knows it. Finally, it leaks the keyword frequency of the database and thus is vulnerable to the frequency analysis attack [2]. Bellare *et al.* [3] formally studied the notion of deterministic encryption for secure database search in cryptographic sense. Bellare *et al.* provided a "strongest possible" notion of security for deterministic encryption and proposed efficient constructions achieving the notion in the random oracle model. Even in the strongest possible notion of security, deterministic encryption can only protect privacy for plaintexts that have high min-entropy. Boldyreva *et al.* [4] proposed a weaker notion compared to that of Bellare *et al.* and efficiently constructed schemes in the standard model.

2.2.2 Order preserving encryption and range query

Order preserving encryption (OPE) was initiated by Agrawal *et al.* [5] from the database community to allow range queries on encrypted numeric values. Simply speaking OPE preserves the order of plaintexts. Specifically for an OPE scheme and two plaintexts p_1, p_2, the following equation holds:

$$\text{OPE}(p_1) \leq \text{OPE}(p_2) \Leftrightarrow p_1 \leq p_2. \tag{2.1}$$

Boldyreva *et al.* [6] initiated the cryptography study of OPE. They show that a nature relaxation of the standard indistinguishably notion of security cannot be achieved by OPE. Then they proposed a notion for OPE called IND-OCPA (Indistinguishability under ordered chosen plaintext attack), relaxing the IND-CPA notion. The notion IND-OCPA is indistinguishable under ordered CPA. Compared with the standard IND-CPA notion, IND-OCPA restricts the queries asked by the CPA adversary to satisfy the same order relations when the CPA adversary tries to distinguish two ciphertexts. The notion of IND-OCPA is the ideal security notion for OPE. However, Boldyreva *et al.* proved that no stateless OPE can achieve this notion, i.e., an OPE with IND-OCPA security must maintain states in the scheme thus require the client to store a large amount of information.

Further development of OPE has constructed schemes satisfying the ideal security of IND-OCPA. Popa *et al.* [7] used the mutable ciphertext technique to propose the first OPE scheme achieving IND-OCPA security. Popa *et al.*'s OPE scheme incurs communication between a client and a server in the complexity of $O(n \log n)$ where n is the total number of records in the encrypted database. Later, Kerschbaum *et al.* [8] improved over Popa *et al.*'s work to reduce the communication complexity to $O(n)$ on average supposing the plaintexts are uniformly distributed. But since OPE leaks the order of plaintexts, it is essentially vulnerable to frequency attacks [2]. Kerschbaum [9] proposed frequency-hiding OPE. The frequency-hiding OPE is proven to be a stronger primitive than ordinary OPE. Boneh *et al.* recently introduced a new primitive related to OPE called order-revealing encryption (ORE). ORE generalizes OPE by breaking the restriction of structures of ciphertexts of POE. Thus, Boneh *et al.* were able to construct a stateless ORE scheme with the ideal IND-OCPA security. However, their scheme uses multi-linear map and is thus far from practical. Efficiency improvement of ORE can be found in the works of Chenette *et al.* [10] and Lewi *et al.* [11].

2.2.3 *Scalar-product-preserving encryption and nearest neighbor query*

Wong *et al.* [12] proposed a scheme for privacy preserving nearest neighbor query. In this scheme, Wong *et al.* constructed an encryption primitive called asymmetric scalar-product-preserving encryption (ASPE). ASPE uses an invertible matrix M as the key to encrypt data records in the database as well as the query vector. Set the database as $D = \{d_1, \ldots, d_n\}$ with n records, where every record d_i is a vector of length m in Euclidean space. We briefly describe the main steps of ASPE as follows:

- **KeyGen($\cdot$)** $\to$ ky: The key generation algorithm randomly generates an $(m+1) \times (m+1)$ invertible matrix M as the secret key.
- **DBEnc(ky, d)** $\to$ d': The database encryption algorithm takes the key ky and a data point p as input and outputs the encryption of d as $d' = M^T(d, -0.5||d||^2)^T$, where $||p||^2$ is the Euclidean norm and $(\cdot)^T$ denotes the transpose of a vector or a matrix. We also use **DBEnc(ky, D)** $\to$ D' to denote the encrypted database D, where encryption is done record by record.
- **QueryEnc(ky, q)** $\to$ q': The query point encryption algorithm takes the key ky and a query point q as input and outputs the encryption of q as $q' = rM^{-1}(q, 1)^T$, where r is a random positive number.

Note that the encryption keys for data record and query vector are different but related. The ASPE scheme has a nice property called scalar-product preservation, which we introduce as the following theorem.

Theorem 2.1 (Scalar product preservation of ASPE). *The ASPE encryption scheme preserves the scalar products between a query vector and two data vectors. Specifically, $\forall d_i, d_j \in D$, let $d_i' = $ **DBEnc(ky, d_i)** and $d_j' = $ **DBEnc(ky, d_j)**, and $\forall q'$ with $q' = $ **QueryEnc(ky, q)**, we have:*

$$d_i'q' - d_j'q' = -0.5r(||d_i||^2 - 2d_iq^T) + 0.5r(||d_j||^2 - 2d_jq^T)$$
$$= 0.5r(dis(d_i, q)^2 - dis(d_j, q)^2) \tag{2.2}$$

The above property enables distance comparison on encrypted database since one can compute the scalar products of an encrypted query point with two encrypted data points and tell which one is closer to the query point based on the sign of the difference of these two scalar products. Precisely, for two encrypted data points d_i', d_j' and an encrypted query point q', we have $d_i'q' - d_j'q' > 0 \Leftrightarrow dis(d_i, q) > dis(d_j, q)$. Wong *et al.* used ASPE to design a privacy-preserving k-nearest neighbor (kNN) query scheme.

The ASPE scheme has enormous impact on the design of privacy-preserving data analysis beyond the application of nearest neighbor query. Since the essential property of ASPE enables distance comparison over encrypted ciphertexts, any data-analysis task that needs comparison can utilize ASPE to design a privacy-preserving solution. Many privacy-preserving multi-keyword search schemes [13,14] have used ASPE as their core building blocks. ASPE can also be used to build privacy-preserving ranked keyword search [15].

At the time of proposing the ASPE scheme, Wong *et al.* thought ASPE is secure against CPA. Unfortunately, Yao *et al.* [16] have shown that ASPE is not secure against CPA. They proposed an attacking method allowing a CPA attacker to fully recover the whole database. Another limitation of ASPE is that since the distance comparison of ciphertexts under ASPE is transformed to scalar product computation, known data structures for efficient distance comparison such as R-tree and kd-tree cannot be employed. Thus privacy-preserving data-analysis schemes using ASPE as building blocks suffer from linear complexity.

2.2.4 Searchable symmetric encryption

Searchable symmetric encryption (SSE) was initiated by Song *et al.* [1]. They motivated the problem of searching by keyword to retrieve records of an outsourced encrypted database and gave a solution for it which is later referred to SSE. An SSE scheme consists of the following phases:

- **Setup**. In the setup phase, the data owner encrypts her database D as $D' = \mathrm{SSE}(D)$ using some randomly generated key k.
- **Queries**. In the queries phase, the data owner takes as input the key k and a keyword w to generate a token tk. Data owner sends the token tk to the cloud server.
- **Response**. In the response phase, upon receiving the token tk, the cloud server searches the encrypted database and returns the identifiers of matching records.

Song *et al.* proved that their scheme is provable secure. But unfortunately, their security model is too weak in the sense that they did not provide the ability of searching the database to the cloud server. In actual applications, a cloud server can search the database. In that case, Song *et al.*'s scheme is no longer secure.

From the above motivating example, we can see the importance of formal security definition in cryptography. Goh [17] refined the security definition of SSE and formulate a security model for SSE as semantic security against adaptive chosen keyword attack (IND2-CKA). IND2-CKA allows a malicious cloud server to adaptively choose keyword and launch search queries on an SSE-encrypted database. One limitation of IND2-CKA is that it does not provide query privacy. The adversarial cloud server might be able to deduce information about keywords of the data record. Chang and Mitzenmacher [18] proposed another simulation-based security notion for SSE, which is supposed to be stronger than IND2-CKA since it requires secure trapdoor. Unfortunately, Curtmola *et al.* [19] observed that the simulation-based security of Chang and Mitzenmacher can be easily satisfied even by an insecure SSE. Curtmola *et al.* thus gave new security definitions of SSE and corresponding constructions.

The area of SSE keeps developing at a fast pace. Kamara *et al.* [20] proposed dynamic SSE which enables dynamic update of the database. Richer query types for SSE are also proposed by researchers. For example, Kamara *et al.* [21] proposed an SSE supporting any Boolean query over the encrypted database. Moreover, their scheme can achieve sublinear search time in the worst case.

We refer the interested readers to some excellent surveys [22,23] on SSE.

2.3   Schemes based on secure computation

Pioneered by the work of Lindell and Pinkas [24], secure computation found its great applications on privacy-preserving data mine in the last decade. This line of research aims to provide solutions for distrusting parties to mine useful information on their joint database while being guaranteed that no information about their private database can be leaked to other parties. Since secure computation is generic in the sense that roughly speaking any efficient computable function can be securely implemented, it is not surprising that it can be used to design privacy-preserving schemes for data analysis. One important advantage of secure computation is that it works for mutually distrusting participants. This implies that we can use secure computation protocols to design schemes *where the data owner and query client distrust each other*.

2.3.1   Secure computation

Secure multiparty (two-party) computation allows a set of mutually distrusting parties to collaborate together in a distributed manner to compute a function $f(x_1, x_2, \dots)$ on their private inputs x_i. The computation is done in such a way that every party gets the output of the function, or the restricted projection of the output for the specific party, while at the same time, every party learns no other information on others' inputs beyond what can be inferred from the output and her own input. For ease of presentation, throughout this chapter, we use secure computation to refer both secure multi-party and secure two-party computation.

Yao's work on the millionaires' problem [25] initiated the study of secure two-party computation. Further on, Yao gave a generic construction [26] for secure two-party computation called garbled circuit which is nowadays the most popular construction in use. Later on Goldreich *et al.* [27] and Ben-Or *et al.* [28] generalized secure two-party computation to the setting of secure multiparty computation and gave generic constructions for secure multiparty computation, respectively. The former is called GMW protocol and is computationally secure. The latter is called BGW protocol and is secure in the secure channel setting (information theoretically secure). Previously generic constructions were thought to be inefficient and impractical for real-life applications. But continuous development on the implementations of generic constructions, especially the garbled circuit construction, has illustrated that generic constructions can be efficient and practical. Somewhat surprisingly, it seems that in most applications, generic constructions are a better choice than handcrafted constructions made for special-purpose tasks.

Bellare *et al.* [29] presented a systematical review of garbled circuits and formally defined a system called garbling scheme which abstracts and generalizes the original garbled circuit proposed by Yao. We follow the description by Bellare *et al.* [29] (with some simplification) to briefly introduce garbled circuit. See Figure 2.2 for an

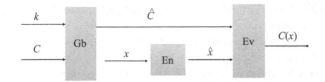

Figure 2.2   Components of a garbling scheme

illustration of a garbling scheme. A garbling scheme $G = $ (Gb, En, Ev) consists of the following algorithms.

- The garbling algorithm Gb$(k, C) \rightarrow \hat{C}$ takes a key k and a circuit description C as inputs and outputs a garbled circuit $\hat{C}$.
- The encoding algorithm En$(x) \rightarrow (\hat{x})$ takes an input x of the circuit C as input and outputs a encoded input $\hat{x}$ for the garbled circuit $\hat{C}$.
- The evaluating algorithm Ev$(\hat{C}, \hat{x}) = C(x)$ takes a garbled circuit $\hat{C}$ and an encoded input $\hat{x}$ as inputs and outputs the evaluation result of x on circuit $C(x)$.

In 2004, Malkhi *et al.* [30] presented the first implementation of secure two-party computation system, Fairplay, based on garbled circuit construction. Being the first of its kind, Fairplay stimulated a subsequent of works aiming at improving the efficiency of secure computation systems. Specifically Kolesnikov and Schneider [31] proposed free-XOR (exclusive or) method for garbled circuit. The free-XOR construction can decrees the cost of XOR gate in a garbled circuit to a degree that is almost free. Pinkas *et al.* used row-reduction technique to reduce the cost of non-XOR gate by 25%. Ishai *et al.* [32] and Asharov *et al.* [33] proposed oblivious transfer (OT)-extension, which can dramatically speedup the time consumption of OT protocol. The OT protocol is a necessary component of garbled circuit construction. Bellare *et al.* [34] proposed to implement garbled circuit using fixed-key blockcipher. Their implementation can compute a garbled Advanced Encryption Standard (AES) circuit within just 900 μs. Zahur *et al.* [35] proposed to break an AND gate into two half-gates. Each half-gate can be garbled using one ciphertext. Thus, they reduce the cost of garbled AND gate from previously four ciphertexts to two ciphertexts. And their technique is fully compatible with the free XOR technique. Songhori *et al.* [36] reported their effort using logic synthesis to compress the garbled circuit which results in lower computational and communication costs.

2.3.2 Scalability of secure computation

Big data provides us great opportunity and at the same time massive challenges. One particular challenge regarding privacy-preserving data analysis is that the scalability of secure computation is quite low. Though the community has made great efforts to continuously push the efficiency of secure computation systems from both theoretical point and practical implementations, these improvements are essentially constant. They are indeed dramatically impressive in practice, reducing the communication cost and computation time by thousands of times. Nonetheless, such improvements still cannot cover the rate at which big data is growing. In order to make secure computation effectively scalable, some tricks that can reduce the complexity of the underlying tasks are essential.

Computer scientists are very familiar with the tools to reduce complexity of certain problems—efficient algorithms and better data structures. In fact there are lots of attempts using effective data structures to design efficient secure computation based privacy-preserving data-analysis schemes. For example, Xia *et al.* [14] built a tree style index to reduce the searching time of their proposed multi-keyword search scheme. Sun *et al.* [37] proposed to use tree index to implement efficient outsourcing of similarity-based multi-keyword search. Cheng *et al.* [38] used R tree to design sublinear privacy-preserving kNN query using OPE as building block. Wang *et al.* [39] also proposed a new scheme using OPE and R tree for privacy-preserving nearest neighbor query. However, all the above mentioned schemes are insecure. These schemes leak at least the trace, formally coined as access pattern, of the underlying secure computation protocols.

We explain now why it is difficult to use efficient data structures in secure computation protocols. Specific data structures for certain problems can reduce the time complexity essentially because it enables pruning some branches of the data structure. In other words, by carefully designing the structure of the data collection, the algorithm on longer needs to examine all the data to compute the result. But an inherent contradiction lies in between this property of branch and bound algorithm and the requirements of secure computation. In fact, garbled circuit construction requires the algorithm for the underlying task being converted to a binary circuit using only Boolean gates. Sometimes, the conversion from RAM algorithm to binary circuit may incur exponential penalty in complexity. For example, in a RAM model, we can access the ith element of an array A of length n in constant time, but in the garbled circuit construction, we have to implement a binary circuit of using at least n gates. This is because the binary circuit used in garbled circuit construction must be static so that it evaluates obliviously to any input. We must ensure that for any value of i, the garbled circuit can successfully access the ith element of A without leaking information about the value of i. One option to solve the inherent confliction between random access pattern and security requirements of secure computation is to employ a primitive called oblivious RAM (ORAM).

2.3.3 Secure computation on top of ORAM

Goldreich and Ostrovsky [40] presented a primitive called ORAM to protect the access pattern of a RAM program running on an insecure memory. They proposed a e hierarchical construction for ORAM. Figure 2.3 shows a schematic of ORAM. In an ORAM scheme, the trusted CPU runs some program on the untrusted memory. We can also model the two parties as an ORAM client and an ORAM server. The client is trusted, so every operation done by the client can be viewed as secure. If the server is untrusted, any operation including any communication between the client and server is insecure. The general idea of how ORAM works is that the client organizes its data as she likes and encrypts the data before putting them on the untrusted memory. The client makes sure that the content on the memory is uniformly distributed. When logically

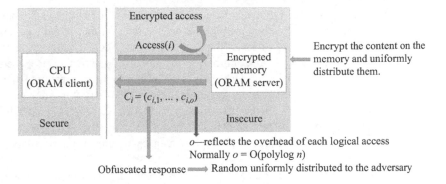

Figure 2.3   Schematic of oblivious RAM

accessing the ith location of the memory, the client will instead physically access o locations from the memory. Since the contents are encrypted and the distribution of them is uniformly random. The access operation does not leak any information about the location to the server. The number o reflects the overhead of each logical access and it is normally of the complexity of $O(\text{polylog} n)$.

The rise and prosperity of cloud computing make researchers to realize that ORAM proposed decades ago is a very nice tool for secure outsourcing in cloud computing. Thus, the research of ORAM boomed again. Two of the influential work on the improvement of ORAM comes from Shi *et al.* and Stefanov *et al.* Shi *et al.* [41] creatively employed a binary tree design to construct the SCSL-ORAM with poly-logarithmic worst case cost, while consuming constant client-side storage. Stefanov *et al.* [42] further improved over SCSL-ORAM by reducing the overhead from $O(\log N)^3$ to $O(\log N)$.

In order to improve the efficiency of secure computation, Gordon *et al.* [43] proposed to combine tree-based ORAM and garbled circuit to construct sublinear secure computation framework. The idea behind the work of Gordon *et al.* is that since ORAM can achieve random access of memory in sublinear time complexity (actually $O(\log N)$ if using Path-ORAM), we can use ORAM to design oblivious data structures achieving random access structure. But in the setting of ORAM, the client is trusted, which is different from the setting of secure computation where the participating parties mutually distrust each other. Thus, Gordon *et al.* proposed to simulate an ORAM scheme using garbled circuit so that the operations of ORAM can be performed between mutual distrust parties. The problem with Gordon *et al.*'s generic construction is that it has heavy overhead and it assumes that all functions can be represented using a generic iterative circuit. While this assumption is justified since that is what compilers do all the time, for real-life applications, the conversion from RAM algorithms to generic iterative circuit is difficult and cumbersome and sometimes might require to construct a circuit containing a whole set of CPU instructions. Wang *et al.* [44] designed oblivious data structures, including oblivious array, oblivious stack, oblivious queue and oblivious AVL tree, based on Path-ORAM. They also realized that in the existing works of ORAM, the client is trusted so that the criteria for evaluating the performance of ORAM schemes are not suitable for ORAM schemes used in secure computation. So they proposed a new evaluation metric [45] called circuit complexity of ORAM to measure the performance of ORAM schemes used for the pop-ups of constructing secure computation protocols. They further proposed circuit-ORAM which achieves better performance regarding to the new metrics they proposed. Keller and Scholl [46] also implemented oblivious data structures designed specifically for secure computation based on tree style ORAM. Xu *et al.* [47] used the secure computation on top of ORAM approach to design a secure *k*NN query scheme over encrypted database achieving sublinear query complexity and simulation-based security.

We take the schematic from Xu *et al.* to show the readers a brief taste of how it works in the conceptual level. Figure 2.4 shows the components of Xu *et al.*'s privacy-preserving *k*NN query scheme. The spatial data structure *k*d-tree is used to achieve sublinear complexity for *k*NN query. Xu *et al.* used the technique of oblivious data structures from Wang *et al.* [44] to build an oblivious *k*d-tree using circuit-ORAM. Then they convert the recursive *k*NN query algorithm using *k*d-tree to an iterative *k*NN query algorithm. Note that this step is necessary due to some technique subtlety. Next with the help of oblivious bounded priority queue, they turned the iterative *k*NN query algorithm into an oblivious algorithm whose execution trace does not depend on the distribution of input data. Finally, all the algorithms and data structures are simulated by a garbled circuit construction.

The simple form of non-recursive tree-based ORAM constructions require the client to store locally a position map with linear length $O(n)$, where n is the largest possible number of accesses to the memory. One can reduce the length of position map to a constant by recursively constructing ORAMs to store the position map. This typically needs a logarithmic number of recursion. In order to achieve sublinear complexity for secure computation, the recursive ORAM must be used. The non-recursive ORAM requires the client to store a position map of linear length. In secure computation, all the operations of ORAM must be simulated by a garbled circuit. Hence, simulating the client's operation to retrieve one element from the position map is equivalent to obliviously accessing a random element of an array. When the

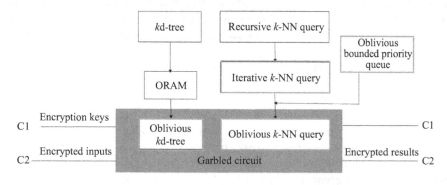

Figure 2.4   Schematic of privacy-preserving kNN by Xu et al. [47]

position map is of linear length, the resulted garbled circuit has at least linear number of gates just for the very task of simulating the client's retrieving the position map. In a nutshell, it only makes sense to design sublinear secure computation protocols using recursive ORAM schemes. A disadvantage of using recursive ORAM is the high round complexity since recursive ORAM needs at least logarithm number of interactions between the ORAM client and ORAM server.

2.4 Features of reviewed solutions

We reviewed some recent works on the area of privacy-preserving data analysis. This area is so broad that our review just touched the tip of the iceberg. For example, we did not mention the famous primitive called fully homomorphic encryption [48] which is born for privacy-preserving data analysis on the cloud. The selection of the material is of course biased due to the author's knowledge and experience.

Our opinions on the limitations of the abovementioned works as shared as follows:

- Property-preserving encryption schemes are efficient but less secure. Deterministic encryption, OPE and scalar-product-preserving encryption can be unified as property-preserving encryption. This kind of encryption schemes have a common feature, the ciphertexts preserve certain property of the plaintexts. For example, deterministic encryption preserves equality relation between plaintexts and OPE preserves order relation between plaintexts. These encryption schemes are naturally less secure since they expose certain property of the plaintexts by definition. Now the standard practice of property-preserving encryption uses a leakage function to explicitly point out the possible leakage of the encryption scheme. However, the leakage function along docs not solve the concern since it is not clear what implication of the leakage function is in particular applications. Some cryptanalysis [2,49,50] have shown that certain leakage would in fact break the security of the whole system.
- SSE is a broad area of research, the schemes are proven secure in different models and thus not directly comparable. Recent research on SSE focus one three lines: (1) query expressiveness of SSE; (2) query efficiency of SSE and (3) security of SSE. SSE now covers lots of subject that we do not have space to discuss in this chapter. Almost all SSE schemes are provably secure nowadays, but they are proven secure under different models, and thus it is difficult to compare different schemes. SSE shares a similar problem with property-preserving encryption regarding the leakage function. Many provably secure SSEs do not take into consideration the leakage during or after a search query. SSE only enables the data owner who has the secret key to query the database, thus it is not suitable for the setting where the data owner and query client distrust each other.
- Schemes based on secure computation provide best security guarantee but are less efficient. Though researchers have pushed the efficiency of generic construction of secure computation such as garbled circuit to the extent that they are

Table 2.1   Features of the reviewed solutions

Solutions	Advantages	Limitations
PPE	1. Easy to implement 2. Efficient and practical	1. Various security issues
SSE	1. Good trade-off between security and efficiency 2. Formal definition of security 3. Rich query expressiveness	1. Different models of security 2. No support for distrusting parties
SC	1. Excellent security guarantee 2. Support for all types of queries	1. Heavy overhead 2. Difficult to design and implement

The abbreviation "PPE", "SSE" and "SC" in the table stand for property-preserving encryption, searchable symmetric encryption and secure computation, respectively.

the most practical solutions for most applications, the security requirements of secure computation rules out trivial use of randomized algorithm. ORAM can be employed for the rescue. But the use of recursive ORAM incur a logarithmic overhead of interaction. This round complexity is much more significant than computational and communication complexity in real applications since it is usually the latency that becomes a bottleneck rather than the computing time or the bandwidth in a network.

We summarize the features of the solutions we reviewed in Table 2.1.

2.5   Summary

Big data has brought us a huge challenge on the scalability of privacy-preserving data analysis. As we discussed in Section 2.4, the solutions based on secure computation provide best security and is capable of tackling any desired data-analysis task. Moreover, the development of secure computation has established a universal model of evaluating proposed protocols. Thus, it is the author's belief that solutions based on secure computation might be the most suitable choice.

But generally it is not easy to design secure computation-based schemes for privacy-preserving data analysis. In our opinion, random algorithms are one of the biggest difficulty in designing efficient secure computation protocols for certain tasks. We show this by the following example: Figure 2.5 shows an example of two random algorithms. We assume the code snippets in Figure 2.5 involve two mutually distrusting parties, and D1 and D2 are their private inputs, respectively.

Checking Lines 3 and 5 of Algorithm 1, we find that the program chooses different executing path based on the condition of the "if" statement in Line 2. Further assume that the algorithm is designed in a way such that the case where the "if" statement is true is limited by a constant. Then the total time complexity of Algorithm 1 is $O(n)$.

Algorithm 1 f(D1,D2)	Algorithm 2 g(D1,D2)
...	...
1 while $(i < n)$:	1 while(*condition*):
2 if $(h(D1[i], D2[i]) > 0)$:	2 $\Delta T = h(D1,D2)$
3 codes with linear complexity	3 while($\Delta T \mathrel{!=} \emptyset$):
4 else:	4 some operations
5 codes with constant complexity	5 $T = T \cup \Delta T$
...	...

Figure 2.5   Examples of two random algorithms

However, in secure computation model, since we cannot leak the truth value of the "if" statement, we must execute both branches (Lines 3 and 5) every time and obliviously choose the correct result according to the truth of the "if" statement. Thus the time complexity of Algorithm 1 under secure computation model increases to $O(n^2)$.

Let us look at Algorithm 2. Assume T, as an array, is the final output of Algorithm 2. Algorithm 2 iterates on the *condition* (Line 1) and incrementally inserts some data to T based on some condition (Lines 2 and 5). Further assume that the algorithm is designed so that the final output T has length $O(n)$. Then the total time complexity of Algorithm 2 is $O(n)$. However, in secure computation model, since we cannot leak the information of the size of ΔT in each iteration, we have to allocate at least linear space for ΔT in each iteration. Thus, the time complexity of Algorithm 2 under secure computation model increases to $O(n^2)$.

In order to improve the scalability of secure computation-based solution, the following research directions can be taken:

- Make further progress on transferring random algorithms in the RAM model to binary circuits, i.e., effectively solving the difficulties we showed in the above example.
- Reduce the round complexity of secure computation protocols using recursive ORAM.
- Take into consideration some classic data condensation techniques and feature extraction algorithms so that the costly secure computation protocols do not need to be built for the whole dataset but a representative of it.

2.6   Summary

Big data has great potential to revolutionize our lives through its predictive power and provide insights far beyond what we know about ourselves. It has become a necessity in today's world. It is expected to grow exponentially in the coming years. Big data has brought us great benefits; however, it can also cause great privacy issues. This chapter surveys various attacks that happened on different types of dataset and different application scenarios, the privacy technologies and privacy metrics that how to evaluate the privacy level based on different privacy-preserving methods. Most privacy-preserving methods can only deal with single type of privacy attack, while new attack models keep coming up. Therefore, it is a very big challenge to design the privacy-preserving methods that can deal with multiple types of attack and defend the new developed attack.

References

[1]   Song DX, Wagner D, and Perrig A. Practical techniques for searches on encrypted data. In: Security and Privacy, 2000. S&P 2000. Proceedings. 2000 IEEE Symposium on. IEEE; 2000. p. 44–55.

[2]   Naveed M, Kamara S, and Wright CV. Inference attacks on property-preserving encrypted databases. In: Proceedings of the 22nd ACM SIGSAC Conference on Computer and Communications Security. ACM; 2015. p. 644–655.

[3]   Bellare M, Boldyreva A, and O'Neill A. Deterministic and efficiently search-able encryption. In: Annual International Cryptology Conference. Springer; 2007. p. 535–552.

[4]   Boldyreva A, Fehr S, and O'Neill A. On notions of security for deterministic encryption, and efficient constructions without random oracles. In: Annual International Cryptology Conference. Springer; 2008. p. 335–359.

[5]   Agrawal R, Kiernan J, Srikant R, *et al.* Order preserving encryption for numeric data. In: Proceedings of the 2004 ACM SIGMOD International Conference on Management of Data. ACM; 2004. p. 563–574.

[6]   Boldyreva A, Chenette N, Lee Y, *et al.* Order-preserving symmetric encryp-tion. In: Annual International Conference on the Theory and Applications of Cryptographic Techniques. Springer; 2009. p. 224–241.

[7]   Popa RA, Li FH, and Zeldovich N. An ideal-security protocol for order-preserving encoding. In: Security and Privacy (SP), 2013 IEEE Symposium on. IEEE; 2013. p. 463–477.

[8]   Kerschbaum F, and Schroepfer A. Optimal average-complexity ideal-security order-preserving encryption. In: Proceedings of the 2014 ACM SIGSAC Con-ference on Computer and Communications Security. ACM; 2014. p. 275–286.

[9]   Kerschbaum F. Frequency-hiding order-preserving encryption. In: Proceed-ings of the 22nd ACM SIGSAC Conference on Computer and Communications Security. ACM; 2015. p. 656–667.

[10] Chenette N, Lewi K, Weis SA, *et al.* Practical order-revealing encryption with limited leakage. In: International Conference on Fast Software Encryption. Springer; 2016. p. 474–493.

[11] Lewi K, and Wu DJ. Order-revealing encryption: New constructions, appli-cations, and lower bounds. In: Proceedings of the 2016 ACM SIGSAC Conference on Computer and Communications Security. ACM; 2016. p. 1167–1178.

[12] Wong WK, Cheung DW, Kao B, *et al.* Secure kNN computation on encrypted databases. In: Proceedings of the 2009 ACM SIGMOD International Conference on Management of Data. ACM; 2009. p. 139–152.

[13] Cao N, Wang C, Li M, *et al.* Privacy-preserving multi-keyword ranked search over encrypted cloud data. IEEE Transactions on Parallel and Distributed Systems. 2014;25(1):222–233.

[14] Xia Z, Wang X, Sun X, *et al.* A secure and dynamic multi-keyword ranked search scheme over encrypted cloud data. IEEE Transactions on Parallel and Distributed Systems. 2016;27(2):340–352.

[15] Fu Z, Sun X, Liu Q, *et al.* Achieving efficient cloud search services: Multi-keyword ranked search over encrypted cloud data supporting parallel computing. IEICE Transactions on Communications. 2015;98(1):190–200.

[16] Yao B, Li F, and Xiao X. Secure nearest neighbor revisited. In: Data Engineering (ICDE), 2013 IEEE 29th International Conference on. IEEE; 2013. p. 733–744.

[17] Goh EJ. Secure Indexes; 2003. https://eprint.iacr.org/2003/216. Cryptology ePrint Archive, Report 2003/216.

[18] Chang YC, and Mitzenmacher M. Privacy preserving keyword searches on remote encrypted data. In: International Conference on Applied Cryptography and Network Security. Springer; 2005. p. 442–455.

[19] Curtmola R, Garay J, Kamara S, *et al.* Searchable symmetric encryption: improved definitions and efficient constructions. Journal of Computer Security. 2011;19(5):895–934.

[20] Kamara S, Papamanthou C, and Roeder T. Dynamic searchable symmetric encryption. In: Proceedings of the 2012 ACM Conference on Computer and Communications Security. ACM; 2012. p. 965–976.

[21] Kamara S, and Moataz T. Boolean searchable symmetric encryption with worst-case sub-linear complexity. In: Annual International Conference on the Theory and Applications of Cryptographic Techniques. Springer; 2017. p. 94–124.

[22] Bösch C, Hartel P, Jonker W, *et al.* A survey of provably secure searchable encryption. ACM Computing Surveys (CSUR). 2015;47(2):18.

[23] Poh GS, Chin JJ, Yau WC, *et al.* Searchable symmetric encryption: Designs and challenges. ACM Computing Surveys (CSUR). 2017;50(3):40.

[24] Lindell Y, and Pinkas B. Privacy preserving data mining. In: Annual International Cryptology Conference. Springer; 2000. p. 36–54.

[25] Yao AC. Protocols for secure computations. In: 23rd Annual Symposium on Foundations of Computer Science. FOCS'82. IEEE; 1982. p. 160–164.

[26] Yao ACC. How to generate and exchange secrets. In: Foundations of Computer Science, 1986., 27th Annual Symposium on. IEEE; 1986. p. 162–167.

[27] Goldreich O, Micali S, and Wigderson A. How to play any mental game. In: Proceedings of the Nineteenth Annual ACM Symposium on Theory of Computing. ACM; 1987. p. 218–229.

[28] Ben-Or M, Goldwasser S, and Wigderson A. Completeness theorems for non-cryptographic fault-tolerant distributed computation. In: Proceedings of the Twentieth Annual ACM Symposium on Theory of Computing. ACM; 1988. p. 1–10.

[29]   Bellare M, Hoang VT, and Rogaway P. Foundations of garbled circuits. In: Proceedings of the 2012 ACM Conference on Computer and Communications Security. ACM; 2012. p. 784–796.

[30]   Malkhi D, Nisan N, Pinkas B, *et al.* Fairplay-secure two-party computation system. In: USENIX Security Symposium. vol. 4. San Diego, CA, USA; 2004. p. 9.

[31]   Kolesnikov V, and Schneider T. Improved garbled circuit: Free XOR gates and applications. In: International Colloquium on Automata, Languages, and Programming. Springer; 2008. p. 486–498.

[32]   Ishai Y, Kilian J, Nissim K, *et al.* Extending oblivious transfers efficiently. In: Annual International Cryptology Conference. Springer; 2003. p. 145–161.

[33]   Asharov G, Lindell Y, Schneider T, *et al.* More efficient oblivious transfer and extensions for faster secure computation. In: Proceedings of the 2013 ACM SIGSAC Conference on Computer & Communications Security. ACM; 2013. p. 535–548.

[34]   Bellare M, Hoang VT, Keelveedhi S, *et al.* Efficient garbling from a fixed-key blockcipher. In: Security and Privacy (SP), 2013 IEEE Symposium on. IEEE; 2013. p. 478–492.

[35]   Zahur S, Rosulek M, and Evans D. Two halves make a whole. In: Annual International Conference on the Theory and Applications of Cryptographic Techniques. Springer; 2015. p. 220–250.

[36]   Songhori EM, Hussain SU, Sadeghi AR, *et al.* TinyGarble: Highly compressed and scalable sequential garbled circuits. In: Security and Privacy (SP), 2015 IEEE Symposium on. IEEE; 2015. p. 411–428.

[37]   Sun W, Wang B, Cao N, *et al.* Privacy-preserving multi-keyword text search in the cloud supporting similarity-based ranking. In: Proceedings of the 8th ACM SIGSAC Symposium on Information, Computer and Communications Security. ACM; 2013. p. 71–82.

[38]   Cheng X, Su S, Teng Y, *et al.* Enabling secure and efficient kNN query processing over encrypted spatial data in the cloud. Security and Communication Networks. 2015;8(17):3205–3218.

[39]   Wang B, Hou Y, and Li M. Practical and secure nearest neighbor search on encrypted large-scale data. In: Computer Communications, IEEE INFOCOM 2016—The 35th Annual IEEE International Conference on. IEEE; 2016. p. 1–9.

[40]   Goldreich O, and Ostrovsky R. Software protection and simulation on oblivious RAMs. Journal of the ACM (JACM). 1996;43(3):431–473.

[41]   Shi E, Chan THH, Stefanov E, *et al.* Oblivious RAM with O((logN)3) Worst-Case Cost. In: Lee DH, Wang X, editors. Advances in Cryptology – ASIACRYPT 2011. Berlin, Heidelberg: Springer Berlin Heidelberg; 2011. p. 197–214.

[42]   Stefanov E, Van Dijk M, Shi E, *et al.* Path ORAM: An extremely simple oblivious RAM protocol. In: Proceedings of the 2013 ACM SIGSAC Conference on Computer & Communications SACM; 2013. p. 299–310.

[43] Gordon SD, Katz J, Kolesnikov V, *et al.* Secure two-party computation in sublinear (amortized) time. In: Proceedings of the 2012 ACM Conference on Computer and Communications Security. ACM; 2012. p. 513–524.

[44] Wang XS, Nayak K, Liu C, *et al.* Oblivious data structures. In: Proceedings of the 2014 ACM SIGSAC Conference on Computer and Communications Security. ACM; 2014. p. 215–226.

[45] Wang X, Chan H, and Shi E. Circuit ORAM: On tightness of the Goldreich–Ostrovsky lower bound. In: Proceedings of the 22nd ACM SIGSAC Conference on Computer and Communications Security. ACM; 2015. p. 850–861.

[46] Keller M, and Scholl P. Efficient, oblivious data structures for MPC. In: International Conference on the Theory and Application of Cryptology and Information Security. Springer; 2014. p. 506–525.

[47] Xu R, Morozov K, Yang Y, *et al.* Efficient outsourcing of secure k-nearest neighbour query over encrypted database. Computers & Security. 2017;69: 65–83.

[48] Gentry C. A fully homomorphic encryption scheme. PhD Thesis, Stanford University, 2009.

[49] Durak FB, DuBuisson TM, and Cash D. What else is revealed by order-revealing encryption? In: Proceedings of the 2016 ACM SIGSAC Conference on Computer and Communications Security. ACM; 2016. p. 1155–1166.

[50] Grubbs P, Sekniqi K, Bindschaedler V, *et al.* Leakage-abuse attacks against order-revealing encryption. In: Security and Privacy (SP), 2017 IEEE Symposium on. IEEE; 2017. p. 655–672.

Chapter 3

Big data security in Internet of Things

Yongjun Zheng[1], Haider Ali[2], and Umair Ullah Tariq[3]

The Internet-of-Things (IoT) paradigm is an emerging twenty-first century techno-logical revolution, a concept that facilitates to communicate with objects, devices, and machines at unprecedented scale. Nowadays, IoT is extensively applied to numerous applications such as intelligent transportation, smart security, smart grid, and smart home. Now, considering that in the near future, millions of devices will be interconnected and will be producing enormous data, the privacy and security of data going to be challenged and private information may leak at any time. This chapter presents an overview of the IoT and security concerns on big data while we discuss privacy and security approaches for big data with reference to infrastructure, application, and data.

3.1 Internet-of-Things

IoT paradigm has enabled embedded systems (smart nodes, sensors, actuators) to interconnect them to the Internet using networking technologies for physical and/or environmental conditions monitoring/control purposes [1]. A basic application of IoT is smart homes where heating, ventilation, air conditioning, and thermostats are controlled and monitored. There are also numerous other domains and environments where IoT plays a remarkable role and improves the quality-of-life (QoL). These applications include health care, pollution monitoring, industrial automation, trans-portation, and agriculture. The IoT applications are mainly categorized into three domains, i.e., society, environment, and industry as listed in Table 3.1 [2]. It is estimated that by 2020, the IoT market will worth hundreds of billion dollars and according to Market and Market report, IoT market surpassed US\$ 1 trillion in 2017 as illustrated in Figure 3.1, and it is expected that it will cross US\$ 1,266 billion by 2019 [3]. In IoT applications, the information is gathered from users and/or smart things through sensors, wearable devices, and cameras known as edges or sensor nodes (SNs). The data gathered is transferred, processed, and stored in the cloud for further processing, visualization, and recommendations as shown in Figure 3.2 [1].

---

[1] School of Computing and Engineering, University of West London, London, United Kingdom
[2] Department of Electronics, Computing and Mathematics, University of Derby, Derby, United Kingdom
[3] School of Computer Science and Engineering, University of New South Wales, Sydney, Australia

Table 3.1   IoT applications domain

Domain	Description	Application
Society	Activities related to the development and betterment of the city, society, and people	Smart cities, smart agriculture, smart animal farming, health care, independent living, home automation, smart buildings, smart grid, smart transportation, medical technology
Environment	Activities related to monitoring, protection, and natural resources development	Smart environment, smart water, smart metering, recycling, disaster alerting and management
Industry	Activities related to commercial transactions between organizations, companies, and other entities	Retail, supply chain management automotive, logistics, industrial control and automation, aerospace and aviation

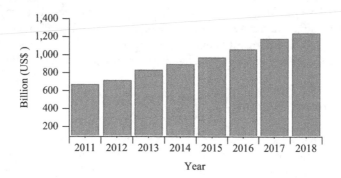

Figure 3.1   IoT market revenue, 2011–18 [4]

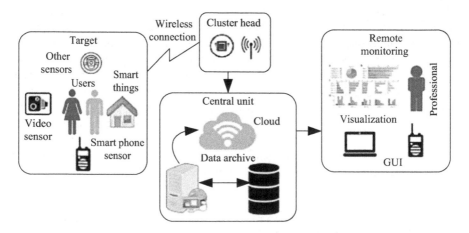

Figure 3.2   IoT connecting devices and users for various applications

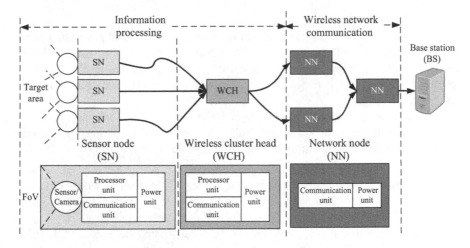

Figure 3.3   Wireless sensor network architecture

3.1.1   Wireless sensor network

Wireless sensor network (WSN) is an integrated part of the IoT and provides a virtual layer to collect information from the physical world, i.e., field-of-view (FoV) [5]. A typical WSN structure consists of four main components as shown in Figure 3.3.

3.1.1.1   Sensor nodes

Recent advances in micro-electro-mechanical systems technology, wireless communications, and digital electronics have enabled the development of low-cost, low-power, multifunctional SNs that are small in size and communicate untethered in short distances. They are the endpoints of the WSN, and each SN comprises sensor, processing unit, and a communication unit. WSNs may consist of different types of sensors, for example, seismic, thermal, low sampling rate magnetic, visual, acoustic, radar, and infrared [6].

3.1.1.2   Wireless cluster head

In WSNs, a process called clustering is performed for achieving better energy efficiency, where several SNs are grouped into one cluster, and one specific SN often referred as wireless cluster head (WCH) is selected. The WCH gathers the data from each node in the cluster and performs further processing to compress the data and then transmits the aggregated data wirelessly to the base station (BS). A WCH contains processing, power, and communication units [5,7].

3.1.1.3   Wireless network node

A wireless network node (WNN) has a power unit and a communication unit. The WNNs have no processing units and only relay the data between the nodes until the BS receives the aggregated data [5].

3.1.1.4   Base station

The BS in WSN is usually a conventional computer with powerful processing capabilities, it basically collects the information from WNNs. The BS provides WAN connectivity and data logging. The BS connects to database replicas across the internet. Finally, the data is displayed to the professionals and/or other users through a user interface [5,8].

The modern technologies have produced SNs with high performance, low cost, and small size for both the scalar and multimedia content. The various units inside the nodes have different functionality that are explained as follows [5]:

1. Sensing unit: It detects the physical occurrences using a single or multiple sensors in analogue form and converts it into digital signals for the processing unit.
2. Processing unit: It is a microcontroller and/or microprocessor with a memory that performs intelligent processing on the data received from FoV.
3. Communication unit: It is a transceiver typically using IEEE 802.14.3, IEEE 802.15.4, or ZigBee standard protocols.
4. Power unit: It supplies regulated DC voltage for data collection, intelligent processing, and transmission purposes.

3.1.2   Cloud

Cloud computing, often referred as simply "the cloud." All the data from different cluster heads is accumulated in the cloud. The cloud provides a massive data/information storage and processing infrastructure [9,10]. The cloud promises high scalability, reliability, speed, performance, autonomy, and low-cost for the IoT applications. In simple words, cloud delivers computing services, storage, networking, databases, software, intelligence, and analytics. The cloud is an essential part of IoT system [11], and the collected data that arrives in big amounts often reaches at real-time. Amazon EC2, Microsoft Azure, Google App Engine, Nimbus, IBM Blue Cloud, and 3Tera are some of the examples of cloud-computing systems [9].

3.1.2.1   Big data

Big data definitions evolved rapidly, which has created some confusion. Some definitions focus on what big data is, while others explains what it does. The first characteristic of big data that comes into mind is size; however, recently few other characteristics of the big data have emerged such as volume, variety, and velocity. Therefore, big data can be described on the basis of these 3Vs shown in Figure 3.4 [12,13]. Gartner, Inc. describes big data in similar words:

"Big data is high-volume, high-velocity and high-variety information assets that demand cost-effective, innovative forms of information processing for enhanced insight and decision making" [14].

Similarly, TechAmerica Foundation explains/defines big data as follows:

"Big data is a term that describes large volumes of high velocity, complex and variable data that require advanced techniques and technologies to enable the capture, storage, distribution, management, and analysis of the information" [12].

1. Volume in the 3Vs shows the magnitude of data. Large volume of digital information is generated from millions of applications and devices (smart devices, ICTs,

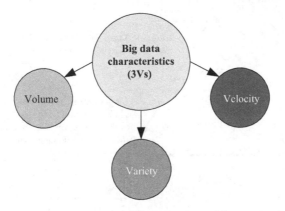

Figure 3.4 Big data characteristics

products' codes, smartphones, sensors, social networks, and logs) [15]. The size of big data is mostly reported in multiple terabytes and petabytes. A terabyte contains 1,024 GB data, while a petabyte is equivalent to 1,024 TB. One TB can store a data that would fit on 220 DVDs or 1,500 CDs in other words enough to store approximately 16 million Facebook photographs. Earlier estimates indicate that Facebook stores 260 billion photos utilizing a storage space of 20 PB [12,16].

2. Variety indicates the structural heterogeneity in dataset. There are various types of data, i.e., structured, semi-structured, and unstructured. The structured data constitutes approximately 5%–7% of all the existing data. It refers to the data in tabular form found in relational databases or spreadsheets. Unstructured data lacks the structural organization needed by the machines for analysis purposes. The examples of unstructured data include text, images, audios, and videos. Semi-structured data is between structured and unstructured data. This format of data does not conform to any strict standards [12,17].

3. The term velocity refers to the data generation rate from SNs and the speed required to be analyzed and acted upon. The advancement in sensor technology and proliferation of digital devices, e.g., smartphones, has initiated an unprecedented rate of data generation. This is driving an ever growing urgency for real-time analytics. IoT deals with thousands of streaming data sources (devices/sensors) that demand real-time analytics. The traditional data management systems cannot handle this huge data feeds instantaneously, thereby making big data technologies in IoT come into play [12,17,18].

3.1.2.2 Cloud services

Cloud provides an easy way to access servers, databases, storage, and various application services over the Internet. The service model of the cloud computing environment comprises three core options as shown in Figure 3.5 [19].

1. Software as a service (SaaS): It is a multi-tenant platform comprising end user applications that are delivered as a service. The examples of SaaS providers include Salesforce.com, Oracle, Microsoft, NetSuite, and IBM. These platforms

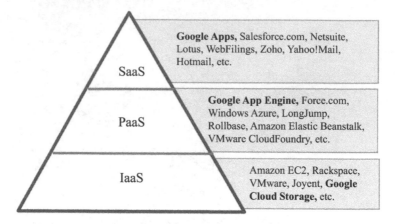

Figure 3.5   Cloud services (Source: Gartner AADI Summit Dec, 2009)

are built to accept the massive volumes of data (big data) generated by the sensors, devices, applications, websites, and customers [19–21].

2. Platform as a service (PaaS): It provides middleware or an application PaaS on which the developers build, deploy, and test custom applications. The Microsoft's Windows Azure platform services are generally referenced as PaaS solutions at this middleware tier [19,22,23].

3. Infrastructure as a service: This primarily circumscribes the technology and hardware for computing power, operating systems, storage, or other infrastructure, delivered as off-premises, on-demand services, for example, the Amazon Simple Storage Service (Amazon S3), or Amazon Elastic Compute Cloud (Amazon EC2) or rather than as dedicated, on-site resources [19,22,23].

3.1.2.3   Cloud types

There are three types of cloud: (1) private, (2) public, and (3) hybrid as illustrated in Figure 3.6.

1. Private cloud: It is only available to a company, organization, and/or person. Processes and data are managed within the same organization. Some of the benefits of a private cloud service include improved insurance, unlimited bandwidth, and low risk of security issues [24].

2. Public cloud: It is a computing model which is available to everyone. It provides services to each user using the same infrastructure. Basically, the users pay for the resources they use. Some benefits of utilizing public cloud service include simple scalability, high reliability, and cost potency [24,25].

3. Hybrid cloud: It is a computing environment that uses a mix of private and public cloud services with composition between the two platforms. By allowing workloads/jobs to move between the public and private clouds as computing costs and needs change subsequently, hybrid cloud can give businesses more data deployment options and greater flexibility [24,26].

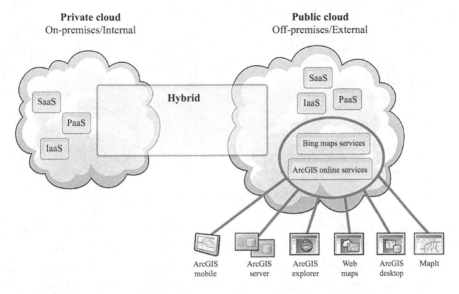

Figure 3.6   Cloud types and layered architecture [23]

3.1.3   Big data analytics

Big data analytics is basically a complex process of examining big data (varied and large data sets) to uncover the information including hidden patterns and unknown correlations that can help the professionals and/or organizations to make informed decisions. The process of extracting insights/information from big data can be categorized into five stages as shown in Figure 3.7 [12,27]. These five stages can be broken down into two main subprocesses: (1) data management and (2) analytics.

1.   Data management: It involves processes and technologies to collect and store data and to prepare data and retrieve it for further analysis.
2.   Analytics: It refers to the techniques being used to acquire and analyze intelligence from the big data. Therefore, big data analytics can be considered as a subprocess in the "insight extraction" from big data.

In the following sections, a brief overview of the big data analytical techniques considering structured and unstructured data are presented. An exhaustive list of the techniques is beyond the scope of this chapter. Therefore, the following few techniques subset of the tools are discussed that are available for big data analytics.

3.1.3.1   Text analytics
Text analytics also known as text mining is a technique that extracts valuable information from textual data. Social network feeds, blogs, emails, online forums, corporate documents, news, survey responses, and call center logs are some of the examples of

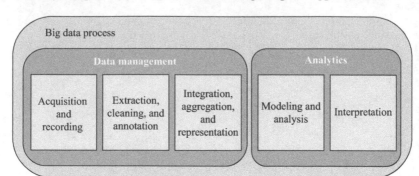

Figure 3.7   Big data processes to extract insights [12]

textual data. Text analytics involve computational linguistics, statistical analysis, and machine learning. Some of the text analytics methods are given as follows [28]:

1. Information extraction (IE): This technique extracts structured information from unstructured text. For example, IE algorithms that are used to extract structured data such as drug names, dosage, and frequency from a medical prescription. Two significant subtasks in IE include (1) entity recognition (ER) and (2) relation extraction (RE). The ER discovers names in text while classifies them into some predefined categories, e.g., person, location, date, and organization. On the other hand, RE extracts semantic relationship between the entities in the text [12,29].

2. Sentiment analysis: It is also referred as opinion mining. This technique analyzes opinionated text that contains people's opinions for entities such as organizations, products, events, and individuals. Sentiment analysis or opinion mining techniques can be further broken down into three subgroups: (1) document level, (2) sentence level, and (3) aspect based. The document-level technique determines whether the whole document expresses either a positive or negative sentiment. The sentence-level technique attempts to find the polarity of a sentiment about an entity that is expressed in a single sentence. Aspect-based are the techniques which recognize all the sentiments within a document [12,30].

3.1.3.2   Audio analytics

It analyzes and extracts information from audio data (unstructured). When audio analytics is applied to spoken human language, it is also called speech analytics. Since these techniques are mostly applied to spoken audio, therefore, the terms speech analytics and audio analytics are often used interchangeably. Health care and customer call centers are the primary applications of audio analytics [12].

1. Health care: In health care, audio analytics provides support to diagnose and treat certain medical conditions that can affect patient's communication patterns, e.g., schizophrenia, cancer, and depression. Moreover, audio analytics also help to analyze an infant's cries in order to know the infant's emotional and health status.

2. Call centers: In the call centers, audio analytics are used for the efficient analysis of millions and billions of recorded calls hours. Audio analytics improve the

customer experience, enhance sales turnover rates, evaluate agent performance, monitor compliance with various policies, e.g., privacy and security policies, and identify service or product issues among many other different tasks.

Speech analytics adopts two common technological approaches, i.e., (1) transcript-based approach which is also known as large-vocabulary continuous speech recognition (LVCSR) and (2) phonetic-based approach. These approaches are explained below.

1. LVCSR: The LVCSR systems work based on a two-phase process, i.e., indexing and searching. In the indexing, the speech content in the audio is transcribed. This is performed deploying automatic speech recognition algorithms to match sound to words. In search phase, standard text-based approaches are used to determine the search terms in the index file.

2. Phonetic-based systems: These approaches transcript phonemes or sounds into visual representation. The phonemes are distinct units of sound in a language that differentiate different words from another, e.g., the phonemes/k/and/b/ distinguish the meanings of a cat and bat. Like LVCSR, phonetic-based systems consist of two phases, i.e., (1) phonetic indexing and (2) searching. Indexing translates the speech into a phonemes sequence. Searching finds the phonetic representations of the search terms.

3.1.3.3 Video analytics

Video analytics also called video-content analysis; it involves different techniques to monitor, extract, and analyze the information from video streams [31]. Closed-circuit television cameras and video-sharing websites are the main contributors of computerized video analysis. In video analytics, a key challenge is the size of the video data. One data in one second of high-definition video is approximately equal to 2,000 pages of text. Video analytics in IoT is widely used in the recent years for surveillance and automated security. Automated surveillance systems are cost effective, cheaper, and remain focused as compared to labor-based surveillance systems. Video analytics can be used for human recognition, face recognition, object detection, recognizing suspicious activities, and detecting breach of restricted zones [32].

In terms of the IoT architecture, two approaches can be adopted for video analytics, namely, (1) server-based and (2) edge-based as explained below [12].

1. Server-based architecture: In this approach, captured video using cameras is transmitted to the centralized and dedicated server where video analytics is performed. The generated video is usually compressed to reduce the frame rates or the image resolution due to limited bandwidth availability. In this configuration, the compressing may result in the loss of information which can adversely affect analysis overall accuracy. However, the server-based approach facilitates easier maintenance.

2. Edge-based architecture. In this configuration, analytics are applied at the SN level or "edge" of the system. In other words, video analytics is performed on the raw data gathered from the camera in the SNs. In this approach, the entire

content/data of the video stream remains available for the video analysis. Therefore, no loss of information occurs and enables efficient and effective content analysis. However, edge-based systems are more costly to maintain and possess lower processing power capability compared to server-based systems.

3.2 Big data security

Nowadays, big data related to the service of Internet companies grow rapidly. Large data volumes are generated daily at unprecedented rate from different heterogeneous sources (e.g., health, industries, government, marketing, social networks, financial) [15,33]. For instance, Facebook generates log data of approximately 10 PB per month, Google processes hundreds of petabyte data, and similarly Alibaba is generating tens of terabyte of data for online trading in a single day. Figure 3.8 demonstrates the

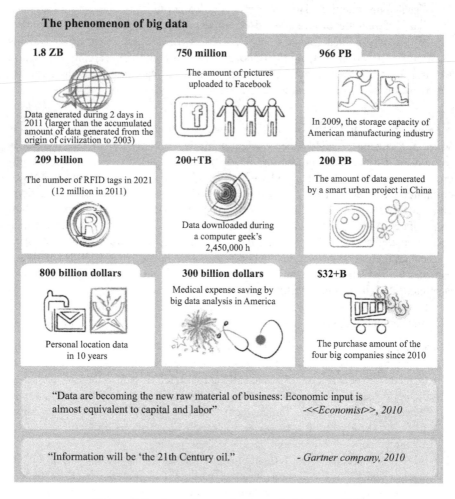

Figure 3.8   A continuous increase in big data [34]

boom in the global data volume generation. The quick growth of the IoT has further promoted a sharp growth in big data. The cloud computing is providing access sites and channels to the data asset. In the IoT paradigm, sensors collect and transmit the data to be stored in the cloud. As mentioned, IoT is a significant source of big data. Among the smart cities which are constructed on the basis of IoT, big data may also come from industry, traffic, agriculture, transportation, medical care, crowed monitoring, public departments, and families. The data generated by IoT possesses the following features [34]:

1. Large-scale data: In IoT, many data-acquisition sensors/devices are deployed, which acquire different types of data from a simple numeric data, e.g., location to a complex multimedia data, e.g., surveillance videos. Therefore, to meet the analysis and processing demands, both current acquired data and historical data (within a certain time frame) must be stored. Thus, data generated from IoT is characterized by large scales.
2. Heterogeneity: As there are variety of data acquisition digital devices and sensors therefore, the acquired data in IoT is different and features heterogeneity.
3. Strong time and space correlation: Every data acquisition device in IoT is positioned at a particular geographic location and every chunk of data/information has its time stamp. Therefore, time and space correlation is a significant property of data in IoT.
4. Effective data: A small portion of effective data contains in the big data. A large portion of data represents noise which occurs during the process of acquisition and transmission in IoT. Among the datasets collected by acquisition devices, a small amount of data is valuable, e.g., during traffic video acquisition, the few video frames capturing traffic violation and traffic accidents are important than capturing normal flow of traffic.

Apart from the factors such as scalability, complexity, and real-time response, privacy of the big data is one of the biggest challenge [34]. Critical and personal information of an individual, people, or an organization can be leaked and/or hacked. Therefore, security of the data is important. Traditional solutions are inadequate to deal with big data in order to ensure privacy and security. Access permissions, firewalls, encryption schemes, and transport layer security can be broken [35]. Therefore, advanced technologies and techniques are developed to monitor, protect, and audit big data processes considering the infrastructure, application, and data [18]. After thorough consideration of the literature, privacy and security issues for big data can be categorized in five titles as demonstrated in Figure 3.9.

The Cloud Security Alliance divided big data privacy and security challenges into four categories: (1) infrastructure security, (2) data privacy, (3) data management, and (4) integrity and reactive security [18].

1. Infrastructure security: It consists of security practices and secure distributed programming in non-relational data stores.
2. Data privacy: It refers to preserving encrypted data center analytics, and granular access control.

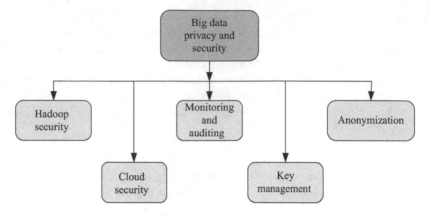

Figure 3.9   Privacy and security categorization of big data [18]

3.   Data management: It deals with how to collect data, integrate, and store. It manages to provide a secure data storage, auditing, and data provenance.
4.   Integrity and reactive security: It includes validation, filtering, and real-time monitoring.

3.2.1   Hadoop security

"The Apache Hadoop software library is a framework that allows for the distributed processing of large data sets across clusters of computers using simple programming models. It is designed to scale up from single servers to thousands of machines, each offering local computation and storage. Rather than rely on hardware to deliver high-availability, the library itself is designed to detect and handle failures at the application layer, so delivering a highly-available service on top of a cluster of computers, each of which may be prone to failures" [36].

Apache Hadoop provides distributed processing framework, and originally it was not developed for security purposes. Several security precautions have been developed on this popular platform recently [18]. Several companies such as Facebook, Yahoo, and Amazon store and process the data on Hadoop which proves its robustness and popularity [37].

Hadoop consider a network by default as trusted and the Hadoop clients use local user names. In default method, no encryption mechanism is involved between the Hadoop and client host, while in Hadoop distributed file system (HDFS), files are stored in a clear text which are controlled by a central server known as NameNode. HDFS basically manages file system namespace while regulating the access to files by clients. In other words, HDFS is data storage system, and it supports hundreds of nodes in a cluster, while it facilitates reliable and cost-effective storage. It can handle both structured and unstructured data and hold huge volumes (i.e., stored files can be bigger than a terabyte) [38]. The HDFS has no security appliance against the storage servers that can peep at data content. To solve these privacy and security issues, few mechanisms and techniques have been included into Hadoop.

3.2.1.1 Authentication and authorization

Authentication is a process to identify the user that is accessing the big data. Adluru *et al.* in [39] proposed two techniques to prevent a hacker to accumulate all the data in cloud. A trust mechanism between the user and NameNode is implemented. NameNode is basically a master server and a preliminary component of HDFS. First, the user authenticates itself before to access NameNode and sends a hash function. The NameNode also generates a hash function and compares it with user's hash function. If both, the hash functions are identical and correct, and access to the system is provided. SHA-256 a hashing technique for authentication is deployed and Rivest Shamir Adleman (RSA), Rijndael, Advanced Encryption Standard (AES), RC6 encryption techniques are used to protect the data from the hackers. MapReduce is used as encryption/decryption process, and finally these two techniques are integrated and tested on twitter streams.

The HDFS is another unit that may cause to reduce the privacy and security of the big data. Saraladevi *et al.* in [40] first increased the security of HDFS using Ticket Granting Ticket or Service Ticket, Kerberos mechanism for authentication. Second Bull Eye algorithm is deployed to monitor all sensitive information. Eye algorithm ensures data security as well as manages a relationship between the replicated and original data. This algorithm allows only authorized people to read or change the data. The issue of NameNode is handled using master and slave NameNodes. In case if an error occurs in the master node, the data is provided from the slave node by the permission of NameNode Security Enhance. This allows lower latency and abrupt response in a secure way.

3.2.2 Cloud security

The extensive deployment of the cloud computing for on-demand services, broad network access, and resource pooling have initiated a suitable environment for big data; however, clouds are prone to attacks and threats [41]. Therefore, a secure mechanism is needed on the clouds for big data sharing. There are different methods that are being deployed to ensure secured big data storing and sharing listed as follows:

1. Authentication
2. Encryption
3. Decryption
4. Compression.

Like any other computing environment, cloud security also involves maintaining sufficient preventative protections ensuring the following:

1. The data and systems both are safe.
2. It allows to insight into current state of security.
3. It responds and/or informs immediately if anything unusual occurs.
4. It traces and responds to the unexpected events.

The classical encrypted techniques are not sufficient to secure big data on cloud. Therefore, new schemes and approaches have been developed and proposed. For example, Hongbing *et al.* in [42] used cryptographic virtual mapping in order to create data path. Big data is separated into different parts and each part is on different storage provider. The storage path is encrypted if the big data encryption is not possible or computational extensive. This approach generates multiple copies of each data part to ensure the data availability.

3.2.3 Monitoring and auditing

Security monitoring is the process of investigating network events to detect the intrusions. The following two elements play a significant role in active security.

3.2.3.1 Intrusion detection

Intrusion detection and prevention applied on the entire network traffic is a tough job. Therefore, security monitoring architecture are developed to analyze domain name system (DNS) traffic, Hypertext Transfer Protocol (HTTP) traffic, IP flow records, and honeypot data. Marchal *et al.* in [43] developed a data-correlation scheme. This scheme calculates three likelihood metrics and identifies whether domain name, packet, or flow is malicious. In the case of malicious activity, an alert occurs in the detection system or the process terminates through prevention system.

3.2.3.2 Event monitoring

Abnormalities can occur in the network-security systems; therefore, big data security event-monitoring system model is required. Lan and Jun in [44] developed big data security event-monitoring system model which comprises four modules: (1) data collection, (2) integration, (3) analysis, and (4) interpretation.

1. Data collection: It includes network devices and security logs and event information.
2. Data integration: This process is performed for data filtering and classifying purposes.
3. Data analysis: In this module, association and correlations rules are determined to capture events.
4. Data interpretation: This module generates visual and statistical outputs and provides them to knowledge database that takes decisions, predict network behavior, and respond events.

The separation of suspicious and non-suspicious data behavior is another issue in monitoring the big data. A self-assuring system that contains four modules is presented by Gupta *et al.* in [45]. In the first module, there are keywords, i.e., library that represents suspicious data. The identification information are recorded in module second named low critical log (LCL) when a suspicious behavior occurs. The third module termed high critical log counts LCL occurrence frequency and determines whether LCL reaches the thresholds value. The last module is a self-assuring system and prevents the user to access the data if the user is detected as suspicious.

3.2.4   Key management

Key generation and sharing with other servers, users is also a security concern in big data. Therefore, to address this security issue, big data centers and authentication protocols are developed.

Thayananthan and Albeshri in [46] proposed a layered model using quantum cryptography for key generation with lower complexity. The authors also used PairHand protocol for the purpose of authentication in fixed or mobile data centers. The developed model consists of front end, data reading, quantum key processing, quantum key management, and application layers. This model enhances the efficiency while also reducing the search operations and passive attacks. Moreover, big data services contain multiple groups, and for secure communications, these groups need key transfer protocols. Hsu *et al.* in [47] developed a novel protocol based on Diffie–Hellman key agreement and linear secret sharing scheme. The protocol counter attacks through ensured key freshness, key confidentiality, and key authentication to reduce overall system's overhead.

Conditional proxy re-encryption (CPRE) is another approach that is being deployed for secure group data sharing. Son *et al.* in [48] developed an outsourcing CPRE scheme cloud environment. This scheme reduces the overhead and encrypts the data without downloading the data from cloud. When a group membership changes, the key generation and decryption execute on the outsourcing server and a changing key is generated. The cloud storage uses this key for data transfer.

3.2.5   Anonymization

Data harvesting for analytics can cause severe privacy concerns. Therefore, protecting personally identifiable information (PII) has become difficult as the data is shared quickly. To remove these privacy and security concerns, the individual and company involved in the agreement must be determined by some policies. Personal data should be anonymized and transferred into secure channels [18,49]. Sedayao *et al.* in [50], removed PII from the Intel Circuit web portal logs in order to protect user's privacy. The developed architecture anonymizes the sensitive fields in log data using AES symmetric key encryption while storing log data in HDFS for further analysis. When de-anonymization is required, the logs are moved and masking areas are decrypted. With the increasing concern of organizational and individual privacy, privacy-preserving data mining gained a tremendous attention. However, this technique adversely affects the success of applications. Subsequently, an adaptive utility-based anonymization is proposed for security and privacy by Panackal and Pillai in [51]. The authors enhanced the classification accuracy using the proposed iterative process.

Though researchers and companies have proposed many solutions as listed in Table 3.2, none of the models provides a complete solution for privacy and handling security attacks as each mechanism has some benefits and hindrance [52]. There is huge potential and opportunities for the researchers in the future to address the privacy and security challenges of big data in IoT.

Table 3.2   Big data privacy and security studies categorization

Reference	Category	Aim	Methodology
[39]	Hadoop security	Privacy and security of Hadoop	Trust mechanism between name node and user, a random encryption approach
[40]		HDFS security	NameNode approach, Kerberos mechanism and Bull Eye Algorithm approach
[42]	Cloud security	Secure data storage on cloud	Identity-based encryption algorithm and key establishment scheme
[43]	Monitoring and auditing	Intrusion detection architecture	Maliciousness likelihood metrics
[44]		Predict network behavior	Data collection, integration, analysis, and interpretation
[45]		Detect abnormal user behavior	Self-assuring system
[46]	Key management	Generates keys and authenticates data centers	PairHand protocol and quantum cryptography
[47]		Secure group key transfer	Online key generation based on Diffie–Hellman key agreement
[48]		Secure group data sharing	Outsourcing conditional re-encryption scheme
[50]	Anonymization	Anonymization of sensitive fields	K-anonymity-based metrics
[51]		Privacy preserving data mining	Adaptive utility-based anonymization model

3.3   Summary

IoT is a technological revolution and plays a significant role to improve our QoL. As per literature, approximately 4.4 trillion GB data will be generated by IoT in 2020. With the rapidly growing number of connected digital devices, it is possible that by 2020, around 10 billion of sensors/devices would be connected to the Internet. Furthermore, all of these sensors and devices will collect, analyze, transmit, and share data in real time. Subsequently, without the data, IoT connected devices will not hold capabilities and functionalities which made them popular and brought worldwide attention. The role of big data considering IoT is important and provides a mechanism to store, process, and analyze large volume of data using different technologies. Big data safety, privacy, and security is one of the biggest issues. Though the area of privacy and security is thoroughly studied, more effective and efficiency techniques, solutions, and technologies are required to be developed in the future.

References

[1]   Ali H, Tariq UU, Zheng Y, *et al.* Energy-aware real-time task mapping on NoC based heterogeneous MPSoCs. IEEE Access. 2018;6:75110–75123.

[2]   Al-Fuqaha A, Guizani M, Mohammadi M, *et al.* Internet of things: A survey on enabling technologies, protocols, and applications. IEEE Communications Surveys & Tutorials. 2015;17(4):2347–2376.

[3]   Marvin S, and Luque-Ayala A. Urban operating systems: Diagramming the city. International Journal of Urban and Regional Research. 2017;41(1): 84–103.

[4]   Ahmed E, Yaqoob I, Hashem IAT, *et al.* The role of big data analytics in Internet of Things. Computer Networks. 2017;129:459–471.

[5]   Ang LM, Seng KP, Chew LW, *et al.* Wireless multimedia sensor network technology. In: Wireless multimedia sensor networks on reconfigurable hardware. Berlin, Heidelberg: Springer; 2013. p. 5–38.

[6]   Akyildiz IF, Su W, Sankarasubramaniam Y, *et al.* Wireless sensor networks: A survey. Computer Networks. 2002;38(4):393–422.

[7]   Shen Y, and Ju H. Energy-efficient cluster-head selection based on a fuzzy expert system in wireless sensor networks. In: Proceedings of the 2011 IEEE/ACM International Conference on Green Computing and Communications. IEEE Computer Society; 2011. p. 110–113.

[8]   Mainwaring A, Culler D, Polastre J, *et al.* Wireless sensor networks for habitat monitoring. In: Proceedings of the 1st ACM International Workshop on Wireless Sensor Networks and Applications. ACM; 2002. p. 88–97.

[9]   Stojkoska BLR, and Trivodaliev KV. A review of Internet of Things for smart home: Challenges and solutions. Journal of Cleaner Production. 2017;140: 1454–1464.

[10] Fox A, Griffith R, Joseph A, *et al.* Above the clouds: A Berkeley view of cloud computing. Rep UCB/EECS-2009-28(13). Dept Electrical Eng and Comput Sciences, University of California, Berkeley; 2009.

[11] Gubbi J, Buyya R, Marusic S, *et al.* Internet of Things (IoT): A vision, architectural elements, and future directions. Future Generation Computer Systems. 2013;29(7):1645–1660.

[12] Gandomi A, and Haider M. Beyond the hype: Big data concepts, methods, and analytics. International Journal of Information Management. 2015;35(2): 137–144.

[13] Kwon O, Lee N, and Shin B. Data quality management, data usage experience and acquisition intention of big data analytics. International Journal of Information Management. 2014;34(3):387–394.

[14] Gartner. IT glossary (nd). Retrieved from http://www.gartner.com/it-glossary/bigdata/.

[15] Oussous A, Benjelloun FZ, Lahcen AA, *et al.* Big Data technologies: A survey. Journal of King Saud University-Computer and Information Sciences. 2018;30(4):431–448.

[16]   Beaver D, Kumar S, Li HC, *et al.* Finding a needle in Haystack: Facebook's photo storage. In: OSDI. vol. 10; 2010. p. 1–8.

[17]   Economist T. Data, data everywhere: A special report on managing information. The Economist. 17 April 2010.

[18]   Terzi DS, Terzi R, and Sagiroglu S. A survey on security and privacy issues in big data. In: Internet Technology and Secured Transactions (ICITST), 2015 10th International Conference for. IEEE; 2015. p. 202–207.

[19]   Rimal BP, Choi E, and Lumb I. A taxonomy and survey of cloud computing systems. In: INC, IMS and IDC, 2009. NCM'09. Fifth International Joint Conference on. IEEE; 2009. p. 44–51.

[20]   Mell P, and Grance T. The NIST definition of cloud computing; 2011.

[21]   Wu L, Garg SK, and Buyya R. SLA-based resource allocation for software as a service provider (SaaS) in cloud computing environments. In: Proceedings of the 2011 11th IEEE/ACM International Symposium on Cluster, Cloud and Grid Computing. IEEE Computer Society; 2011. p. 195–204.

[22]   Jamsa K. Cloud computing. Burlington, MA: Jones and Bartlett Publishers, Inc.; 2012.

[23]   esri. The new age of cloud computing and GIS. 2018. Retrieved from https://www.esri.com/news/arcwatch/0110/feature.html.

[24]   Jadeja Y, and Modi K. Cloud computing-concepts, architecture and challenges. In: Computing, Electronics and Electrical Technologies (ICCEET), 2012 International Conference on. IEEE; 2012. p. 877–880.

[25]   Li A, Yang X, Kandula S, *et al.* CloudCmp: Comparing public cloud providers. In: Proceedings of the 10th ACM SIGCOMM Conference on Internet Measurement. ACM; 2010. p. 1–14.

[26]   Li J, Li YK, Chen X, *et al.* A hybrid cloud approach for secure authorized deduplication. IEEE Transactions on Parallel and Distributed Systems. 2015; 26(5):1206–1216.

[27]   Labrinidis A, and Jagadish HV. Challenges and opportunities with big data. Proceedings of the VLDB Endowment. 2012;5(12):2032–2033.

[28]   Chung W. BizPro: Extracting and categorizing business intelligence factors from textual news articles. International Journal of Information Management. 2014;34(2):272–284.

[29]   Aggarwal CC, and Zhai C. A survey of text clustering algorithms. In: Mining text data. Boston, MA: Springer; 2012. p. 77–128.

[30]   Feldman R. Techniques and applications for sentiment analysis. Communications of the ACM. 2013;56(4):82–89.

[31]   Abraham A, and Das S. Computational intelligence in power engineering. vol. 302. Berlin, Heidelberg: Springer; 2010.

[32]   Hu W, Xie N, Li L, *et al.* A survey on visual content-based video indexing and retrieval. IEEE Transactions on Systems, Man, and Cybernetics, Part C (Applications and Reviews). 2011;41(6):797–819.

[33]   Khan N, Yaqoob I, Hashem IAT, *et al.* Big data: Survey, technologies, opportunities, and challenges. The Scientific World Journal. 2014;2014:1–19.

[34]   Chen M, Mao S, and Liu Y. Big data: A survey. Mobile Networks and Applications. 2014;19(2):171–209.

[35]   Matturdi B, Xianwei Z, Shuai L, *et al.* Big data security and privacy: A review. China Communications. 2014;11(14):135–145.

[36]   Apache Hadoop. What Is Apache Hadoop?; 2014.

[37]   Jam MR, Khanli LM, Javan MS, *et al.* A survey on security of Hadoop. In: Computer and Knowledge Engineering (ICCKE), 2014 4th International eConference on. IEEE; 2014. p. 716–721.

[38]   White T. Hadoop: The definitive guide. Sebastopol, CA: O'Reilly Media, Inc.; 2012.

[39]   Adluru P, Datla SS, and Zhang X. Hadoop eco system for big data security and privacy. In: Systems, Applications and Technology Conference (LISAT), 2015 IEEE Long Island. IEEE; 2015. p. 1–6.

[40]   Saraladevi B, Pazhaniraja N, Paul PV, *et al.* Big data and Hadoop – A study in security perspective. Procedia Computer Science. 2015;50:596–601.

[41]   Hashem IAT, Yaqoob I, Anuar NB, *et al.* The rise of "big data" on cloud computing: Review and open research issues. Information Systems. 2015;47:98–115.

[42]   Hongbing C, Chunming R, Kai H, *et al.* Secure big data storage and sharing scheme for cloud tenants. China Communications. 2015;12(6):106–115.

[43]   Marchal S, Jiang X, State R, *et al.* A big data architecture for large scale security monitoring. In: 2014 IEEE International Congress on Big Data. IEEE; 2014. p. 56–63.

[44]   Lan L, and Jun L. Some special issues of network security monitoring on big data environments. In: Dependable, Autonomic and Secure Computing (DASC), 2013 IEEE 11th International Conference on. IEEE; 2013. p. 10–15.

[45]   Gupta A, Verma A, Kalra P, *et al.* Big data: A security compliance model. In: IT in Business, Industry and Government (CSIBIG), 2014 Conference on. IEEE; 2014. p. 1–5.

[46]   Thayananthan V, and Albeshri A. Big data security issues based on quantum cryptography and privacy with authentication for mobile data center. Procedia Computer Science. 2015;50:149–156.

[47]   Hsu C, Zeng B, and Zhang M. A novel group key transfer for big data security. Applied Mathematics and Computation. 2014;249:436–443.

[48]   Son J, Kim D, Hussain R, *et al.* Conditional proxy re-encryption for secure big data group sharing in cloud environment. In: Computer Communications Workshops (INFOCOM WKSHPS), 2014 IEEE Conference on. IEEE; 2014. p. 541–546.

[49]   Tene O, and Polonetsky J. Big data for all: Privacy and user control in the age of analytics. Northwestern Journal of Technology and Intellectual Property. 2012;11:xxvii.

[50]   Sedayao J, Bhardwaj R, and Gorade N. Making big data, privacy, and anonymization work together in the enterprise: Experiences and issues. In: Big Data (BigData Congress), 2014 IEEE International Congress on. IEEE; 2014. p. 601–607.

[51]   Panackal JJ, and Pillai AS. Adaptive utility-based anonymization model: Performance evaluation on big data sets. Procedia Computer Science. 2015;50: 347–352.

[52]   Arora S, Kumar M, Johri P, *et al.* Big heterogeneous data and its security: A survey. In: Computing, Communication and Automation (ICCCA), 2016 International Conference on. IEEE; 2016. p. 37–40.

Chapter 4

A watermark-based *in situ* access-control model for image big data

Liangli Ma[1], Jinyi Guo[2], Wei Ren[3,4], and Yi Ren[5]

When large images are used for big data analysis, they impose new challenges in protecting image privacy. For example, a geographic image may consist of several sensitive areas or layers. When it is uploaded into servers, the image will be accessed by diverse subjects. Traditional access-control methods regulate access privileges to a *single* image, and their access-control strategies are stored in servers, which impose two shortcomings: (1) fine-grained access control is not guaranteed for areas/layers in a single image that needs to maintain secret for different roles and (2) access-control policies that are stored in servers suffer from multiple attacks (e.g., transferring attacks). In this chapter, we propose a novel watermark-based access-control model in which access-control policies are associated with objects being accessed (called an *in situ* model). The proposed model integrates access-control policies as watermarks within images, without relying on the availability of servers or connecting networks. The access control for images is still maintained even though images are redistributed again to further subjects. Therefore, access-control policies can be delivered together with the big data of images. Moreover, we propose a hierarchical key-role-area model for fine-grained encryption, especially for large-sized images such as geographic maps. The extensive analysis justifies the security and performance of the proposed model.

4.1 Preliminaries

Access control is a primary method to solve this problem. Usually, access control distributes different privileges of files to different users, thus data can be safer. In other words, different safety levels data have their corresponding users, and every user has his specific privileges to operate data. Access-control model can be classified to

[1]College of Electronic Engineering, Naval University of Engineering, Wuhan, P.R. China
[2]School of Computer Science, China University of Geosciences, Wuhan, P.R. China
[3]Hubei Key Laboratory of Intelligent Geo-Information Processing, China University of Geosciences, Wuhan, P.R. China
[4]Guizhou Provincial Key Laboratory of Public Big Data, Guizhou University, Guiyang, P.R. China
[5]School of Computing Science, University of East Anglia, Norwich, UK

role-based access control (RBAC) model [1], task-based access-control model [2], and object-based access-control model [3].

Remote-sensing image mainly divided into aerial photograph and satellite photograph. It can be used to monitor land cover, forest cover, and grassland. Geographic image contains wider information than remote-sensing image, including normal atlas, topographic map, city-planning diagram, geographic environment information, and even biological information in different areas.

To ensure digital images can be spread freely in network, but only ones who have specific privileges can visit them, we should encrypt images. Image-encryption technique can be classified into two types, which are airspace image encryption technology and compression image encryption technology. Discrete chaotic encryption technology [4] is a typical method of airspace image encryption technology, and it processes images as a two-dimensional data. Compression image encryption technology based on some certain compression technique, such as JPEG (2008), arithmetic coding [5], and wavelet compression technology [6]. These encryption techniques process digital images at data level, instead of content analysis. They cannot process images in different areas/layers according to diverse situations.

4.2 Introduction

The development of deep learning enables the analysis of a massive amount of image data. During these processes, how to analyze the image data while protecting images from leakage and exposure is a big challenge. Traditional access-control policies may be invalid when images are stored again in different servers. For example, 4G and incoming 5G techniques enable smart phone users to share their images easily. When an image is uploaded to a service provider (e.g., Facebook), a user can set access privileges to control the access rights for the image so that the image can only be accessed by "friends" or the public. However, when the accumulated images are redistributed to other parties for further analysis (e.g., the Facebook–Cambridge Analytica scandal[1]), the access-control policies which were stored in its original servers are lost. Thus, desired protection solutions should integrate access-control policies with the image itself. In other words, even if the image is redistributed, the access-control polices will be attached (*in situ*) as well. In addition, a simple "yes" or "no" access control on an image does not work well. For example, when taking a photo with a smart phone, additional information such as location data, latitude/longitude, map, and date and time are also included. Various privileges should be attached for that information. Consider geographic or remote sensing images as another example. A geographic image may consist of several areas/layers. Thus, differentiating access control for various areas/layers requires fine-grained and flexible access-control policies.

Recently, centrally regulated access-control models (e.g., [7,8]) have been intensively studied. However, they are not suitable for image data sharing and redistribution

[1]https://wwwtheguardiancom/technology/2018/apr/04/facebook-cambridge-analytica-user-data-latest-more-than-thought. 2018.

for the following reasons: distributed data can be accessed with two modes: "Yes" for all or "No" for all. For data that cannot be accessed publicly, the data cannot be distributed. Once data is distributed, it can be accessed by all accessors. Besides, for those data that must be in access control (classified data), control policies are difficult to define and change, especially when the data volume is large. For example, for different areas in a single image with different access policies, we must set up different regulations in central control servers. Moreover, classified data can be accessed only when remote policy conformance servers are available. The accessibility of the data relies on the availability of networks and the workload of central control servers. It constrains the convenience of remotely accessing data. Furthermore, access-control regulation for a large volume of data results in a large delay. Each time accessors request images, they must first fetch access-control policies on servers. In big data scenarios, accessing a response on servers results in a large burden and access delay. Finally, once data is distributed, the control domain is changed. Thus, the old management authority may not be available to control the data.

Therefore, with the development of big data sharing and redistribution, traditional access-control models based on central conformance should be improved to cater to the new requirements.

In this chapter, we design a novel access-control model in which access control is conducted by specific clients and access policies are carried together with access objects themselves. Our proposed access-control model has the following advantages: access-control policies are attached with image data. Regardless of how many times the data are further redistributed, access-control policies are still incorporated with the data. Additionally, access control is fine-grained. For images with large size (e.g., geographic or remote-sensing images), control strategies must be specific to different partial areas instead of the entire image. In other words, different parts in one image must conform to different access privileges. Furthermore, accessing classified data does not rely on remote servers or available network connections. The control flow is made more lightweight due to reshaping regulations at clients (we also call it *in situ* control).

Based on the above observations and analysis, we propose a new access-control model for big image data sharing and redistribution. The major contributions of this chapter are listed as follows:

1. We propose a watermark-based access-control model, allowing objects being accessed to integrate together with access-control strategies.
2. We propose a hierarchical key-role-area access-control model for images with large size such as geographic graphs and remote sensing graphs. We also propose a hierarchical key generation method that can guarantee fine-grained access privileges.

The rest of the chapter is organized as follows: Section 4.3 surveys related work. Section 4.4 formulates the research problems and challenges. Section 4.5 elaborates on the proposed models. Extensive analysis of the proposed scheme is presented in Section 4.6, and we conclude the chapter in Section 4.7.

4.3   Related work

The topic of watermarks has been explored for decades. Due to powerful software and personal computers, there has emerged considerable unauthorized copying and distribution of digital content, such as e-books, videos, and digital images. To solve this problem, watermarks are usually used to verify and protect the copyrights [9–12]. Watermark can be classified into robust watermark and fragile watermark. A major problem of digital watermark is that watermark can be extracted and be used to verify even if it is changed intentionally or unintentionally. This kind of change is geometric transformation, photometric transformation, or damage in transmission. In "A robust watermark authentication technique based on Weber's descriptor" [13], a watermark technique was proposed which is able to authenticate the presence of watermark in the watermarked image, even when it is distorted due to geometric and photometric attacks. In addition to this, this technique is found to be robust against noise, cropping, and compression attacks. Su [14] suggested a new blind watermarking algorithm, which embeds the binary watermark into the blue component of a RGB image in the spatial domain, to resolve the problem of protecting copyright. Usually, fragile watermark is used to detect whether original image has been tampered, and distinguish areas which are tampered and untampered. In "An image fragile watermark scheme based on chaotic image pattern and pixel-pairs," a general framework for fragile watermark is proposed, and then a novel fragile watermarking scheme for image authentication is presented. Simulation results and performance analysis show that the presented method is fast, secure, and capable of detecting and localizing modification. In the above methods, both fragile watermarks and robust watermarks are coded as a legal label instead of as a control technique. Additionally, many methods have been evaluated to detect the modification of images [15,16]. Also, watermark can be categorized into visible watermark and invisible watermark. Invisible watermark is not visible to our eyes, so it does not affect the view quality of images. "Robust watermark technique using masking and Hermite transform" [17] evaluated a watermark algorithm designed for digital images by using a perceptive mask and a normalization process; thus, it can prevent human eye detection. Since visible watermark will decrease image quality, Hu [18] proposes a reversible visible watermarking algorithm to satisfy a new application scenario where the visible watermark serves as a tag or ownership identifier but can be completely removed to resume the original image data. However, these measures are unable to find the modifier or prevent such modifications.

In recent years, several watermark schemes have been claimed for access control. In "Watermark based access control to copyrighted content" [19], methods which utilize the embedding redundancy to maximize robustness and the security of the system while maintaining low implementation cost are proposed. This model combines watermark with access control to protect copyright. In 2011, Yang [20] investigated embedding binary watermarks in digital images in dual-tree complex wavelet transform domain for access control of digital image, due to its rich direction selection, shift invariance, and higher robustness. Watermarks used for permitting hierarchical access control and protecting the content of visual medical information were proposed [21]. However, original images are not encrypted in this scheme. A removable and visible watermark by combining block truncation coding and chaotic map is proposed in "A secure removable visible watermarking for BTC compressed images" [22], which can be applied in copyright notification and access control in mobile communication. They proposed two-stage watermarks that blur original images before visitors pass access control, and only authorized visitors can attain clear images. However, they are not a hierarchical access control. Phadikar suggested a quality access control in "Data hiding based quality access control of digital images using adaptive QIM and lifting" [23]. It means that images are encrypted to a vague state at first, and the people who own privileges can obtain clear image. In addition, he proposed a data-hiding scheme for access control and error concealment in digital images [24]. He also proposed a data-hiding method that integrates access control and authentication in a single platform, especially for cover images [25]. Jana [26] presented a hardware implementation of a reversible watermarking system that can insert invisible, semi-fragile watermark information into digital image in real time. Furthermore, removal of watermark signal from the watermarked image by reversible process realizes quality access control by authentic used. To summarize, the schemes above display images in lower quality formats before visitors obtain permission. The access-control strategies are still not coded in watermarks.

Quality-access control is also used in audio watermarks. Datta *et al.* proposed a combination of both encryption and audio watermark. This method is used for the safe distribution of audio content over public networks, whereby only authorized users can access the high-quality content, while other users can only access a low-quality content [27]. "Principles of Audio Watermarking" [28] contains a brief overview of modern methods for embedding additional data in audio signals. It is based on watermark and is used for access control or identification related to particular type of audio. A multipurpose digital speech watermark was designed by Nematollahi [29], which is applied to embed semi-fragile and robust watermarks simultaneously in the speech signal, respectively, to provide tamper detection and proof of ownership. This method is developed by a combination of personal identification number, one time password, and speaker biometric through the speech watermarks. Moreover, watermarks can be used in video files to identify pirates, which can be extracted at the decoder and used to determine whether the video content is watermarked [30]. With the concern of copyright protection, access control and coding efficiency for 3D content, Wang [31] proposed quantized Discrete Cosine Transform (DCT) expansion which hides the depth information into the texture image/video by a reversible watermarking algorithm. "An approach to embed image in video as watermark using a mobile device" [32] analyzes bitstream video watermarking technique, a study of spatial and temporal domain watermarking. The method evaluated in it can be implemented in computers and mobile phones. Besides, watermark can be used on documents in cloud computing. Tseng [33] utilized the watermark and RSA algorithms (a kind of asymmetric encryption algorithm) for increasing security of file-sharing in the clouds. This design applies the Authentication, Authorization, Accounting (AAA) certification mechanism to enhance the authentication security control. We stress that our proposed scheme for integrating access-control policies as watermarks can also be applied in audio files or video files, although we concentrate on images in this chapter.

Geologic mapping and the design of geologic (thematic) maps are currently supported by Geographic Information System (GIS). In order to gain a high degree of efficiency and to allow the exchange of a common structured framework, map data models have been designed by agencies and individuals in order to support their mapping process. File-based geo-databases are much more accessible but still suffer from a number of administrative limitations [34]. A new access-control mechanism that combines trust and RBAC models is presented in [35]. Kim proposes a multilayer based access-control model for GIS mobile web services [36]. The objective of such spatially aware access-control models is to regulate the access to protect objects based on the position information. Kirkpatrick proposed RBAC with spatial constraints [37]. Ma *et al.* proposed a fine-grained access-control model for spatial data in a grid environment based on an RBAC model [38]. Furthermore, a multi-granularity spatial access-control model was proposed that introduces more types of policy rule conflicts than single-granularity objects [39]. The model can manage and enforce the strong and efficient access-control technology in large-scale environments. However, all of these access-control strategies are not encoded into watermarks, and access control still relies on servers.

In recent years, quick response (QR) codes have been popular due to their efficiency and security. They are widely used in mobile phones (e.g., applications of instance messaging, user login, and mobile payment). QR codes cannot only store large information but also have error-correction ability [40]. A high-performance optical encryption (OE) scheme was proposed in "High performance optical encryption based on computational ghost imaging with QR code and compressive sensing technique" [41], based on computational ghost imaging (CGI) with QR code and compressive sensing technique, named QR-CGI-OE scheme. This scheme enhances the robustness of QR code significantly. In addition, QR codes have high recognition rate, and there are massive algorithm libraries to invoke [42]. Liu [43] designed a high-speed, high-accuracy binarization method, in order to adapt various sizes, various gray-level values, and under various lighting conditions of real bar code image. This technique can also locate the finder pattern accurately and integrate the local threshold method with global threshold. For these reasons, we chose the QR code as a case study for our model.

4.4 Problem formulation

4.4.1 System model

Figure 4.1 depicts the traditional access model, which includes four entities: servers, accessors, images, and access-control unit. The access-control unit is located with servers. Traditional access-control processes include four steps: (1) accessors request to fetch some data (e.g., images) from servers; (2) servers inquire access-control strategies from the access-control unit to determine corresponding accessible objects (e.g., images); (3) the access-control unit regulates access privileges as well as accessible objects accordingly; and (4) servers return accessible objects to accessors corresponding to designated privileges.

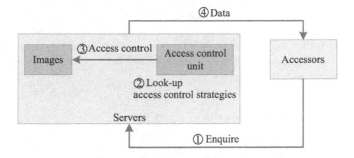

Figure 4.1 Existing traditional access-control model

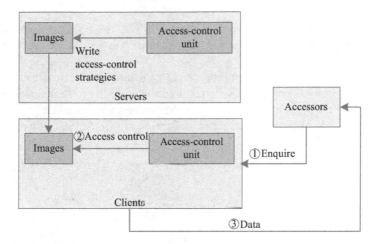

Figure 4.2 Existing traditional access-control model

Once accessors enquire servers for data, servers first have to search access-control strategies. According to the access-control policies, servers then decide what data can be provided to accessors.

In big data publication scenarios, we move the access-control unit to clients, so as to provide persistent control. We change the access-control processes as follows: (1) servers incorporate access-control strategies into images as watermarks; (2) accessors request to fetch some data (e.g., images), and servers publish image big data to accessors; (3) the access-control unit in clients' parses access-control strategies in watermarks to determine access to objects in images; and (4) the access-control unit regulates access privileges and returns accessible objects to accessors.

Figure 4.2 depicts our proposed new access-control architecture.

Note that embedding methods for access-control policies are independent with the above architecture. Watermarks or other associated tags can also be workable if they can reveal access-control policies. In most cases, invisible watermarks may be preferred.

Access-control policies are embedded with big data, and thus the access-control unit is moved to clients for persistent control, regardless of how many times the data are redistributed. Additionally, access control can be accomplished without assuming the availability of servers and networking connections, which also mitigates the workload of servers and shortens the access delay.

4.4.2 Attack models

4.4.2.1 Transferring attack

Existing access-control models invite the transferring attack. In a transferring attack, if accessor "A" can access image "P," then accessor "A" can transfer image "P" to others, such as accessor "B." Thus, accessor "B" can easily gain the access privileges of accessor "A."

To tackle this attack, we propose the use of a watermark-based access-control model where access policies are embedded with objects and move the access-control unit from servers to clients.

Besides, transferring attacks cannot be accountable. That is, it is impossible to trace back to original leaking accessors if many accessors can access the same objects. In other words, the provenance of leakage is lost. To provide provenance, we can also rely on watermarks that can reveal the identification of originators or leakers.

Proposition 4.1. *For persistent access control, access-control policies need to be associated with accessible objects, and the objects can only be accessed upon parsing policies at clients. Additionally, the objects need to return back to inaccessible status after the allotted time of authorized access.*

Proof. If objects do not retain inaccessible status after being accessed, others can also access those objects when they are transferred to others.

If access-control policies are not associated with accessible objects, clients will not be able to enforce access policies. □

Proposition 4.2. *For the provenance of distributed data, data must carry the identification information of originators.*

Proof. If data do not carry any of the originators' identification information, the provenance of who distributes data cannot be determined. □

4.4.2.2 Distributed denial of service (DDoS) attack

Traditional access-control models rely on the availability of servers and access-control units. The availability can be damaged by distributed denial of service (DDoS) attack. If servers or access-control units cannot be accessed, access processes or services will be terminated. It is much easier to let clients be available than servers, thus access-control that is migrated to clients will be more scalable and durable.

4.4.2.3 Coarse access

In traditional access-control models, servers are confronted with a large volume of data and access requests, and fine-grained access control will experience much difficulty due to workload. It is not fine grained if access control is specific to an entire image, instead of a specific area or layer in the image—especially for those images that have large size such as geographic graphs or remote sensing graphs. Traditional models may have to tackle fine-grained access by extra control, which further increases the overhead of servers.

4.4.2.4 Physical copy attack

In image big data distribution, the most difficult attack to defend against is physical copy attack, in which images are copied by physical manners such as screen capture or outside photo shooting. After accessors gain access to images, those images are totally displayed and out of (access) control. This attack must be tackled, especially if certain areas or layers in images must remain confidential. It cannot be defended against by access control because it is a kind of proactive defense before events. This attack can be traced back by watermark-based schemes for further provenance, as that is a kind of reactive defense after events.

Proposition 4.3. *Physical copy attack cannot be defended against by any access-control schemes, but it can be traced back to the source of image leakers, which is called provenance. The provenance can only be achieved by associated watermarks in images.*

Proof. As images can be uncovered and viewed by authorized accessors, physical copy attack such as screen capture and photo shooting is also possible.

The provenance can be achieved by embedding watermarks in images, as watermarks are also carried by images during and after physical copy attack.

Only when some watermarks associated with the identity of originators are embedded with uncovered images can the provenance of originators who exposed the images be accomplished from leaked images. □

4.4.3 Design goals

We list design goals as follows: design a novel access-control flow that migrates the control unit from servers to clients. Design a watermark-based access-control model that provides fine-grained access control for various areas or layers in a single image. Defend against attacks imposed by traditional access-control models and propose a tailored design for big data sharing and redistribution of images with large sizes.

Remark 4.1. *Images can be downloaded only from servers who embed access policies into images via watermarks.*

Images can only be viewed via particular client tools, such as an image browser that can extract watermarks, parse watermark semantics into policies, and enforce access-control policies before viewing. The context of watermarks can be recognized by corresponding clients.

Accessors may register their roles on servers at first, and their roles can be affirmed by client tools before viewing images.

The client tool can transparently decrypt images by asking for the correct keys. After accessors view their corresponding partial areas, those areas are encrypted again by client tools transparently.

If a hard copy of images is obtained by screen capture or photo shooting, watermarks in images can facilitate the trace back to the accessor who was the last authorized viewer.

4.5   Proposed scheme

4.5.1   Basic settings

We first describe a concrete process to explain our scheme, which consists of three steps as follows:

1. Accessors registration. Accessors register for data access on servers. They are assigned a role or multiple roles by servers.
2. Data publication. Servers who are data publishers or distributors embed access-control policies via watermarks in data such as images. Data is published, in which certain areas or layers may be encrypted by secret keys related to control policies.
3. Client conformance. Accessors request images via particular client tools, such as image browsers. Client tools ask accessors to present their roles and secret keys. Client tools enforce control policies by parsing from watermarks that are embedded in images, and decrypt corresponding areas or layers in images by responding secret keys.

Obviously, data publication and client conformance are critical in the design. Next, we propose a hierarchical encryption model as a concrete scheme.

4.5.2   Hierarchical key-role-area access-control model

The encryption (and decryption) of various areas in a single image can be conducted by the following proposed hierarchical models:

$HKRAGraph ::= \langle V, E \rangle$;
$V = \{KEY, ROLE, AREA\}$
$E = \{E_{k2k}, E_{r2k}, E_{a2r}\}$;
$E_{k2k} = \langle from, to \rangle, from, to \in KEY$;
$E_{r2k} = \langle from, to \rangle, from \in ROLE, to \in KEY$;
$E_{a2r} = \langle from, to \rangle, from \in AREA, to \in ROLE$.

1. Hierarchical keys
   i. $KEY ::= \langle l, c \rangle$, where $l \in \mathbb{N}$ is a key level, and $c \in \mathbb{N}$ is a key column. Keys should be classified into different levels. In other words, a key has two metrics: one is key level denoted as l and the other is key column denoted as c.

ii. $K2L : k \in KEY \to l \in \mathbb{N}$, where KEY is a set of keys; l is a natural number representing key level. It is a function. It does not need to be one-to-one. That is, multiple keys may map to one level. It is on-to. We denote the $k \in KEY$ with level l as $k[l, \cdot]$. If multiple keys map to the same level l, we distinguish them as $k[l, c], c \in \mathbb{N}$.

iii. $K2C : k \in KEY \to c \in \mathbb{N}$, where KEY is a set of keys and c is a natural number representing key column. It is a function. It does not need to be one-to-one. That is, multiple keys may map to one column index. It is on-to. We denote the $k \in KEY$ with index c as $k[\cdot, c]$. If multiple keys map to the same column c, we distinguish them as $k[l, c], l, c \in \mathbb{N}$.

iv. $k[l + 1, c] \Leftarrow g(k[l, c])$, where $k[l, c] \in KEY$ and $\forall l \in \mathbb{N}$. That is, $\forall l \in Set_l = \{\ell | \ell = K2L(k[l, c] \in KEY)\}, c \in Set_c = \{c' | c' = K2C(k[l, c])\}$. $g(\cdot)$ is a one-way function. It is computationally infeasible to obtain x from $g(x)$, where $x \in KEY$.

v. $k[j, c]$ can be computed from any $k[i, c]$ $(i < j)$ by $k[j, c] = g^{j-i}(k[i, c])$, where $\forall i, j \in Set_l, c \in Set_c, g^{m+1}(\cdot) = g(g^m(\cdot)), m \in Set_l, g^1(\cdot) = g(\cdot)$. Similarly, $\forall j > i, k[j, c]$ can be computed from $k[i, c]$ by $k[j, c] = g^{j-i}(k[i, c])$, where $\forall i, j \in Set_l, c \in Set_c, g^{m+1}(\cdot) = g(g^m(\cdot)), m \in Set_l, g^1(\cdot) = g(\cdot)$.

Simply speaking, a key with a larger key level can be derived from any key with smaller key levels in the same key column. If accessors possess a key of a smaller level, they can derive all keys with larger key levels in the same key column. Thus, a larger level key can decrypt the data encrypted by a smaller level key, but not inversely.

2. Hierarchical roles

   i. $ROLE ::= \langle l, c, u \rangle$, where l is a key level, c is a key column, and u is an identification to distinguish multiple roles for the same key. As multiple roles may map to the same key with $k[l, c]$, multiple identifications (e.g., u) are required for the distinction of multiple roles.

   ii. $R2K : r \in ROLE \to k \in KEY$, where $ROLE$ is a set of roles and KEY is a set of keys. It is a function. It does not need to be one-to-one. That is, multiple roles may map to one key. We denote $r \in ROLE$ that maps to the same key $k[l, c]$ as $r[l, c, u], l, c, u \in \mathbb{N}$. $R2K(\cdot)$ is on-to.

   Simply speaking, multiple roles may be related to one key. Regarding the privileges for images, the mainly one is "read." A role with smaller (higher) levels can access all objects that can be accessed by roles with larger (lower) levels. Each role will be mapped to a key.

   iii. $R2L : r \in ROLE \to l \in \mathbb{N}$, where $ROLE$ is a set of roles; l is a natural number representing a key level. Note that $\forall r \in ROLE, R2L(r) \Leftarrow K2L(R2K(r))$. That is, roles are also hierarchically classified into different levels.

   iv. $R2C : r \in ROLE \to c \in \mathbb{N}$, where $ROLE$ is a set of roles and c is a natural number representing a column number. Note that $\forall r \in ROLE, R2C(r) \Leftarrow K2C(R2K(r))$. This function returns a key index (in terms of key column) for a role, which can be used for guaranteeing derivative relationship between keys.

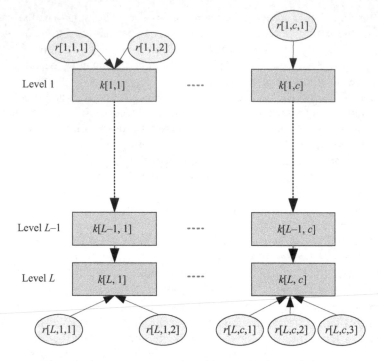

Figure 4.3   Hierarchical key and role model

    v. $R2U : r \in ROLE \rightarrow u \in \mathbb{N}$, where *ROLE* is a set of roles and *u* is a natural number representing users who are associated to the same key. Note that $\forall r_1, r_1 \in ROLE$, if $R2K(r_1) = R2K(r_2)$, then $R2U(r_1) \neq R2U(r_2)$.

The model proposed above is illustrated in Figure 4.3.

3.   Differentiate areas by roles

    i. $AREA ::= \langle l, c, u, i \rangle$, where *l* is a key level, *c* is a column number, *u* is an identification to distinguish multiple roles for the same key, and *i* is an identification to distinguish multiple areas for the same role. Note that $\cap_{l,c,u,i} a[l, c, u, i] = \emptyset$.

    ii. $A2R : a \in AREA \rightarrow r \in ROLE$ is a function. It does not need to be one-to-one. That is, multiple areas may be assigned to one role. As *r* is a tuple with three elements, *a* is a tuple with four elements.

    iii. $A2K : a \in AREA \rightarrow k \in KEY$ is a function. It does not need to be one-to-one. Note that $\forall a \in AREA, A2K(a) \Leftarrow R2K(A2R(a))$.

    iv. $A2L : a \in AREA \rightarrow l \in \mathbb{N}$. Note that $\forall a \in AREA, A2L(a) \Leftarrow R2L(A2R(a))$.

    v. $A2C : a \in AREA \rightarrow c \in \mathbb{N}$. Note that $\forall a \in AREA, A2C(a) \Leftarrow R2C(A2R(a))$.

    vi. $A2U : a \in AREA \rightarrow u \in \mathbb{N}$. Note that $\forall a \in AREA, A2U(a) \Leftarrow R2U(A2R(a))$.

Remark 4.2. *Note that, AREA can also be replaced by LAYER. In geographic images, there may be multiple layers in a single image.*

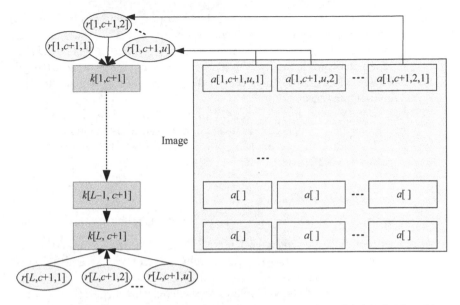

Figure 4.4   Hierarchical key-role-area access-control model (HKRAGraph)

a ∈ *AREA could be any shapes (e.g., circles or rectangles), which are indepen-dent of the design of this chapter. The details on areas can be embedded in watermarks, such as one-point locations with two rectangular edges. Areas for different roles can be overlapped. For different roles with the same R2K, the areas may be different, and one area information for one role may not be available for the other role.*

If we remove the constraints of R2K from a function to any mapping, then one role may map to multiple keys.

The proposed access-control model is illustrated in Figure 4.4.

4.5.3   Image publication

Images can be processed before publication as follows:

1. Servers select an image to publish. Corresponding areas (e.g., $a \in AREA$) in this image are split according to security concerns and assigned to different roles. Areas are layered into different security levels, such that roles who can access higher security level (with larger key level) will be able to access cor-responding or lower security levels (with smaller key level). Servers formulate access-control strategies by $ACL ::= \langle ROLE, AREA \rangle$, where $\forall a \in AREA, \exists r = A2R(a) \in ROLE$.
2. Servers code access-control strategies into watermarks and embed them into pub-lished images. For example, QR codes can be used as watermarks and strategies are coded into QR codes.

3. Servers maintain a table for the image $TBL ::= \langle a \in AREA, f(A2K(a)) \rangle$, and encrypt specific areas in images with corresponding keys. For example, servers encrypt a by $f(A2K(a))$. $f(\cdot)$ is a one-way function. $f(A2K(a))$ instead of $A2K(a)$ is stored for better confidentiality. $A2K(\cdot)$ is initialized by servers in *HKRAGraph*.
4. $\forall a \in AREA$ in this image, a is encrypted by $f(A2K(a))$, and all identical $K2C(A2K(a))$ must be noted.
5. $\forall a_1, a_2 \in AREA$ in an image, we have $A2C(a_1) = A2C(a_2)$. Simply speaking, for all areas in one image, encrypt keys must be in the same column index.
6. $\forall a_1, a_2 \in AREA$ in an image, if $A2L(a_1) = A2L(a_2)$, then $A2K(a_1) = A2K(a_2)$ due to $A2C(a_1) = A2C(a_2)$.

4.5.4 Client conformance

Client conformance for access control can be processed as follows:

1. Accessors request images via a particular client tool (e.g., image browser).
2. The browser prompts to ask for and obtain a secret key k' and a role r' corresponding to an accessor.
3. The browser extracts a QR code, obtains access-control strategies (i.e., $ACL ::= \langle ROLE, AREA \rangle$). All $a \in ACL.AREA$ are obtained for $r' \in ACL.ROLE$. That is, $A2R(a) = r'$.
4. The browser computes $f(k')$ and decrypts all areas for r' (i.e., a). Note that the key is not stored in the browser, and only $f(k')$ is computed temporarily by the browser and destroyed after browsing.
5. Calculate all $j > l$, $k[j, c] \Leftarrow g^{j-l}(k[l, c])$, $k[l, c] = k'$ and decrypt left areas at lower levels. That is, $a \in ACL.AREA, A2R(a) \neq r'$ by $k[j, c]$.
6. The browser displays all a to the accessor.
7. Accessors close the browser, and the browsed image returns to its original encryption status.

Remark 4.3. *Servers will maintain consistency with client tools for function $f(\cdot)$ (i.e., the same $f(\cdot)$). Once the consistency is retained, $f(\cdot)$ can be evolved further regularly to provide forward security. Alternatively, an extra pairwise key (e.g., key_p) between servers and client tools can be introduced into $f(\cdot)$ as $f(\cdot, \cdot)$ (e.g., $f(\cdot, key_p)$). We stress that client tools do not locally and permanently store accessor keys. Instead, decryption keys for encrypted areas in images are computed temporally upon browsing.*

4.5.5 Case study

It is a trend to incorporate multiple maps from one location into one map as multiple layers. For a better explanation, we separate a combined map with multiple layers into three individual maps. In this case study, three maps of Shanghai are displayed in Figure 4.5, which include a remote-sensing image, a geologic map, and a city planning map. These three maps describe three aspects of the same location. A combinative map can provide various aspects of one location in one map by multiple layers, which facilitates fast linkages to relevant information within one area.

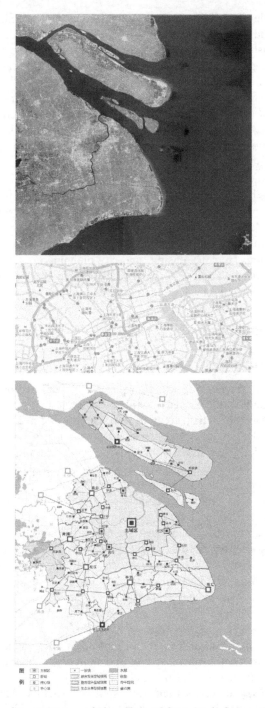

Figure 4.5   A combinative map of Shanghai with multiple layers. The first one is sensing image. The second one is a geologic map. The third one is a city planning map.

The security levels of roles and corresponding layers are embedded into maps as watermarks, and thus access-control strategies can be obtained from distributed maps without consulting servers. Accessors present their roles to a dedicated client tool such as an image browser, and specific areas that can be accessed by presented roles will be determined by the client tool.

In one map, accessible areas are encrypted by corresponding keys (e.g., a_i is encrypted by k_i ($i = 1, 2, \ldots, n$)). Only someone who presents the correct key (e.g., k_i) can view the corresponding encrypted areas (a_i). We also provide a kind of hierarchical access by hierarchical encryptions for areas. That is, keys at lower security levels can be derived by keys at higher security levels (e.g., k_{i+1} can be derived by k_i). Thus, areas for roles in lower security levels can also be decrypted and viewed by roles with higher security levels. Upon request for images by an accessor, the image browser will prompt the accessor to present their key (e.g., k_i). The image browser will compute $f(k_i)$ and use it to decrypt corresponding areas.

In combinative maps, one area consists of multiple aspects presented in layers. For example, geology, remote sensing, and city planning are the three layers of a single city, Shanghai. Some accessors may only be able to access one layer among them. Accessors present their roles and keys to reveal corresponding layers.

4.6   Security and performance analysis

4.6.1   Security analysis

Defending against transferring attack. Images are encrypted by designated keys related to corresponding roles or accessor identifications, and accessors must present the correct keys to enable client tools to decrypt images for browsing. Encrypted images cannot be decrypted without keys, even if images are transferred to others again. Moreover, decrypted images can only be decrypted and displayed in client tools. Images will return to their original encrypted status after browsing.

The control unit migrates to client tools, and it maintains control even though images are redistributed again. The control policies are associated with images as watermarks, which specify what areas can be viewed for given roles. The decryption can only occur upon browsing, and the encrypted area returns back to confidential status after images are browsed in the client tools. That is, the encrypted areas (layers) are transparently decrypted and ephemerally displayed upon browsing.

Defending against DDoS attacks. As access-control logics are embedded in watermarks together with images, client tools can control access policies without consulting servers and relying on networking connections. Thus, DDoS attacks for servers and networking connections are not workable.

Defending against coarse access. Our model can differentiate the access privileges for various areas in a single image, and similarly, further access control for various layers in a single area is also possible iteratively.

Defending physical copy attack. As visible watermarks such as QR codes or invisible watermarks are incorporated with images, anyone who obtains physical copies of images by screen capture or outside camera shooting will be traced back by watermarks. The roles and identifications can be revealed by decrypted areas in captured images and control policies in watermarks.

Proposition 4.4. *It is hard to compute k_j from k_i if $k_j = g(k_i)$, where $f(\cdot)$ is a one-way function.*

Proof. Straightforward. We use a one-way function to drive keys in lower security levels from keys in higher security levels. As the function is one way, the derivation of keys will be also one way. That is, it is hard to compute x from $g(x)$.   □

4.6.2   Performance analysis

Computation cost. The major computations in the scheme are as follows: encoding and decoding watermarks, encrypting and decrypting areas in images, and one-way function computation. However, encoding watermarks can be conducted only once. Encryption is conducted once for each image, and decryption is conducted once for each instance of image browsing. Note that encryption and decryption cannot be avoided for image-access control, as some contents must be encrypted for confidentiality. One-way function computation is lightweight (e.g., cryptographically secure hash function).

Higher access throughput and less access delay. The access-control policies are embedded into watermarks and distributed with images, thus it is not mandatory to consult servers for corresponding areas that can be accessed. This improves the scalability of data access. Besides, the access delay is decreased due to the absence of consulting communications latency between servers and clients.

Efficiency. A balance between servers and clients is preferred, instead of only relying on servers. Servers only need to attach a watermark to an image and encrypt designated areas upon data publication, which can be accomplished in a batch. Client tools only need to decode a watermark and decrypt corresponding areas. The decryption is conducted at the client side, which is much more lightweight than at the server side. The encryption and decryption are mandatory because some areas are confidential.

Convenience. The deployment is convenient. Particular client tools can be deployed as middle-ware over normal image browsers. Besides, communication channels and networks are not required, which brings more convenience for accessors.

QR codes can be used for fast generation and decoding of watermarks. It presents the advantages of large capacity, fault tolerance, easy generation, and fast decoding. Thus, the overhead of attaching and decoding watermarks is manageable.

Table 4.1 compares the advantages and disadvantage between ours and existing schemes.

4.7   Conclusions

In this chapter, we propose a watermark-based access-control model. In contrast to current access-control methods, we attach access-control strategies within accessed

Table 4.1   The comparisons between proposed scheme and other existing related work

Performance	Our scheme	Wolfgang [15]	Kountchev [21]	RVM [22]	Phadikar [24]
1. Hierarchical access control	✓	✗	✓	✗	✗
2. Code access-control strategies in watermarks	✓	✗	✗	✗	✗
3. Access control can take effect without servers	✓	✗	✗	✗	✗
4. Watermarks are used for access control	✓	✗	✓	✓	✓
5. Record modifiers in watermarks	✓	✗	✗	✗	✗
6. Copyrights protection	✓	✓	✓	✓	✓
7. Quality access control	✓	✗	✗	✓	✓
8. Fine-grained	✓	✗	✗	✗	✗

objects (e.g., images) as watermarks, instead of storing access-control strategies on servers. Our proposed model makes it possible to let accessors view images without accessing servers. This can ease the burden of servers and shorten the access delay. In addition, our model also defends against several dedicated attacks for accessing big image data, such as transferring attack, DDoS attack, coarse access, and physical copy attack. Moreover, we also propose a hierarchical key-role-area access-control model. In this model, multiple areas in an image can be mapped to one role, and each role is associated with a hierarchical key. Hierarchical keys are classified into levels, and keys at higher security levels can derive keys at lower security levels. Thus, various areas that can be accessed by different roles in one image can be encrypted by hierarchical keys. Because of the above key-role-area model, fine-grained access control can be achieved in a more complicated and customized manner. Especially, the above method can also be applied for different layers in a single image (e.g., geographic maps). Furthermore, further traceability of image leakage (e.g., areas, layers) becomes possible due to embedded watermarks.

Acknowledgments

The research was financially supported by Major Scientific and Technological Special Project of Guizhou Province under Grant No. 20183001, the Open Funding of

Guizhou Provincial Key Laboratory of Public Big Data under Grant No. 2017BDK-FJJ006, Open Funding of Hubei Provincial Key Laboratory of Intelligent Geo-Information Processing with under Grant No. KLIGIP2016A05, and National Natural Science Foundation of China under Grant No. 61502362. Preliminary results are presented in doi:10.3390/'10080069, July 29, 2018, MDPI Future Internet.

References

[1]   Ferraiolo D, and Alturi V. Role-Based Access Control; 2011.

[2]   Periorellis P, and Parastatidis S. Task-based access control for virtual organizations. Scientific Engineering of Distributed Java Applications. 2005;3409: 38–47.

[3]   Chen SS, Choo CY, and Chow RY. Internet security: A novel role/object-based access control for digital libraries. Journal of Organizational Computing and Electronic Commerce. 2006;16(2):87–103.

[4]   Liu Z, Xia T, and Wang J. Image encryption technology based on fractional two-dimensional triangle function combination discrete chaotic map coupled with Menezes–Vanstone elliptic curve cryptosystem. Discrete Dynamics in Nature and Society. 2018;2018:1–24.

[5]   Kim HKH, Wen JWJ, and Villasenor JD. Secure arithmetic coding. IEEE Transactions on Signal Processing. 2007;55(5):2263.

[6]   Zhao WJ, Zhao MJ, and Pan J. The image compression technology based on wavelet transform. Advanced Materials Research. 2014;1078:370–374.

[7]   Xiong H, Choo KKR, and Vasilakos AV. Revocable identity-based access control for big data with verifiable outsourced computing. IEEE Transactions on Big Data. 2017:1.

[8]   Xiao M, Wang M, Liu X, *et al.* Efficient distributed access control for big data in clouds. In: 2015 IEEE Conference on Computer Communications Workshops (INFOCOM WKSHPS); 2015. p. 202–207.

[9]   Wang Y, Doherty JF, and Dyck REV. A wavelet-based watermarking algorithm for ownership verification of digital images. IEEE Transactions on Image Processing. 2002;11(2):77–88.

[10] Moulin P. The role of information theory in watermarking and its application to image watermarking. Signal Processing. 2001;81(6):1121–1139.

[11] Gunjan R, Laxmi V, and Gaur MS. Detection attack analysis using partial watermark in DCT domain. In: International Conference on Security of Information and Networks; 2012. p. 188–192.

[12] Al-Nu'Aimi AT. Gray watermarks to prove the rightful ownership for digital coloured images. In: International Conference on Intelligent Semantic Web-Services and Applications; 2010. p. 27.

[13] Walia E, and Suneja A. A robust watermark authentication technique based on Weber's descriptor. Signal Image and Video Processing. 2014;8(5):859–872.

[14] Su Q, and Chen B. Robust color image watermarking technique in the spatial domain. Soft Computing. 2017;22(1):1–16.

[15]   Wolfgang RB, and Delp EJ. A watermark for digital images. In: Proceedings of 3rd IEEE International Conference on Image Processing. vol. 3; 1996. p. 219–222.

[16]   Wong PW. A public key watermark for image verification and authentication. In: Proceedings 1998 International Conference on Image Processing. ICIP98 (Cat. No.98CB36269). vol. 1; 1998. p. 455–459.

[17]   Coronel SLG, Ramírez BE, and Mosqueda MAA. Robust watermark technique using masking and Hermite transform. SpringerPlus. 2016;5(1):1830.

[18]   Hu Y, and Jeon B. Reversible visible watermarking and lossless recovery of original images. IEEE Transactions on Circuits and Systems for Video Technology. 2006;16(11):1423–1429.

[19]   Petrovic R, and Atti V. Watermark based access control to copyrighted content. In: International Conference on Telecommunication in Modern Satellite, Cable and Broadcasting Services; 2014. p. 315–322.

[20]   Yang H, Jiang X, and Kot AC. Embedding Binary Watermarks in Dual-Tree Complex Wavelets Domain for Access Control of Digital Images. In: Transactions on Data Hiding and Multimedia Security VI, eds., Shi YQ, Emmanuel S, Kankanhalli MS, Chang SF, and Radhakrishnan R. Springer, Berlin, Heidelberg; 2011.

[21]   Kountchev R, Milanova M, and Kountcheva R. Content protection and hierarchical access control in image databases. In: 2015 International Symposium on Innovations in Intelligent SysTems and Applications (INISTA); 2015. p. 1–6.

[22]   Yang H, and Yin J. A secure removable visible watermarking for BTC compressed images. Multimedia Tools and Applications. 2015;74(6):1725–1739.

[23]   Phadikar A, and Maity SP. Data hiding based quality access control of digital images using adaptive QIM and lifting. Signal Processing: Image Communication. 2011;26(10):646–661.

[24]   Phadikar A, Maity SP, and Delpha C. Data hiding for quality access control and error concealment in digital images. In: IEEE International Conference on Multimedia and Expo; 2011. p. 1–6.

[25]   Phadikar A, and Maity SP. A cost effective scheme for content verification and access control of quality of an image. In: IEEE Region 10 and the Third International Conference on Industrial and Information Systems; 2008. p. 1–6.

[26]   Jana P, Phadikar A, Maity GK, *et al.* Reversable data hiding for content verification and quality access control of image and its hardware implementation. In: 2016 International Conference on Electrical, Electronics, and Optimization Techniques (ICEEOT); 2016. p. 3324–3329.

[27]   Datta K, and Gupta IS. Partial encryption and watermarking scheme for audio files with controlled degradation of quality. Multimedia Tools and Applications. 2013;64(3):649–669.

[28]   Hrncar M, and Krajcovic J. Principles of audio watermarking. Advances in Electrical and Electronic Engineering. 2008;7(1–2):247.

[29]   Nematollahi MA, Gamboa-Rosales H, Martinez-Ruiz FJ, *et al.* Multifactor authentication model based on multipurpose speech watermarking and

online speaker recognition. Multimedia Tools and Applications. 2017;76(5): 7251–7281.

[30]   Asikuzzaman M, and Pickering MR. An overview of digital video watermarking. IEEE Transactions on Circuits and Systems for Video Technology. 2017; 28(9):2131–2153.

[31]   Wang W, and Zhao J. Hiding depth information in compressed 2D image/video using reversible watermarking. Multimedia Tools and Applications. 2016; 75(8):4285–4303.

[32]   Venugopala PS, Sarojadevi H, and Chiplunkar N. An approach to embed image in video as watermark using a mobile device. Sustainable Computing: Informatics and Systems. 2017;15:82–87.

[33]   Tseng CW, Liu FJ, and Huang SH. Design of document access control mechanism on cloud services. In: Sixth International Conference on Genetic and Evolutionary Computing; 2013. p. 99–102.

[34]   Gasselt S, and Nass A. Planetary map data model for geologic mapping. Cartography and Geographic Information Science. 2011;38(2):201–212.

[35]   Xing HF, Cui BL, and Xu LL. An mixed access control method based on trust and role. In: Second IITA International Conference on Geoscience and Remote Sensing; 2010. p. 552–555.

[36]   Kim J, Jeong D, and Baik DK. A multi-layer based access control model for GIS mobile web services. In: International Conference on Consumer Electronics; 2009. p. 1–2.

[37]   Kirkpatrick MS, Damiani ML, and Bertino E. Prox-RBAC: A proximity-based spatially aware RBAC. In: ACM SIGSPATIAL International Symposium on Advances in Geographic Information Systems, ACM-GIS 2011, November 1–4, 2011, Chicago, IL, USA, Proceedings; 2011. p. 339–348.

[38]   Ma F, Gao Y, Yan M, *et al.* The fine-grained security access control of spatial data. In: International Conference on Geoinformatics; 2010. p. 1–4.

[39]   Zhang A, Ji C, Bao Y, *et al.* Conflict analysis and detection based on model checking for spatial access control policy. Tsinghua Science and Technology. 2017;22(5):478–488.

[40]   Kao YW, Luo GH, Lin HT, *et al.* Physical access control based on QR code. In: 2011 International Conference on Cyber-Enabled Distributed Computing and Knowledge Discovery; 2011. p. 285–288.

[41]   Zhao S, Wang L, Liang W, *et al.* High performance optical encryption based on computational ghost imaging with QR code and compressive sensing technique. Optics Communications. 2015;353:90–95.

[42]   Melgar MEV, Zaghetto A, Macchiavello B, *et al.* CQR codes: Colored quick-response codes. In: 2012 IEEE Second International Conference on Consumer Electronics – Berlin (ICCE-Berlin); 2012. p. 321–325.

[43]   Liu Y, and Liu M. Automatic recognition algorithm of quick response code based on embedded system. In: Sixth International Conference on Intelligent Systems Design and Applications. vol. 2; 2006. p. 783–788.

Chapter 5

Blockchain-based security and access control for BIM big data

Rongyue Zheng[1], Jianlin Jiang[1], Xiaohan Hao[2], and Wei Ren[2]

5.1 bcBIM: a blockchain-based big data model for BIM modification audit and provenance in mobile cloud

5.1.1 Introduction

Building information modeling (BIM) is a set of interacting policies, processes, and technologies, which produce a methodology to manage the essential building design and project data throughout the building's life cycle [1]. It can provide a unified presentation, data framework, and organization. In construction automation, the architecture enables information and communication technology (ICT) to manage the life cycle information of buildings. During a whole life of a building, the essential features of BIM can be summarized into four aspects, namely integrating with various databases, facilitating document management, visualizing analytical processes and results, and providing sustainability analyses and simulation [2]. The most recent ICT architecture application for BIM is the traditional client–server architecture, some of which still work as a single workstation pattern. We argue that the future development of BIM technology must be combined with advanced communications technology and computer technology in order to greatly improve the efficiency of the construction industry, such as blockchain, mobile cloud computing, big data, and the Internet of things (IoT). Blockchain is a distributed database system that acts as an "open ledger" to store and manage transactions. Each record in the database is called a block and contains details such as transaction timestamp and links to the previous block. This characteristic makes it impossible for anyone to change the information about the records retrospectively. In addition, since the same transaction is recorded on multiple distributed database systems, the technology is safe in design. As a hot topic in the world at present, cloud computing has become the strategic direction of the future development of information industry and an important engine

[1]Faculty of Architecture, Civil Engineering and Environment, Ningbo University, Ningbo, China
[2]School of Computer Science, China University of Geosciences, Wuhan, China

to promote economic growth, which not only provides new impetus for transformation and innovation of the information industry itself but also provides great opportunities for the upgrading of traditional industries and the development of new industries.

With the rapid development of society, more and more difficulties appear in current models. The main difficulty is that they cannot safely track revisions. For example, the design may be modified due to budget or host requirements. The revision of BIM data is usually updated, rather than retaining the revision history. Even if the updated records are stored, it is difficult to guarantee the integrity of historical data. In addition, recorded updates depend on the complete trust of the central operator. Once the internal operators misbehave, the data will lead to construction rework, or even disaster.

However, the marriage of them with BIM has been explored by few related work. The BIM cloud will significantly reduce the latency of information access, making BIM information available to all users. It provides a high-capacity storage, fast retrieval, and on-demand calculations for building information. As a result, mobile cloud architectures can make BIM information popular and available to a large number of users. Although the mobile cloud for BIM provides conveniences of information accessing, it also raises several security issues [3–5]. In this chapter, we mainly solve the following problem: the audit of BIM modification. The current challenges are as follows: (1) keep only the last modification record, (2) the source of the modified item cannot be traced, and (3) attacks from the central operator cannot be recorded and tracked. In order to solve the above challenges, we combine BIM with blockchain to provide a BIM data-organization method, which can track, prove, and prevent the tampering of BIM historical data. At the same time, a unified format is generated to support the open sharing of future data. In addition, BIM models and parameters may be modified during smart construction. If the chain of revision history is stored for later audit, the provenance, and accountability will be possible. However, current BIM architecture pays insufficient concerns for the data audit. In this chapter, we propose a bcBIM model customized for BIM data audit and mobile cloud BIM architecture. The contributions of the chapter are listed as follows:

1. We make the first attempt to propose a bcBIM model enhanced by blockchain for BIM data audit, provenance, and accountability.
2. We propose traceable and authenticated bcBIM model via blockchain that can satisfy traceability by timestamp for recording BIM-modification history.

5.1.2   Related work

In view of the combination of architecture with BIM, Nassiri *et al.* [6] combined BIM with decision method (entropy-topsis) to scientifically optimize the choice of sustainable building materials during the conceptual design phase of a building project. Oti and Tizani [7] provided a BIM-integrated system that combined three green metrics: life cycle costs, ecological footprint, and carbon footprint, to help structural engineers conduct sustainability assessments of alternative designs. Inyim *et al.* [8] introduced an optimization tool combining BIM with construction environmental impact simulation to help designers achieve multiple sustainable goals in the decision-making process, such as those related to construction time, initial construction costs, and CO_2 emissions. Wang *et al.* [9] discussed and investigated how BIM can be extended to the site via the "practical arm" of augmented reality (AR). Kokorus *et al.* [10] used BIM technology to design innovative approach to the substation. Dawood *et al.* [11] combined BIM with genetic algorithm to find the optimal design with minimum life cycle cost in the service life of buildings. Pasini *et al.* [12] built information-modeling framework for management of cognitive buildings to explore how BIM practices and technologies could improve a data-driven asset management. Zhu *et al.* [13] combined BIM construction with other building technologies and greatly shortened the time of modeling development and significantly improved the efficiency of modeling. Isikdag *et al.* [14] proposed a BIM-oriented service-oriented architecture design pattern. Yoon *et al.* [15] put forward a design method of energy-saving building based on BIM. On the specific practice of BIM, the practical implementation of BIM framework is proposed by Jung and Joo [16]. Linderoth *et al.* [17] understood adoption and used BIM as the creation of actor networks. Lu and Li [18] established information modeling and changed construction practice. Desogus *et al.* [19] presented preliminary performance monitoring plan for energy retrofit: the "Mandolesi Pavillon" at the University of Cagliari.

Considering the combination of big data and BIM, Arslan *et al.* [20] developed a prototype system using Hadoop for data storage and processing. The results of processing BIM and sensor data in a Hadoop architecture have demonstrated that the system can effectively provide data visualizations to facility managers. Building life cycle assessment of energy consumption is an important issue in the field of sustainable development and green building. Yuan *et al.* [21] summarized the features of building life cycle energy consumption data, proposed the method of information exchange and integration management by BIM, and utilized cloud-computing technology to achieve wide-area building life cycle (BLC) energy data management. Ferguson *et al.* [22] presented an application of linked data views (or semantic views) as part of a larger, modular, and extensible framework that provided a method to automatically query, understand, and translate BIM instances into linked data, for better supporting more accurate decision. Bottaccioli *et al.* [23] proposed building energy modeling and monitoring through the integration of IoT equipment and building information model. Razavi *et al.* [24] proposed using BIM to realize multi-sensor data fusion of material tracking in construction site.

The mobile cloud or blockchain marries with BIM model is a new topic and the literatures are very limited. Park *et al.* [25] and ASCE presented a framework for this safety-monitoring system as a cloud-based real time on-site application. The system integrates Bluetooth low-energy-based location detection technology, BIM-based hazard identification, and a cloud-based communication platform. Garcia-Fernandez *et al.* [26] discussed the different approaches to date on the BIM generation chain: from 3D point cloud data collection to semantically enriched parametric models. In this chapter, we proposed a bcBIM model via blockchain which can not only satisfy traceability by timestamp for recording BIM modification history but also enhance BIM data audit, provenance, and accountability.

5.1.3   Problem formulation

5.1.3.1   System model

In this section, we briefly describe how the bcBIM model implements our proposed scheme before discussing the adversary model.

BIM can collect a large amount of information throughout the life cycle of a project by creating a database. Through the adjustment, addition and modification of the data information, the overall status of the project can be accurately reflected. Through the association with the data, faster decision-making progress can be achieved, and the quality of decision-making can be improved, thereby improving project quality and increasing project profit. However, the main weaknesses of BIM in terms of security are given next.

The audit and provenance of revised BIM data. Some revision for BIM data may not be avoided in construction, for example, design may be revised due to budgets, or requirements of hosts. The major difficulties in current model is that the revision cannot be traced securely. The revision of BIM data is usually updating, not remaining the revision history. Even the updating record is stored, the integrity for historical data is difficult to be guaranteed. Furthermore, the updating of record relies on the complete trust of central operators. Once internal operators conduct misbehavior, the data will lead to construction rework, or even disaster.

To solve the overcome weakness, we consider using blockchain technology to improve BIM. Blockchain can be roughly divided into three categories: public blockchain, private blockchain, and consortium blockchain. Public blockchain is open to all which means anyone can participate in it; private blockchain is open to individual or entity; and consortium blockchain is open to specific organizations and groups. Although the above three blockchains are all based on consensus mechanisms to ensure the security and reliability of blockchain technology operations, satisfying traceable and non-tamperable, they also have significant differences. From private blockchain, consortium blockchain to public blockchain, the degree of decentralization has gradually increased, and the scope of authority has been expanding. Different levels of information disclosure and central control help blockchain meet different types of application requirements. Table 5.1 makes comparison of three blockchains.

In the basic model, we discuss our proposal with private blockchain, which can be signed by a trusted center. However, if applying in consortium blockchain, it can be signed by the federation node. Private blockchain refers to the write rights that are entirely in the hands of an organization, and all the nodes involved in the chain are strictly controlled. In some cases, some rules in the private blockchain can be modified by the organization, such as restoring the transaction process. Compared with public blockchain, private blockchains have the greatest advantage of encrypting audit and public-identity information. That is, no one can tamper with the data; once some errors occur, it is possible to track the source of errors. Therefore, private blockchain is common in internal system or network. Due to its privacy, some private chains also omit the function of "mining," which greatly improve the efficiency of implementation. Private blockchain can not only prevent a single node in an organization from deliberately concealing or tampering with data but also quickly

Table 5.1 A comparison of three kinds of blockchain

	Application of decentralized degree	Access mechanism	Transaction speed	Transaction cost	Execution efficiency	Application example
Private	Centralize	Specific individuals or entities	Fast	Low	High	Acrblock
Consortium	Partial decentralization	Authorized organizations or institutions	Mid	Mid	Mid	R3, Hyperledger
Public	Complete decentralization	All	Slow	High	Low	BTC, ETH, NEO

identify sources whenever there are occurrences of some errors. Different from the open and semi-open characteristics of public blockchain or consortium blockchain, private blockchain emphasize privacy, which are limited to user access and transactions within an enterprise, between two organizations, such as Acrblock. For example, some financial and auditing institutions are used to store books and databases, and only users with relevant authority can access and modify the data. The advantages of private blockchain are as follows:

1. Private blockchain has fast transaction speed. Its transaction progress only requires a few generally recognized high-power nodes rather than requiring the confirmation of all network nodes.
2. Transaction costs are very low compared with public and consortium blockchain.
3. Since the privacy of receipts is limited, it is difficult for participants to obtain data on private blockchain, that is, the privacy protection is better than others.

The disadvantage of private blockchain is as follows: the risk of receiving attacks is higher because it can be manipulated price or modified code.

Unlike private blockchain, consortium blockchain has several organizations or institutions which participate in the management. Each organization or institution controls one or more nodes, and they record transaction data together. Only organizations and institutions which have relevant authorities can read, write, or send transaction data on consortium blockchain. Since it only opens parts of functions to members, the permissions and accounting rules on consortium blockchain are "customized" according to the consortium. The consensus process is controlled by preselected nodes on consortium blockchain. It is suitable for B2B scenarios such as interagency transactions, settlement, and liquidation. For example, many financial institutions connect their blockchain networks together to form a consortium network, which facilitates data docking and collaboration. For example, R3, Hyperledger, and Golden Chain Consortium, each node has its corresponding entity or organization on consortium blockchain. In addition, it is also suitable for scenarios such as transaction and settlement between different entities. Consortium blockchain is maintained by the participating member organizations and provides a complete set of safety-management functions, such as management, certification, authorization, monitoring, and auditing of the participating members. For example, the R3 consortium is a consortium blockchain of banking industry which was established in 2015. At present, it has joined more than 40 members, including world famous banks such as JPMorgan Chase, HSBC, and Goldman Sachs. Each bank can become a node, but the transfer behavior of one bank must be confirmed by other bank nodes (2/3 number) in order to make the block effective. Nowadays, BIM is usually used internally, such as a bridge design institute, architectural design institute, and a large group company. In addition, almost no proof of work (POW) consensus mechanism is used in consortium blockchain, but consensus algorithms such as proof of rights or Practical Byzantine Fault Tolerance (PBFT) are used. The advantages of consortium blockchain are as follows:

1. As the number of nodes has been streamlined, consortium blockchain has faster transaction speed and lower cost.
2. Compared with public blockchain, consortium blockchain requires more transactions to be confirmed per unit time.

The disadvantage of consortium blockchain is as follows: the safety and performance requirements are relatively high.

Considering that contemporary green construction is assembled building, we discuss how to establish a BIM-shared component library. One of the applications of public blockchain is recording BIM database which can be added by anyone, that is, it can form BIM-shared component library. We propose this scheme as an advanced model with POW mechanism. In addition, public blockchain is a kind of non-tampering account book, and it is the most widely used blockchain at present. In addition, public blockchain establishes a centralized autonomous organization which can be books, electricity transactions, big data transactions, or BIM database. Bitcoin and Ethernet are the most popular public blockchain which means the behavior of public blockchain is open. However, it is neither controlled by anyone nor owned by anyone, it is a "completely decentralized" blockchain. The advantages of public blockchain are as follows:

1. The access threshold is so low that any user with an internet-connected computer can access it.
2. Open and transparent, since the whole system is "completely decentralized," the process of running the system is open and transparent.
3. Anonymity, since nodes do not need to trust each other, all operations can be performed anonymously, that is, the privacy is well protected.
4. Free from the influence of the developer, reading and writing public blockchain data are not controlled by any organization or individual, so it can also protect users from programmers.

The disadvantages of public blockchain are as follows: low efficiency, large power consumption, long time required to validate and complete transactions.

5.1.3.2   Adversary model

In this section, we identify four potential vulnerabilities that can be exploited by our opponents to undermine our solutions: (1) the modified content cannot be traced to its source; (2) the integrity of the historical data is tampered with the last modification record; (3) attacks from the central operator cannot be recorded and tracked. Some modifications of BIM data may be unavoidable in construction, for example, design modifications due to budget or host requirements. The revision of BIM data is usually updated, rather than retaining the revision history. Therefore, attackers may be able to modify the source of BIM data. In our scheme, we combine BIM with blockchain to ensure that the source of BIM data is not modified.

As mentioned above, the traditional BIM model only retains the last modification record. In the process of revising BIM data, even if the update record is stored, the historical data can be modified by attackers, and the integrity of the historical data is difficult to guarantee. In our model, the integrity of historical data can be guaranteed by using the traceability of blockchain and the non-tampering characteristics of information. In traditional BIM model, recording updates depends on the full trust of the central operator; once improper behavior of internal operators occurs, the data will lead to construction rework or even disaster. In our scheme, we combine BIM with blockchain and take advantage of the decentralization of blockchain. In addition, the data blocks in BIM system are maintained by the nodes with maintenance function in the whole system.

5.1.4   Proposed scheme

Our solution is briefly described in the above section, and the details of our solution are described in this section.

5.1.4.1   Proposed basic architecture

In this section, we propose the mobile cloud BIM architecture for further ICT paradigms.

BIM as a service—BIMaaS

BIMaaS is a cloud service for providing outsourced BIM data storage and computation. It can be looked as a united virtual central server by harvesting multiple computing resources, which provides an on-demand storage and computation service. BIMaaS is managed by a dedicated cloud-computing software. It can smoothly respond any storage and computation requests by migrating or redistributing the tasks to a resource pool, which is transparent to users. Thus, users do not need to care about the implementation details on BIMaaS and just look at it as a virtual server.

The BIMaaS can be further classified into two folders:

1.   BIM data are outsourced to a public cloud that is provided by cloud service companies such as AWS, Azure, and AliYun. Such public cloud service is paid according to the resource requirements. The initial investment for hardware and

software is avoided, as both of them are rented from the public BIMaaS. It can obviously decrease the startup budget for small business in AEC industry. Besides, the management of BIMaaS can also be outsourced to public BIMaaS, the personnel enrollments and cost for human resources may also be alleviated.
2. For some giant companies in AEC industry, it may be possible to integrate private BIMaaS by themselves. Such companies have already deployed an information infrastructure such as data center before. They usually have their ICT division and have a large number of human resources for ICT supports. Thus, they construct their private BIMaaS services via some publicly available software tools such as OpenStack.

Big data sharing among BIMaaS

With the development of BIMaaS, BIM data is accumulated with time elapsing and project conducting. Even for one building, a large volume of BIM data is aggregated. Once revision occurs during a construction life time, all historical data may also be snapshot and stored for further audit. For example, once a design for a model is modified, all legacy versions may also be stored respectively for tracing revised model locations and parameters. When such traceability is required for critical structures or components, an additive data organization with provenance capability will be required. In addition, BIM data sharing should be a trend once the data accumulated is sufficiently large. For example, for different buildings in the same category, BIM data can be mutually accessed or referenced among them. Some validated best practices and design experiences can be migrated from one project (building) to another. Some common characteristics in design can be abstracted by data mining or machine learning. Information exchanges between BIM data will let users form a global view of specific design in multiple projects.

Pervasively accessing by mobile terminals

Anyone can access BIM data and revoke the BIM computation service such as model visualization from BIMaaS or big data pool. Mobile terminal is a convenient tool for mobile users, especially field engineers in smart construction. It is a handheld device that can access the BIM information anytime anywhere by wireless. It can divided into the following two folders:

1. Mobile terminals can be handheld devices such as smart phones, tablets, and laptops. Currently, such devices are largely used as personal computing tools. By them, designers can verify the conformation of engineering regulation; the monitors can check the schedules of engineering procedures; the suppliers can consult the future requirements for material resources.
2. Mobile terminals can be wearable devices such as smart watches, smart glasses, and smart helmets. Those are equipped with sensors for instant information collection, or displayers for smooth human–machine interaction. For example, wireless sensors for environmental monitors, 3D information presentation such as virtual reality (VR) or AR. It can improve operational efficiency, especially for field engineers in a limited space. It can support smart and automatic construction scenarios. For example, smart helmet for engineers on constructing fields may

access BIM data remotely, and reconstruct VR by the latest data. Construction robots may access BIM data and collect sensing information from sensors in constructing fields to evaluate sustainable design parameters for green houses.

Automatically exchanging by Internet of Things

IoTs is a network with wireless sensors. In smart construction, those sensors may deploy with facilities in operational fields, with Internet accessing via wireless communications such as 4G or NB-IoT. Those sensors can collect the construction environmental data and upload them into BIMaaS server, once those data can help the revision or improvement of the design in BIM. For example, wind and sunshine design evaluation for green construction can be justified or amended after analysis from the field-sensing data during the construction. Those feedback will enhance the initial design in BIM that only relies on simulation or emulation and not manipulates from realistic on-site parameters. Moreover, the construction engineering machines (e.g., crane) that are equipped wireless devices can also access BIM data in BIMaaS. They may access the BIM information automatically and display the result to operators to guide the future instructions. Some equipment such as surveillance video cameras can automatically set up the direction of lens by fetch specific installation data from BIMaaS.

In summary, BIMaaS provides a storage and computation service for BIM data, including data retrieval, data updating, and data computation. BIM big data is accumulatively merged and shared to form a unified resource pool for responding on-demanded requests from traditional desktop PCs or especially mobile terminals in construction fields. Some special wearable devices such as helmets may provide more enhancement for BIM information presentation. BIM data can be accessed anytime and anywhere, not only by mobile devices but also by wireless sensors. Those sensors create IoTs to collect critical data about on-site construction on time. The analysis on those data can help reevaluate the quality of design or construction and provide amending feedback. Moreover, IoT devices on construction machine can access and display BIM data to empower the intelligence of construction machines. Those architecture not only enables the pervasive retrievals of BIM information but also supports the ubiquitous information exchanging or cooperatively constructing. It provides a promising framework for the exchanging and sharing of BIM data in smart construction.

Structure of blockchain

Blockchain is a distributed ledger; a technical solution to collectively maintain a reliable database through decentralized, trusted ways, and blockchain is a distributed database that is almost impossible to change. "Distributed" here is not only a distributed storage of data but also a distributed record of data (i.e., shared by the system participants), blockchain is not a single technology, but a result of a variety of technology integration; these technologies in a new structure together to form a new way of data recording, storage, and expression. Combined with these technologies, the contents of the scheme after adopting the present invention will be difficult to be modified, and the security can be improved.

Data stored using blockchain technology is also time-series, tamper-proof, forged, and privacy-pending, which is proven in many documents. bcBIM also inherits these features and guarantees the absolute security of the information data from two aspects: one is to ensure that the pseudo-block does not appear on the blockchain.

Because each chunk contains the hash value of the previous chunk, if the malicious node changes a chunk of data, you must change the chunk behind all the blocks that are changed, but also in the future with their own pseudo-branched chain to cover the correct blockchain, in terms of modern computer capabilities, which is also an impossible task.

The basic processing unit of blockchain technology is a data block that stores all transaction data and related verification information for a certain period of time. The blockchain is combined into a specific data structure in chronological order, which forms the non-tamper and non-falsification data-sharing information guaranteed by cryptography and uses the SHA 256 algorithm and the Merkle tree to realize the data-management system with simple and safe storage, successive relation and efficient and fast verification, etc. [27].

Block is the basic unit of blockchain, which is composed of blocks. The block header contains block ID, version number, previous block hash value, timestamp, Merkle root, the block target hash value, and so on. The main body of the block contains the main data information of the block, including identity certificate, transaction content, amount of breach of contract, and so on (Figure 5.1).

The characteristic of BIM data organization method based on blockchain is that each newly generated block saves the hash value of the previous block. Therefore, we combine BIM with blockchain to provide BIM data organization method which can track, prove, and prevent tampering of BIM historical data. At the same time, it can generate unified format to support open sharing of future data.

Blockchain-based model for audit and provenance

In this section, we propose to use blockchain to facilitate the audit and provenance of historical BIM data.

Blockchain consists a data structure with cryptographic hash value to guarantee the integrity of a serial data. The major items in proposed blockchain-based model is as follows (::= denotes "is defined as"):

1. **Block** ::= $\langle BlockHead, Data \rangle$. *BlockHead* guarantees the integrity (non-modification) of *Data* and modifying history of *Data*.
2. **BlockHead** ::= $\langle PreviousBlockHash, DataHash, Nonce, Difficulty, Timestamp \rangle$. The *PreviousBlockHash* is the hash value of the intermediate previous block head. *DataHash* is the hash value of *Data* in this block. *Nonce* is a value to be determined by randomly checking whether
   $Zero(Hash(PreviousBlockHash \| DataHash \| Timestamp \| Nonce)) \geq Difficulty$.
   $Zero(\cdot)$ is a function that returns the number of left consecutive zeros in an inputting string in bytes. *Difficulty* is an integer to tell the requirement on how

Block header	
Field	Description
Version	Block version number
Previous block hash	Hash of the previous block in the chain
Merkle tree root	Hash of the merkle tree root $root_M$
Timestamp	Creation time of this block
Targeted difficulty	The proof-of-work difficulty target
Nonce	A counter for the proof-of-work

Figure 5.1   Format of block

many consecutive zeros in the head of hash result. For example, *Difficulty* $= 2$ means the first 2 byte of target hash outputting is 0. That is, the first 2 byte of *Hash*($\cdot$) is 0. *Timestamp* is the time snapshot of current packaging block.

3. **Data** $::= \langle Metadata, BIMdata \rangle$. *Metadata* is an optional tuple for data description on *BIMdata*, which can be empty. The *BIMdata* is a mandatory tuple for concrete BIM data. Once BIM data is modified, *Data* will be created and wait for being appended into blockchain in a batch.

4. *PreviousBlockHash* $=$ **Hash**(*BlockHead*), where *BlockHead* is the previous blockhead where *PreviousBlockHash* tuple is located. That is, the hash value of previous blockhead is embedded into next block head. It can also be looked as a link of two adjacent block heads.

5. *DataHash* $=$ **Hash**($BIMdata_1 \| BIMdata_2 \| \cdots \| BIMdata_n$). Suppose the number of BIM in this time-span is n, that is, it is the numbers of BIM data that will be packaged in blockchain during a block generation period. *DataHash* guarantees the integrity of block contents consisting of modified BIM data.

The purpose of blockchain is to record the historical process of BIM record modification. A blockhead is composed of multiple BIM data, which can speed up the uplink of BIM record modification. The necessary BIM data need to record the history of modification, but the ordinary BIM cannot implement it. The method of calculating block hash values can get hash values of all uplink BIM data more quickly and efficiently than calculating Merkle tree roots. We propose a BIM via blockchain to storage data, which solve the problem of tracing, proving, and preventing tampering with BIM historical data. At the same time, it can generate a unified format to support

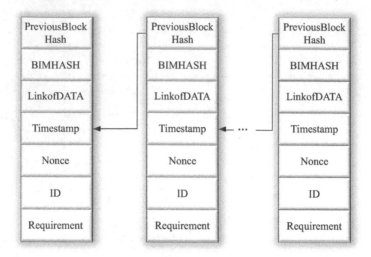

Figure 5.2   Public blockchain block data structure diagram

future open sharing. This method uses the hash structure of blockhead to ensure the integrity of all block data. In addition, block integrity is guaranteed by hash value, and the signature guarantees blockhead's integrity. The value of hash and nonce in blockhead guarantees fair consensus and non-tampering.

5.1.5   Example—public blockchain bcBIM

In this scene, the blockchain-based BIM data organization method is based on a decentralized measure, also known as a public blockchain method. The block data structure is shown in Figure 5.2.

Each newly generated block holds the hash value of the previous block. Therefore, the data uploaded by users cannot be tampered. Besides, *Nonce* is a random number which causes the block hash value having a number of 0 before it, and the number of 0 is determined by the value of *Requirement*, such as *Requirement = 5*.

5.1.6   Example—private blockchain bcBIM

bcBIM on the public blockchain is primarily used for autonomous organizations, but private blockchain may be easier to build for companies.

In this scene, the BIM data organization method based on blockchain is based on a central method, also known as a private blockchain or consortium blockchain method, which is shown in Figure 5.3. Besides, the resulting block data structure is shown in Figure 5.4.

The purpose of blockchain is to record the historical process of BIM record modification. A blockhead is composed of multiple BIM data, which can speed up

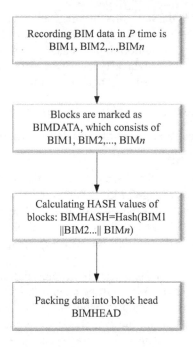

Figure 5.3   *Flow chart of BIM data organization method based on blockchain*

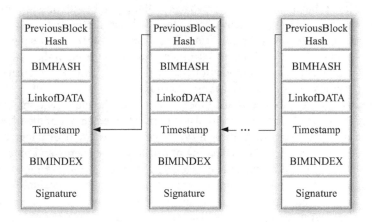

Figure 5.4   *Private blockchain block data structure diagram*

the uplink of BIM record modification. The necessary BIM data need to record the history of modification, but the ordinary BIM cannot implement it. The method of calculating block hash values can get hash values of all uplink BIM data more quickly and efficiently than calculating Merkle tree roots. We propose a BIM via blockchain to storage data, which solve the problem of tracing, proving, and preventing tampering with BIM historical data. At the same time, it can generate a unified format to support future open sharing. This method uses the hash structure of blockhead to ensure the integrity of all block data. In addition, block integrity is guaranteed by hash value, and the signature guarantees blockhead's integrity. The value of hash and nonce in blockhead guarantees fair consensus and non-tampering.

5.1.7 Security analysis and performance analysis

In this section, we will analyze the security and performance of bcBIM.

5.1.7.1 Security analysis

If a blockhead is changed, the hash value of the block head, denoted as Hash(*BlockHead*), will be changed too. It is computationally intractable to compute a block that is distinct with the original block but has the same hash value. That is, given Hash(*BlockHead*) $= a$, it is computationally intractable to compute *BlockHead'* such that Hash(*BlockHead'*) $= a$. In cryptography, it is called as second pre-image resistance.

Similarly, if a block data is changed, the hash value of block data will be changed. That is, if *Data* is altered, *DataHash* will be altered too. It will consequently alter related *BlockHead* and corresponding *PreviousBlockHash*, as well as all later influenced blocks in whole blockchain. In other words, once one *Data* is changed, some items in blockchain must be changed for consistence. Otherwise, it is very likely to detect such changes and inconsistences in blockchain.

The blockchain cannot be modified by any attackers. If any modification of any tuple in blockchain occurs, *Nonce* will be fault with high probability (that will be explained later) because anyone can detect the inconsistence by verifying whether Zero(Hash(*PreviousBlockHash*∥*DataHash*∥*Timestamp*∥*Nonce*)) $\geq$ *Difficulty*. If attackers try to find corresponding *Nonce* to maintain the consistence, it will cost a large amount of computation and is almost impossible to recreate a fake blockchain that is longer than original blockchain.

The separation of blockhead and block data will let the blockhead maintain the same size. The size of block data is varied and related to the number of modified BIM data. It can also make the computation of *PreviousBlockHash* more efficient, because the fix length of block head. The searching of *Nonce* will be energy and time saving.

The details of BIM data depend on the context, such as specific storage modes in underlying BIM systems, whose semantics is independent with our design. For example, if a model or parameter is changed, the location of modified value in terms of specific table, column, or tuple will be also recorded, depending on the specific selection of underlying database system in concrete BIM systems waiting for blochchain enhancement.

DataHash is generated by concatenation instead of Merkel tree root. Concatenation can reduce the hash computation from $O(n^2)$ to 1, which will be analyzed in details later.

Data and *DataHash* have an implicit linkage between themselves. Given *DataHash*, there exists one and only one *Data* such that *DataHash* $=$ Hash(*Data*). Inversely, given *Data*, there exists one and only one *DataHash* such that

DataHash = **Hash**(*Data*). In implementation, an explicit linkage can be added for fast jumping such as a variable with point type in C programming language.

Similarly, *PreviousBlockHash* and previous *block* have an implicit linkage between them. Given *PreviousBlockHash*, there exists one and only one *Block* such that *PreviousBlockHash* = **Hash**(*BlockHead*). Inversely, given *PreviousBlockHash*, there exists one and only *Block* such that

PreviousBlockHash = **Hash**(*BlockHead*). In implementation, an explicit linkage can be added for fast fetching such as a variable with point type in C programming language.

The block size can be tuned by setting different period of packaging blocks into blockchain. The period influences the timestamp gap between adjacent revision.

Proposition 5.1. *In BlockHead, the Nonce is computed by*
Zero(**Hash**(*PreviousBlockHash*‖*DataHash*‖*Timestamp*‖*Nonce*)) ≥ *Difficulty and only by random trials.*

Proof. *Nonce* is computed by
Zero(**Hash**(*PreviousBlockHash*‖*DataHash*‖*Timestamp*‖*Nonce*)) ≥ *Difficulty* after given *PreviousBlockHash*‖*DataHash*‖*Timestamp*. As the value of **Hash**(·) is unpredictable and almost random (normal distribution in outputting range), **Hash**(· ‖*Nonce*) is almost random. It can only be achieved by brute force trials to find satisfying *Nonce* such that **Zero**(**Hash**(· ‖*Nonce*)) ≥ *Difficulty*. □

Difficulty can be tuned by default regulations such as letting the searching period for *Nonce* to *p* where *p* depends on the requirements on modification audit or revision frequency (e.g., 24 h).

Proposition 5.2. *In private blockchain, blockhead could be*
BlockHead ::= ⟨*PreviousBlockHash, DataHash, Sig, Timestamp*⟩, *where Sig is the signature of blockchain generator, and*
Sig = **Sign**(*PriKey, PreviousBlockHash*‖*DataHash*‖*Timestamp*), *where* **Sign**(·) *is a signing function of an asymmetric cryptography.*

Proof. Straightforward. In private blockchain that all blocks are packaging by generators, blockchain generators are trustworthy. It signs the blockhead with its signature to guarantee the integrity of blockchain. All other users can check the integrity of blockchain by verifying the signature. □

In general, the blockhead is composed of multiple BIM data, which can accelerate the updating speed of BIM record modification. In addition, the important BIM data needs to record the history of modifications. However, ordinary BIM cannot record the history of modifications. The scheme proposed in this chapter can improve the security of BIM. The method of calculating block hash values can obtain all the hash values of upstream BIM data faster and more effectively than that of Merkle tree roots. In this chapter, a method of BIM data storage based on blockchain is proposed, which solves the problem of tracking, proving, and preventing tampering of BIM historical data. At the same time, it can also generate a unified format to support future open sharing. This method uses the chain hash structure of block heads to ensure the integrity of all block data. In addition, block integrity is guaranteed by block hash value, block signature guarantees block integrity, block hash and Nonce guarantees fairness, consistency and non-tampering.

5.1.7.2 Performance analysis

In this section, we mainly perform performance analysis on transaction throughput and up-link delay.

On the one hand, transaction throughput mainly tests one indicator: call contract system throughput (TPS). For blockchain systems, TPS is a new transaction record generated every second. In theory, Bitcoin can only handle seven transactions per second, one block per 10 min, which is equivalent to seven transaction throughput. Bitcoin's transaction processing speed is 6–7 transactions per second for public chains. However, this transaction throughput cannot meet the business needs of enterprises. For consortium chains, thousands of transactions can be processed per second. Miners pack blocks and submit them to the network, and each blockchain contains a certain number of transaction records. Thus, in the bcBIM system, we can also calculate TPS: TPS = the number of transactions contained in a block/block generation time. Take Bitcoin as an example, one block size is 1 MB, and the average size of each transaction record is 495 byte. The average number of transactions per block $= 1 \times 1,024 \times 1,024$ byte/495 = 2,118. Block generation time is about 10 min, that is, TPS $= 2,118 /(10 \times 60) = 3.53$.

On the other hand, in terms of up-link delay time, the inherent property of blockchain leads to transaction delay. The time of public chain is fixed, and the transaction delay is 10 min. In order to be safe, it is necessary to wait for at least six blocks to confirm the validity of payment. The generation of a block takes about 10 min, and the confirmation time is at least 1 h. Besides, private blockchain is faster, the main delay is one signing time.

5.1.8 Conclusions

In this chapter, we proposed a novel BIM model for enhancing current BIM ICT architecture called bcBIM by a component—a blockchain-based BIM data audit mechanism for BIM data aggregation in time serials. bcBIM model can guarantee the BIM data integrity and provenance by adding blockchain in current BIM database and facilitate mobile computing and pervasive accessing for BIM information. bcBIM is very likely an inevitable trend because of the development of mobile devices such as smart phones and tablets, cloud computing, IoT, and BIM big data sharing. The proposed bcBIM model can guide the design for further BIM information system and foster more interesting applications in BIM ICT systems, for example, accessing BIM cloud securely by engineering machines, construction robots, and wearable helmets in constriction area.

We designed a blockchain-based method for BIM data aggregation including data structure and basic computation for consensus. We analyzed its system parameters such as security strength, block size, packaging period, and hashing time cost. This method uses blockchain record BIM to modify history to ensure the integrity and unverifiability of messages. Blockchain technology can greatly improve the security and quality of BIM data and solve the hidden security risks of modifying BIM model and parameters in intelligent structure. Therefore, the use of blockchain will greatly promote the development of BIM technology.

5.2 CaACBIM: a context-aware access control model for BIM

5.2.1 Introduction

BIM (building information model) has been envisioned as a key approach for smart construction, such as construction automation, construction supply chain management, building information exchange, and building data sharing [28]. BIM can provide a uniform presentation, data framework, and organizing architecture to enable ICT to manage the full life-time information of a building in smart construction. BIM information can be accessed to facilitate engineering procedures such as design, construction, maintenance, reconstruction, and even destruction.

The recent ICT architecture for BIM applications is usually traditional client/server mode or single work station mode. It is worth noting that mobile cloud computing becomes pervasive in current personal computing. For example, cloud servers provide storage for the large volume of BIM data, which can be accessed remotely. Mobile-computing devices help designers, monitors, construction workers or suppliers access BIM information in cloud servers, anytime and anywhere. The BIM cloud can greatly shorten information accessing delay, and make BIM information available to all demanders. In other words, mobile cloud architecture allows BIM information to be pervasively accessible and is scalable for a large number of users.

However, access control of BIM data is subtle in mobile cloud environment. For example, consider entities in a construction project as follows: owners of a bank building are members of a bank company; designers are engineers in design institute; contractors are managers in contracting companies; and builders are workers of construction companies. They may access BIM information with different privileges. Even for the same information and entity, the privileges may be different at various times or locations, as, in mobile cloud, access may occur anytime and anywhere.

RBAC (role-based access control) is a mainstream model in current access control research [29–32], in which roles are assigned to each user. When the number of users grows, the management complexity obviously increases. Besides, RBAC may be inflexible due to the restriction of user's login authority. Mobile cloud for BIM provides the convenience of information access, but it also raises several security issues.

Access control for critical and sensitive BIM data presents the following challenges: (1) users are mobile and access may be anytime, thus requiring a more efficient and secure enhancement in access-control mechanism. (2) When the number of users is much larger than that in traditional RBAC, it experiences difficulties in scalability assigning each user privileges. (3) An attack is possible in which the credential of a role is leaked, whether due to intentional attacks or unintentional mistakes and random failure.

To tackle the above challenges, in this chapter, we propose a context-aware access control (CaAC) model called CaAC for BIM data auditing in mobile cloud BIM architecture. CaAC can support many users with fewer roles. Although the number of roles is decreased, CaAC can guarantee access control within the same role by differentiating contexts, which provides fine-grained control. We group users and user groups (UG) are granted roles. The contributions of the chapter are listed as follows:

1. We propose a CaAC mechanism to guarantee pervasive access control in mobile cloud paradigm that provides scalable storage and fast retrieval.
2. We propose a user grouping method to improve scalability and efficiency. We also propose an authentication scheme by dynamic electronic signature to reduce the aggressiveness of role leakage attacks.

5.2.2   Related work

BIM model is largely used in smart construction and sustainable buildings. Ren *et al.* [33] discussed BIM model for sustainable construction, such as energy saving, pollution reduction, costs saving, and construction efficiency. They proposed a BIM-based system that can be scheduled to be built by reducing the amount of energy. Vozzola *et al.* [34] described a practical application of BIM in the construction processes.

Regarding BIM application potential, Ding *et al.* [35] proposed a BIM application framework, which describes the process of expanding from 3D to computable *n*D. BIM is the simulation tool to generate the building design and dynamical analysis for the energy consumption of houses. According to the measures and characteristics of BIM barriers in China, Pan *et al.* [36] drafted a road map for the adoption and application of BIM in China. Mohd *et al.* [37] discussed the application of BIM in architectural planning. BIM was used to conduct semi-structured interviews with customers. The interviews revealed the necessity and benefits of BIM implementation in construction planning, as well as the challenges faced by customers in implementing BIM. Ferreira *et al.* [38] used a simplified method, combining the location information generated by interaction between beacon propagation signals and mobile device sensors (accelerometers and gyroscopes) with local building information to provide real-time positioning and guidance for users in buildings.

We observe that some upcoming computing paradigms are promising to be integrated with BIM system as a new architecture, such as mobile cloud computing, blockchain, and IoT. However, the marriage of them with BIM has been explored by few related works. The handheld devices such as smart phones and tablet computers have already been pervasively used as an ordinary computing tool for many engineers. Those devices perform as convenient productivity tools, because hardware capabilities grow sufficiently powerful, and more productivity applications are available at application stores. The work on the marriage between mobile cloud and BIM model is few. Betarte *et al.* [39] proposed a framework—ACTkit—for the definition and enforcement of dynamic access control. Their work is independent of ours.

5.2.3   Problem formulation

5.2.3.1   System model

The main weakness in security for current BIM are as follows: the access control of BIM data is not fine-grained. BIM data can be accessed by roles, but same roles may have different privileges for the same subject. In addition, with the development of pervasive data sharing in BIM data, access control becomes more critical because some data may not be accessible to the same role in different contexts, e.g., times or locations. For some sensitive buildings, such as cross-sea bridges and critical infrastructures, it is necessary to carry out fine-grained access control of BIM data.

Five basic elements are concerned: users, roles, objects, operations, and permissions. At least one permission is assigned to each role, and at least one role is assigned to each user. The same access rights can be assigned to different roles. Users and roles are many-to-many, which means users can have different roles in different scenarios. For example, a project manager can also be a designer. Certainly, a role can be given to multiple users. The separation of user and role can make authorization be more flexible. Roles and permissions are also many-to-many, which means roles can have multiple rights and the same right can be delegated to multiple roles. RBAC refers to the association of a user with permissions through roles, where a user has multiple roles and each role has multiple permissions. In this way, an authorization model such as user-role permissions is built. In this model, ordinary people have many-to-many relationships between users and roles, as well as roles and permissions.

When the number of users is large, it is cumbersome to give each user authorization (to delegate roles) one by one. Thus, we consider organizing multiple users in one group, and authorizing users by authorizing groups. As a result, all permissions that a user possesses consist of permissions possessed by the user personally and permissions possessed by the UG. The model is shown in Figure 5.5, and the specification is discussed in details in the following.

In addition, we propose two models on grouping rules: basic model and advanced model. In the basic model, grouping is based on user's privileges. That is, the user knows the privileges upon login. Once the basic model is not sufficiently flexible, the advanced model is proposed in which grouping corresponds to context requests.

It is worth stressing that the main difference between a role and a UG is that a UG is a group of users, instead of a group of permissions. In contrast, a role is a group of users and permissions, and it indeed connects two groups as a mediation. In a system where permissions and members of a UG can only be modified by system administrator, user-grouping mechanism is very similar to role mechanism. Roles can also be implemented based on UGs, in which a role links to the privileges of the UG.

5.2.3.2   Adversary model

In this section, we pinpoint three potential weaknesses that could be exploited by adversaries as follows: role credential leakage, administrator compromise, and a mismatch between the number of users and roles.

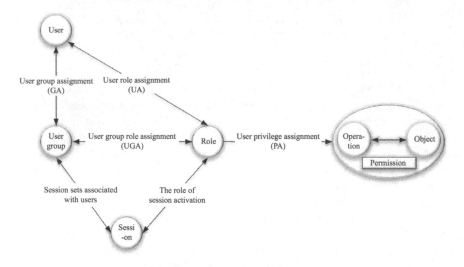

Figure 5.5   Context-aware access control with grouping

The role's credential may be disclosed, whether it is an intentional attack, an unintentional error, or a random failure. Attackers can impersonate designated roles to obtain unauthorized permissions by obtaining the credentials, e.g., a login password.

During the grouping process, all UGs are grouped by administrators. We assume that administrators may be compromised. As a result, attackers can be included into any groups they want to join. Although it is difficult in reality, it is preferable to assume stronger adversary for better security.

We observe that, in the BIM model, the number of users may be much larger than the number of roles, thus mismatch exists between them. This mismatch leads to potential risks for BIM models. For example, some critical models (e.g., architecture, construction, and infrastructure data) may be revealed by unintended users and exposed to potential attackers that intend to access data illegally.

5.2.4   Proposed scheme

5.2.4.1   Context-aware access control

As BIM data are stored in cloud servers, the data may be accessed by requestors, or be updated by corresponding users who are responsible to the information. A secure data management issue thus arises: access control for the BIM data in cloud servers.

The access control has been explored for many years, and the mechanism becomes mature in traditional ICT domains. For example, RBAC is a typical one in which access rights are controlled according to requestor's roles. The data have different access rights, such as read, write, and execute (if applicable), and a user is assigned one role or multiple roles, corresponding to access rights to specified data. The key advantage of RBAC access control mechanism is that it can support a large number of users within much fewer roles, and access control tables can be created easily. Furthermore, assigning rights to roles is more flexible than assigning rights to users

Table 5.2   Notation

CS	Cloud servers
MC	Mobile clients
RRA	Role-revealing attack
BIM	Mobile cloud BIM (with blockchain enhancement)
RBAC	Role-based access control
CaAC	Context-aware RBAC
U	User
R	Role
S	Subject
P	Permission
SA	Subject assignment
PA	Permission assignment
C	Context

directly. For example, if the right for accessing certain data is changed for a user, it can be done easily by changing the role of the user to another role.

We observe that the number of roles in BIM system context is usually rare. There exist four main roles in the BIM model:

1. Host: It represents investors for a building construction.
2. Designer: It represents building devisers or revisers.
3. Constructor: It represents executive and concrete builders of the building.
4. Supplier: It represents material providers for the constructors.

It is straightforward to deploy RBAC to facilitate access control in BIM. However, we observer that the numbers of users and subjects in terms of BIM models are usually large, but the number of roles is usually small, thus there exists a mismatch between them. Such mismatch will induce certain risks of BIM model breach. Besides, passwords for designated roles may be incidentally exposed or hacked by attackers intentionally. As there are much fewer roles than users, it may not be flexible to change the accessing privileges of a role. (It will influence all users in this role.) To tackle these problems, we propose incorporating the context information along roles in access control for BIM in the following.

We list certain major notations used in the remainder of the chapter in Table 5.2.

For better understanding and emphasis, we induce the following notation:

Definition 5.1. *Role-revealing attack (RRA). It works for leaking the credential of a role, whether by intentionally attack or by unintentionally mistakes and random failure.*

Next, we present our access control model.

Definition 5.2. *User (U): It represents users who will access BIM data.*

Definition 5.3. *UG: It represents user groups who will access BIM data.*

Definition 5.4. *Subject (S): It represents data in BIM servers awaiting for accessing.*

Definition 5.5. *Role (R): It represents a title with an authority level for accessed subject.*

Definition 5.6. *Operation (O): It represents the operating right for an accessed subject, for example, read, write, and execute.*

Definition 5.7. *Permission (P): It represents the operation combinations for an accessed subject.*

Definition 5.8. *Subject assignment: A subject is assigned to a role.*

Definition 5.9. *Permission assignment (PA): A permission is assigned to a role.*

Definition 5.10. *User assignment (UA): A user is assigned to a role.*

Definition 5.11. *UG assignment (UGA): A UG is assigned to a role.*

Definition 5.12. *Context (C): The extra condition for regulating the access permission for a role with respect to a subject.*

We propose a context-aware RBAC called CaAC model as follows:

1. $UA \subseteq U \times R$, where UA is a user-assignment relation; U is a set of users; and R is a set of roles. The UA is a relation of users and roles. A user may possess multiple roles and a role may be possessed by multiple users.
2. $UGA \subseteq UG \times R$, where UGA is a UG assignment relation; UG is a set of user groups; and R is a set of roles. The UA is a relation of UGs and roles. A UG may possess multiple roles and a role may be possessed by multiple groups.
3. **AssignedUser**$(\cdot) : r \in R \to 2^U$. **AssignedUser**$(\cdot)$ is a function to describe UA procedure. It is a function from R to 2^U, which means a role is assigned to a user or multiple users. 2^U is a set of sets in which elements are users. It cannot be onto, as some users may not be an image of a role. It can be one-to-one, as some users may be an image of multiple roles. It is a function, as one role can only map to one set of users.
4. **AssignedUsergroup**$(\cdot) : r \in R \to 2^{UG}$. **AssignedUser**$(\cdot)$ is a function to describe UGA procedure. It is a function from R to 2^{UG}, which means a role is assigned to a UG or multiple UGs. 2^{UG} is a set of sets in which elements are UGs. It cannot be onto, as some UGs may not be an image of a role. It can be one-to-one, as some UGs may be an image of multiple roles. It is a function, as one role can only map to one set of UGs.
5. **AssignedUser**$(r) = \{u \in U | (u, r) \in UA\}$. It is a set of users for a given role. It can also be seen as the range of function **AssignedUser**$(\cdot)$ for given r. That is, they are all users who are assigned a given role r. The range of the function is all $u \in U$ where $(u, r) \in UA$.
6. **AssignedUsergroup**$(r) = \{ug \in UG | (ug, r) \in UGA\}$. It is a set of UGs for a given role. It can also be looked as the range of function **AssignedUsergroup**$(\cdot)$ for given r. That is, they are all UGs who are assigned a given role r. The range of the function is all $ug \in UG$ where $(ug, r) \in UGA$.

7. $P = 2^O$, where P is a set of permissions and O is a set of operations such as read, write, and execute. P is a set of sets in which elements are operations.

8. $PA \subseteq P \times R$, where PA is a permission-assignment relation. PA means a relation of permission set P and role set R.

 Instead, $PA_c \subset P \times R \times C$. A permission is assigned to a combination of R and C. The $R \times C$ can define a proper permission for the further access. Roughly speaking, when and only when the specification of role and that of context are both guaranteed, assigned permission will be possessed.

 Note that, this part is only for CaAC, but the traditional RBAC is the previous one. This presentation way can point out the distinction between the two methods.

9. **AssignedPermission**$(\cdot) : r \in R \to 2^P$, where **AssignedPermission**$(\cdot)$ is a function to assign a permission or multiple permissions to a role.

 Instead, **AssignedPermission**$(\cdot) : r \in R \times c \in C \to 2^P$, where **Assigned Permission**$(\cdot)$ is a function to assign a permission to a combination of role and context. Note that, when and only when the specification of role and that of context are both satisfied, the permission will be possessed.

10. **AssignedPermission**$(r) = \{p \in P | (p, r) \in PA\}$. It is a set of privileges for a given role. It can also be looked as the range of function **AssignedPermission**$(\cdot)$ for a given inputting. The range of the function for a given r is all $p \in P$ where $(p, r) \in PA$.

 Instead, **AssignedPermission**$(r, c) = \{p \in P | (p, r, c) \in PA_c\}$. It describes the range of function **AssignedPermission**$(\cdot)$ for given r and c. The range of the function is all $p \in P$ where $(p, r, c) \in PA_c$.

11. **UserSubjects**$(\cdot) : u \in U \to 2^S$, where U is a set of users and S is a set of subjects.

12. **SubjectRoles**$(\cdot) : s \in S \to 2^R$, where S is a set of subjects and R is a set of roles.

13. **SubjectRolesContexts**$(\cdot) : s \in S \to 2^R \times 2^C$, where S is a set of subjects, R is a set of roles, and C is a set of context.

14. $\bigcup_{r \in \text{SubjectRoles}(s)}$ **AssignedPermision**(r). This set includes all permissions of the roles that can access the subject s, that is, all permissions for the subject s.

15. $\bigcup_{r, c \in \text{SubjectRolesContexts}(s)}$ **AssignedPermision**(r, c). This set includes all permissions of the roles that can access the subject s in all related context, that is, all permissions for the subject s.

16. **creatnewUG**$(\cdot)$: This is a function to create a new UG. When it is found that the original UG does not meet the use requirements, a new UG is created.

5.2.4.2 Proposed authorization rules

Rules for basic model: when a user initiates a request to access BIM data, servers first obtain the permissions of the user according to users and permissions mapping table. Second, the user is added to corresponding UGs based on permissions. In addition, the user's permissions are also added to the UG's permissions. However, if there exists no permission relationship between the user and others, a new UG is immediately created. The next step is granting roles to the UG which activates by launching a session. When the user requests to access BIM data again, the permissions are assigned according to the roles of the UG. Finally, servers compare the user's requirements with permissions and determine whether the requirements are satisfied. Access is allowed if they are satisfied, otherwise access is not allowed.

Rules for advanced model: when a user initiates a request to access BIM data, servers first obtain the requirements of the user according to corresponding contexts. Second, the user is added to the corresponding UGs based on requirements. In addition, the user's permissions are also added to the UG's permissions. However, if there are no requirements relationships between the user and others, a new UG is immediately created. The next step is granting roles to the UG that activates by launching a session. When the user requests access to the BIM data again, the permissions are assigned according to the roles of the UG. Finally, servers compare the user's requirements with permissions and determine whether the requirements are satisfied. Access is allowed if they are satisfied, otherwise access is not allowed. Besides, to defend against RRA, we propose using dynamic electronic signature in advanced model.

Aiming at the problem of strong attack on RRA, we propose dynamic electronic signature over access control. Considering signing a data file in BIM system, due to the uncertainty of the number of directories, the directory page after the signature page cannot be effectively determined. We use dynamic signature key and feature recognition technology in BIM system to achieve accurate identification of signature page. It can also effectively ensure uniqueness, correctness, and validity of BIM data.

The BIM master data generated in electronic signature is usually original information for entire building life cycle, e.g., architectural design drawings, while data attribute document is attribution information, including creators, creation time, construction stages, technical status, data classification, level of secrecy, etc. Figure 5.6 describes the method of dynamic electronic signature. The process of obtaining dynamic page number is included, and the key feature set F and signature page number p are added to the electronic configuration template.

5.2.4.3 Examples: location-aware or time-aware

BIM data may include the following BIM models at different stages of a life cycle of a building:

1. Design models: Building, structure, hydropower and wind, performance simulation, environment, and infrastructure.
2. Construction model: Subdivide the design model according to the construction steps.
3. Schedule model (4D): Linking model objects in a project according to schedule.
4. Cost model (5D): Linking objects to the cost and time of the project.
5. Manufacturing models: Using 3D models instead of traditional plane drawings to manufacture building components.
6. Operational model: Used to simulate operations management, maintenance, and midterm updates.

As the access of BIM cloud servers is always pervasive at different locations, we propose using location information of accessors to further constrain the access right so as to provide a fine-grained access control.

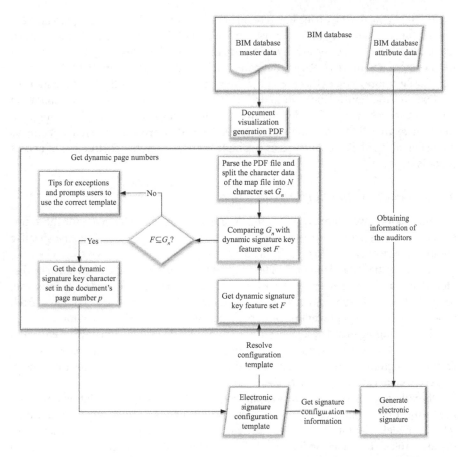

Figure 5.6 Dynamic signature method

For example, a designer may access the BIM data at the construction fields, at home, or in the offices. In traditional RBAC, no matter where she is, she will be granted the same permission for accessing the BIM data. It may provide certain convenience in some situations, but it may also create risk in terms of privilege leakage, for example, the malicious codes at home computer may steal the password for the role. In CaAC, the designer can access 3D data in offices, which cannot be accessed in construction fields, while 2D data can be accessed in construction fields. Thus, to specify the permission for a role in different locations, a location information may be induced to distinguish, e.g., contexts. That is, the permission is related to not only roles but also locations. The administrators can group users in different areas according to location context and then assign roles.

Another context that may be encountered is time, i.e., the time of accessing BIM data. Similarly, we propose a time-aware RBAC that can incorporate time constraints into access control, especially with respect to the same role. Material suppliers may access BIM data during office hours or on holidays. MCBIM server can guarantee the successful access during office hours, but not on holidays. According to the context, the users in this time period are divided into a group and the roles are granted. It cannot be accomplished in naive RBAC but can be achieved in time-aware RBAC model.

Furthermore, context-aware can be further extended to other instantiation of context. In addition to location and time, the context can be any other condition related to access right. The detailed model for context-aware RBAC is similar to location-aware RBAC and time-aware RBAC. The latter two are presented not only as an instantiation of CaAC but also as a sample for the concrete construction of access models.

5.2.5 Security and performance analysis

In this section, we compare two models proposed in this chapter with the traditional RBAC model in five aspects and analyze security and feasibility. The specific comparison results are shown in Table 5.3.

Confidentiality and integrity: The former means data are guaranteed not to be disclosed to unauthorized users. The latter means data cannot be tampered (e.g., insertion, modification, deletion, and reordering) without authorization during storage. Both proposed models can prevent unauthorized access and tampering behavior.

Defending against RRA: We propose dynamic electronic signature over access control. That is, BIM system equips accurate identification of signature pages. Key feature recognition can effectively solve the risks of RRA and ensure the uniqueness, correctness, and validity of BIM data.

Flexibility: Flexibility refers to the convenience of mapping relations between users and roles, and reconfiguring roles and privileges on demand. In traditional RBAC model, flexibility imposes difficulties in recreating sessions and activates updated roles. In basic model, flexibility is improved. Since grouping rules stem from permissions upon login, they still need to be grouped if the permissions change. In advanced model, it is not necessary to re-perform all the steps, even if roles or login permissions change. It is independent of the permissions upon login and only depends on contexts.

Efficiency: When data volume is huge or the number of users is large, traditional RBAC model may be inefficient in authorizing each user in the system sequentially. Thus, grouping users and authorizing UGs in a batch will be more efficient. Furthermore, advanced model is less efficient than the basic model. The specific quantitative analysis process is as follows:

1. Worst case: There is no inclusion relationship between users and user requests, thus grouping needs n times.
2. Average case: If there are p users and other q users with inclusion relationship $(p + q < n)$, the remaining $(n - p - q)$ users need to group $(n - p - q)$ times. $(p + q)/2$ coincidence elements are generated in the inclusion relationship. The efficiency is improved by $n/(n - p - q + (p + q)/2) = 2n/(2n - p - q)$.
3. Best case: All users and user requests have inclusion relationship, thus grouping only occurs once. The efficiency increases n times.

Table 5.3 A comparison between the CaAC model and the traditional RBAC

Characteristic	Model		
	RBAC	**Basic CaAC**	**Advanced CaAC**
Privilege management	Constraints are set for each permission, which is prone to errors in the process of permission allocation. With the increase of functional modules in the system, the number of permissions is huge, and it is difficult to achieve effective management	Grouping rules are based on user login permissions, more fine-grained than RBAC	Grouping according to context user request, more fine-grained than RBAC
Flexibility	Flexibility is extremely poor. If any part of the session changes, the user needs to recreate the session and activate the user role	Flexibility is at a moderate level, and if user's permissions change upon login, she needs to be grouped again	The user's roles or login permissions have changed without requiring all steps in the model to be repeated
Data security	With the increasing number of people involved and the growing size of databases, this model obviously can not meet the security of data	Because of adopting grouping strategy, data security can be satisfied	Dynamic electronic signature is adopted to ensure the security of data
Efficiency	Efficiency and its inefficiency, to give each user of the system one-by-one authorization (role), is a very cumbersome thing	Efficiency is the highest. Privileges and roles should be set first to form access control tables. Grouping and authorization only need to look up tables upon requests	Efficiency is moderate. Users login first and then be grouped according to requests, while permissions can be granted directly to each group

5.2.6   Conclusions

We analyzed the limitation in traditional role-based only access-control mechanism. As the number of mobile users is much larger than the number of roles, naive RBAC may not be suitable in BIM situations. We thus propose a context-aware fine-grained access control, called CaAC. We describe the functions of CaAC by formal method and present several illustrations on contexts via location-CaAC and the time-aware access control. CaAC can guarantee the access control within the same role by differentiating contexts, which is more fine-grained than current role-based only access control. We also present grouping algorithms of two models. By comparing the proposed models with traditional RBAC model, we analyze the security and feasibility. As a result of analysis, we conclude that the average efficiency is improved by $2n/(2n - p - q)$, and the time complexity of the proposed algorithm is $O(n)$.

Acknowledgment

The research was financially supported by the National Key R&D Program of China with No. 2016YFC0702107. Preliminary results are presented in *Information*, 10(2):47, and *Mathematical Problems in Engineering*.

Data availability statement

1. The [code] data used to support the findings of this study have been deposited in the [IEEE DATAPORT] repository ([10.5072/7h0n-3g73]).
2. The [code] data used to support the findings of this study have been deposited in the [IEEE DATAPORT] repository ([10.5072/6mv1-jx31]).

References

[1]   B. Succar. Building information modelling framework: A research and delivery foundation for industry stakeholders. *Automation in Construction*, 18(3): 357–375, 2009.

[2]   Y. Lu, Z. Wu, R. Chang and Y. Li. Building information modeling (BIM) for green buildings: A critical review and future directions *Automation in Construction*, 83:134–148, 2017.

[3]   J. Zhao, L. Wang, J. Tao, *et al.* A security framework in G-Hadoop for big data computing across distributed Cloud data centres. *Journal of Computer and System Sciences*, 80(5): 994–1007, 2014

[4]   C. Perera, R. Ranjan and L. Wang. End-to-end privacy for open big data markets. *IEEE Cloud Computing*, 2(4):44–53, 2015

[5]   C. Perera, R. Ranjan, L. Wang, S.U. Khan and A.Y. Zomaya. Big data privacy in the Internet of Things era. *IT Professional*, 17(3):32–39, 2015

[6]   A. Jrade and M. Nassiri. Integrating decision support system (DSS) and building information modeling (BIM) to optimize the selection of sustainable building components. *Journal of Information Technology in Construction*, 20(25):399–420, 2015.

[7]   A.H. Oti and W. Tizani. BIM extension for the sustainability appraisal of conceptual steel design. *Advanced Engineering Informatics*, 29(1):28–46, 2015.

[8]   P. Inyim, J. Rivera, Y. Zhu, *et al.* Integration of building information modeling and economic and environmental impact analysis to support sustainable building design. *Journal of Management in Engineering*, 31(1):A4014002, 2015.

[9]   X. Wang and P. E. Love. BIM + AR: Onsite information sharing and communication via advanced visualization. *Proceedings of the 2012 IEEE 16th International Conference on Computer Supported Cooperative Work in Design (CSCWD'12)*, Wuhan, 2012, pp. 850–855.

[10]   M. Kokorus, W. Eyrich and R. Zacharias. Innovative approach to the substation design using building information modeling (BIM) technology. *2016 IEEE/PES Transmission and Distribution Conference and Exposition (TD16)*, Dallas, TX, 2016, pp. 1–5.

[11]   M.H. Dawood. BIM based optimal life cycle cost of sustainable house framework. *2016 3rd MEC International Conference on Big Data and Smart City (ICBDSC'16)*, Muscat, 2016, pp. 1–5.

[12]   D. Pasini, S.M. Ventura, S. Rinaldi, P. Bellagente, A. Flammini and A.L.C. Ciribini. Exploiting Internet of Things and building information modeling framework for management of cognitive buildings. *2016 IEEE International Smart Cities Conference (ISC2'16)*, Trento, 2016, pp. 1–6.

[13]   W. Zhu, B. Eynard, M. Bricogne, S. Remy and W. Wan. Framework for information modeling of an integrated building. *2015 International Conference on Smart and Sustainable City and Big Data (ICSSC'15)*, Shanghai, 2015, pp. 139–144.

[14]   U. Isikdag. Design patterns for BIM-based service-oriented architectures. *Automation in Construction*, 25:59–71, 2012.

[15]   S. Yoon, N. Park and J. Choi. A BIM-based design method for energy-efficient building. In *2009 Fifth International Joint Conference on INC, IMS and IDC (NCM'09)*, August 2009, pp. 376–381.

[16]   Y. Jung and M. Joo. Building information modelling (BIM) framework for practical implementation. *Automation in Construction*, 20(2):126–133, 2011.

[17]   H.C.J. Linderoth. Understanding adoption and use of BIM as the creation of actor networks. *Automation in Construction*, 19(1):66–72, 2010.

[18]   W. Lu and H. Li. Building information modeling and changing construction practices. *Automation in Construction*, 20(2):99–100, 2011.

[19]   G. Desogus, E. Quaquero, A. Sanna, *et al.* Preliminary performance monitoring plan for energy retrofit: A cognitive building: The "Mandolesi Pavillon" at the University of Cagliari. *2017 AEIT International Annual Conference*, Cagliari, 2017, pp. 1–6.

[20] M. Arslan, Z. Riaz and S. Munawar. Building information modeling (BIM) enabled facilities management using Hadoop architecture. *2017 Portland International Conference on Management of Engineering and Technology (PICMET17)*, Portland, OR, 2017, pp. 1–7.

[21] Y. Yuan and Z. Jin. Life cycle assessment of building energy in big-data era: Theory and framework. *2015 International Conference on Network and Information Systems for Computers*, Wuhan, 2015, pp. 601–605.

[22] H. Ferguson, C. Vardeman and J. Nabrzyski. Linked data view methodology and application to BIM alignment and interoperability. *2016 IEEE International Conference on Big Data (Big Data'16)*, Washington, DC, 2016, pp. 2626–2635.

[23] L. Bottaccioli, A. Aliberti, F. Ugliotti, *et al.* Building energy modelling and monitoring by integration of IoT devices and building information models. *2017 IEEE 41st Annual Computer Software and Applications Conference (COMPSAC17)*, Turin, 2017, pp. 914–922.

[24] S.N. Razavi and C.T. Haas. Multisensor data fusion for on-site materials tracking in construction. *Automation in Construction*, 19(8):1037–1046, 2010.

[25] J. Park, K. Kim and Y.K. Cho. Framework of automated construction-safety monitoring using cloud-enabled BIM and BLE mobile tracking sensors. *Journal of Construction Engineering and Management*, 143(2):05016019, 2017.

[26] J. Garcia-Fernandez, J. Anssi, Y. Ahn and J.J. Fernandez. Quantitative + qualitative information for heritage conservation an open science research for paving 'collaboratively' the way to historical-BIM. *2015 Digital Heritage*, Granada, 2015, pp. 207–208.

[27] Y. Yuan and F.-Y. Wang. Blockchain: The state of the art and future trends. *Acta Automatica Sinica*, 42(4):481–494, 2016.

[28] K. Barlish and K. Sullivan. How to measure the benefits of BIM—A case study approach. *Automation in Construction*, 24:149–159, 2012.

[29] E. Coyne and T. Weil. An RBAC implementation and interoperability standard: The INCITS cyber security 1.1 model. *IEEE Security and Privacy*, 6:84–87, 2008.

[30] D. Ferraiolo, R. Kuhn and R. Sandhu. RBAC standard rationale: Comments on "a critique of the ANSI standard on role-based access control." *IEEE Security and Privacy*, 5:51–53, 2007.

[31] V.N.L. Franqueira and R.J. Wieringa. Role-based access control in retrospect. *Computer*, 45:81–88, 2012.

[32] M. Xu, D. Wijesekera and X. Zhang. Runtime administration of an RBAC profile for XACML. *IEEE Transactions on Services Computing*, 4:286–299, 2011.

[33] Q. Ren, D. Tan and C. Tan. Research of sustainable design based on technology of BIM. *Proceedings of the 2011 International Conference on Remote Sensing, Environment and Transportation Engineering (RSETE'11)*, Nanjing, China, 24–26 June 2011, pp. 4322–4324.

[34] M. Vozzola, G. Cangialosi and M.L. Turco. BIM use in the construction process. *Proceedings of the International Conference on Management and Service Science (MASS'09)*, Wuhan, China, 20–22 September 2009, pp. 1–4.

[35] L. Ding, Y. Zhou and B. Akinci. Building information modeling (BIM) application framework: The process of expanding from 3D to computable nD. *Automation in Construction*, 46:82–93, 2014.

[36] J.Y. Pan and Y.Y. Zhao. Research on barriers of BIM application in China's building industry. *Journal of Engineering Management*, 1:6–11, 2012.

[37] S. Mohd and A.A. Latiffi. Building information modeling (BIM) application in construction planning. *Proceedings of the 7th International Conference on Construction in the 21st Century (CITC-VII)*, Bangkok, Thailand, 19–21 December 2013.

[38] C. Ferreira, R. Resende and S. Martinho. Beacons and BIM models for indoor guidance and location. *Sensors*, 18:4374, 2018.

[39] G. Betarte, A. Gatto, R. Martinez and F. Zipitria. ACTkit: A framework for the definition and enforcement of role, content and context-based access control policies. *IEEE Latin America Transactions*, 10:1742–1751, 2012.

Chapter 6
Security of marine-information system

Lin Mu[1] and Jun Song[2]

This chapter starts from the security demand of marine-information system to emphatically introduce the main problems in the marine-information system, including wireless-communication security, secure sharing of information, big data security and military–civilian coordination, centers on the marine information security system to discuss the technology and method of guaranteeing the security of marine-information system from the aspects of communication network security, computing environment security, data and application security, security monitoring and forewarning and security support. In addition, it lays emphasis on analyzing and introducing the required key theories and technologies of the network space security for marine-information-system design.

6.1 Background and significance of marine information security

Digital ocean connects the remote-sensing technology, geographic information system (GIS), sensing and information collection technology, automation and network technology with the human need of constant and deep ocean development, thus providing a basic framework for marine informatization, which refers to informationalized ocean in essence. With the constant development of cloud computing and mobile internet application, the world has entered the era of big data, while the "digital ocean" system needs to constantly adapt to the development of new technology in the aspects of marine information acquisition, massive information analysis and processing as well as scaled service and application; besides, its information system security guarantee also faces new challenge.

Marine-information-system development is the most important component of national marine information infrastructure. Marine space information security refers to the information defense technology which works in the marine space, takes the combination of the marine technology and information security technology as the means and is based on the purpose of maintaining marine information security. Owing to the unique geographical situation of marine space, the globalization relies on the

[1]College of Marine Science and Technology, China University of Geosciences, Wuhan, P.R. China
[2]School of Computer Science, China University of Geosciences, Wuhan, P.R. China

ocean strongly; therefore, sea right has become the important component of the overall national strategy capability. Researching the characteristics of marine space information security and developing the marine space information security technology is not only of urgency but also of profound strategy significance.

6.2   The characteristics and design objective of marine-information system

The marine space information system has become more and more complicated, usually including the marine meteorological environment and marine-information system, marine communication system, marine navigation system, marine alert, forewarning system, identification friend or foe system as well as command and control system [1], which has the following characteristics:

1. The marine space information system has close reliance on the outer space [2]. It usually cannot leave from the support of space base and is also a component of space-information system. Therefore, it also has the characteristics of space communication, including exposure, vulnerability, long distance of link and high bit error rate. It is clear that the marine space information system has much similarity with space-information-security technology.
2. Marine space information system is of great mobility. The sea target is in a state of motion; therefore, the establishment and maintaining of marine information link is usually dynamic and featured with mobile communication, namely, the marine space information system is in a dynamic change which makes marine space information security technology complicated, variable and difficult.
3. The marine network communication mode is diversified [2]. The marine link includes wireless transmission, cable-based and cable-free transmission. Wherein, the wireless transmission bases on wide frequency spectrum and covers the transmission media from sound wave to light wave and from sea water to outer space. Its transmission feature varies largely. Owing to the large state change of sea target, the antenna beam is generally wide and the like exposure and openness are dominant; besides, the marine space information security channels mostly base on the technology means of sonar security, electronic security and photoelectric security.
4. The marine space information network nodes are dispersed with small scale [2]. Owing to the massive sea scope, data collection usually relies on the disperse data-collection platform (containing buoy) which has low data rate. However, the formation of ship generally has low scale and weak network link layer as well as special marine space communication network agreement; therefore, marine space network security relies on special research.
5. The marine space signal environment density is low [4]. Because the sea scope is massive and the sea target density is relatively low, the background environment of electromagnetic signal is not as complicated as the land, but instead, the radio interference source on the ocean is few, there hardly exists with industrial interference and electromagnetic interference. The wireless signal density is low,

the electromagnetic signal environment is relatively wide and the information source security protection is relatively to be realized.

The marine information is of complex acquisition channel, multiple data types and large data scale and is actually a typical big data system. Therefore, digital marine-information system adapting to the marine strategy development demand should be established fully based on the characteristics of big data. Generally, the main design objectives of marine-information system include five aspects:

   i.   Features of overall, large-scale and multichannel marine information data acquisition, storage and high-speed concurrent processing capability [2,3].

   ii.   Its data acquisition, analysis and processing should be featured with dynamics and real-time response.

   iii.   It should possess the capability to conduct data mining and intelligent analysis on massive marine information data sources to form overall marine trend, thus providing support for various marine-information system applications [2].

   iv.   It should provide platform-based and open marine informatization application support and have information sharing and multi-business coordination capability.

   v.   It should have perfect information-security-guarantee capability [2].

6.3   Marine information security risk analysis

The digital marine information processing system and platform design need to form a complete link in the whole process from marine information collection, data mining and analysis to marine information service, besides, the data in the links of big data processing all exist with the risks of data losing, data unauthorized access and data tampering or losing. Combined with the general characteristics of digital marine information processing system and the characteristics of marine information research, the digital marine-information system mainly has the following five aspects of security risks:

1.   Disclosure risk of marine information. When the marine information is obtained and transmitted to the digital marine-information system, there exists, with the sensitive information disclosure risk, the wrong information and marine affairs analysis and decision risks caused from incredible information source and information tampering as well as the information security risk caused from hosted virtualization and network virtualization existed in the cloud-computing platform relied by the digital marine-information system [3].

2.   Secure storage risk of massive data. For the massive marine information and diversified data sources, the traditional storage system cannot satisfy the demand of big data application. For example, the massive data from different marine business systems are collected and stored in the digital marine-information system, which utilizes HBase-based Not only Structured Query Language (NoSQL) storage technology to implement the fetching, managing and processing of big

data. In terms of the different sensitivity of transactions, the mechanisms of authentication, access control and data-security management supported by HBase do not meet the requirement of hierarchical data protection. Therefore, massive distributed data storage increases the risk of out of control caused by data access [2,3].

3. Authority division risk of marine-information system. In the digital marine-information system, the authorities of data owners and users, operators and administrators should be divided, besides, the life cycle of much data is temporary, the dynamic development and parallelization of data storage and processing, the dynamic development of environmental boundary processing, complexity and diversification of data operation behavior all bring challenges to information security of digital marine-information system [3].

4. Security protection risk of mobile equipment. The digital marine-information system needs to obtain marine information from land, sea and air through multiple-businesses and multi-platforms and also needs to connect with internet of things and mobile internet application. More and more sensitive analysis data are transmitted between mobile equipment and put forward challenges to mobile data-security prevention capability and digital marine mobile user terminal security protection [3].

5. Marine-information sharing and synergy risk. The digital marine-information system users are also the important providers of marine information; besides, the related information systems have different design objectives and information security ratings. Hence, it is necessary to study how to realize the information sharing and business synergy according to demands; how to design open, platform-based and shared information system and how to avoid non-authorized or exceeding use of related services and prevent information disclosure or system service invalidness [3].

6.4 Analysis on marine-information system security demand

6.4.1 Wireless network communication security

Marine communication network mainly serves for the offshore fixed platform (marine engineering platform and fixed buoy), mobile platform (ship, plane and mobile buoy) and communication guarantee between marine platform and shore base. The marine communication platforms are far from the shore-based land, mostly of which are mobile platforms and adopt wireless communication and satellite communication to realize communication guarantee [2]. Therefore, the marine-information system mostly adopts the wireless communication means based on short wave, ultrashort wave, microwave, satellite or underwater. The wireless network adopts open channel, and the attackers can launch various security attacks on the network by aid of the openness of wireless channel, which are diversified in types and channels [2]. For example, the attack modes such as eavesdropping, resetting and tampering are hard to be prevented in the wireless network; some modes even cannot be inspected. Therefore, the marine communication network faces more severe security challenge.

6.4.2   Marine data security

The marine historical data have been accumulated for hundreds of years and have a large quantity. As more and more real-time marine observation systems are established, the marine big data are increasing based on an index-level trend. With the enhancement on massive data analysis capability, the big data system can explore knowledge from data, find the hidden rule of data and even predict the future trend. For example, the attackers can collect metadata to spy upon privacy through big data analysis technology and even steal the confidential information. In addition, the big data processing framework lacks of reliable security mechanism. For example, the security mechanism of big data processing framework represented by Hadoop is unsatisfactory.

6.4.3   Marine-information-sharing security

The marine information network tends to be military–civilian information network, for example, marine satellite includes sea-viewing satellite, marine dynamics environment satellite and marine forewarning and monitoring satellite. However, fierce competition exists between countries or departments and causes the marine-information sharing to face large difficulty. Therefore, it is needed to guarantee the marine information security and, meanwhile, consider the channel and mode of marine data sharing which are beneficial to international and departmental cooperation. Currently, it is especially needed to carry out research on marine-information system application security access control technology and solve the identity certification, authority management and responsibility confirmation in the multi-department and cross-region access process.

6.4.4   Marine-information-systematization security

In recent years, information security technology development has presented the characteristics of systematic and diversified confrontation. It has gradually expanded from anti-disturbance and anti-capture of information system to multiple-level protection, including basic transmission password protection, network and boundary protection, computing environment security protection, application security protection and data-security protection [2]. Marine-information system is a big system containing multiple subsystems. It not only involves transmission and exchange but also involves various application services and command-management systems, and even involves the national information infrastructure. Therefore, aiming at the multiple-level security protection demand of complicated system, it is very necessary to carry out research on marine information security system.

6.5   Marine information security system

According to the function and usage, marine-information-system security mainly consists of five main parts, including communication network security, computing environment security, data and application security, security monitoring forewarning and security infrastructure.

6.5.1   Marine communication and network security

The communication and network security provides safe and reliable network-operating environment for various-level application information systems and establishes the "complete-chain" safe and reliable mechanism from server, host, terminal, wired network and wireless network to realize the security connection of marine communication link and prevent the wireless intrusion and cross-network penetrated attacks from network interconnection. The air, water-surface and underwater, ship-communication security cannot completely copy the shore-based communication security means, instead, the design of reasonable and effective security mechanism and solutions aiming at the problems of network isomerism, dynamic topology change, wireless access control and performance efficiency are needed [2].

Generally speaking, because there exists large difference in military–civilian security-protection system, algorithm and security-protection rating, intercommunication is difficult to be conducted. In addition, the underwater communication has low transmission rate; therefore, the underwater communication and its security transmission and protection is a problem needing to be solved urgently.

6.5.2   Marine system computing environment security

Computing environment security can effectively enhance the resistance and protection capability on known/unknown attacks of various computing facilities in the marine-information system; therefore, the security management and control capability of computing environment should be strengthened. Besides, it is needed to start from the marine-information system design and network-system structure to establish the trust chain based on hardware trusted root, make timely forewarning before the intrusion behavior affects the information system and establish elastic prevention system in real time to avoid, transfer and reduce the risks of information system. Moreover, it is crucial to base on the intrusion source defense to conduct certification and control on each node on the internet, to establish point-to-point trust mechanism, to provide trusted measurement of entity and behavior and to establish safe and creditable computing environment.

6.5.3   Big marine data and application security

In the view of big marine data security, it is needed to implement protection on various stages including data establishment, storage, usage, sharing, filing and destruction to guarantee data security and controllability within the life cycle. Data-security provides safe support for marine data usage and storage and also provides the functions of disaster recovery backup and safe data destruction. The application security protects the access process of marine-information service, data storage and exchange processes to guarantee information resource controllable and shared and prevent the attacked destruction and exceeding access aiming at the application system. It is also important to adopt the technologies, e.g., big data content monitoring, data recognition and filtering, data leakage inspection and protection, information protection and control, to trace and protect the whole life cycle of data, to prevent unauthorized usage of data and to guarantee the secrecy and completeness of big data.

6.5.4 Marine-information-sharing security

With the development of the big data analysis technology, cloud computing technology, software defined network (SDN) technology and artificial intelligence (AI) technology, the marine-information system undertakes large number of important business data and key data resources, and its security position is increasingly highlighted. It is needed to carry out researches on marine-information-sharing security technology, provide data-security protection capability of data-distribution access control according to different sharing requirements, thus providing support for military–civilian information sharing and internal marine cooperation, and to promote the marine information security service industry capability enhancement. Currently, marine data resource openness and sharing has become a hot issue. Due to the lack of powerful security guarantee the contradiction between marine data resource openness and sharing and security protection will exist for long time.

6.5.5 Marine security monitoring and forewarning mechanism

With the development of big data analysis technology and AI technology, security monitoring and forewarning system have become the key link for various part linkage of information security system in the field of marine, which gives play to the roles of dynamic systematization and defensiveness through the system synergy. Besides, it collects and senses the various security factors of marine-information system in real time, conducts loophole exploring and abnormal threat inspection through the means of static analysis, dynamic analysis, comparison analysis and connection exploring, monitors and judges the security loophole and intrusion behavior of information system, rapidly finds the security loophole, prevents the intrusion behavior timely and provides accurate monitoring and forewarning. Furthermore, it adopts effective prevention measures to strengthen the monitoring and forewarning mechanism of marine-information system in data collection, trend perception and emergency response.

6.5.6 Marine security infrastructure

Establish the military–civilian security support infrastructure to be used for not only guaranteeing the civilian field including marine management, marine scientific research, marine forecasting and marine disaster reduction and prevention but also guaranteeing the military field including battlefield environment and even objective monitoring. The information security in the field of marine supporting capability construction includes hierarchical and regional information certification infrastructure as well as trust-service system construction, related infrastructure construction and so on [2].

6.6 Key security theory and technology

The realization of marine-information system security relies on various network-information security technology. According to the application mode and technology method, these network information security technologies are composed of two types, information exchange technology and network system security.

Information security exchange technology is mainly to guarantee the information-exchange security in the network environment and prevent illegal stealing, tampering, resetting and counterfeiting in the information-transmission process. It is realized through the security mechanism including data secrecy, data completeness and authenticity of user identity. Its key technology lies in cryptographic technology and security protocol, involving the main technology methods of various encryption equipment, virtual private network (VPN), security server and certification authority (CA) certification system.

Network-system-security technology is mainly used to guarantee the security of various application systems and information resource in the network environment, prevent illegal log-in system of unauthorized users and also prevent illegal network resource access, information stealing or destruction. It mainly lays emphasis on researches on attack behavior and feature, attack behavior inspection and prevention, and system protection and disaster recovery, involving the technology methods of firewall, access control, intrusion detection, loophole scanning, identity certification, disaster recovery and security management, which can be summarized as network protection, network inspection, disaster recovery and security-management technology.

The mainly involved basic and key theories and technologies of marine-information system design, including password and cryptographic protocol, intrusion detection, data backup and recovery, are analyzed and introduced as follows.

6.6.1   Password and security protocol

6.6.1.1   Foundations of cryptography

Cryptographic technology is the basis for designing cryptographic protocol and is the interdisciplinary application of computer, electronics and communication. It is one of the main means to protect information security.

The basic approach of cryptographic technology is to transform one form of information to another, making the unauthorized personnel unable to obtain actual plain texts. Cryptographic technology not only has the function of information encryption but also has the functions of digital signature, identity certification and key distribution. It can not only guarantee information secrecy but also guarantee information completeness and prevent information tampering or counterfeiting. It consists of two types from the perspective of principle: single-key cryptosystem (also called symmetric cryptosystem or private key cryptosystem) and public-key cryptosystem (also called nonsymmetric cryptosystem or dual-key cryptosystem). Generally speaking, the encryption algorithm used in the password mechanism is public; thus, the security of password mechanism only relies on the key secrecy.

1. Single-key cryptosystem. In the single-key cryptosystem, encryption key and decryption key are same; therefore, it is also called symmetric cryptosystem. Compared with public-key cryptosystem, the keys in the single-key cryptosystem are all private keys; therefore, it is also called private key cryptosystem. It is

mainly used for data encryption but can also be used for simple information certification, for example, it can verify the user identity in the password certification system.

The classical algorithm of single-key cryptosystem includes simple replacement, multi-list replacement, homomorphic replacement, product cipher and so on; modern cryptographic algorithm includes Data Encryption Standard, Advanced Encryption Standard and so on.

The single-key cryptosystem has the main characteristic of high secrecy intensity. Meanwhile, it has the main disadvantage that the communication parties should transmit the key through safe and reliable channels before having secret communication. In addition, the main role of single-key cryptosystem is to protect information secrecy. It has not the features of providing information authentication and solving the difficulty of digital signature.

2. Public-key cryptosystem. In 1976, W. Diffie and M. E. Hellman first put forward the concept of public-key cryptosystem in the article of New Directions in Cryptology [5]. The basic idea of public-key cryptosystem is as follows: each user has an encryption key Ke (public key in short) and a corresponding decryption key Kd (private key in short), besides, solving the decryption key Kd through the encryption key Ke is not feasible in computing.

The main characteristic of public-key cryptosystem is to separate the encryption and decryption capabilities to realize one user decryption for encryption information of multiple users or encryption information of one user for information decryption of multiple users; therefore, the public-key cryptographic algorithm can also realize the functions of digital signature and certification, especially suitable to the user-communication network and open environment, which simplifies the key management largely.

The security of most public-key cryptographic algorithms bases on related mathematical difficulties. Currently, the mathematical difficulties used for establishing safe and effective public-key cryptographic algorithm are mainly composed of following three types: problem based on integer factorization (RSA system), discrete logarithm problem based on finite field multiplicative group (ElGamal system) and discrete logarithm problem based on elliptic curve (ECC system). The public-key cryptosystem provides new theory and technology foundation for the development of cryptology and has profound influence on information secrecy, completeness, key distribution and certification. The main disadvantage of public-key cryptosystem is that it is difficult to generate keys, and the speed of encryption and decryption is slower than that in single-key cryptosystem, especially under the situation of large encryption data quantity.

6.6.1.2 Concept and function of cryptographic protocol

Cryptographic protocol (also called security protocol or cryptographic scheme) is a kind of interactive communication protocol established based on cryptosystem. It realizes the purpose of key distribution and identity certification by aid of cryptographic algorithm. Cryptographic protocol is the protocol of cryptology, while the cryptographic technology is one basic tool to establish cryptographic protocol. Its basic functions include the following:

1. Establish dialog key. Establish or distribute the keys for safe dialogs of users between the entities of the protocol.
2. Complete entity certification: Guarantee the communication parties to be the expected entities.
3. Complete the distributed key distribution. This includes the following four meanings:
   i.   Guarantee the distributed entities of key to be expected.
   ii. Guarantee the entities having the key to be expected.
   iii. Guarantee the entities thinking they have the key to own the key actually.
   iv. Guarantee the identity of two parties sharing the key to be the expected user entity.

In addition, a complicated cryptographic protocol also has the functions of non-repudiation and secure group communication. According to the demand of computer-network information system on the password service function, the cryptographic protocol is mainly composed of key distribution protocol, encryption protocol, signature protocol and authentication protocol. Considering the most basic function of the cryptographic protocol, it can be divided into two types:

1. Key-exchange protocol
   Key-exchange protocol is generally to establish shared key between the two or multiple entities participating in the agreement, which is usually used for establishing the dialog key used in the communication process. Based on the difference of key-generation modes, it can be divided into key transmission protocol, key distribution protocol and key negotiation protocol. In addition, according to the difference of the number of protocol participants and protocol objectives, it can be divided into key-exchange protocol with two parties and key-exchange protocol with multiple parties.
2. Authentication protocol
   Authentication protocol which includes entity authentication (identity authentication) protocol, information authentication protocol, information source authentication and information purpose authentication protocol is used for preventing counterfeit, tampering and contradiction. It generally adopts nonsymmetric cryptographic technology. According to the difference of cryptographic algorithms used in the protocol, it can be divided into nonsymmetric password-based authentication protocol and one-way function-based authentication protocol. According to the number of protocol entity participants, it can be divided into dual-authentication protocol and multi-authentication protocol. According to the authentication orientation, it can be divided into single-authentication protocol and dual-authentication protocol. For the complicated cryptographic protocol, it can be divided into e-commerce protocol and group key distribution protocol from the perspective of application purpose.

6.6.2 *Intrusion detection*

Intrusion Detection is an important means, which refers to that collecting and analyzing the information of several key points in the computer network or computer system in order to find whether there exists with security strategy violation behavior and attack in the network or system thus to make response. The intrusion detection system (IDS) is the combination of series of software and hardware to realize the IDS. IDS are viewed as a classifier from the perspective of its most basic form; it conducts classified processing on the collected event and status information based on the system security strategy to judge the intrusion and nonintrusion behaviors.

6.6.2.1 Main functions and components of IDS

The main functions of IDS include monitoring and analyzing the activities of users and system, inspecting system configuration and loophole, inspecting the completeness of key system and data document, recognizing the activity modes of known attacks, conducting statistical analysis on abnormal behaviors and managing the operating system to judge whether there exists with user activities destroying security. A successful intrusion system can make system administrators to know the network system (including procedure, document and hardware equipment) change in real time to provide guidance to formulate network security strategy. Besides, it relies on simple management and configuration to make nonprofessional personnel to obtain network security guarantee very easily. In addition, the intrusion detection scale should change with the change of network threat, system construction and security demand.

IDS is generally composed of information collection module, information analysis module and user interface.

1. Information collection. The first step of intrusion detection is information collection, including the status and behavior of system, network, data and user activity. The information application of intrusion detection generally sources from following four aspects: system and network interface document, catalog and unexpected change in document, expected behavior of procedure implementation and intrusion information based on physical form.
2. Information analysis. The four types of collected information related to system, network, data as well as the status and behavior of user activity are conducted through three kinds of technical means: mode matching, statistical analysis and completeness analysis, wherein the previous two methods are used for real-time intrusion detection, while completeness analysis is used for post-event analysis.
3. User interface. The user interface of IDS makes users easier to observe the output signal of the system and make them control the system.

6.6.2.2 Classification of intrusion-detection technology

According to different classification standards, IDS can be divided into different types. For IDS, the following factors should be considered: information source, intrusion, event generation, event processing, inspection method and so on. According to the source of original data, it can be divided into host-based IDS, network-based IDS and application-based IDS. In actual application, the mixed application of these three systems is generally conducted. According to the attribute of intrusion behavior, it can be divided into abnormal intrusion detection and misuse intrusion detection. According to the system structure, it can be divided into centralized model, ranking model and collaborative model.

In recent years, intrusion detection technology has presented the development trend of totalization, systematization and integration. The main development orientations include distributed intrusion detection and universal intrusion detection architecture, intelligent intrusion detection, testing and evaluation methods of intrusion detection and systematic intrusion detection scheme.

6.6.3 Data backup and recovery technology

6.6.3.1 Introduction to data backup and recovery

Data fault may appear in the case of data transmission, data storage and data exchange. Data backup and data recovery are the final and most important means for data protection, wherein data backup refers to the periodical work to strengthen the data availability and security to prevent data failure. Data recovery is the process that recover the original system by aid of the backup data or other means to guarantee data security and business continuity in the case of disasters and accidents. A complete data backup and recovery system includes four parts: backup hardware, backup software, backup system and disaster recovery plan.

6.6.3.2 Classification of data-backup system

The data-backup system can be divided into data-level and application-level data-backup systems according to the guarantee content. According to the data backup and recovery function realization distance, it can be divided into distant backup and recovery system and local backup and recovery system. A complete data-backup system should consist of the following parts: local backup system, data-security mechanism, data distant backup system and data recovery processing system. The mode of data backup mainly includes synchronization mode and non-synchronization mode. And the data backup has two channels: hot backup (online backup) and cold backup (off-line backup).

The backup includes two kinds of realization technologies, physical backup and logic backup, wherein the physical backup is also called "block-based backup" or "device-based backup." The logic backup is also called "file-based backup." The above two kinds of backup realization technologies have respective advantages, but the file-based backup is commonly used, because it conforms to the logic thought and usage demand of people. Some current famous backup software conduct backup based on the file level, such as Backup Exec series product of VERITAS Company and Bounce Back Professional software of CMS Peripherals Company.

6.6.3.3 Data backup and data-recovery strategy

Backup strategy refers to determining the needed backup content, backup time and backup mode. The backup data tend to be determined based on the demands of enterprises or organizations. For the backup data, one or combination of several modes of the complete backup, incremental backup or differential backup can be adopted. Data recovery should be conducted if/when data was destructed. It consists of three types: complete recovery, individual file recovery and reorientated recovery.

At present, the backup trend tends to be unattended automated backup, manageability and disaster recovery, which are enhanced aiming at the high efficiency of system, and the high availability of data and business.

In addition, the network storage technology is closely related to data-backup technologies, which is a universal network term based on data storage. The network storage structure consists of three types: direct attached storage, network attached storage and storage area network.

6.7 Marine information security development trend and discussion

In the future, marine network security threat tends toward three dimension and integration, including three-dimensional space development based on different physical features of seabed, deep sea, shallow sea, sea surface and sea air, multidimensional and integrated space development crossing the air, land and sea, which expands from sea space to near space to outer space. Therefore, it should combine different network space environments and natural situations, aim at the problems of complicated network environment, lack of collaborative management of data and space communication exposure, vulnerability, long link distance and high error code rate and adopt different schemes to form multilevel and three-dimensional network-security protection system.

Besides, marine network security threat develops toward unmanned mode. Unmanned technology is widely applied in the marine detection field. Marine unmanned aerial vehicle (UAV) and underwater UAV have been widely applied in underwater objective search and detection, and marine information acquisition, including key marine parameters, such as a series of environment parameters and dynamics parameter: temperature, salinity, density and so on. The means for unmanned marine information acquisition is flexible with diversified functions; however, the unmanned equipment security and stability of remote control of equipment are all problems needing to be researched in the current marine network security field.

Under the situation that the countries in the whole world are paying more and more attention to the ocean, marine information security is an important component of national network space security and an important component of national security. Marine-information system is not a fresh security problem, which has similarity with the security problem of other information systems. The relationship between marine information security and traditional information security is not separated, instead, it is a relationship of inheritance and promotion. Many problems need to rely on the traditional security technology to be solved. However, marine information security has some new characteristics. In order to satisfy the new application scenes and environments, the traditional and current methods cannot be helpful enough; deeper researches should be conducted by the scholars in different fields.

References

[1] Xu W, Yan S-F, Ji F, *et al.* Marine information gathering, transmission, processing, and fusion: Current status and future trends. Science China (Information Science), 2016,46(08):1053–1085.

[2] Mei L-R. Research on marine information system security system. Communication Technology, 2017, 50(8):1822–1825.

[3] Li J. Research and Development on the Key Technology of Marine Data Sharing Platform. Tianjin: Tianjin University, 2008.

[4] Dong G-S, Wang Z, and Liu Z-J. Digital marine system and its security requirements based on big data. Communications Technology, 2015, 48(05):573–578.

[5] Stallings W. Cryptography and Network Security: Principles and Practice, 6th Edition, Upper Saddle River, NJ: Prentice Hall, 2013.

Chapter 7

A layered security architecture based on cyber kill chain against advanced persistent threats

Pooneh Nikkhah Bahrami[1], Ali Dehghantanha[2],
Tooska Dargahi[3], Reza M. Parizi[4],
Kim-Kwang Raymond Choo[5], and Hamid H.S. Javadi[6]

Inherently, static traditional defense mechanisms which mostly act successfully in detecting known attacks using techniques such as blacklisting and malware signature detection are insufficient in defending against dynamic and sophisticated advanced persistent threat (APT) cyberattacks. These attacks are usually conducted dynamically in several stages and may use different attack paths simultaneously to accomplish their commission. Cyber kill chain (CKC) framework provides a model for all stages of an intrusion from early reconnaissance to actions on objectives when the attacker's goal is met which could be stealing data, disrupting operations or destroying infrastructure. Achieving the final goal, an adversary must progress all stages successfully. Any disruption at any stage of the attack by the defender would mitigate or cease the intrusion campaign. In this chapter, we align 7D defense model with CKC steps to develop a layered architecture to detected APT actors tactics, techniques and procedures in each step of CKC. This model can be applied by defenders to plan resilient defense and mitigation strategies against prospective APT actors.

7.1 Introduction

APTs, a relatively recent emerging class of threats to computer networks, targets not only military organizations but also high-profile companies and governments with the risk of security breaches [1]. APT groups are generally directly or indirectly supported by governments or other state-linked organizations with considerable financial and other resources (e.g., access to individuals with the right skillset and

[1]Department of Computer Science, University of Tehran, Tehran, Iran
[2]Cyber Science Lab, School of Computer Science, University of Guelph, Ontario, Canada
[3]School of Computing, Science and Engineering, University of Salford, Manchester, UK
[4]College of Computing and Software Engineering, Kennesaw State University, Marietta, USA
[5]Department of Information Systems and Cyber Security, University of Texas at San Antonio, San Antonio, USA
[6]Department of Computer Science, Shahed University, Tehran, Iran

background) [2,3]. They encompass skillful individuals who access to advanced tools, costumed malware and sometimes 0-day exploits that are not found in the cybercriminal black markets [4,5]. As organizations mainly rely on conventional computer-network defense mechanisms, their security systems are not able to detect or prevent such sophisticated and dynamic attacks. APT attackers are easily bypassing conventional network defense mechanisms to successfully exploit target systems [4]. APT actors are known for using advanced malware targeting Internet of Things networks [6], Internet of Battlefield of Things [7], and OSX platform [8], or even developing ransomware merely disrupting targets operation [9,10]. To deal with this issue, more advanced and proactive measurements should be taken to address risk of APT actors activities. That is, the threat must be detected and denied before any serious impact is made. Countermeasures should be dynamic to cope with risks which continuously and persistently evolve.

There are several researchers [11–15] who proposed detection and protection techniques against APT actors. Most of the proposed techniques are relatively abstract and only suggest general measures such as network-based intrusion-detection systems (NIDSs) or host-based intrusion detection systems (HIDSs). Although these approaches are essential and should be applied to detect and prevent sophisticated attacks, most of them are already in place and APT actors have bypassed them.

Modeling of APT attacks using CKC [16] is an effective way to reach a new understanding of the intrusion life cycle as phased progressions rather than singular events. Using this model, an APT intrusion is divided into seven stages, namely, (1) reconnaissance, (2) weaponization, (3) delivery, (4) exploitation, (5) installation, (6) command and control and (7) action on objects. By progressing each stage, the attacker gets more privileges, information and power to compromise the organization. However, disrupting operation at any stage could undermine APT actors attempts and stop their operation.

In this chapter, we adopted the 7D model (also called course of action (CoA) matrix) [16] to offer a layered defense architecture to protect networks against APT actors attacks. The 7D model is composed of seven stages, namely, discovery, detection, deny, disrupt, degrade, deceive and destroy. We mapped each phase of the CKC model into corresponding defense method suggested in the 7D to develop a layered network-defense architecture. Using this model, defenders can develop mitigation methods against intruders and intelligently prioritize investments in new technologies or processes.

This chapter is organized as follows. Brief overview to preliminaries on intelligence-driven defensive model is presented in Section 7.2. In Section 7.3, the proposed defense mechanism is explained. Defense plan for considered six APT groups based on their disclosed attacks are illustrated in Section 7.4. Finally, Section 7.5 concludes the chapter and outlines possible future work.

7.2   Driven defensive model (course of actions)

By processing and analyzing APT intrusion attacks, as an APT attacker usually carries out multiple attacks during its lifetime to reduce system exposure to attacks, each phase of the intrusion has been mapped to CoAs. This will help analysts and security experts within organizations to protect their network by knowing what to look for at each stage of the CKC. Defensive model, also called 7D matrix, consists of six dimensions, namely, detect, deny, disrupt, degrade, deceive and destroy. Table 7.1 maps each phase of the CKC model to an action in defensive model using defender tools.

The matrix illustrates that in the delivery phase, for example, HIDSs can passively detect malicious payload, and mail filter could be helpful in identifying potential tampering of e-mails. In exploitation phase, data execution prevention (DEP) can disrupt the exploit once it initiates. Altogether, the matrix is a collection of proactive and post-active measurements and capabilities that defenders can utilize them to plan an investment roadmap to compensate any cyber defense gaps.

The critical point of this matrix is related to 0-day exploit attacks, i.e., previously undisclosed exploits, which are not detectable by traditional security tools. However, this weakness does not destroy completeness of the defensive model. The main reason is that the major objective of defenders is to keep the resiliency of the entire network. An intruder may deploy an undetectable 0-day exploit but upon using a detectable tool or infrastructure in other phases of the CKC, the entire process will interrupt by defender(s), provided that the defenders have mitigation for the disclosed exploits and repeated infrastructures. By this way, defenders have built a robust defense model against attackers. While it cannot certainly ward off all of the attacks to the network, it will surely increase cost of executing successful intrusions by adversary.

Here we briefly explain defensive mechanisms, which are mentioned in Table 7.1, which can be used against particular cyberattacks:

- Firewall ACL (access control list): Establishing network perimeter defenses to detect and block download of executable files, block access to known malware and phishing domains. As a matter of fact, it acts as a security interface and prevents direct communication of user's system with the Internet.
- NIDS, HIDS and HIPS (host intrusion prevention system): Detection of both Network and Computer (Host) intrusions can be done by monitoring systems or network activities based on anomaly behavior (often relies on machine learning) or signature (pattern detection). The performance of intrusion detection systems (IDSs) relies on the differences between the behavior of an intruder and a legitimate user. The detective mechanism of NIDS is on Network traffic, while the main source of input to monitor in HIDS is operating system audit traits [17,18]. Some IDSs have the ability to respond to detected intrusions. Systems with response capabilities are typically referred to as an HIPS. The HIPS technology examines network traffic flow to detect and prevent vulnerability exploits [19].
- Patch management: Known vulnerabilities in applications and operating system are usually the first target of the attackers. By installing the latest version of a software, attacks which exploit known software bugs can be prevented.
- Vigilant user: Users of any organization with high-value information should be trained, regarding possible threats. They should learn what information about the organization can reveal potential vulnerabilities to the attacker (such as used software and configuration details, profiling information like name, title, e-mail address and anything of value to an attacker).

Table 7.1 An example of defensible actions matrix aligned to the cyber kill chain

Phase	Detect	Deny	Disrupt	Degrade	Deceive	Destroy
Reconnaissance	.NIDS .Router logs .Web logs .Valiant user	.Firewall ACL	.Active defenses	.Active defenses .Honeypot .Redirect loop	.Honeypot .Restrict loops .Active defenses	
Weaponization	.NIDS	.NIPS				
Delivery	.NIDS .HIDS .Vigilant user .Antivirus	.Mail filter .Web filter .File converting	.Mail filter .Web filter .File converting	.Sinkhole	.Honeypot	
Exploitation	.NIDS .HIDS .Antivirus .Patching .Behavior-based protection	.HIDS .DEP .Antivirus .Patching .Hardened systems .Disabling macros	.HIPS .Antivirus .Hardened systems	.Highly restrict user accounts	.Honeypot	
Installation	.HIDS .Application logs .Antivirus	.App whitelisting .Blocked execution	.Antivirus .HIPS		Honeypot	
C2	.HIDS .NIDS .Antivirus .DNS monitoring	.Egress filter .Firewall ACL .Sinkhole .Disable/Limit FTP	.DEP .Sinkhole	.Sinkhole	.Honeypot .Sinkhole	
AOO	.HIDS .NIDS .Antivirus .DEP .Application logs	.Egress filter .Firewall ACL .Network segmentation	.Network segmentation .DEP .HIPS	.Network segmentation	.Honeypot	

- DEP: This security feature monitors and performs additional checks on memory to prevent malicious code execution on a system. Memory location has been reserved for windows and other authorized programs which have made DEP compatible version of the program. If DEP detects NIDS, a malicious usage of memory by a program, it will then raise an exception.

7.3 Defense mechanism

According to the defensible actions matrix in Table 7.1, the activities that take place in each phase of an attack chain can be mitigated by security mechanism(s). Defenders can measure the performance as well as the effectiveness of these actions and plan investment roadmaps to rectify any capability gaps. It should be taken into consideration that an APT attacker utilizes various techniques and methods to achieve his objectives; consequently, the attacker cannot be defeated by any single technology. To gain more effective results, combination of techniques is recommended. Next, we describe security mechanisms that can be performed in each phase and then propose CoA matrix for each campaign based on their analyzed CKC model which can be find in Section 7.4.

7.3.1 Mitigation for each phase of CKC model

7.3.1.1 Mitigating of reconnaissance phase

Some basic information of an organization can be a source of potential vulnerabilities. Before sharing and publishing any information, one must be sure that such action will not reveal anything of value to an attacker (such as used application or name and title of individuals in an organization).

The main approach must be training and educating the officials. Users should be aware of the risks of publishing information about system, discussing work-related topics on social media and the potential ways of being targeted by phishing attacks. It has been seen that some APT campaigns by applying some unsophisticated approaches were be able to deceive an unaware user to open a malicious e-mail. For instance, APT1 which attributed to the government of the Republic of China, in an attack to Mandiant employees, created e-mail accounts using familiar names to the given recipient, like their colleagues, a company executive, an IT department employee, or company counsel and sent spear phishing e-mails. If anyone had clicked on the link that day, their computer would have downloaded a malicious ZIP file which contained a malicious executable that installs a custom APT1 backdoor that was called WEBC2-TABLE [20]. While with a little accuracy of users, they could prevent such an attack.

Port scanning is one of the main tools that have been used by attackers to find open ports of a given target to exploit known vulnerabilities of services associated with open ports. Firewall can check which ports are open and block them when they expose to any attack. HIPS can detect port scans in progress and block them before the attacker can gain a full map of the network. Therefore, they can be applied as a proactive measurement in the network.

7.3.1.2   Mitigating of weaponization phase

Because this phase is out of defenders accessibility, defensive mechanism cannot propose any solution to mitigate it.

7.3.1.3   Mitigating of delivery phase

E-mail spear phishing has been the predominant vector of delivery for APT attacks; 84% of organizations have been the victim of successful spear-phishing attack in 2015 [21]. Organizations need a robust e-mail security solution that automatically detects and blocks advanced targeted campaigns that involve spear phishing, the harvesting of credentials or the impersonation of legitimate senders. The used methods of delivery by advanced attackers against target's systems and network can be significantly dwindled by applying secondary controls. To gain more effective results, combination of them is proposed.

Up-to-date antiviruses (including signatures database, reputation ratings and other heuristic and behavioral detection capabilities) may detect, block or remove malicious e-mail attachments; they prevent known malware being downloaded directly or from a malicious domain. They also block malicious file being executed from a removable media. However, Australian Cyber Security Center stated in [21] that the effectiveness of antivirus software against malicious e-mail attachments is minimal. Their restricted approach is to convert attachments to another file type to remove malicious content or render it ineffective. For example, by converting Microsoft Office documents to PDF documents or converting a JPEG to Bitmap to remove potential threats embedded within the file. To diminish the cost of file type conversion, it is proposed to check files by antivirus engines because known threats can be still detectable by anti-virus (AV) and convert potentially risky types of files into different types to remove embedded threats. This approach can be a proactive measurement for 0-day exploits. Most of the APT campaigns which have a 0-day exploit to penetrate in victim's system like APT16 [22], APT17 [23,24], APT1 [20,25], APT15 [26], APT12 [27], APT28 and APT29, has leveraged e-mail spear phishing to deliver their payload.

In addition whitelist attachments based on file typing has excellent effectiveness in blocking malicious phishing e-mails. It guaranties just specified file types can be received and prevents all others. File extensions are changeable and thus a mismatch between a file type and its stated extension would be regarded as a suspicious activity and prevented. This form of subterfuge has been previously employed by some Middle Eastern threat actors such as "Desert Falcons," reported by Kaspersky [28], CopyKittens [29], and by elements operating in Syria [30] that could be detected and denied by this mechanism. However, it can cause so many limitations for some organizations. Educating officials is a beneficial proactive measurement that informed them of phishing attacks and other methods of malware delivery.

NIDS by blocking access to e-mail from malicious actors can reduce the likely of successful delivery. E-mail and web filtering based on the subject and content of the e-mail can degrade attacker's efficiency.

Some defenders benefit Honeypot e-mail to monitor e-mails from unknown and malicious users and deceive attackers to get access to their malware.

Defending air-gapped systems using signature-based antivirus is far less useful and effective; traditional antivirus solutions require signature update every so often, which is a significant challenge in systems with no internet connectivity. While a sophisticated antivirus, which is able to identify threat, based on artificial intelligence and machine learning is an effective solution. Proactive measurements can be included plugging unused USB slots with the USP port blocker and encrypting data.

At first glance, it may seem that due to the variety of defense mechanisms, high profile targets like government institutions, embassies, oil and gas industry, research institutes, or military contractors and activists will never be attacked by any APT campaign. Nevertheless, surprisingly, it has been seen that an unsophisticated attacker like NetTraveler has infected hundreds of high profile targets around the world through spear-phishing attacks using Office documents, which exploit two publicly known vulnerabilities, CVE-2012-0158 and CVE-2010-3333 [31] that could be easily detected by an updated antivirus.

7.3.1.4 Mitigating of exploitation phase

As with the delivery phase, by few security controls, it is possible to highly mitigate exploitation of known vulnerabilities, which are again best to be deployed together.

Effective patch management and an up-to-date antivirus are fundamental approaches to detect and block any known vulnerability. Exploits are predominantly based on known and patchable software flaws. Actually, more than 90% of the attacks today are exploiting known vulnerabilities. Updating systems with the latest security patches protects against attacks that exploit vulnerabilities.

Macro malware leverages the scripting mechanism of Microsoft Office. While Microsoft has disabled macros by default, attackers may use social engineering techniques to convince the user to re-enable them. A simple approach to protect the system is to disable macros simply but is not always a practical option as they are necessary in some organizations. One option to avoid macro attacks is to educate users just enable macros for document which they have confidence about its destination. IDSs, IPS, DEP and advanced AV have the ability of detecting directly in-memory executed malicious code by using an array of detection engines including an advanced signature-based engine with heuristic just-in-time memory scanning and machine-learning scans, where traditional AV cannot detect in-memory malicious code executions. However, this is not a definitive solution for any APT attack. For example, in operation Aurora attack, the PDF file attached to the e-mail exploits the Adobe Reader "CoolType.dll" TTF Font Remote Code Execution vulnerability (CVE-2010-2883). It uses a technique known as return-oriented programming to bypass DEP using code in icucn36.dll module. This module is not compatible with the address space layout randomization so the module will be loaded in the same virtual address space every time the reader loads it [32]. This attack could be blocked and prevented by disabling JavaScript support in PDF reader or by converting to another type like Microsoft Word Office in delivery phase as a proactive action.

The mitigation approaches for 0-day exploits have been less efficient. Traditional security tools rely on malware binary signatures or the reputation of URLs and servers. In fact, they can only detect known threats. Moreover, several 0-day exploits have bypassed the operating system-level protections such as NIDS, HIDS and DEP [33]. There are some approaches to degrade the attacks like using inline HIPS that, for example, checks unexpected potentially legitimate traffic or substantial scanning activity originating from a client or a server. However, applying all security updates as soon as their patches are released can be an effective proactive measurement. By patching a new disclosed vulnerability of an application by its vendor, some unknown flaws might proactively be addressed which could have been potentially exploited by attackers. For example, one 0-day vulnerability exploit (CVE-2015-2545) in Microsoft Office used by PLATINUM [34] was addressed immediately in September 2015. Subsequently, in November, Microsoft also released a proactive security update for the same component that could ultimately mitigate other exploits surfacing in the wild after the first attack. Customers who updated their application in November immediately would have been protected against the second wave of exploits.

Exploitation using SQL injection vulnerabilities can be avoided using some simple proactive measurements like the use of prepared statements (with parameterized queries), use of stored procedures, white list input validation, enforcing least privilege or escaping all user supplied input [35]. VOHO campaign, as one of the largest and most successful watering-hole attacks to date which impacted hundreds of organizations, was actually formed by a simple SQL injection at first [36] which could be prevented by SQL injection prevention mechanisms (SQLi-PM).

Credential stuffing attacks can usually be prevented by some simple authentication mechanisms like using a password manager to create strong password, changing password every few times, enabling two-factor authentication or enabling login notifications via text or e-mail to proactively monitor any suspicious account activity and login attempts [37]. However, some sophisticated APT attackers gain access to credentials using more sophisticated approaches that hardly can be prevented using basic client-side defense mechanisms. For example, Shell_Crew penetrated a victim network through CVE-2010-2684 exploitation (an Adobe ColdFusion directory transversal vulnerability) and obtained the password of "ColdFusion" administrator account [38].

7.3.1.5   Mitigating of installation phase

Appropriately checking of memory and hard disk can significantly help to detect and block executing and installing malicious files.

Enabling operating-system level protection like HIDS, HIPS and DEP can monitors and perform additional checks on memory to prevent malicious code execution or installation on a system. Moreover, antivirus can detect and block malicious files and programs in system storage. Application whitelisting uses a checklist to specify which applications (and application components like libraries and configuration files) are allowed to be present or run on a host [39]. In fact, it creates a list of known or approved file hashes and block potentially malicious software to execute through memory or registry key persistence [40]. Whitelisting tools can also detect and block potentially malicious software that may be executed through search order hijacking or COM hijacking. Regularly updating Software can decrease the DLL side-loading vulnerabilities in software. Monitoring registry keys to detect potential changes caused by unknown software can degrade the like hood of persistence malware. Checking start folder and start-up programs may show up suspicious programs that have not seen before [41]. Attackers of APT12 campaign dropped a shortcut of their malware with lure name (adobe reader) in the start-up folder without even changing the registry key. Checking up the start-up folder could easily disrupt this persistent malware [42].

To prevent modification of boot sectors by bootkits and their persistence in the infected system trusted platform module (TPM) technology can be used; it can highly assure the integrity of a platform [43,44].

Restricting user's account-access level within a network can reduce the level of authority of the adversary who has established persistence in the system by creating a local account. Moreover, using a multifactor authentication is a proactive measurement as APT1 attackers leverage the weakness of single-factor authentication in systems to access their accounts [4].

Creation and execution of Launch Daemons/Agents are done under user or administrator level privileges. In order to deny malware persistence using the user's privileges should be limited through group policy. In addition, creation of new Launch Daemons should be dedicated only to an authorized administrator [45,46].

As some adversaries establish persistence using scheduled tasks, monitoring process execution from launchd and cron tasks in Linux and Apple systems or Windows Task Scheduler in windows OS (svchost.exe or tasking.exe) can detect abnormal or unknown applications and behavior [47,48]. Although Windows has some tools such as Sysinternals Autoruns which lists current scheduled tasks, it can be used to check what abnormal changes has been made on tasks which are not related to known applications [49]. Moreover, limiting the privileges of user accounts can be done to degrade the persistence [47,48].

7.3.1.6   Mitigating of command and control phase

Unauthorized command and control network traffic can be detected and controlled using NIDS and HIDS. More over Firewall can control out band traffic.

Monitoring domain name service (DNS) traffic can be applied to pretend leak of data. Some points should be checked in DNS monitoring. DNS data is usually publicized and does not have any personally identifiable data. Moreover, DNS traffic is generally "low volume" when compared to data-carrying Internet protocols. Therefore, anything contrary to this can be a suspicious case. Two-factor authenticating of DNS administrator account is another way of mitigating this type of attacks.

CopyKittens [29], which launched at least three waves of cyberattacks such as Israel's Ministry of Foreign Affairs and some well-known Israeli academic researchers in 2015, usually manipulate DNS protocol to connect to their C2 server. The group uses a substitute cipher to obscure the data before it is sent to the C2. This technique makes traffic analysis and detection more complicated. They also tried to camouflage the DNS traffic using IPs from address blocks of Microsoft and McAfee in the C2 responses. Upon receiving a command from the C2 server in the DNS response, the RAT will turn it to a corresponding command. For instance, when the C2 sends a DNS response with the IP address 155.1168.145.10, the RAT will try to steal outlook passwords. C2 mitigation mechanisms could help resist these semi-sophisticated attacks easily. Disable FTP or limited access of FTP to specific IP can be used to block and prevent data leakage using this protocol.

Data-loss prevention (DLP) is a security countermeasure technology which monitors and protects data breach across e-mail and web protocols. It scans and inspects the stream of outgoing communications to get aware of sender authentication, the destination of outgoing data and the authentication of the receiver as well to protect data from being leaked or stolen [50].

Proper deep packet inspection (DPI) or log review can be helpful to detect ICMP tunneling through the network. Although by blocking ICMP traffic, this type of tunneling can be eradicated totally, the functionality of the network will lose significantly. There are legitimate reasons that a user or an administrator needs to use ICMP in the network environment such as troubleshooting Internet connection in diagnose utilities. Another method for mitigating this type of tunneling is to allow only fixed sized ICMP packets through firewalls, which can impede or eliminate this type of behavior.

7.3.1.7   Mitigating of action on objectives phase

If all the measures for the phases are consistently in place, the majority of attacks using known threats are likely to be unsuccessful. However, if an adversary is able to use 0-day attacks, then they will likely evade the security system and get into target systems. In theory, it is necessary to establish what constitutes a "normal" activity on the network; moreover, effective security monitoring should detect any unusual activity. Once a professional attacker gains full access to the systems, it would not be much easier to identify their actions and eliminate their presence; thus, a full defense-in-depth strategy would be most needed.

7.4   Mapping 7D, CKC and APT actors activities

Technical analysis of CKC model of APT groups shows that these groups usually have commonalities in their attack methods. For instance, APT1 [20,51,52], APT15 [26], APT29 [53], Desert Falcons [28] and Red October [54] used spear phishing as the initial vector to deliver their malware to the target. In exploitation phase, attackers vastly make use of vulnerabilities in software such as Microsoft Word Office or PDF for command execution or privileged escalation. However, it should take into account that some APT attackers used novel methods to intrude target systems which can significantly complicate the job of network defenders. For example, Hurricane Panda [55] employed tricky technique to conceal their command and control traffic. They hijacked legitimate domains such as adobe.com and used public DNS resolvers to redirect command and control traffic. Due to the complexity of APT attacks and the multiple attack paths, finding a single security remedy is not possible. However, based on their commonalities, a comprehensive multilayer robust defense plan would mitigate attack effects considerably. In the following, defense plan of six APT groups, namely, Ice Fog, APT17, APT28, APT3, Project Saurom and CopyKittens based on disclosed attacks of them are illustrated in Tables 7.2–7.7.

Table 7.2 *Defense plan of Ice Fog*

Phase	Detect	Deny	Disrupt	Degrade	Deceive	Disrupt
Reconnaissance				.Vigilant user .Honeypot	.Honeypot .Redirect loops	
Delivery	.AV .NIDS .Vigilant user	.AV .NIDS .Mail/Web filter	.Mail filter .Web filter			
Exploitation	.Patching .AV .HIDS .Vigilant user	.Patching .AV .HIDS .Macro disabling	HIPS	Vigilant user		
Installation	.HIDS .Monitoring registry key .App whitelisting	.AV HIPS .App whitelisting	HIPS	.Enable safe DLL search mode .User restrict account .Multifactor authentication		
C2	.NIDS .DLP	.Firewall .IP/Domain blocking	.DLP			
AOO	.Active monitoring			Network segmentation		

Table 7.3 Defense plan of APT17

Phase	Detect	Deny	Disrupt	Degrade	Deceive	Disrupt
Reconnaissance	.Vigilant user			.Vigilant user	.Honeypot .Redirect loop	
Delivery	.AV .NIDS	.AV .NIDS .E-mail filter .Web filter		.Vigilant user .E-mail filter .Web filter	.Fake e-mail .Honeypot	
Exploitation	.NIDS .HIDS .AV	.NIDS .HIDS .AV .Patching .HIPS .SQLi-PM	.HIPS .AV	.Highly restricted user account SQLi-PM		
Installation	.HIDS Monitoring registry key .App whitelisting	.AV .HIPS .App whitelisting	.HIPS			
C2	.NIDS	.Firewall			.Sinkhole	
AOO	.Active monitoring			.Network segmentation		

Table 7.4 Defense plan of APT28

Phase	Detect	Deny	Disrupt	Degrade	Deceive	Disrupt
Reconnaissance				.Vigilant user .Honeypot	.Honeypot .Redirect loops	
Delivery	.Patching .Sophisticated AV .HIDS .NIDS Vigilant user	.Patching .Sophisticated AV .HIDS .NIDS .Web/Mail filter	.Sophisticated AV .HIPS -Web/Mail filter .Convert .Whitelist attachments	.Data encryption .Block unused USB port		
Exploitation	.NIDS .HIDS .Patching .AV .Behavioral-based protection	.HIPS .AV	.HIPS .AV	.Highly restricted user account .Inline HIPS .Vigilant user	.Honeypot	
Installation	HIPS DEP	.Application whitelisting .Blocked execution .TPM	HIPS DEP TPM			
C2	NIDS HIDS Proxy DLP	NIDS HIDS .Block unused USB port	HIPS DLP			
AOO	NIDS HIDS DEP Application log		DEP HIPS Network segmentation	Network segmentation .Data encryption .Data backup		

Table 7.5 Defense plan of APT3

Phase	Detect	Deny	Disrupt	Degrade	Deceive	Disrupt
Reconnaissance				.Vigilant user .Honeypot	.Honeypot .Redirect loops	
Delivery	AV NIDS Firewall DNS monitor Vigilant user	AV NIDS Firewall DNS monitor E-mail/Web filter	E-mail/Web filter	Vigilant user	Honeypot e-mail	
Exploitation	Patching AV NIDS HIDS Inline-HIPS	AV NIDS HIDS	HIPS Inline-HIPS			
Installation	.HIDS .Monitoring registry key .Monitoring process execution .App whitelisting .Sysinternals Autoruns	.AV .HIPS .App whitelisting	HIPS	.Restrict user account .Multifactor authentication		
C2	NIDS HIDS	NIDS HIDS Firewall	HIPS			
AOO	.Active monitoring			Network segmentation		

Table 7.6 Defense plan of Project Sauron

Phase	Detect	Deny	Disrupt	Degrade	Deceive	Disrupt
Reconnaissance						
Delivery	Sophisticated AV .HIDS NIDS Vigilant user DPI	.Patching .Sophisticated AV .HIDS NIDS ICMP blocking	.Sophisticated AV .HIPS	.Data encryption .Block unused USB port		
Exploitation	.NIDS .HIDS .Patching .AV .Behavioral-based protection	.HIPS .AV	.HIPS .AV	.Highly restricted user account .Inline HIPS .Vigilant user	.Honeypot	
Installation	.HIDS .NIDS	.AV .HIPS .Firewall	HIPS			
C2	NIDS HIDS DEP DNS monitoring Proxy DPI	Firewall ID/Domain block NIDS HIDS FTP disabling DNS monitoring ICMP blocking .Block unused USB port	HIPS	.FTP limiting .DNS monitoring .fixed size of ICMP packets	Sinkhole	
AOO	NIDS HIDS DEP Application log		DEP HIPS Network segmentation	.Network segmentation .Data encryption		

Table 7.7 Defense plan of CopyKittens

Phase	Detect	Deny	Disrupt	Degrade	Deceive	Disrupt
Reconnaissance				.Vigilant user .Honeypot	.Honeypot .Redirect loops	
Delivery	.AV .NIDS .Vigilant user	.AV .NIDS Mail/Web filter .Whitelist attachments	.Mail filter .Web filter	.Vigilant user		
Exploitation	.Patching .AV .HIDS .Vigilant user	.Patching .AV .HIDS .Disable macro SQLi-PM	HIPS	Vigilant user SQLi-PM		
Installation	.NIDS	.Firewall .IP/Domain blocking			.Honeypot	
C2	.NIDS .HIDS .DNS monitoring	.NIDS .HIDS .Firewall .DNS monitoring .Two-factor authentication of DNS administrator account	HIPS	.DNS monitoring		
AOO	.NIDS .HIDS .DEP .Application log		.DEP .HIPS .Network segmentation	.Network segmentation .Data encryption		

7.5 Conclusion

In the foreseeable future, APT attacks will continue to be an attack vector of choice and relevance to nation states. Hence, given the evolving nature of APT actors and attacks, in this chapter, we proposed a dynamic defense plan to mitigate such threats, using the CKC model. The latter allows us to map APT attacks into a step-phased model to illustrate their commonalities in attacks.

References

[1]   Mwiki H, Dargahi T, Dehghantanha A, *et al.* Analysis and Triage of Advanced Hacking Groups Targeting Western Countries Critical National Infrastructure: APT28, RED October, and Regin. In: Critical Infrastructure Security and Resilience. Cham: Springer; 2019. p. 221–244.

[2]   Choo KKR. Organised crime groups in cyberspace: A typology. Trends in Organized Crime. 2008;11(3):270–295.

[3]   Kiwia D, Dehghantanha A, Choo KKR, *et al.* A cyber kill chain based taxonomy of banking Trojans for evolutionary computational intelligence. Journal of Computational Science. 2018;27:394–409.

[4]   van der Ende R. M-trends®2015: A View From the Front Lines. Mandiant; 2015.

[5]   Advanced Persistent Threat Groups [homepage on the Internet]. Chicago: FireEye, Inc.; 2018 [updated 2019; cited 2019 Jan 12]. Available from: https://www.fireeye.com/current-threats/apt-groups.html.

[6]   HaddadPajouh H, Dehghantanha A, Khayami R, *et al.* A deep Recurrent Neural Network based approach for Internet of Things malware threat hunting. Future Generation Computer Systems. 2018;85:88–96.

[7]   Azmoodeh A, Dehghantanha A, and Choo KKR. Robust malware detection for Internet of (Battlefield) Things devices using deep eigenspace learning. IEEE Transactions on Sustainable Computing. 2018;4:88–95.

[8]   Pajouh HH, Dehghantanha A, Khayami R, *et al.* Intelligent OSX malware threat detection with code inspection. Journal of Computer Virology and Hacking Techniques. 2018;14(3):213–223.

[9]   Homayoun S, Dehghantanha A, Ahmadzadeh M, *et al.* DRTHIS: Deep ransomware threat hunting and intelligence system at the fog layer. Future Generation Computer Systems. 2019;90:94–104.

[10]   Homayoun S, Dehghantanha A, Ahmadzadeh M, *et al.* Know abnormal, find evil: Frequent pattern mining for ransomware threat hunting and intelligence. IEEE Transactions on Emerging Topics in Computing. 2017.

[11]   Bhatt P, Yano ET, and Gustavsson P. Towards a framework to detect multi-stage advanced persistent threats attacks. In: Service Oriented System Engineering (SOSE), 2014 IEEE 8th International Symposium on. IEEE; 2014. p. 390–395.

[12]   Chen P, Desmet L, and Huygens C. A study on advanced persistent threats. In: IFIP International Conference on Communications and Multimedia Security. Springer; 2014. p. 63–72.

[13] Hutchins EM, Cloppert MJ, and Amin RM. Intelligence-driven computer network defense informed by analysis of adversary campaigns and intrusion kill chains. Leading Issues in Information Warfare & Security Research. 2011; 1(1):80.

[14] Sood AK, and Enbody RJ. Targeted cyberattacks: A superset of advanced persistent threats. IEEE Security & Privacy. 2013;11(1):54–61.

[15] Virvilis N, and Gritzalis D. The big four-what we did wrong in advanced persistent threat detection? In: Availability, Reliability and Security (ARES), 2013 Eighth International Conference on. IEEE; 2013. p. 248–254.

[16] Ussath M, Jaeger D, Cheng F, *et al.* Advanced persistent threats: Behind the scenes. In: Information Science and Systems (CISS), 2016 Annual Conference on. IEEE; 2016. p. 181–186.

[17] Basicevic I, Popovic M, and Kovacevic V. The use of distributed network-based IDS systems in detection of evasion attacks. In: Null. IEEE; 2005. p. 78–82.

[18] Mukherjee B, Heberlein LT, and Levitt KN. Network intrusion detection. IEEE Network. 1994;8(3):26–41.

[19] Jackson GM. Intrusion prevention system. Google Patents; 2008. US Patent 7458094.

[20] APT1: Exposing One of China's Cyber Espionage Units; 2013 [cited Online; accessed 12-January-2019]. Available from: https://www.fireeye. com/content/dam/fireeye-www/services/pdfs/mandiant-apt1-report.pdf.

[21] Australian Cyber Security Centre (ACSC). Malicious Email Mitigation Strategies [White Paper]. Australian Cyber Security Centre (ACSC); 2016 [cited Online; accessed 12-January-2019]. Available from: https://acsc. gov.au/publications/protect/Malicious_Email_Mitigation.pdf.

[22] Winters R. The EPS Awakens – Part 2 [homepage on the Internet]. Fire-Eye Threat Intelligence; 2015 [cited Online; accessed 12-January-2019]. Available from: https://www.fireeye.com/blog/threat-research/2015/12/the-eps-awakens-part-two.html.

[23] Symantec Security Response. Hydraq – An Attack of Mythical Proportions [homepage on the Internet]. Symantec Security Response; 2010 [cited Online; accessed 12-January-2019]. Available from: https://www.symantec.com/connect/blogs/hydraq-attack-mythical-proportions.

[24] O'Gorman G, and McDonald G. The Elderwood Project. Symantec Corporation; 2012.

[25] Wilhoit K. The SCADA That Cry Wolf – Who's Really Attacking Your ICS Equipment? (Part 2) [White Paper]; 2013 [cited Online; accessed 12-January-2019]. Available from: http://www.trendmicro.com/cloud-content/us/pdfs/security-intelligence/white-papers/wp-the-scada-that-didnt-cry-wolf.pdf.

[26] Villeneuve N, Bennett JT, Moran N, *et al.* Operation "KE3CHANG" Targeted Attacks Against Ministries of Foreign Affairs [White Paper]; 2014 [cited Online; accessed 12-January-2019]. Available from: https://www.fireeye. com/content/dam/fireeye-www/global/en/current-threats/pdfs/wp-operation-ke3chang.pdf.

[27] Sancho D, dela Torre J, Bakuei M, *et al.* IXESHE – An APT Campaign [White Paper]; 2012 [cited Online; accessed 12-January-2019]. Available from: http://www.trendmicro.com/cloud-content/us/pdfs/security-intelligence/white-papers/wp_ixeshe.pdf.

[28] Saad G, and Hasbini MA. The Desert Falcons Targeted Attacks [homepage on the Internet]; 2015 [cited Online; accessed 12-January-2019]. Available from: https://securelist.com/the-desert-falcons-targeted-attacks/68817/.

[29] Minerva Labs LTD and ClearSky Cyber Security. CopyKittens Attack Group [White Paper]. Minerva Labs LTD and ClearSky Cyber Security; 2011 [cited Online; accessed 12-January-2019]. Available from: https://s3-eu-west-1.amazonaws.com/minervaresearchpublic/CopyKittens/CopyKittens.pdf.

[30] Syrian Malware. Samples from the Conflict in Syria [White Paper]. A Catalog of Malware Used in the Syrian Civil War; 2017 [cited Online; accessed 12-January-2019]. Available from: http://syrianmalware.com/.

[31] Global Research and Analysis Team. The NetTraveler (aka "Travnet" [White Paper]. Global Research and Analysis Team; 2011 [cited Online; accessed 12-January-2019]. Available from: https://kasperskycontenthub.com/wp-content/uploads/sites/43/vlpdfs/kaspersky-the-net-traveler-part1-final.pdf.

[32] Selvaraj K. Hydraq (Aurora) Attackers Back? [homepage on the Internet]; 2014 [cited Online; accessed 12-January-2019]. Available from: https://www.symantec.com/connect/blogs/hydraq-aurora-attackers-back.

[33] FireEye, Inc. Less Than Zero: A Survey of Zero-day Attacks in 2013 and What They Say About the Traditional Security Model [White paper]; 2014 [cited Online; accessed 12-January-2019]. Available from: https://www.fireeye.jp/content/dam/fireeye-www/global/en/currentthreats/pdfs/wp-zero-day-attacks-in-2013.pdf.

[34] Windows Defender Advanced Threat Hunting Team. PLATINUM Targeted attacks in South and Southeast Asia [homepage on the Internet]. Windows Defender Advanced Threat Hunting Team; 2016 [cited Online; accessed 12-January-2019]. Available from: https://download.microsoft.com/download/2/2/5/225BFE3E-E1DE-4F5B-A77B-71200928D209/Platinum%20feature%20article%20-%20Targeted%20attacks%20in%20South%20and%20Southeast%20Asia%20April%202016.pdf.

[35] Berkeley Information Security and Policy. How to Protect Against SQL Injection Attacks [homepage on the Internet]. Berkeley Information Security and Policy; 2014 [cited Online; accessed 12-January-2019]. Available from: https://security.berkeley.edu/resources/best-practices-how-articles/system-application-security/how-protect-against-sql-injection.

[36] Doherty S, Gegeny J, Spasojevic B, *et al.* Hidden Lynx–Professional Hackers for Hire. Symantec, Tech Rep; 2013.

[37] OWASP. Credential Stuffing Prevention Cheat Sheet [homepage on the Internet]. OWASP; 2017 [cited Online; accessed 12-January-2019]. Available from: https://www.owasp.org/index.php/Credential_Stuffing_Prevention_Cheat_Sheet.

[38] RSA Incident Response. Emerging Threat Profile: Shell Crew [White Paper]. RSA Incident Response; 2014 [cited Online; accessed 12-January-2019]. Available from: http://www.emc.com/collateral/white-papers/h12756-wp-shell-crew.pdf.

[39] Sedgewick A, Souppaya M, and Scarfone K. Guide to application whitelisting. NIST Special Publication. 2015;800:167.

[40] Jim B. Application Whitelisting: Panacea or Propaganda. Global Information Assurance Certification Paper SANS Institute; 2010.

[41] Corporation TM. Registry Run Keys / Start Folder; 2018. [Online; accessed 25-August-2018]. https://attack.mitre.org/wiki/Technique/T1060.

[42] Sancho D, dela Torre J, Bakuei M, *et al.* IXESHE: An APT Campaign. Trend Micro Incorporated; 2012.

[43] Perez R, Sailer R, van Doorn L, *et al.* vTPM: Virtualizing the trusted platform module. In: Proc. 15th Conf. on USENIX Security Symposium; 2006. p. 305–320.

[44] Trusted Platform Module Technology Overview Microsoft Support. [homepage on the Internet]; 2018 [cited Online; accessed 12-January-2019]. Available from: https://docs.microsoft.com/en-us/windows/security/ information-protection/tpm/trusted-platform-module-overview.

[45] The MITRE Corporation. Launch Agent [homepage on the Internet]. The MITRE Corporation; 2018 [cited Online; accessed 12-January-2019]. Available from: https://attack.mitre.org/wiki/Technique/T1159.

[46] The MITRE Corporation. Launch Daemon [homepage on the Internet]. The MITRE Corporation; 2018 [cited Online; accessed 12-January-2019]. Available from: https://attack.mitre.org/wiki/Technique/T1160.

[47] The MITRE Corporation. Local Job Scheduling [homepage on the Internet]. The MITRE Corporation; 2018 [cited Online; accessed 12-January-2019]. Available from: https://attack.mitre.org/wiki/Technique/T1168.

[48] The MITRE Corporation. Scheduled Task [homepage on the Internet]. The MITRE Corporation; 2018 [cited Online; accessed 12-January-2019]. Available from: https://attack.mitre.org/wiki/Technique/T1053.

[49] Microsoft Support. Russinovich M. Autoruns for Windows v13.91 [homepage on the Internet]. Microsoft Support; 2018 [cited Online; accessed 12-January-2019]. Available from: https://docs.microsoft.com/ en-gb/sysinternals/downloads/autoruns.

[50] Wu JS, Chong S, and Kuo CT. Sensitive data discrimination method and data loss prevention system using the sensitive data discrimination method. Google Patents; 2018. US Patent 9965646.

[51] Narang S. Backdoor.Barkiofork Targets Aerospace and Defense Industry [homepage on the Internet]. Symantec; 2013 [cited Online; accessed 12-January-2019]. Available from: https://www.symantec.com/connect/blogs/backdoorbarkiofork-targets-aerospace-and-defense-industry.

[52] Coogan P. Targeted Attacks Make WinHelp Files Not So Helpful [homepage on the Internet]. Symantec; 2012 [cited Online; accessed 12-January-2019].

Available from: https://www.symantec.com/connect/blogs/targeted-attacks-make-winhelp-files-not-so-helpful.

[53] Krebs B. Russian 'Dukes' of Hackers Pounce on Trump Win [homepage on the Internet]. Krebs On Security; 2016 [cited Online; accessed 12-January-2019]. Available from: https://krebsonsecurity.com/2016/11/russian-dukes-of-hackers-pounce-on-trump-win/.

[54] Global Research and Analysis Team. "Red October" Diplomatic Cyber Attacks Investigation [homepage on the Internet]. Kaspersky; 2013 [cited Online; accessed 12-January-2019]. Available from: https://securelist.com/analysis/publications/36740/red-october-diplomatic-cyber-attacksinvestigation/.

[55] Moran N, Scott M, and Homan J. Operation Poisoned Hurricane [homepage on the Internet]. FireEye; 2014 [cited Online; accessed 12-January-2019]. Available from: https://www.fireeye.com/blog/threat-research/2014/08/operation-poisoned-hurricane.html.

Chapter 8
Privacy-aware digital forensics

Ana Nieto[1], Ruben Rios[1], and Javier Lopez[1]

Digital forensics and privacy are the two naturally conflicting concepts. While privacy can be defined as the desire of people to decide for themselves when, how and to what extent their personal information is shared with others, digital forensics is aimed at acquiring and analysing relevant data from devices in the scope of digital forensic investigations, following a set of procedures to comply legal proceedings.

Digital forensic investigations are usually carried out after seizing the devices from investigated suspects or third parties, who consequently lose control over the data being accessed by the investigator. Moreover, digital forensic tools are even capable of retrieving information which is apparently no longer present in the device because the user decided to delete it. These tools also have the ability of correlating information from different sources giving rise to new actors in the investigation whose privacy can be affected. Also, the lack of context to determine when and why the user intentionally deleted some of the contents may result in wrong accusations.

All things considered, even when digital investigations are conducted by responsible professionals, the data collected from personal devices may result in dreadful invasions to individual privacy. Inevitably, this leads to a controversial debate on the need for strong privacy guarantees in the context of digital forensics. This chapter aims to shed some light into this imperative and highly demanded debate given the fundamental role that the user and his/her personal data play in current and future digital investigations.

8.1 Introduction

Digital forensics dates back to the early 1970s when two experts were capable of recovering a highly fragmented database file that was mistakenly deleted from a computer system [1]. At that time, the variety of devices was rather limited and their capacity was considerably smaller compared to current systems. Also, most electronic devices were not interconnected, and when connected, data transfers were

[1]Network, Information and Computer Security (NICS) Lab, Computer Science Department, University of Málaga, Málaga, Spain

minimal because of the low capacity of the networks at that time. Since then, technology has evolved at a tremendous pace and so did digital forensics in an attempt to keep up with the technology changes. In the current picture of digital forensics, the users, their devices and the communication infrastructure are strongly related to each other, more than ever before, resulting in an extremely complex ecosystem (Figure 8.1).

Given the plethora of devices owned by most people and the amount of information stored in them, privacy-preserving digital investigations have been recognised among the key challenges that must be overcome by digital forensics in the near future [2]. While the amount of data collected for an investigation is increasing, usually only a small portion of this data is relevant to the investigation. Moreover, during the process of extracting data for an investigation, some personal data, irrelevant to the investigation, may be exposed. This data may not only be stored in personal devices but also in remote machines, such as Cloud servers and Internet of Things (IoT) devices. Even more so, given the multi-tenant nature of current computer systems, a single device may not only contain data from the individual being investigated but also from other users not even related to the investigation, thus leading to what is referred to as third-party privacy breach (TPPB) [3].

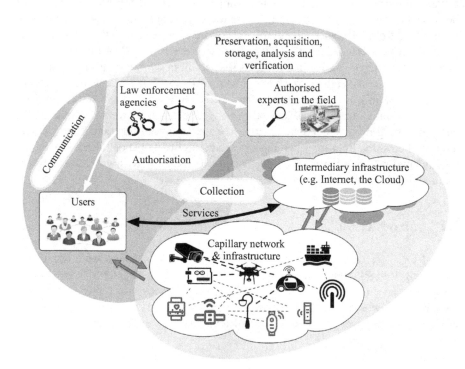

Figure 8.1   Actors in a digital forensic ecosystem

Some solutions have been devised to prevent violating users' privacy during digital investigations, thereby protecting both the users and the investigators from being accused of privacy invasions. Unfortunately, as we will show next, privacy-preserving digital forensics is still in its infancy and much work still needs to be done in this area. In fact, although it has been widely recognised as one of the major challenges in digital forensics, current tools and methodologies are mostly oblivious to this problem and provide no support for dealing with privacy issues.

In the following sections, we will delve into the role of privacy in digital forensics investigations. We start by describing these two disciplines separately to understand their requirements and principles. This will provide the reader with a solid base on how digital forensics and privacy conflict with each other but also show that there is room for privacy-respecting digital investigations. This is followed by a detailed analysis of the current state-of-the-art in privacy-aware digital forensic (PADF) approaches. In addition, this chapter gives insight into the social, contextual and technological changes affecting digital investigations.

8.2 Digital forensics

Digital forensics can be defined as the *scientific tasks, techniques, and practices used in the investigation of stored or transmitted binary information or data for legal purposes* (ISO/IEC 27037:2012).

Before the explosion of the Internet and the widespread adoption of social networks, the digital forensics ecosystem was limited to personal computers seized by law-enforcement officers in the context of digital investigations. The extraction and analysis of digital evidence could be complex, but the lack of security mechanisms (e.g. secure data erasure or encryption) allowed a large amount of information to be recovered and analysed. In addition, the availability and predominance of certain operating systems and applications facilitated the procedural analysis of data. Thus, the most typical actions in digital forensics were related to data recovery with non-repudiation guarantees and the analysis of digital artefacts (e.g. pictures or other digital files) for cases of fraud or copyright violations. However, the scope of this discipline is broader.

Digital forensics can also help to determine the timeline of events carried out in an entire system to better understand the casuistry or the motivations of an attacker and thus help to prevent future attacks. In fact, there are multiple tools available to forensic professionals for this purpose. The most common ones are software applications aimed to conduct general-purpose digital investigations (e.g. Access-Data FTK, MPE+, EnCase, Autopsy) or applications specific to a particular domain (e.g. volatility for memory analysis). There are also preconfigured environments with tools available to conduct digital investigations (e.g. Kali Linux, Blackarch Linux, SANS DFIR, CAINE). Other utilities are hardware-dependent such as disk copy utilities or specific hardware (e.g. JTAGulator). Finally, some environments and devices, such as smartphones and cars, require the use of manual techniques. An example of this is the chip-off technique which consists of extracting embedded chips for analysis.

The set of tools to be used will be determined by the type of investigation (public or private/administrative) and the specific requirements of the context being analysed (devices, volatility, etc.). All this knowledge requires specific training in the use of methodologies and tools which is not always easy or possible to provide. Some of the reasons for this may be limitations on hardware resources, on the time to conduct practical cases or licence requirements.

The volume of data and devices susceptible to analysis is continuously growing. Aside from the operational problems that dealing with vast amounts of data causes to law-enforcement agencies (LEAs), this has also resulted in the specialisation of certain areas in the field of digital forensics due to the emergence of data from new contexts. These include among other, the Cloud and the IoT, which in turn have led to Cloud- and IoT-forensics, respectively. The way in which digital forensics has evolved with the development of new scenarios is analysed in Section 8.2.1.

Cybercrime evolution

According to the Internet Crime Compliant Center (IC3), in 2013–17, there were a total of 1,420,555 Internet scams affecting victims across the globe, causing around $5.52 billion losses [4]. The motives of the criminals are similar to those that had been years ago (e.g. cyberespionage, financial crime, revenge and cyberterrorism), but the means to commit crimes, especially the telematic means, are much more powerful [5]. Nowadays, there are multiple cyberweapons or offender resources such as key-loggers, exploit kits or botnet kits, some of which have been developed to affect even the most recent IoT devices. Intrusion-detection systems do their best effort to stop these threats, but they are not enough.

In recent years, digital forensics has begun to be an area reinforced by different learning courses (either specialised courses or as part of the academic program of various universities) without a lack of consensus in the training methodologies. One of the reasons is that the specific procedures of a digital forensics professional depend on the law of the country where he/she will practice and the type of investigation he will focus on. The technical background of a digital forensic practitioner should be the same, but the legal procedures to commit his/her work can be completely different depending on the context in which the professional is performing his investigation. Another reason that probably affects the training methodologies is the evolution of the digital ecosystem.

8.2.1   Evolution of digital forensics

The evolution of digital forensics has been motivated by contextual changes. While many researchers consider digital forensics and computer forensics as equivalent terms, the latter is only a portion the former; as new devices and technologies appear and become more complex, it is more difficult to cover all different aspects of the discipline. Figure 8.2 shows specific areas that can be grouped under the term digital forensics.

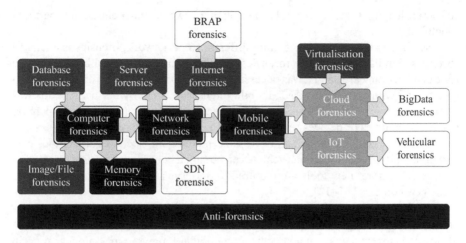

Figure 8.2   Evolution of topics in digital forensics

Computer forensics has its origin in the analysis of evidences that are in digital form, typically found in a computer. This means that it is not necessary to be an expert to perform some of the basic operations considered of forensic nature, such as applying techniques to identify modifications in images or files. Indeed, this is a natural step when analysing digital evidence found in a crime scene or provided by a claimant. This raises the following questions: (i) what makes computer forensics a discipline? and (ii) when is it possible to consider that a certain 'X-forensics' discipline is *mature*?

There are some indicators that can help answer the previous questions. First, unlike image/file forensics or database forensics, *computer forensics* groups the entire context of a computer and is a term widely used by a group of experts who have defined the problem in books and standards. Moreover, the materialisation of a new discipline typically includes other existing disciplines (now sub-disciplines). For example, memory forensics can be considered as part of computer forensics since, after all, there is memory inside a computer. However, *memory forensics* must be considered as a mature discipline by itself which, in fact, can be applied to other devices and not just computers, for instance, mobile devices [6,7]. Indeed, there are specific tools developed for memory forensics (e.g. DumpIt, Volatility) and new emerging areas, such as malware analysis, are very dependent on this domain because there are attacks that avoid leaving traces by using only volatile memory. In the same way, *network forensics* started to be analysed because of intrusions and attacks to computer systems that caused great harm in the 1980s. Today, there is a wide range of tools and techniques to capture and analyse network traffic, as well as the artefacts and digital evidence generated from network communications [8].

Figure 8.2 depicts the evolution of digital forensics by relating consolidated disciplines (i.e. properly defined, accepted by the experts and practitioners, well documented and with solid tools) with other sub-disciplines (e.g. image/file forensics, database forensics, server forensics) or emergent ones (e.g. Cloud forensics and

IoT-forensics) that are acceptably described or whose challenges are partially identified.

Notably, mobile forensics is quite different from network forensics or memory forensics. Similar to computer forensics, mobile forensics emerged because a new type of device appeared and it was necessary to develop the right tools and methodologies to deal with them. Nowadays, mobile forensics is properly defined but this was an inflexion point. New forensic disciplines (e.g. IoT-forensics [9]) are also emerging because new types of devices (e.g. sensors nodes) are being developed.

New use cases, scenarios and devices keep emerging, such as autonomous cars and drones [10]. An autonomous vehicle can be stolen or used maliciously by external entities. Therefore, new tools are required to preserve and store digital evidence in these new contexts [11–13].

It is important to highlight that, unlike computer forensics, new emerging areas are analysing privacy as a requirement from their inception. This is a clear example of how the current social context is changing digital forensics, making new areas in digital forensics incorporate privacy as a requirement.

8.2.2   Digital forensics rules

Digital investigations are governed by a set of principles and standards that define the procedures accepted by a broad community of experts in the field. In this section, both principles and standards for digital forensics are detailed in order to provide a solid foundation that helps to understand this discipline.

8.2.2.1   Digital forensics principles

Digital investigations are conducted following a set of well-defined methodologies and processes accepted by a broad community of experts in the field (see Section 8.2.2.2 for further information). Although there are various methodologies covering different contexts, all of them respect a set of basic principles:

Integrity: The actions carried out during the seizure of digital evidence should not change the evidence itself.

Competence/Expertise: Any person accessing the original digital evidence must be forensically skilled and competent.

Availability: The whole digital-evidence-management process (seizure, access, storage or transfer) must be fully documented, preserved and available for review.

Responsibility: Those individuals in possession of digital evidence are responsible for all actions taken with it during the period in which it is guarded by them.

Agreement: Any agency that is responsible for conducting digital forensic processes must comply with these principles.

Repetitiveness: An independent third party should be able to repeat the entire process applied to digital evidence and achieve the same result.

Most of the previous principles are defined by the *International Organization on Computer Evidence* (IOCE 1999). In particular, the principle of repetitiveness is not defined by the IOCE, but it is assumed that this principle should be ensured through compliance with the rest of principles. There is one exception which justifies not including such principle among the previous four principles: when volatile data is acquired (e.g. a memory dump during live forensics) it is very difficult, if not impossible, to repeat the process with the same results because the data could be rewritten precisely due to the tools used to make the acquisition of the data in memory.

It should be noted that there are legal principles that depend on the country where the digital investigation is carried out and also on the ethical principles of the investigator. In particular, anything not explicitly considered by law (cf. Section 8.3.2.1) is subjective and depends on the interpretation of the investigator. Additional precautions can be taken before the digital investigation starts by establishing contracts (commitment rules and acceptable use policies) between the digital investigator and the client.

8.2.2.2 Digital forensics standards

A set of international standards have been developed to define the guidelines for the management of digital evidence and digital forensics processes. One example is the ISO/IEC 27037:2012 standard, which provides guidelines for four basic processes in the management of digital evidence: (i) identification, (ii) collection, (iii) acquisition and (iv) preservation. After this, it is assumed that the digital evidence will be analysed in the laboratory. Precisely, the ISO/IEC 27042:2015 standard describes steps for (v) investigation, (vi) analysis, (vii) interpretation and (viii) reporting. Also, other important aspects, such as analytical models to be considered, and the mechanisms and techniques to demonstrate the competence and proficiency are provided.

It is important to highlight that, depending on the model or methodology chosen to conduct the digital investigation, more or less phases/processes are considered. However, six phases are generally considered [14]: planning, identification, collection, preservation, examination, analysis and report. Typically, the planning phase has to be done before the field work – selection of procedures, legal and ethical considerations (e.g. responsibilities, authorisations, etc.), tools and so on; the identification, collection and preservation occur at the crime scene; and the examination, analysis and report can be done at the laboratory, once the digital evidence has been collected, thus preserving the chain of custody.

Chain of custody (ISO/PC 308)

The technical committee (TC) ISO/PC 308 (created in 2016) is currently working on the standardisation of what is referred to as the chain of custody (CoC). This is a term applied beyond digital evidence management. In words of the ISO/PC 308 TC, 'a chain of custody is a succession of responsibilities for processes as a product moves through each step of the supply chain. Each supply actor has to implement and document a set of measures in order for the chain of custody to function'. The goal is to guarantee the traceability and integrity of the product, which in the context of digital forensics is the digital evidence. If the integrity and authenticity of the digital evidence is put in question, the entire digital investigation can be rendered useless.

The ISO/IEC 27043:2015 and ISO/IEC 30121:2015 standards can be considered horizontal to the previous ones. The former encapsulates 'idealised models for common investigation processes across various investigation scenarios', therefore covering all the previous steps or processes of any digital investigation. The latter describes how to conduct digital forensics within an organisation to take legal actions after a security breach or in the case of any other incident in which information technology is a decisive factor.

In addition, the ISO/IEC 27050:2016 – Electronic discovery – standard is closely related to digital investigations. This standard is decomposed in four parts: (i) overview and concepts, (ii) guidance for governance and management of electronic discovery, (iii) code of practice for electronic discovery and (iv) ICT readiness for electronic discovery. In this standard, *electronic discovery* is defined as the 'discovery (3.4) that includes the identification, preservation, collection, processing, review, analysis or production of Electronically Stored Information'. These are, in fact, the typical steps or processes already defined for digital-evidence management. This standard emphasises the cost associated with the managing electronically stored information (ESI). It considers there are ESI that must be preserved (e.g. logs) while other ESI that can be considered expendable (e.g. deleted data or unallocated space on hard drives). However, this is in conflict with digital forensics.

According to the ISO/IEC 27037:2012 standard, digital evidence is defined as 'information or data stored or transmitted in binary form that **may be relied upon as evidence**'. This is different from ESI, defined in ISO/IEC 27050-1:2016, as 'data or information of any kind and from any source, whose temporal existence is evidenced by being stored (3.26)' (volatile storage or non-volatile storage) 'in or on any electronic medium'. Then, a digital evidence is, by nature, the ESI that is *relevant* to a digital investigation.

8.2.3 Digital forensics challenges

The challenges in digital forensics have also evolved over the years. A good summary of the history of digital forensics is provided in [1]. According to the author, the history of digital forensics can be divided into three stages, which helps to understand the evolution of the challenges in this field.

Thus, during the first stage, 1970s–1990s, digital forensic professionals worked with LEAs 'on an ad-hoc, case-by-case basis' and the need to perform digital forensics was rather limited, because as the capacity of the disk was smaller, users saved less data and printed more. In the second stage, 1999–2007, denoted as 'the golden age', multiple vendors began to develop specific digital forensic tools that required relatively limited training, allowed to recover deleted files – basic file carving – or to analyse e-mail messages. It was then when new disciplines such as Network and Memory Forensics were born to answer to some specific challenges: obtain data that allows to understand the network events and obtain memory data that would allow us to circumvent the security controls of the computers (cf. Section 8.5). Furthermore, it was during the *golden age* when the research in digital forensics had rapid growth and the professionalisation of the sector began. This resulted in the acceptance on the use

Table 8.1   Digital forensics challenges

Characteristic	Digital forensic challenge
Growing **size** of storage devices	Insufficient **time** to create a forensic image or to process the data
Prevalence of **embedded** flash storage and proliferation of HW interfaces	Storage devices can no longer be easily removed or imaged. **Embedded storage is routinely ignored** during forensic investigations (e.g. persistent memory inside GPUs)
Proliferation of **operating systems and file formats**	Increase the requirements, **complexity and cost** of digital forensic **tools**
Multiple devices in a single case	**Correlation** of digital evidence is needed
Pervasive **encryption**	Hinders or **avoids the processing** of data
Cloud for remote processing and storage	Complicates the **identification and acquisition** of digital evidence. Makes **impossible to perform basic forensic methodologies** of data preservation and isolation
Malware not written in persistent storage and capable of using **anti-forensic** techniques	Need for RAM forensics tools which are more difficult to create than disk tools and new systems to **capture the malware for in-depth analysis**
Law and privacy	Limits the scope of forensic investigations

of specific tools and procedures to conduct digital investigations by the community of experts.

The third stage considered in [1] is from 2007 to 2010 (the year in which the paper was published), but the environmental characteristics and the challenges in digital forensics are basically the same as today (see Table 8.1).

It is important to emphasise that, regardless of the clear value of technical challenges, the challenges motivated by social changes (e.g. the *need* for privacy) are usually not so prominent in the literature and, nevertheless, play a crucial role given the new areas highlighted in the previous section and summarised in Figure 8.3. For example, one of the major challenges is to make the new areas and methods used (cf. Section 8.2.2.2) understandable by an audience that is not an expert in the field and that is increasingly involved in digital investigation [15].

In particular, privacy is a major concern in digital forensics, because (i) digital forensic tools will be more and more proactive; the inference of user's information will be fundamental to speed up the processing of data, and (ii) privacy tools, in general terms, affect the acquisition and analysis of digital evidence, being considered as anti-forensic mechanisms in many cases [16]. Nevertheless, although the confrontation between digital forensics and privacy is intuited, it is unfair to make an assessment of the influence of privacy in digital investigations without first knowing the nature of data privacy. In order to fully understand the said relationship, the basic characteristics of digital privacy will be addressed below. Furthermore, Section 8.3.3 will return to the digital forensic challenges but from the point of view of privacy.

8.3 Digital privacy

Privacy is a difficult concept to explain. There have been many definitions throughout history, each of which consider different aspects and perspectives of this convoluted concept. For example, an extensively used definition of privacy was formulated at the end of the nineteenth century by Warren and Brandeis [17], who described it as 'the right to be let alone'. However, this definition of privacy covers only a single dimension of the term, and many other jurists, scholars, philosophers and sociologists have considered and introduced new aspects which broadens its scope.

One of the main problems in reaching a satisfactory definition for privacy is the fact that it is a very subjective term. Privacy has to do with the desires and expectations of people. Moreover, desires and expectations evolve and change over time although they are very much conditioned by the past and current situation. For example, a person may be willing to share his religion believes when living in his/her home country but may be reluctant to do so when travelling to a different state or country.

Consequently, privacy is about giving people a feeling of security and confidence. People need to feel in control of what personal information is known to others and want to have the ability to decide how much information and in which circumstances. These arguments lead to another widely accepted definition of privacy by Westin [18], who describes it as the desire to determine under what circumstances and to what extent personal information is exposed to other entities.

Note that no matter which is the most accurate definition of privacy, what is really important here is the observation that people feel vulnerable and insecure without it. And because of this, privacy has been recognised as an individual right in numerous laws, regulations and treaties all over the world, including the *Universal Declaration of Human Rights*.

8.3.1 Evolution of digital privacy

As previously mentioned, privacy encompasses many different aspects and it very much depends on the context. In the early days when privacy started to be considered as a serious matter, concerns were mostly about physical privacy. That is, the right of people to be free from intrusions into one's physical space, property or solitude.

According to Holvast [19], people could be arrested in England for peeping and eavesdropping, as early as 1361. Also, personal correspondence was protected from reading invasions already in 1624. And, since privacy depends on context, by that time, privacy invasions were mostly perpetrated by acquaintances in close contact with the individual, typically from the same town or village.

With the growth in popularity of the newspaper and the more recent invention of photography, the reach and impact of privacy invasions grows. These technologies made it possible to publish information from individuals without their consent and the audience was considerably bigger. Fortunately, this led to an interesting privacy debate that gave rise to the publication of 'The Right to Privacy' by Warren and Brandeis [17], which has been fundamental to the development of privacy laws, mostly in the United States.

As a matter of fact, the emergence of new technologies has been inevitably followed by new ways of invading privacy, which in turn fuelled the privacy debate. For example, the development of telephony led to communication wiretapping and the creation of laws to protect from it, such as the Wiretapping Act in the United States. Other technologies went through a similar process, but it was not until the development of the computer and the widespread use of the Internet that the number and magnitude of privacy invasions reached a whole new dimension.

The ability of computers to collect, store, analyse and disseminate massive amounts of information opened the door to unique opportunities to violate privacy. Information was no longer just local, it could be transmitted and shared with anyone, anywhere in the world almost instantly. Communications exploded in number and size. People started to use their computers, smartphones, and other types of devices to get online. Nowadays, people upload comments, pictures and videos to social networks and the Cloud. All these communications leave traces of what they do, what they like, where they are and whatnot. These traces can potentially be collected and analysed for different purposes by companies, governments and even criminals.

However, this situation is far from finished. New technologies and paradigms are being developed, such as the IoT [20], which promises to expand the Internet to the physical world by fitting everyday objects with computational, sensing and communication capabilities. In such scenario, the ubiquitous deployment of billions of smart devices will bring countless opportunities to invade privacy. Personal data will be more distributed than ever before, stored in all types of devices, local and remote. People may not even realise of being subject to data collection, who is collecting data and for which purposes. Furthermore, data collection will happen in situations hitherto unsuspected, even in the intimacy of our homes. All this, together with the increase in computing capabilities, advances in data mining and machine-learning algorithms (see Figure 8.3) bring unprecedented challenges to privacy protection.

8.3.2 Privacy protection

There are basically two ways to protect privacy. The first means of protection consists of implementing privacy enhancing technologies (PETs) and privacy-by-design principles. This allows to minimise the collection of personally identifiable information (i.e. data that is linkable to the identity of an individual) and also promote client-side data storage and processing. These approaches aim to anonymise and/or reduce the quality of data before it is released. In this way, the user retains some level of control over the data being offered to third parties. Later in this chapter, we will see some PETs applied to digital forensic investigations.

The other means of privacy protection is not technological but legal and regulatory. These are extremely important, especially in situations where the user can be subject to data collection even without taking an active role in the system. This is the case, for example, when a person is in a smart environment surrounded by different types of sensors, cameras and so on. In situations like these, the user cannot control with technological means the amount of personal information that is being collected.

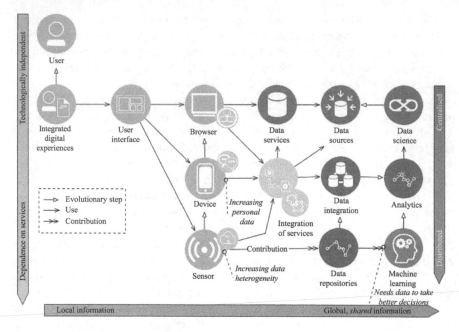

Figure 8.3   Contextual changes for privacy and digital forensics

Therefore, to prevent data-hungry entities from invading individual privacy, laws, regulations, audits, and sanctions must be in place.

8.3.2.1   Privacy laws

The importance of protecting privacy was acknowledged around the globe after a long history of privacy invasions. Privacy is now seen as a fundamental right in the constitution of most countries all over the world [21] and, in 1948, the United Nations recognised privacy in the *Universal Declaration of Human Rights* [22].

> **Universal Declaration of Human Rights, Article 12:**
> No one shall be subjected to arbitrary interference with his privacy, family, home or correspondence nor to attacks upon his honour and reputation. Everyone has the right to the protection of the law against such interference or attacks.

Two years later, the Council of Europe created the European Convention on Human Rights [23], which also included the right to privacy. However, there are no universally accepted privacy laws. Still, there are agreements between countries in relation to the movement of personal data [24], such as the EU–US Privacy Shield and the US–Swiss Safe Harbour Framework.

In most countries, the legal basis for the protection of privacy is defined by constitutional laws. In the United States, the Fourth Amendment of the Constitution protects individuals from unreasonable searches and seizures without a warrant, which can only be obtained upon probable cause. In other words, individual privacy is protected unless there is sufficient evidence to believe that the person has committed a crime. Like the United States, some countries (e.g. Canada, Germany or Japan) do not explicitly mention the word privacy in their constitutions [21]. In those countries, the courts usually recognise the privacy right as implicit. Other countries like Brazil, South Africa and South Korea directly refer to the inviolability of privacy in their constitutions. Besides constitutional laws, each country has its own specific laws related to privacy protection.

In the United States, privacy provisions in constitutional laws are complemented by statutory privacy laws [25]. The main restrictions to privacy invasions come from the Electronic Communications Privacy Act (previously the Wiretap Act), the Pen Register Act and the Stored Communications Privacy Act. The first two are related to the protection of all forms of private communications and the metadata generated from these communications, while the latter regulates access to the information stored by Internet Service Providers. However, it is important to note that when people share information and files with others, they usually lose the reasonable expectation of privacy [26]. Additionally, privacy is considered in tort laws, and there is a number of sector-specific laws, such as the Health Insurance and Accountability Act for the health sector.

On the contrary, in Europe, there is a general framework for the protection of privacy regardless of the sector. The European Data Protection Directive from 1995 (Directive 95/46/EC [27]) was devised as a mechanism to homogenise and unify the privacy laws from different member states. However, being a directive, each member state was free to decide how to transpose its provisions into national laws. In recent years, however, the European Union has been developing a regulation (not a directive) for the protection of personal data. The General Data Protection Regulation 2016/679 (GDPR [28]) has recently superseded Directive 95/46/EC. This regulation not only entered into force in May 2018 in all member states simultaneously with legal binding but also introduces some notable changes. For example, it introduces bigger fines to organisations not complying the GDPR, which can reach up to 4% of their annual global turnover or €20 million, whichever is bigger. Another relevant change introduced by the GDPR is that it extends its data-protection scope to any organisation processing personal information of European citizens, regardless of its location. Also, the GDPR recognises new rights to data subjects, such as the right to erasure, also known as the right to be forgotten.

Clearly, covering all existing privacy laws is virtually impossible and well beyond the scope of this section. The goal is solely to give a brief overview of some well-known privacy laws. The interested reader is referred to [24] for more details on privacy laws around the world with a special focus on the United States.

8.3.2.2 Privacy principles

Most privacy laws identify a set of principles that determine the responsibilities of organisations that handle personal data and at the same time shape the rights of individuals. How to successfully comply with these principles depends on each particular organisation and is not covered by the law, but at least these principles define some general guidelines.

The first law to introduce privacy principles was probably the US Privacy Act of 1974 [29]. This law established a set of guidelines to govern the practices of federal agencies in the maintenance, processing and dissemination of personal data records. A few years later, the Organisation for Economic Co-operation and Development published eight principles for the protection of privacy and transborder flows of personal data. These principles, which were revised in 2013 by a group of experts and remained unchanged [30], can be summarised as follows:

Collection limitation: Personal data should be collected by lawful means and with the consent of the data subject.

Data quality: Personal data should be accurate, complete and relevant to the purpose for which it was collected.

Purpose specification: The data subject should be aware of the purpose for which personal data is collected not later than at the time of data collection.

Use limitation: Personal data should not be used for purposes other than the ones specified at the time of collection.

Security safeguards: Personal data should be protected against loss, attacks and misuse.

Openness: The data subject must be aware of the policies, procedures and practices of the data holder with regard to personal data.

Individual participation: The data subject must be able to access his/her own data as well as to ask for corrections within reasonable time.

Accountability: The data controller is made responsible for non-compliance with any of the above principles.

Although not all privacy laws consider the same principles, most of them revolve around the same ideas of data minimisation, use limitation, individual participation and access, plus security and accountability. These principles usually change in name or number but not in form. For example, the EU Directive 95/46/EC [27, Chapter II] adopted all these principles, and the same happened with the more recent GDPR 2016/679 [28], which references all principles in Article 5 except for individual participation. Notwithstanding, data subject's rights are addressed in part III (articles 15 to 17), which include the rights of access, the right to rectification and the right to be forgotten. All three, can be regarded as sides of the same coin, namely individual participation.

Note that all these laws include some limitations and restrictions to the privacy principles considered in them. These restrictions are included as a mechanism to, among other things, protect national or public security, assure the rights and freedoms of others, or prevent and prosecute criminal activities.

8.3.2.3   Privacy standards

A technical standard is a document that provides a series of rules, instructions or methods for achieving uniform results across different products or systems. Standards are mostly developed by standard organisations after a rigorous process involving a number of technical experts in the area.

Some organisations have developed standards with a focus on data protection and privacy in different domains. One of the most prolific standards organisations in this respect are the International Organisation for Standardisation (ISO) and the International Electrotechnical Commission (IEC), with several standards. The devised standards cover several aspects including the establishment of a common framework defining privacy terminology, actors and principles (ISO/IEC 29100:2011), the description of architectural components for systems that process personally identifiable information (ISO/IEC 29101:2013), and the definition of a set of controls for implementing measures to protect personal data (ISO/IEC 27018:2014) in accordance with the privacy principles defined in the aforementioned standard. It is also worth mentioning that a technical committee of experts from the ISO, the ISO/PC 317, is currently working on a new standard (ISO/NP 23485) to ensure the compliance with new regulations during the whole life cycle of products or services.

Other organisations, such as the British Standards Institute (BSI), the European Committee for Standardization (CEN) and the National Institute of Standards and Technology (NIST) from US Department of Commerce, have also delved into the protection of personal data and privacy with various standards and recommendations. Some of them are the BSI BS 10012:2009, the CEN CWA 16113:2010 and the NIST 800-122.

8.3.3   Privacy challenges in digital forensics

Considering the main characteristics of the current ecosystem of technologies and the digital forensics challenges summarised in Table 8.1, a list of privacy challenges motivated by digital forensics is provided in Table 8.2.

Some of the papers analysed during this chapter (cf. Sections 8.5–8.7) partially cover some of said challenges. For example, the (unnecessary) privacy exposure of third parties which are not directly related with the digital investigation is widely discussed in Section 8.5.2.3. There are also some challenges that are closely related to each other. For example, a user giving consent to access his/her personal devices may in turn reveal data from other users related to him or her; therefore, even with an informed consent, there will be a high risk of TPPB to occur. Besides, informed consents must be simple and clear, and this is increasingly difficult due to the different jurisdictions, laws, standards and the users themselves.

Also, different jurisdictions can affect data privacy. For example, in Cloud computing environments, a PADF solution must consider the jurisdiction of the country where the data is stored and be able to understand that this data cannot be moved to another country that does not meet the same privacy requirements. At the same time, forensic tools in this area should understand these premises.

In addition, there are clear digital forensics and privacy trade-offs in new areas such as Cloud forensics, IoT-forensics or more recently, vehicular/automotive forensics, that must be further explored. For example, renting a car with an on-board computer and synchronising our device with it (e.g. to listen to music or to make a call),

Table 8.2   Digital forensics practices and privacy concerns

Digital forensic procedures	Privacy issues
Indiscriminate acquisition/collection of digital data	**Third party privacy** breach (TPPB) must be avoided
Full disk images are created and analysed	Deleted files can lead to **false accusations**
Data can be collected from personal devices	Need for **informed consents** complete and understandable by the users
During the investigation, the data to be acquired may be hosted on servers in different countries	Different **jurisdictions** can understand privacy differently
Warrants can be necessary during private investigation	Matching of **privacy policies** and **warrants** (formally defined) for automated analysis
Correlation is needed in order to build a timeline	**Multi-device** context (more and more data)
Digital forensics tools and methodologies must be accepted and tested by a broad group of experts in the field	Privacy requirements must be integrated by design in **existing tools and methodologies**
Digital forensic principles must be guaranteed	The **manipulation of data** (e.g. encryption) to protect privacy must be done considering digital forensic principles Section 8.2.2.1

nothing guarantees that these preferences will be erased or that our list of contacts will not be recorded in the car. In contrast, the existence of such mechanisms to secure erasure would eliminate digital evidence that can help establish liability in an accident (e.g. if data from accelerometers are removed) or from other events (e.g. the location of the individual's car at the time of a fine as exculpatory evidence). Moreover, in general, multi-device context and/or multi-tenant architectures implies the access of multiple users to the same platform, compromising the privacy of the individuals sharing data in case a digital investigation is required. Besides, relevant information to the investigation can be divided as pieces of a complex puzzle between multiple personal devices. Therefore, when the digital forensics mechanisms are applied (e.g. based on a warrant) surpassing the security measures, these particular cases must be taken into account.

Considering the previous initial list of PADFs challenges, during the rest of the chapter, solutions that consider privacy in different digital forensics scenarios are analysed in order to identify the degree of satisfaction of these requirements.

8.4   Law, privacy and digital forensics

One of the expected skills of a digital forensic investigator is to understand the laws and comply with them. Laws help to narrow down the scope of forensic investigations.

However, it is possible that due to ignorance or imprudence, the forensic investigator exceeds some limits and ruins all the investigation. For that reason, some authors have tried to make these limits more evident by presenting an analysis of privacy laws in different countries.

The authors in [26] concentrate on investigations in the United States. They start by introducing the laws restricting forensic investigations, including the Fourth Amendment and several acts in the United States Code. But their main contribution is on the presentation of situations where investigators need or need not a court order to conduct the investigation. In general, a search warrant/court order/subpoena is necessary to gather the evidence legally. However, if the investigation does not violate a person's reasonable privacy, does not break the law or falls into an exception of law, then the evidence can be legally obtained without search warrant/court order/subpoena and the evidence will be accepted in court.

Another paper that analyses American law is [25]. The authors describe nine legal areas where more research in digital forensics is necessary. Privacy is only considered in two out of the nine areas (constitutional law and tort law), and unfortunately, the authors do not give details on how to approach specific privacy issues. A more privacy-focused analysis is provided in [31]. In this paper, the authors concentrate on the relation of privacy laws with forensic tools. In particular, the analysis is based on the reliability of the tools and how they can protect privacy. The authors claim that one desirable requirement for digital forensic tools is the ability to provide individual accountability through logins. This would help to ascertain who was using the tool during the acquisition or analysis of the data. In addition, the authors propose the inclusion of mechanisms to ensure (by design) that the tool is only used for the purpose the search warrant was granted.

Some authors have looked beyond American laws and have analysed how laws and regulations in Europe and/or Asia-Pacific countries affect digital investigations. This is done, for example, by the authors in [32]. They also present a survey of three areas of research related to privacy and digital investigations: (i) analysis of privacy policies, (ii) modelling of privacy policies and (iii) technologies for privacy-respecting investigations.

Some relevant changes introduced by the European GDPR with respect to digital investigations are introduced in [33]. For example, the paper discusses about the influence of the new regulation on the legal proceedings for e-discovery. They observe that with the GDPR, there will be problems in the way cross-border litigations were performed before since data was typically collected on-site and sent to a central e-discovery provider from where lawyers from different countries could access the data. This may no longer be possible with the new data-protection regulation. However, the authors conclude that the impact of the GDPR on digital investigations is still unclear.

Finally, the authors in [34] present a state-of-the-art analysis of legal aspects regarding security, privacy and digital forensics in Future Internet scenarios like Smart Cities and the IoT. After reviewing some relevant pieces of legislation in various countries and major cities adopting these novel technologies (Hong Kong, South Korea, Budapest, USA and Europe), the authors observe some of them lack a solid legal framework for data protection being the European GDPR the best structured piece of legislation. The authors also recognise the need for international agreements and cooperation towards a common security and privacy framework that may be paved by GDPR mandates on protecting transnational flows of data related to European citizens.

8.5 Privacy-aware computer forensics

This section is divided in two broad areas where most of the research on privacy solutions has concentrated over the years, namely database and computer forensics. Very few works consider privacy and memory forensics [6,35,36]. These works are mostly devoted to compromising data privacy when it is decrypted in memory and for that reason they are not included here.

8.5.1 Database

As mentioned at the beginning of the chapter, the digital forensic discipline emerged as a problem closely related to data recovery and databases [1]. Privacy problems in the database forensics have been considered from the following points of view: (i) the right to protect the access to data, (ii) to ensure the secure erasure of data and (iii) to protect the data of honest users during post-mortem investigations towards the definition of specific frameworks for data storage. See Figure 8.4 for a visual summary of PADFs solutions in this area.

In general, most of the solutions in this section use encryption to restrict the access to data, that can be stored in multiple devices or be used for different purposes, as shown in Figure 8.5.

Nowadays, there are database solutions for both servers and mobile devices, and data protection covers not only large servers but also storage devices that can connect to any computer. In this ecosystem, there are personal devices, used (theoretically) by a single user and devices shared by multiple users or multi-tenant architectures. All these systems need data to be stored following certain criteria.

In the following sections, the contributions in the area of privacy-aware database forensics are analysed. However, it is very important to keep in mind that some of

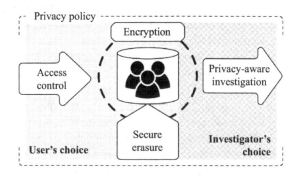

Figure 8.4   PADF database approaches

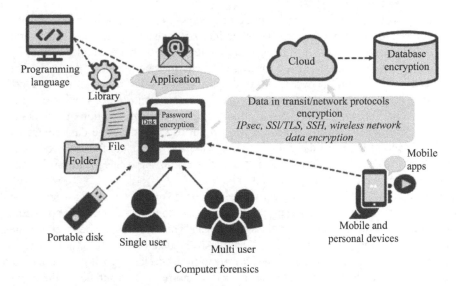

Figure 8.5   Encryption to protect different scenarios

these solutions are also applied to other areas because it is part of the evolution of digital forensics as described in Figure 8.2.

8.5.1.1   Access control

Access control has been used for two main purposes in digital investigations: as a security mechanism for preventing unauthorised access to data and as a mechanism to control the whole digital forensic investigation. For example, in [37], access control mechanisms are developed to protect individuals' privacy in DNA databases. In case the database is accessed by a non-authorised entity, the contents will be unintelligible. Only law agencies officers are capable of accessing this information. The proposed solution uses encryption to ensure that only legitimate queries on the database are allowed. The key to access to the identity of an individual in the database is the result of a set of DNA tests from the specific individual, following a shared secret approach. In this way, only those in possession of the DNA tests, can get access to the data.

Note that, in the previous work, the contribution is focused on access control as a mechanism to limit access to personal data within a forensics database populated by and belonging to forensic experts. This is different from controlling access to a database containing data stored by a system about individuals (or stored by them). Two solutions [38,39] can be found to support the latter case. These solutions are aimed at controlling the data that can be accessed by investigators when performing and investigation. In both solutions, data needs to be first categorised in different sensitivity levels.

In [38], the data is later encrypted in such a way that the forensics investigator only gains access to a more privacy-sensitive level once he proves knowledge of data in the level immediately below. In particular, the forensics investigator queries the data controller with a cryptographically blinded hypothesis. The hypothesis is basically the hash of a predicate regarding the investigation. After checking that the investigator has not exceeded the number of hypothesis test requests for that particular sensitivity level, the data controller returns a message that can be used to unlock the key of the next sensitivity level if the hypothesis of the investigator was correct. However, there are some open issues that should be clarified in future contributions. For example, who is the data controller and when is the categorisation and encryption of data done. This is extremely important from a privacy point of view since the data controller will have access to all the data, thus moving the privacy problem from the forensics investigator to the data controller. It is also unclear how these categorisation is done and how accurate the hypotheses need to be.

Similarly, in [39], privacy levels are defined based on a previous classification of data, which is made considering all possible accesses to the system. In this approach, both the user and the investigator classify the data. The user chooses between private or not private, and the investigator determines if the data is relevant or not relevant, based on the goal and the scope of the investigation. Data classified as private and not relevant is not collected, and data that is private and relevant is subject to the user's choice. In this case, the user can decide whether his/her data will be collected as is or encrypted. The problem of this approach is that by encrypting data, the user alters the digital evidence and therefore could invalidate the digital investigation. Another problem is that the user is in full control and the role of the investigator is extremely limited by the user. This may be in line with privacy principles but not with some of the restrictions included in privacy laws.

8.5.1.2 Secure erasure

Completely eliminating a data set is not as simple as it may seem. The aim of secure erasure techniques is to make sure that data cannot be recovered by any means, and this is the reason why this anti-forensic technique has also been considered as a mechanism to protect privacy. Nowadays, it is increasingly common to include secure erasure as a requirement in the security policy of any organisation that manages digital data, even more so after the entry into force of the GDPR.

Deleted data passes through several phases before it is finally removed from the system, and making data unrecoverable in the context of database systems is even more challenging. The database system usually makes multiple copies of sensitive data in transaction logs, indexes, etc. that may help to recover data. Based on these findings, the authors in [40] analyse four common database systems, including PostgreSQL and MySQL, and reveal they are vulnerable to some of this data leakage problems. They also propose some changes to the storage manager in MySQL for securely removing deleted data. Basically, the changes consist of calling to the *memset*() operation to overwrite those records which are considered no longer necessary. According to the authors, with careful configuration, this imposes insignificant degradation of system performance. On the other hand, they propose to encrypt log records from transaction logs with different keys and simply delete the keys when these log records are no longer necessary.

Some other contributions are focused on the analysis of different tools for secure erasure more closely related to the operating system, and thus they are analysed in the following section, which concentrates on computer forensics.

8.5.2 Computer

Typically, the terms digital forensics and computer forensics have been used interchangeably. Perhaps one of the main reasons is that, for a long time, computer forensics was the area that covered everything necessary in this discipline. As detailed in Section 8.2, numerous contributions have been developed in this area, and, as it could not be otherwise, also contributions regarding privacy. Being computer forensics the propeller of digital forensics, this explains to some extent why most of the privacy-aware contributions analysed have been made in the area of computer forensics. The topics in this area are quite similar to privacy-aware database forensics but tends to be more complex due the heterogeneity of computer architectures, file systems and operating systems available (Figure 8.6).

This is the reason why some contributions in this area focus on particular technologies, contexts or platforms. Also some authors have surveyed the field of privacy-aware computer forensics [41–43]. Although they usually provide different ways of classifying existing solutions, they generally reach similar conclusions.

8.5.2.1 Frameworks and policies

It is extremely complex to control all the factors that may affect privacy during a digital forensic investigation without turning to a framework that guides the investigator throughout the process and gives recommendations on the different issues. For that reason, the PET framework is proposed in [44] to protect the privacy of honest users during a post-mortem digital forensic investigation. Similar to [37], the solution controls the requests to the databases. The paper is extended in [3], where the concept of TPPB is properly defined in the context of computer forensics. This will be further analysed in Section 8.5.2.3.

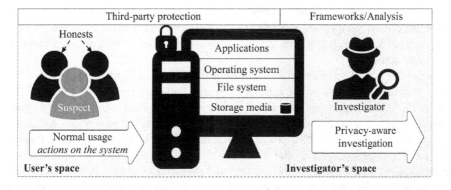

Figure 8.6 PADF computer approaches

The high-level framework proposed in [45] allows enterprises to effectively conduct digital forensic investigations of privacy incidents. The authors extend a general forensic framework to incorporate privacy-related components in the auditing and monitoring of business processes. In particular, the privacy-specific business processes introduced in the framework are borrowed from the *Generally Accepted Privacy Practices* standard. Similarly, the privacy-specific business policies are based on the *Fair Information Privacy Principles*. It is important to highlight that inside an organisation, the type of investigations are private, which may be less restrictive than public ones.

The framework presented in [46] is based on three modules: (i) expert system, (ii) evidence extraction and (iii) ranking. The module for evidence extraction will collect the digital evidence and will be then processed by the expert system. This module decides whether the digital evidence is relevant or not to the case so that it can be processed by the investigator. The decision of the expert system is based on previous investigations that are considered to be similar to the current one. Note that, the solution is very dependent on the learning phase that, as highlighted in previous papers, is critical since (i) it depends on the quantity and quality of the previous investigations and (ii) it represents a privacy issue by itself because it needs access to the case data.

Finally, some authors consider policy-based solutions for preserving privacy in computer forensics. Privacy policies are used to guide the data-treatment process. In this area, [47] proposes a set of privacy policies for guiding the investigator throughout the various phases of a forensic investigation (identification, collection, preservation, analysis and presentation).

8.5.2.2   Secure erasure

In [48], six counter-forensic privacy tools for Windows operating systems are analysed. The authors identify a number of limitations on these tools, which fail to provide a sufficient level of protection to users that wanted to delete sensitive information from their computers. According to the authors, the main problem with these tools is that it is extremely difficult for them to keep up with the number of ways different applications manage data and interact with the operating system. In case the user needs stronger privacy guarantees, the authors point to alternatives to the analysed counter-forensic tools, namely disk encryption and booting from a CD with all disks removed from the computer.

Similar conclusions are reached in [49]. In this case, six privacy software packages are evaluated based on the amount of information recoverable after they are used. Some of these solutions are intended for secure erasure, either using wipe or deleting specific files. The results show that there are tools that do not purge the unallocated space (in case of wipe a disk) and also that these tools tend to leave some trace of the deleted files – stored by the operating system. Besides, they also evaluate the effectiveness of the tools in erasing targeted user and operating system. As in the previous case, the operating system and the applications create files that are obviated by the evaluated software.

To conclude, in [50], the authors highlight the need to consider different types of evidence since most of the works on privacy protection in digital forensics concentrate on e-mails or documents. Moreover, they criticise the incompatibility of the proposed solutions with existing software forensic tools. This is an important issue, given that new solutions are more difficult to be accepted in court without a clear acceptance (and training) by the experts in the field.

8.5.2.3   Third-party privacy breach

A *third party* is usually understood as an entity that is not the main actor (or interested party) in the scene/context/protocol. In the contributions analysed next, a third party is equivalent to the concept of *honest user*. Unfortunately, honest users are very difficult to distinguish from malicious users. The protection of honest users is also a field of study in network forensics (see Section 8.6).

In the area of computer forensics, the problem of protecting honest third parties is defined as a *TPPB* [44]: 'the event that a third party, not culpable in the actions leading to the investigation, may be investigated'. This is possible, for example, when pattern-matching techniques return data about multiple users that must be analysed by the investigator, although they are finally discarded if they are not relevant.

To prevent the aforementioned problem, the same authors [51] propose a solution that forces the investigator to issue focused (i.e. specific) queries in order to get results from the system. The solution consists of various components, one of which is in charge of categorising documents based on their similarity, using *n*-grams and distance measures. Then, a response filter component is responsible for determining whether the result of a query may lead to a privacy violation based on the distance of results (i.e. being very different). In that case, the query is logged and the investigator is suggested to provide a more specific query. This type of solutions do not necessarily assume a dishonest investigator. They prevent this threat but also reduce the risk of an honest investigator violating the privacy of third parties unwittingly. Moreover, they can be useful for reducing the amount of irrelevant data that needs to be processed by the investigation, thus significantly reducing the time to conclude an investigation.

The authors in [52] focus on the problem of discerning honest users from inside attackers. Their goal is to determine the type of data that helps to catch this type of attackers while complying with data-protection laws. They argue that the analysis of data available from physical security systems (e.g. biometrical access control systems) can be crucial to delimit the investigation. Thus, they suggest the data from these systems to be anonymised and only when applying anomaly detection analysis, this data can be partially de-anonymised. This would allow to track down insider attacks without revealing the identity of honest users. The problem is that once the data is partially de-anonymised, it may be possible to identify some particular users.

8.6   Privacy-aware network forensics

This section considers solutions for the protection of privacy in three main domains related to networked systems: servers, networks and browsers. Note that some of the solutions analysed here could fall into some other categories. For example, privacy solutions for server forensics could fall into the category of computer forensics since a server is, in essence, a computer.

8.6.1   Server

A server is a specific-purpose computer optimised to provide a set of services to remote users through the network. Most papers in this area consider web and e-mail servers as case studies. More specifically, web data and e-mails are used to test numerous forensic tools used for pattern recognition (e.g. using keywords). There are two main type of contributions in this area: (i) revocable anonymity and (ii) searchable encryption. In these cases, the digital investigation is focused on server data, as shown in Figure 8.7.

8.6.1.1   Revocable anonymity

Revocable anonymity refers to the process of allowing users to operate or receive services anonymously unless they misbehave, in which case they can be re-identified, typically with the help of a trusted third party.

This is the type of approach followed by PPINA (Protect Private Information, Not Abuser) [53]. The idea is to allow users to connect to the server through an anonymous communication network, but before doing so, they have to generate a public/private key pair and an access token. The access token is cryptographically linked to the public key of the user. Then, the token is sent to a trusted third party (the Forensics Investigation Entity) that verifies the validity of the token and stores it with the identity of the user. The server also receives a copy of this token signed by the trusted third party (TTP). The server verifies the token without knowing the identity of user, who establishes a connection to it through an anonymity network. The server also stores the token and all messages signed with the key corresponding to the token. In case the user misbehaves, the server sends all the messages and the

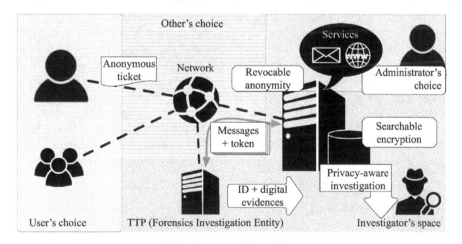

Figure 8.7   PADF server approaches

token to the TTP for it to decide whether an attack occurred or not and if positive reveal the identity of the user.

A similar approach is followed by the ERPINA protocol [54]. This protocol is intended to respect both the desire of the user to remain anonymous while accessing a server and the right of the server to know the actual identity of the user if he misbehaves. The main difference with the previous solution is that, in this case, the anonymous ticket obtained by the user embeds a policy of use. The ticket is sent by the user through an anonymous communication network and has to be validated by the server before granting access to the service. If the server considers the anonymous user is not following the rules defined by the policy of use, it sends the ticket together with the policy to a trusted third party, which, after reviewing the case, decides whether to reveal the identity of the user or not.

8.6.1.2 Searchable encryption

Searchable encryption is a cryptographic technique that allows to issue queries to an encrypted database. This is a promising technique to protect user privacy while conducting digital investigations.

A searchable encryption scheme is used in [55] to allow the forensics investigator to query for data matching some specific keywords in the context of e-mail servers. First, the disk image is analysed and an index file matching keywords to files (or sectors in the disk image) is generated. The index file and the image are encrypted at this point. Then, the forensics investigator generates a list of keywords which are relevant to the investigation and passes the list to the data owner. The data owner can then generate a trapdoor, which is a data structure that allows the investigator to search the encrypted index file for a given keyword or a set thereof. Then the investigator can ask the data owner for that specific location of file in the disk interactively. A notable limitation of this scheme is that the data owner can potentially hide information to the investigator since he/she is in charge of creating the index file, the trapdoor and decrypting the files. Another limitation is that the data owner gains sensitive information about the case from the keywords provided by the investigator to obtain the trapdoor.

The solution proposed in [56] aims to prevent the server administrator from learning what is the investigator looking for. To that end, the investigator generates a public/private key pair and shares the public key with the administrator. Then, the administrator divides the documents into keywords and encrypts them with the public key provided. The investigator encrypts its n keywords with the same public key and transforms them into a polynomial of degree n. After that, the investigator sends the administrator the coefficients of that polynomial to hide the actual encrypted keywords. Finally, the server administrator makes a similar transformation of the files into coefficients, and using the coefficients from the investigator, the administrator can determine which files contained keywords of interest to the investigator. An important point that is not sufficiently discussed in the paper is how can the administrator prevent the investigator from asking for keywords which are irrelevant to the investigation. Also, it seems that if the number of keywords of interest to the investigator is small, the administrator can more easily brute-force the coefficients and obtain the keywords. This is in contradiction with user privacy preservation since the investigator should ask only for the minimum amount of information that allows him or her to close the case.

Finally, in [57], a searchable encryption scheme is provided with the following features: (i) keyword search is non-interactive, meaning that the forensic investigator does not need to contact the data owner every time it wants to issue a query, and (ii) the data owner remains oblivious to the queries (keywords) of interest to the investigator. The data owner determines which are the keywords that can be queried for and establish a threshold of t keywords that need to be present in the file for disclosing it. Very basic keywords, such as pronouns, can be excluded to prevent trivial attacks. The approach is based on Shamir's secret sharing scheme, that is the key for decrypting a file is constructed based on the keywords in that file and t of such keywords reveal the key. The authors acknowledge two main limitations to the scheme. First, the need to have exact keyword matches for searching. Second, there is the possibility that the investigator performs brute-force/dictionary attacks on keywords to reveal the key. In addition to these limitations, there is the problem of a potentially malicious data owner who wants to limit the ability of the investigator retrieving data. This would be as simple as blacklisting some keywords.

8.6.2   Networks

Unlike previous sections, the contributions analysed here concentrate mainly on how to protect data in transit that must be monitored – either by the network equipment or by the investigator – and lately analysed by the investigator.

Interestingly, the first papers in this area were focused on advising practitioners on the best way of performing monitoring actions so as not to have legal repercussions [58], while most of the articles have a wider awareness of privacy. Therefore, there is tendency towards recognising user's rights and the potential impact on the privacy of honest third parties using the same communication channel.

Being the network a shared medium where multiple individuals exchange information, it becomes a great source of evidence and at the same time a great problem for privacy. Figure 8.8 describes the scope of this section. It includes privacy solutions for both the process of traffic capture and traffic analysis.

8.6.2.1   Traffic capture

A solution to network flow recording with partial privacy guarantees is presented in [59]. The authors propose to divide captured network traffic into files containing 5 min of network flows from a single IP. Each of these files are read separately and statistics are extracted from them and imported into a database. After this, each file is encrypted with a random Advanced Encryption Standard (AES) key, and all these keys are identity-based encryption (IBE)-encrypted with the IP-timestamp as public key encryption. Plain text files are deleted from the system. The result is short encrypted files (5 min of activity) so that when law enforcement requires data, they can be provided with all files pertaining to a specific period rather than all the data. Moreover, the authors propose to use a secret sharing approach to divide the IBE key

Figure 8.8   Privacy-aware network forensic approaches

used for decryption of the files into several shares so that files can only be decrypted if all key holders agree to do so.

The authors in [59] also take care when populating the statistical database to prevent sensitive information from being revealed when querying it. This is enforced by replying to queries only when the result satisfies some privacy conditions. For example, requiring a minimum number of bytes being transmitted to prevent website fingerprinting (i.e. recognising the website being accessed by a user based on the bytes transferred).

Tools are an important part in traffic capture. In this respect, Carnivore was a packet sniffer that allowed the use of filters to capture traffic only from a particular individual, instead of collecting all network traffic. This was a tool after which there was controversy because it was secretly used by the FBI from 1999 to 2005. Carnivore was made public in 2000 and several failures were discovered. This caused it to be replaced by commercial products. This tool allowed restricting the capture of traffic, so it was considered that when properly used could help to protect honest users' privacy [31]. Nowadays, most traffic capture tools enable the use of filters.

8.6.2.2 Traffic analysis

The first approach we are going to discuss here is based in searchable encryption, which has also been used in other contexts (cf. Section 8.6.1.2). In this case, the authors propose a scheme [60] based on bilinear pairings that is intended to allow the investigator to collect evidences from network traffic under the assumption that an attack have been perpetrated. The idea is to analyse the traffic without revealing the identity of the potential attacker until there is sufficient evidence. The paper focuses on evaluating the efficiency of searchable encryption scheme, and it is not clear how it can be applied to a real digital forensic investigation.

A network-layer capability named 'privacy-preserving forensic attribution' is proposed in [61] to protect the privacy of users while ensuring data traceability. Using a packet-level cryptographic signature mechanism, a packet is self-identifying and linked to the physical machine that sent it. Privacy is considered as a requirement to avoid non-authorised entities from examining the packets. Another requirement is that packet signatures must be non-identifying; two packets sent by the same source must carry different signatures. The solution uses a hardware chip that is considered a trusted third party if a single third party is required but considers a secret sharing approach otherwise.

8.6.3   Browser and applications

The actions a user performs on the Internet leave a data trace in the user's device, which can be analysed in the context of Internet Forensics (cf. Section 8.2). In particular, the trail left by the user when using a web browser has been analysed in various articles [62–64]. Also, as applications become more Internet-dependant to operate, new challenges arise.

Applications (the browsers among them) have changed the communication habits of the user in the network. They introduce new ways of interacting with other users. The volume of data stored in user devices increases as the applications become more dependent on users' data. Data is usually privacy sensitive as it is related to user relationships and may include locations, photos, chats or other types of data. Also, the way the user interacts with the application may reveal sensitive information, including the identity, mood, etcetera. This led to the emergence of the term BRAP (Browser and Application) forensics [65].

Due to the fact that BRAP-related problems are usually analysed as part of computer forensics, the contribution in the area of BRAP forensics is rather limited or dispersed among different areas, especially in the context of mobile forensics [66]. Figure 8.9 shows the focus of BRAP forensics and its relationship with other forensic disciplines.

Most of the approaches that consider privacy in BRAP forensics are closely related to data storage. For example, [67] presents a solution to identify the keywords that enable the inference of topics which are relevant to the investigation. After performing some data mining experiments on web data and e-mails, the forensic investigators could unintentionally extract sensitive data if their tools fail to associate the keywords to the topics of interest. This problem grows with the amount of data to be processed and will be exacerbated when the data is shared among different organisations.

The challenges of BRAP forensics are detailed in [65], where privacy issues are highlighted. The reason for this is that the concept of BRAP forensics is beyond the

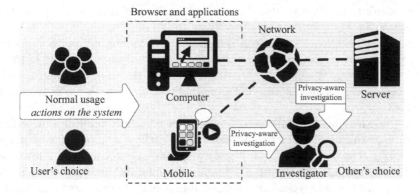

Figure 8.9 BRAP approaches

analysis of logs. The purpose of novel applications is to learn as much information about the user as possible to be much more functional and adapt to user needs. How and where this data is stored depend on each software developer. BRAP forensics will be affected by this and will differ from application to application.

Intuitively, the widespread use of the novel applications raises numerous privacy issues. Therefore, it is worth trying to achieve the same functionality without storing too much personal information. Also, as stated in [65], it is more effective to protect privacy by not storing data than by encrypting them. However, even without storing data, our information can be deduced based on our relationships with other individuals (e.g. appearing with a friend in a picture). Doubtlessly, this is a challenging problem.

Unfortunately, there are currently no comprehensive privacy-respecting forensic solutions for BRAP, beyond the generic frameworks that are not directly applicable to specific applications.

8.7 Beyond computer and network forensics

This section describes the contributions in areas other than computer and network forensics. Unlike previous sections, the following analysis shows an evolution from the traditional concept of computer forensics. Starting with mobile forensics, which required the development of specialised tools, the same happened with the Cloud or the IoT.

Basically, these are new contexts that are being analysed by the scientific community and for which specific privacy challenges are envisioned.

8.7.1 Mobile

Mobile forensics is probably the most mature discipline considered in this section. Intrusions to privacy started to receive attention in this context since mobile phones became an integral part of our lives. However, this area considers also other types of mobile personal devices. Indeed, personal devices have motivated various papers in this field and have also strengthened other areas, such as BRAP forensics (cf. Section 8.6.3).

A common approach in this area is to display a banner to inform the user about privacy expectations and garnet their consent. This is a solution followed in Droid-Watch [68] and digital witness [69] for mobile phones. However, this approach does not protect privacy, it only informs the user about potential privacy problems in some situations.

In [66], the authors analyse existing solutions and methodologies to perform privacy assessments of mobile applications based on how data is stored by mobile applications. The authors follow a forensic methodology to check the information stored by the applications on Android devices. They use the Android Device Bridge for data acquisition and typical unix command-line tools (sqlite3, hexdump, tree and strings) for data analysis.

The authors in [70] also analyse Android devices, but in this case, they focus on the possibility of recovering authentication credentials from volatile memory. One of the observations made by the authors is that password managers can be compromised if the attacker has physical access to the device. Although this problem is independent of the user, in some cases, privacy problems are due to the user behaviour. This is precisely the goal of the research conducted in [71], to show how user decisions affect his/her own privacy in the context of a mobile platform. In this case, the authors use the mobile forensic tools to help users understand how their behaviour affect their privacy.

Finally, it is worth noting that the area of mobile computing is closely related the Cloud and the IoT. Mobile devices generate huge amounts of data, and due to memory limitations, it has to be outsourced to the Cloud. Moreover, mobile devices can serve as gateways or user interfaces to IoT devices and the data produced by them can be also relayed to the Cloud. In addition, the Cloud is used as intermediary in the communication among different devices.

8.7.2   Cloud

To the best of our knowledge, there are not many papers on the topic of privacy-aware cloud forensics. At the time of writing, there are basically two solutions both of which provide cryptographic techniques to limit access to data and resources in the Cloud.

A scheme based on secret sharing and message authentication codes is proposed in [72] to provide a robust logging of Cloud events for forensic investigations. According to the authors, in Cloud environments, there is one (or more) logging servers that collect logs from all attached servers. The data to be written to the log file is accompanied by a message authentication code creating a chain to prevent an attacker from deleting events without being detected. To further complicate the task of the attacker, each event of the log is divided into n shares and distributed into random computers of the Cloud. Finally, they also propose to record these events in an immutable database, meaning a database that not even the system administrator can modify. Thus, making it easier for the investigator retrieve evidence.

The paper [73] aims to provide a cloud-forensic solution that minimises the number of virtual machines to be investigated. The proposed method is based on a set of inputs which define the historical activity data for the virtual machine (e.g. network logs, CPU usage) and an array of characteristics of the investigation. The virtual machines that do not match the previous requirements are removed from the search space of the investigation. The data is protected using anti-forensic techniques (both memory and storage are encrypted), but if a security breach occurs, it is still feasible to conduct an investigation using statistical techniques.

Finally, [74] describes some basic security and privacy problems in edge and fog computing. The authors argue that new laws on data protection, and in particular the European GDPR, may require service providers to delete data they collected and are no longer necessary. However, how to secure erase data and the challenges associated to do so in a highly distributed environment like the one envisioned by edge and fog computing is not described in the paper.

8.7.3 Internet of Things

Although IoT-forensics is becoming a promising area of research (cf. Section 8.2), there are very few contributions that consider privacy in this context.

One of the most recent contributions in privacy-aware IoT-forensics (PRoFITs) is [15]. This paper is based on a previous contribution by the same authors, in which the PRoFIT model is proposed [75]. In addition, the authors define a methodology to integrate privacy properties in accordance with ISO/IEC 29100:2011 throughout the phases of a digital forensic model adapted to the IoT. Unlike previous approaches, the methodology encourages users to collaborate as witnesses in a digital investigation by sharing their digital evidence. The methodology allows the users to collaborate voluntarily with full control on the data they provide to the investigator.

Similarly, the concept of anonymous digital witnessing in IoT environments is defined in [76]. This type of solution is interesting to promote the cooperative approaches in the context of a digital investigation in the IoT. However, the entire process should be part of a reference model or framework in order to ensure consistency, facilitate the traceability of evidence, documentation and identify possible mistakes. These are some of the reasons why PRoFIT is used in [15] to adapt an already defined IoT-forensic solution, the digital witness, to be respectful with privacy. In this article, two case studies were provided to help understand the convergence between privacy and digital forensics in new, challenging scenarios.

In the first scenario, the user in possession of a PRoFIT-compliant digital witness (named Bob) initiates a digital investigation using his device during a dinner in a smart restaurant equipped with IoT devices owned by the restaurant (e.g. smart oven, smart windows) and by clients (e.g. smart watch). Both personal and non-personal IoT devices coexist in the restaurant. To conduct the digital investigation, Bob's device must inform Bob about the digital forensics procedures that will be necessary to acquire its own digital evidences from the environment. Also, Bob's device must ask for collaboration to the rest of IoT devices in the restaurant that are handled by a responsible (the Maître), who must agree with the requests. Furthermore, the Maître will have the right to know the status of the data that has been provided to the digital investigator and can request these rights to be withdrawn at any time. In this case of study, it is possible to determine the source of malicious software that could have affected more clients in the restaurant. The person in charge of the restaurant, the Maître, collaborates in the investigation, and this allows to identify the origin of the problem and also prevents future incidents. In the second scenario, the user who initiates a digital investigation is a police officer (called Max). Max has to search a warehouse where there are several IoT devices (e.g. cameras and temperature sensors). In this case, Max's device contains a search warrant and is able to conduct the digital investigation without asking for the voluntary cooperation of other personal IoT devices. This resembles current proceedings, when there is a reasonable ground to suppose that a charge of criminal conduct is well founded, and thus the approach does not consider privacy preferences or policies. As a matter of fact, it is important to understand the context in which the digital investigation is conducted and the actors involved in it. Otherwise, it will be very difficult to promote solutions flexible enough to be adopted by the different experts.

In addition, there are other solutions that could be considered within the context of PRoFITs. For example, Themis is an architecture aimed to acquire data from sensors in smartphones taking into account privacy requirements [77]. The solution is focused on the platform – the mobile phone – from which the data will be collected. The user is notified about the collection of digital evidence, but this does not protect the privacy of the possible third-party data contained in the device.

In general, current IoT-forensics solutions do not consider third-party privacy notifications because most of the solutions are not cooperative. This is not necessarily wrong, it just means that they were designed for another purpose. For example, the authors in [78] argue that privacy in the Home IoT context 'may not necessarily equate to expectations of privacy in social networks'. However, the cooperation of individuals and their personal devices may be increasingly necessary in digital investigations. This can be pretty similar to a social network in the sense that many individuals can be involved in the same digital investigation.

Finally, smart vehicles can also be considered part of the IoT (cf. Section 8.2). In this area, [12] provides a high-level description of the implementation of a mobile app aimed to give the driver control on the parameters collected by the car's event data recorder. Basically, the app is allowed to connect to the car's internal network (after authentication) and collect event data as a backup mechanism. Consequently, the user has more control on the data collected by the car and its status. The data collected by the app can also be backed up in the Cloud. During a case, the forensics investigator has the option to retrieve the data either from the user, the car or the cloud. Thus, the investigator can check the consistency of the data and the user can at least know which data is being accessed by the investigator.

8.8   Conclusions and final remarks

Digital forensics is an evolutionary discipline but with solid legal and ethical principles. As part of this evolution, privacy has taken an increasingly relevant role. Initially, privacy mechanisms (e.g. encryption, secure erasure) were considered anti-forensic. Over the last few years, the new digital forensics topics (e.g., IoT-Forensics) tend

Table 8.3   Level of accomplishment of privacy-aware digital forensics

Context	Privacy-aware digital forensics solutions					
	Privacy levels, policies and filters	Frameworks, models	Revocable anonymity	Searchable encryption	Secret sharing	User consent
Database	*A*	*NI*	*NI*	*NI*	*N*	*P*
Computer	*A*	*A*	*PA*	*NI*	*N*	*P*
Server	*NI*	*NI*	*NI*	*A*	*N*	*NI*
Networks	*PA*	*A*	*N*	*A*	*A*	*N*
Applications	*N*	*B*	*N*	*NI*	*N*	*A*
Mobile	*N*	*N*	*N*	*N*	*N*	*A*
Cloud	*PA*	*N*	*NI*	*NI*	*A*	*PA*
IoT	*PA*	*A*	*N*	*N*	*N*	*PA*

A, addressed; *P*, partially addressed; *B*, barely addressed; *N* not addressed; *NI*, not addressed but can be learned based on the experience of another context.

to consider the need for a symbiosis between both domains, probably because the contexts are increasingly user centric.

Table 8.3 summarises the results of the analysis made in this chapter. The synthesis of contributions in the area of digital forensics and privacy trade-offs shows that, although privacy solutions have been devised for almost all the topics shown in Figure 8.3, it is not broadly considered in digital forensic scenarios. For example, it is common to examine privacy as a legal requirement and make use of access control solutions, sometimes using cryptographic techniques, to protect access to data. Note that techniques such as revocable anonymity or searchable encryption are used in unrestricted environments, but IoT-based approaches are not considering (yet) these solutions. This is in part due to the hardware limitation of current IoT devices but also because the challenges considered by PRoFIT [15] are different. It mostly focuses on the deployment of cooperative approaches in common frameworks and methodologies.

It is also possible to check in Table 8.3 which solutions or techniques can be reused or adapted to other digital forensic areas (e.g. it can be understood that solutions for computer forensics can be adapted to servers). This adaptation is not always possible or necessary, though. Intuitively, this is either because of the lack of resources or because the new environments have other requirements. Besides, it is possible that open challenges will require very specific solutions for that area. For example, typical privacy user consents will not be directly applicable to Cloud computing because there are additional issues regarding the jurisdictions that must be considered (cf. Section 8.2.3).

Furthermore, note that, in the current ecosystem, not only personal devices but also intermediary platforms, such as the Cloud, have become core elements of forensic investigations. Not all user data is kept in a single location, instead they are stored on third party platforms and shared with other users around the globe. This dispersion of data also leads to possible problems because a common legal framework is lacking for all countries. For example, Europe has the GPDR but the United States has its own laws. Therefore, PADF mechanisms for Europe will be presumably different from those developed in USA.

Doubtlessly, information systems will continue to store increasing amounts of information about users. Nevertheless, we should not fall into the mistake of simplifying PADFs issues to something that governments, organisations or users must resolve by themselves. This is a convoluted problem that can only be addressed if all actors have a common understanding of the problem and they are willing to pay the price of the change.

References

[1]   Garfinkel SL. Digital forensics research: The next 10 years. Digital Investigation. 2010;7:S64–S73. The Proceedings of the Tenth Annual DFRWS Conference. Available from: http://www.sciencedirect.com/science/article/pii/S1742287610000368.

[2]   Caviglione L, Wendzel S, and Mazurczyk W. The future of digital forensics: Challenges and the road ahead. IEEE Security & Privacy. 2017;15(6):12–17. Available from: doi.ieeecomputersociety.org/10.1109/MSP.2017.4251117.

[3]   van Staden WJ. An investigation into reducing third party privacy breaches during the investigation of cybercrime. In: 2014 Information Security for South Africa; 2014. p. 1–6.

[4]   Internet Crime Complaint Center. IC3 2017 Internet crime report; 2018. Available from: https://pdf.ic3.gov/2017_IC3Report.pdf.

[5]   Chon KHS. Cybercrime precursors: Towards a model of offender resources; PhD Thesis, The Australian National University; 2016.

[6]   Thing VL, Ng KY, and Chang EC. Live memory forensics of mobile phones. Digital Investigation. 2010;7:S74–S82.

[7]   Willassen S. Forensic analysis of mobile phone internal memory. In: IFIP International Conference on Digital Forensics. Springer; 2005. p. 191–204.

[8]   Meghanathan N, Allam SR, and Moore LA. Tools and techniques for network forensics. International Journal of Network Security Its Applications (IJNSA). 2009;1(1):14–25.

[9]   Oriwoh E, Jazani D, Epiphaniou G, *et al.* Internet of things forensics: Challenges and approaches. In: Collaborative Computing: Networking, Applications and Worksharing (CollaborateCom), 2013 9th International Conference on. IEEE; 2013. p. 608–615.

[10] Horsman G. Unmanned aerial vehicles: A preliminary analysis of forensic challenges. Digital Investigation. 2016;16:1–11.

[11] Huang C, Lu R, and Choo KR. Vehicular fog computing: Architecture, use case, and security and forensic challenges. IEEE Communications Magazine. 2017;55(11):105–111.

[12] Mansor H, Markantonakis K, Akram RN, *et al.* Log your car: The non-invasive vehicle forensics. In: Trustcom/BigDataSE/ISPA, 2016 IEEE. IEEE; 2016. p. 974–982.

[13]   de Fuentes JM, González-Manzano L, Gonzalez-Tablas AI, *et al.* WEVAN– A mechanism for evidence creation and verification in VANETs. Journal of Systems Architecture. 2013;59(10):985–995.

[14]   Rogers MK, Goldman J, Mislan R, *et al.* Computer forensics field triage process model. Journal of Digital Forensics, Security and Law. 2006;1(2):2.

[15]   Nieto A, Rios R, and Lopez J. IoT-forensics meets privacy: Towards cooperative digital investigations. Sensors. 2018;18(2):492.

[16]   Conlan K, Baggili I, and Breitinger F. Anti-forensics: Furthering digital forensic science through a new extended, granular taxonomy. Digital Investigation. 2016;18:S66–S75.

[17]   Warren SD, and Brandeis LD. The right to privacy. Harward Law Review. 1890;4(5):193–220.

[18]   Westin AF. Privacy and Freedom. New York: Atheneum; 1967.

[19]   Holvast J. 27 – History of Privacy. In: Leeuw KD, Bergstra J, editors. The History of Information Security. Amsterdam: Elsevier Science B.V.; 2007. p. 737–769. Available from: http://www.sciencedirect.com/science/article/pii/ B9780444516084500286.

[20]   Gubbi J, Buyya R, Marusic S, *et al.* Internet of Things (IoT): A vision, architectural elements, and future directions. Future Generation Computer Systems. 2013;29(7):1645–1660. Available from: http://www.sciencedirect.com/ science/article/pii/S0167739X13000241.

[21]   Solove DJ. Understanding Privacy. Cambridge, MA: Harvard University Press; 2008.

[22]   The Universal Declaration of Human Rights; 1948. Available from: https://www.ohchr.org/EN/UDHR.

[23]   European Convention on Human Rights; 1950. Available from: https://www.echr.coe.int/Documents/Convention_ENG.pdf.

[24]   Solove DJ, and Schwartz PM. Privacy Law Fundamentals 2017. International Association of Privacy Professionals; 2017.

[25]   Nance K, and Ryan DJ. Legal aspects of digital forensics: a research agenda. In: System Sciences (HICSS), 2011 44th Hawaii International Conference on. IEEE; 2011. p. 1–6.

[26]   Huang J, Ling Z, Xiang T, *et al.* When digital forensic research meets laws. In: Distributed Computing Systems Workshops (ICDCSW), 2012 32nd International Conference on. IEEE; 2012. p. 542–551.

[27]   The European Parliament and the Council of the European Union. DIRECTIVE 95/46/EC on the protection of individuals with regard to the processing of personal data and on the free movement of such data; 1995. Available from: http://data.europa.eu/eli/dir/1995/46/oj.

[28]   The European Parliament and the Council of the European Union. REGULATION (EU) 2016/679 on the protection of natural persons with regard to the processing of personal data and on the free movement of such data, and repealing Directive 95/46/EC (General Data Protection Regulation); 2016. Available from: http://data.europa.eu/eli/reg/2016/679/oj.

[29]   The US Department of Justice. Privacy Act of 1974; 1974. Available from: https://www.gpo.gov/fdsys/pkg/STATUTE-88/pdf/STATUTE-88-Pg1896.pdf.

[30] Organisation for Economic Co-Operation and Development (OECD). The OECD privacy framework; 2013. http://www.oecd.org/sti/ieconomy/oecd_privacy_framework.pdf.

[31] Adams CW. Legal issues pertaining to the development of digital forensic tools. In: Systematic Approaches to Digital Forensic Engineering, 2008. SADFE'08. Third International Workshop on. IEEE; 2008. p. 123–132.

[32] Dehghantanha A, and Franke K. Privacy-respecting digital investigation. In: Privacy, Security and Trust (PST), 2014 Twelfth Annual International Conference on. IEEE; 2014. p. 129–138.

[33] Ryz L, and Grest L. A new era in data protection. Computer Fraud & Security. 2016;2016(3):18–20.

[34] Losavio MM, Chow K, Koltay A, and James J. The Internet of Things and the Smart City: Legal challenges with digital forensics, privacy, and security. Security and Privacy. 2018;e23:1–11.

[35] Ghafarian A, and Seno SAH. Analysis of privacy of private browsing mode through memory forensics. International Journal of Computer Applications. 2015;132(16):27–34.

[36] Aljaedi A, Lindskog D, Zavarsky P, *et al.* Comparative analysis of volatile memory forensics: live response vs. memory imaging. In: Privacy, Security, Risk and Trust (PASSAT) and 2011 IEEE Third International Conference on Social Computing (SocialCom), 2011 IEEE Third International Conference on. IEEE; 2011. p. 1253–1258.

[37] Bohannon P, Jakobsson M, and Srikwan S. Cryptographic approaches to privacy in forensic DNA databases. In: International Workshop on Public Key Cryptography. Springer; 2000. p. 373–390.

[38] Croft NJ, and Olivier MS. Sequenced release of privacy-accurate information in a forensic investigation. Digital Investigation. 2010;7(1–2):95–101.

[39] Halboob W, Mahmod R, Udzir NI, *et al.* Privacy levels for computer forensics: Toward a more efficient privacy-preserving investigation. Procedia Computer Science. 2015;56:370–375.

[40] Stahlberg P, Miklau G, and Levine BN. Threats to privacy in the forensic analysis of database systems. In: Proceedings of the 2007 ACM SIGMOD International Conference on Management of Data. ACM; 2007. p. 91–102.

[41] Verma R, Govindaraj J, and Gupta G. Data Privacy Perceptions About Digital Forensic Investigations in India. In: Peterson G, Shenoi S, editors. Advances in Digital Forensics XII. Cham: Springer International Publishing; 2016. p. 25–45.

[42] Aminnezhad A, and Dehghantanha A. A survey on privacy issues in digital forensics. International Journal of Cyber-Security and Digital Forensics (IJCSDF). 2014;3(4):183–199. Available from: http://usir.salford.ac.uk/34016/.

[43] Ledbetter EM. Facing the Challenge: Protecting Data Privacy During Forensic Investigations. Master Thesis, Utica College; 2017.

[44] Van Staden W. Third Party Privacy and the Investigation of Cybercrime. Orlando, FL, USA: Springer; 2013.

[45] Reddy K, and Venter H. A forensic framework for handling information privacy incidents. In: IFIP International Conference on Digital Forensics. Springer; 2009. p. 143–155.

[46] Gupta A. Privacy preserving efficient digital forensic investigation framework. In: 2013 Sixth International Conference on Contemporary Computing (IC3); 2013. p. 387–392.

[47] Halboob W, Mahmod R, Udzir NI, *et al.* Privacy policies for computer forensics. Computer Fraud & Security. 2015;2015(8):9–13. Available from: http://www.sciencedirect.com/science/article/pii/S1361372315300750.

[48] Geiger M, and Cranor LF. Scrubbing stubborn data: An evaluation of counter-forensic privacy tools. IEEE Security & Privacy. 2006;4(5):16–25.

[49] Hou S, Uehara T, Yiu SM, *et al.* Privacy preserving confidential forensic investigation for shared or remote servers. In: 2011 Seventh International Conference on Intelligent Information Hiding and Multimedia Signal Processing; 2011. p. 378–383.

[50] Afifah K, and Perdana RS. Development of search on encrypted data tools for privacy preserving in digital forensic. In: 2016 International Conference on Data and Software Engineering (ICoDSE); 2016. p. 1–6.

[51] van Staden W. Protecting Third Party Privacy in Digital Forensic Investigations. In: Peterson G, Shenoi S, editors. Advances in Digital Forensics IX. Berlin, Heidelberg: Springer Berlin Heidelberg; 2013. p. 19–31.

[52] Zimmer E, Lindemann J, Herrmann D, *et al.* Catching inside attackers: Balancing forensic detectability and privacy of employees. In: International Workshop on Open Problems in Network Security. Springer; 2015. p. 43–55.

[53] Antoniou G, Wilson C, and Geneiatakis D. PPINA – A forensic investigation protocol for privacy enhancing technologies. In: IFIP International Conference on Communications and Multimedia Security. Springer; 2006. p. 185–195.

[54] Antoniou G, Sterling L, Gritzalis S, *et al.* Privacy and forensics investigation process: The ERPINA protocol. Computer Standards & Interfaces. 2008;30(4):229–236.

[55] Law FY, Chan PP, Yiu SM, *et al.* Protecting digital data privacy in computer forensic examination. In: Systematic Approaches to Digital Forensic Engineering (SADFE), 2011 IEEE Sixth International Workshop on. IEEE; 2011. p. 1–6.

[56] Hou S, Uehara T, Yiu S, *et al.* Privacy preserving multiple keyword search for confidential investigation of remote forensics. In: Multimedia Information Networking and Security (MINES), 2011 Third International Conference on. IEEE; 2011. p. 595–599.

[57] Armknecht F, and Dewald A. Privacy-preserving email forensics. Digital Investigation. 2015;14:S127–S136.

[58] Yasinsac A, and Manzano Y. Policies to Enhance Computer and Network Forensics; In: Proceedings of the 2001 IEEE Workshop on Information Assurance and Security; 2001. p. 289–295.

[59] Shebaro B, and Crandall JR. Privacy-preserving network flow recording. Digital Investigation. 2011;8:S90–S100.

[60] Lin X, Lu R, Foxton K, *et al.* An efficient searchable encryption scheme and its application in network forensics. In: International Conference on Forensics in Telecommunications, Information, and Multimedia. Springer; 2010. p. 66–78.

[61] Afanasyev M, Kohno T, Ma J, *et al.* Privacy-preserving network forensics. Communications of the ACM. 2011;54(5):78–87.

[62] Marrington A, Baggili I, Al Ismail T, *et al.* Portable web browser forensics: A forensic examination of the privacy benefits of portable web browsers. In: Computer Systems and Industrial Informatics (ICCSII), 2012 International Conference on. IEEE; 2012. p. 1–6.

[63] Satvat K, Forshaw M, Hao F, *et al.* On the privacy of private browsing – A forensic approach. In: Data Privacy Management and Autonomous Spontaneous Security. Springer; 2014. p. 380–389.

[64] Dharan DG, and Nagoor Meeran AR. Forensic evidence collection by reconstruction of artifacts in portable web browser. International Journal of Computer Applications. 2014;91(4):32–35.

[65] Berghel H. BRAP forensics. Communications of the ACM. 2008;51(6):15–20.

[66] Stirparo P, and Kounelis I. The mobileak project: Forensics methodology for mobile application privacy assessment. In: Internet Technology And Secured Transactions, 2012 International Conference for. IEEE; 2012. p. 297–303.

[67] Chow R, Golle P, and Staddon J. Detecting privacy leaks using corpus-based association rules. In: Proceedings of the 14th ACM SIGKDD International Conference on Knowledge Discovery and Data Mining. ACM; 2008. p. 893–901.

[68] Grover J. Android forensics: Automated data collection and reporting from a mobile device. Digital Investigation. 2013;10:S12–S20.

[69] Nieto A, Roman R, Lopez J. Digital witness: Safeguarding digital evidence by using secure architectures in personal devices. IEEE Network. 2016;30(6): 34–41.

[70] Ntantogian C, Apostolopoulos D, Marinakis G, *et al.* Evaluating the privacy of Android mobile applications under forensic analysis. Computers & Security. 2014;42:66–76.

[71] Keng JCJ, Wee TK, Jiang L, *et al.* The case for mobile forensics of private data leaks: Towards large-scale user-oriented privacy protection. In: Proceedings of the 4th Asia-Pacific Workshop on Systems. APSys '13. New York, NY, USA: ACM; 2013. p. 6:1–6:7. Available from: http://doi.acm.org/10.1145/2500727. 2500733.

[72] Weir G, Aßmuth A, Whittington M, *et al.* Cloud accounting systems, the audit trail, forensics and the EU GDPR: how hard can it be?. In: British Accounting & Finance Association (BAFA) Annual Conference 2017; 2017.

[73] Odebade A, Welsh T, Mthunzi S, *et al.* Mitigating anti-forensics in the Cloud via resource-based privacy preserving activity attribution. In: Software Defined Systems (SDS), 2017 Fourth International Conference on. IEEE; 2017. p. 143–149.

[74] Esposito C, Castiglione A, Pop F, *et al.* Challenges of connecting edge and cloud computing: a security and forensic perspective. IEEE Cloud Computing. 2017;(2):13–17.

[75] Nieto A, Rios R, and Lopez J. A methodology for privacy-aware IoT-forensics. In: Proceedings of the 2017 IEEE Conference on Trustcom/BigDataSE/ICESS, Sydney, NSW, Australia; 2017. p. 1–4.

[76] Nieto A, Rios R, and Lopez J. Digital witness and privacy in IoT: Anonymous witnessing approach. In: Proceedings of the 2017 IEEE Conference on Trustcom/BigDataSE/ICESS, Sydney, NSW, Australia; 2017. p. 1–4.

[77] Mylonas A, Meletiadis V, Mitrou L, *et al.* Smartphone sensor data as digital evidence. Computers & Security. 2013;38:51–75.

[78] Oriwoh E, and Sant P. The forensics edge management system: A concept and design. In: Ubiquitous Intelligence and Computing, 2013 IEEE 10th International Conference on and 10th International Conference on Autonomic and Trusted Computing (UIC/ATC). IEEE; 2013. p. 544–550.

Chapter 9

A survey of trust, trustworthiness and trustworthy computing: concepts, models and challenges

Fatos Xhafa[1]

With the fast development of large-scale Internet-based systems and their penetration into every human life activity, trust, trustworthiness and trustworthy computing have become cross-cutting features of all such systems being business, e-commerce, social networking, collaborative systems, etc. Indeed, users' activity in Internet-based systems each time raises more concerns of trust while interacting through and with such systems. The expectations of users, clients, costumers as well as of the communication and collaboration at large scale are based on the premise of trust as a cornerstone of secure, reliable, privacy preserving and integrity of Internet-based systems. While trust and security go hand-by-hand, trust however is very much related to users' experiences and perceptions on system's performance, reliability and privacy. Unfortunately, many recent cases from development of large-scale systems, especially from social networking and from big corporates, have shown important breaches and vulnerabilities causing a devastating effect on users' trust.

In this chapter, we survey most relevant concepts and models for trust, trustworthiness and trustworthy computing and discuss their various forms in business, e-commerce, social networking, etc. We identify main factors that determine trust, trustworthiness and trustworthy computing as well as major research challenges in the field. We also briefly discuss how Blockchain is shaping trust in new Internet-based systems. Current efforts by research community to address them are discussed and new research directions envisaged.

9.1 Introduction

In the Trustwave Global Security Report* for the last 10 years, an increasing number of threats, vulnerabilities and breaches in information security and cybersecurity were pointed out worldwide. It is reported that such threats have fast evolved from

[1]Departament de Ciències de la Computació, Universitat Politècnica de Catalunya, Barcelona, Spain
*2018 Trustwave Global Security Report: https://www2.trustwave.com/GlobalSecurityReport.html.

opportunistic ones aiming at stealing money, card data, login credentials, etc. to very sophisticated threats exercised by skilled professionals and criminal groups. Moreover, security attacks have been becoming more targeted each time not only for classical threats to web applications, emails and servers but also for all sorts of network devices and IoT devices particularly. By analysing various large data sources, it was observed that the trend is that security incidents and vulnerabilities have been increasing significantly.

In addition, it should be noted that due to the increase of population in the digital world and the increase in digitalisation and expansion of knowledge society, the exposure to threats, vulnerabilities and breaches will keep the pace making, thus the information security more challenging. Obviously, due to security incidents and vulnerabilities, the trust of users in Internet-based systems is being eroded, therefore online user's activity being discouraged and reticent. It is in this, landscape where trust, trustworthiness and trustworthy computing play a vital role in cybersecurity arena.

Many research studies as well as numerous experiences show that security threats, vulnerabilities and breaches cannot be solved with technology solutions alone. To date, even most advanced security technological solutions, such as Public Key Infrastructures, have limitations and vulnerabilities that impede the development of complete and overall technological security frameworks. In such a context, it can be said that solutions to cybersecurity are not only technological but also human, as security is primarily a human problem, and as such it can and should be mitigated by a proactive and collaborative human behaviour.

In order to design strategies for humans to contribute to cybersecurity solutions, it is important first to understand trust, trustworthiness and trustworthy computing. These concepts are commonly used in different contexts of everyday life such as business, economics, law and relationship. Common to all these contexts is that trust, trustworthiness and trustworthy assume a belief or certainty on the reliability of some entity being it a person, a machine, a product, a company, a digital platform, a relationship, etc. Beyond their traditional use, these concepts are finding new forms as well as new contexts in the Internet era and are therefore becoming crucial to the Internet applications.

Besides reliability requirement on the trusted entity or relationship, now these concepts comprise requirements on security, privacy and integrity, among others. New forms of trust, trustworthy and trustworthiness have emerged such as 'trust on an online user', 'trust on an Internet connected machine', 'trust on computation', 'trust on a virtual platform', 'trust on a virtual organisation' and 'trust on Internet technology'. Because trust is established based on a relationship among two or more parties, being one of the parties a person, say, an online user, or an entity more generally, we could define the concepts of *active trust* and *passive trust*. The former captures the case when the user as one of the parties involved in the trust actively participates in an activity and therefore trust here is needful to accomplish a task or an objective. For instance, a user wants to make a bank transaction or an online purchase and should therefore trust on the online platform of the bank or the e-commerce platform to complete her/his transaction. On the other hand, a user reading daily news in an online site may trust or not the published news; in this case, as a reader she or he passively uses trust by considering the news worth of trust or not. However, the user can switch to 'active trust' if he is actively engaged in propagating the news either as a trusted news or as a fake news. It is therefore in the user's activity where trust is found and built!

Trust, trustworthiness and trustworthy computing are crucial to Internet applications as they ensure smoothly running daily activity of persons, institutions, organisations, businesses, collaboration, e-learning, etc. In addition, trust has become critical to Internet-based applications due to data generation behind online users' activity. Therefore, trust has become many-fold while (1) interacting with a system, (2) interacting with other users in a system, (3) leaving personal and activity data in a system and (4) trusting data custody in data outsourcing to a system.

It can be said that trust is a disruptive paradigm. Indeed, let us assume that entities A and B operate based on a trusted relationship. For instance, A is a customer and B is an e-commerce platform. If B's properties that define its trust change, then the A's trust on B changes as well and A could interrupt operating with B. Likewise, if A's properties change, then B could stop serving to A. In either case, trust becomes a factor of disruption. In addition, its disruptive nature is fuelled by an array of disruptive underlying technologies (e.g. IoT technologies) through which trust is built!

In this chapter, we analyse basics concepts and models for trust, trustworthiness and trustworthy computing. We aim to identify the main factors that influence trust, trustworthiness and trustworthy computing as well as the challenges to be addressed by researchers and developers in the field. We refer to some key applications and use cases from trust, trustworthiness and trustworthy computing and exemplify the exposition by real life cases such as that of P2P trustworthiness in Virtual Campuses in online learning and collaboration teams.

The rest of the chapter is organised as follows. In Section 9.2, we briefly refer to some basic concepts on trust, trustworthiness and trustworthy computing. Issues about evaluation and prediction on trust, trustworthiness and trustworthy computing are discussed in Section 9.3. In Section 9.4, we overview some recent research work on blockchain and trust. The chapter ends in Section 9.5 with some conclusions and outlook for future research on trust, trustworthiness and trustworthy computing.

9.2 Basic concepts and models for trust, trustworthiness and trustworthy computing

In a general setting, trust can be defined as belief or certainty on the reliability of some entity. The entity is then deemed as trustworthy. When such entity is a computing system, we speak of trustworthy computing. Trustworthiness is defined as the quality of an entity being worth of trust. These definitions can be used and adopted to any context; however, depending on the concrete context, specifics of these definitions can be identified. It can therefore be said that trust is context-aware, contextual or situational.

Let us consider now some concrete contexts and identify specifics of trust, trustworthy and trustworthiness. Of course, our aim is to focus on Internet-based application contexts.

Trust on an online entity (organisation, institution, media, e-commerce, business, etc.): Interacting with an entity through an online platform is subject to trust and users tend to be interested on the trusted value of the platform *a priori* and during the interaction. The trust value or score to the platform on which to judge is 'computed' in various ways, from personal experiences and perceptions or collaboratively from others' experiences and perceptions. In this case, trust can be defined as *uni-directional trust*, namely entity A operates with B according to a trust score.

Trust on an online user: In all Internet-based platforms, users are the crucial actors to trust [1]. It could be a social networking, an online citizens' platform, a discussion forum, etc. Here interaction (either synchronous or asynchronous) is primarily among users. For instance, in an online site selling cars, users interact with users. Trust here is primarily put on users; however, based on users' experiences with the online platform, this can as well receive a trust score. Trust score here is *computed* based on user's activity within the online platform. In this case, trust can be defined as *bi-directional trust*, namely entity A operates with B according to mutual trust scores. It should be noted that many online platforms open to mass users tend to assume that all users are trustworthy (not only at the beginning of user's activity but also during the activity). For instance, Facebook and other online social networks did not worry about the trustworthy activity of their users, perhaps due to rampant competition!

Trust on a computational platform (Cloud, Fog, Edge, IoT computing): Large-scale computing platforms have become a must for the activity of individuals, businesses and institutions. All of them select the platform for their own activity based on trust although trust requirements may vary according to their requirements. Thus, businesses select the computational platform according to its business needs such as resilience and disaster recovery solutions to ensure business continuity. All of them however require service level agreement (SLA) accomplishment. Recently, we are seeing how SLA includes more requirements each time on privacy preserved (individual data, institutional data, client data); recent examples from major IT companies such as Google and Amazon show serious data leakage. Unfortunately, in most cases users are not able to fully check, track or audit the accomplishment of an SLA with the platform provider. Furthermore, the emergence of other Cloud-related platforms such as Fog, Edge and IoT are raising new trust issues, namely such new systems become harder to trust [2].

For instance, IoT devices are poorly secured when compared to large computing systems, requiring huge investments on IoT security. Differently from large-scale systems, in Fog and IoT systems, users are not able to check or track the security level of the IoT devices they are using, say, at home. Trust can be a useful means in a variety of forms, from classifying devices as trustworthy to detecting denial of service attacks [3].

Trust on service and resource selection: Users request services and resources based, among other factors, on trust and trustworthiness. Trust can therefore be used in negotiation of resource allocations [4]. In this context, trust has been used as a key factor from designing service-oriented architectures [5] to optimal selection of services [6–9].

Trust on an online collaborative process: Internet-based applications distinguish for their support to collaborative processes at large in various forms of collaborative work, business collaboration, online learning teams, crowd-sensing, collective intelligence, etc. [10–12]. Obviously, trust is a fundamental issue for a successful collaboration. With the fast development on collaboration platforms, current research focuses on a variety of trust models to capture the dynamics of trust and processes in collaborative contexts.

Trust on social media networks: Internet-based platforms, most notoriously social networking, enable mass creation and sharing of multimedia contents online. The effect of social media shapes the way people, institutions, organisation, business, etc. interact and communicate among them. Since trust is fundamental to communication and given the openness of such platforms the question is to what extent can the social media be trusted? The lack of control and the widespread of fake contents make the trust on social media the most challenging issue: how to measure user's trust and users' trustworthy behaviour, how does trust affect the consumption of social media contents for everyday life activities [13–16].

Trust on a data set: The interaction among the users (as in a discussion forum or a social networking platform), or among the users and the system (when navigating, reading, downloading, etc.), or from sensing of the environment (as in IoT systems) generates huge data sets (*aka* Big Data). Such data sets are considered a valuable source of knowledge for individuals, institutions, organisations, businesses and alike. The critical issue however is if such data sets are trustworthy data at all! For instance, multimedia data posted at Facebook, Twitter are used for opinion mining and can therefore be used to influence the opinion of users on certain topic of interest. If the data source is not reliable, the outcome may distort the reality. The challenging research issue here is how to ensure that data set is trustworthy as well as data sharing, data access and data transmission can be done in a trustworthy way [17–21].

9.2.1 Characteristics of trust, trustworthiness and trustworthy computing

Trust characteristics depend on context such as human context, social context, computing context, business context and e-commerce context. Common to all these contexts are the following characteristics of trust, and hence of trustworthy and trustworthiness: *integrity, consistency, confidentiality* and *availability*. When applied to computing systems, trustworthy computing requires such systems to be secure, available and reliable.

- *Integrity* refers to the ability (of a system, a user, etc.) to maintain or transfer digital objects unaltered. Only authorised parties can modify their content.
- *Consistency* refers to the ability (of a system, a user, a digital object, etc.) to always behave in the expected manner according to its specification.

- *Confidentiality* refers to ability (of a system, a user, a digital object, etc.) to treat information as expected whereby only authorised parties can access to such information.
- *Availability* refers to ability (of a system, a user, a digital object, etc.) to always ensure access to information to authorised parties.

In the literature, there have been identified core properties of trust [22,23], including context-specific, dynamic, propagative, aggregative, non-transitive, subjective, composable, asymmetric, self-reinforcing, event-based [23]. Among these we distinguish the following:

- *Asymmetric:* If entity A trusts entity B, it does not imply vice versa to be true.
- *Non-transitive:* If entity A trusts entity B, and entity B trusts entity C, it does not imply that entity A trusts C.
- *Context-specific:* If entity A trusts entity B in a context, it does not imply that entity A trusts entity B in other contexts. It can be said that trust is situational.
- *Composable:* An entity A can build trust on another entity B through a chain of intermediate entities. This property is suited to social networks where users not directly connected build trust along chains in social networks.

9.2.2 Trust, trustworthy and trustworthiness modelling

An accurate modelling of trust is challenging given that various actors are involved in cyberphysical systems, namely

1. *Trust among users:* For instance, in an online virtual campus, students have to collaborate among them to accomplish some project. The collaboration depends on the level of trust among students. Most notoriously, trust is essential in social networks where unknown users establish communication assuming reciprocal trust.
2. *Trust among users and computing systems:* For instance, a user while completing an online transaction is asked in various steps to provide personal data for authentication.
3. *Trust on computation at different parts/subsystems of computing systems:* For instance, in systems of systems such as a smart city, there has to be a communication among (sub)systems, which comprises disclosure and/or information sharing.
4. *Trust on computing devices:* For instance, on IoT devices at a smart home.

Ideally, a trust model should be able to capture all the above views on trust; however, the complexity of cyberphysical systems makes it very complex to model altogether the above mention views. One specific reason is that cyberphysical systems comprise humans and computing systems. It seems therefore reasonable to consider the trust model according to human-centric trust or non-human-related trust. The difference between the two views, namely human-centric trust vs. non-human-related trust, resides in the fact that human-centric trust is trust based on human behaviour and expectation. It requires humans to trust on humans, computations and devices as well as to be able to monitor and audit the level of trust among such entities. On the other hand, non-human-related trust is trust based on systems or computing devices behaviours alone. It requires systems, agents or devices to establish communication and collaboration trust based on computation, data storage, data transmission, etc.

To exemplify the trust modelling and its complexities, we briefly describe next some trust models presented in the literature.

9.2.2.1 Trust model for collaboration in virtual campuses

Virtual campuses have emerged as large online platforms for learning and teaching. Large open universities of thousands of students are nowadays examples of how online learning and teaching are replacing traditional distance teaching universities. One such example is the Open University of Catalonia[†] (in Barcelona, Spain) accounting for about 50,000 students, running on a fully virtualised campus. Students enrol in online courses arranged in virtual classrooms and within the classroom they engage in one or more discussion forums, collaborative work in online teams, etc. Obviously trust plays an important role for a successful collaboration. Unlike traditional universities, where trust is built through face-to-face communication, in an online setting trust has to be built through online communication. In Miguel *et al.* [24], we take a massive parallel data-processing approach to model the trust and trustworthiness in online virtual classroom. We consider various data sources generated during learning activities as a result of user-to-user communication in Learning Management Systems (LMSs), namely LMS log files of Virtual Campus and of Basic Support for Collaborative Work (BSCW). We also consider other sources such as ratings, questionnaires and reports containing P2P evaluations of students about their contributions in the virtual classroom.

In order to model the trustworthiness, we consider a list of factors that contribute to building trust and factors that contribute to reducing trust (Tables 9.1 and 9.2). These are some of the factors; the list is not exhaustive (S denotes a student as a member of group of students (GS)).

As in this case trust is built through interaction among students, we consider determining the context of interaction between two students (it could be part of discussion forum of the virtual classroom, or it could be part of discussion forum of a group project, etc.) as well as determining the criteria involved in the interaction. In addition, our aim is to model not just a snapshot of the trust but rather its evolution over time; therefore, we consider *Trustworthiness History Sequence*, which shows the evolution of trust over time in the virtual classroom.

Based on the above, a list of atomic variables tw_i for every indicator i expressing trustworthiness according to trustworthiness building factor/trustworthiness reducing factor, resp., is defined. Then, trustworthiness levels Ltw_i are defined and computed as a composition of tw_i for every indicator i. These trustworthiness levels are further normalised following a similar approach as in [25] but modified by using weight vectors in order to ponder particular components that need to be considered of more importance

---

[†]Open University of Catalonia (in Barcelona, Spain): https://www.uoc.edu/.

Table 9.1   Trustworthiness building factor (TBF)

No.	Action
	Student (S) collaborating in the group of students (GS) is building trustworthiness when
1	S communicates honestly, without distorting any information
2	S shows confidence in GS abilities
3	S keeps promises and commitments
4	S listens to and values what GS says, even though S might not agree
5	S cooperates with GS and looks for mutual help and scaffolding

Table 9.2   Trustworthiness reducing factor (TRF)

No.	Action
	Student S collaborating in the group of students (GS) is reducing trustworthiness when
1	S acts more concerned about own welfare than anything else
2	S sends mixed messages so that GS never knows where S stands
3	S avoids taking responsibility
4	S jumps to conclusions without checking the facts first
5	S makes excuses or blames others when things do not work out

than others. A correlation analysis is performed to deduce whether the variables involved in the model are correlated using a Pearson correlation coefficient, which is a suitable measure of strength of relationship (see also [26]). Finally, trustworthiness indicators are grouped into a trustworthiness matrix with the aim of representing the whole relationship table for each indicator. The model is then refined to select those indicators oriented to perform the best similarity and correlation evaluation model.

Due to the large scale of the system (in terms of users, datasets sizes, etc.), a Big Data processing approach is needed to efficiently establish the trust model. An array of technologies, mainly from Apache software ecosystem, such as Hadoop MapReduce, were shown useful to bring the overall computing time to reasonable amount of time and in some cases to nearly real time.

Cheng *et al.* [27] considered trust modelling in a broader scope of computer-mediated collaboration. They consider modelling of trust evolution over time. To that end they considered six factors influencing the trust, namely, *risk, benefit, utility value, effort, power and interest*. Then, two approaches, the scale balance model and the trust spider diagram, were presented and evaluated to investigate individual trust development over time. The former follows a trust development model by Nolan *et al.* [28] for trust in online communities, while the second follows examples of a spider diagram in the area of computer-mediated collaboration [29].

9.2.2.2   Trust model for social networking

Modelling trust in social networks is perhaps the most challenging scenario. This is so due to the openness and informality of such systems, which persist due to lack of rules and control over communication, creation, sharing, etc. It is in this case where social chains are crucial for users to build and propagate trust and extend their list of friends. One concept that captures trusted users is that of influential nodes (*aka* influencers). Trust and influence are intimately related in this case. The more trusted a user is, the more influential can be over other users. Asim *et al.* [22] presented a trust model for nodes in a social network using a local and global trust and investigate the relation between trust and influence in social networks. To that end their model includes both direct trust and indirect trust. The former is based on variables such as *user attributes, degree prestige, the frequency of communication* and *relationship types*, while the later, the indirect trust, is based on different user activities.

Mao *et al.* [1] presented an algorithm for inferring the trust between two individuals in social networks. They propose a *traversal method* to identify the strong trust paths from the *truster* and the *trustee*, which are then aggregated to predict the trust rate between them. The authors consider *variables such as common (weighted) interest topics, topic frequency and topology network metric*.

Zhou *et al.* [30] used *multi-agent learning* and *game theory* approach to study trust emergence in social networks, where agents play an iterative game of stag hunt with their neighbours, namely the stag hunt model was found useful for the formation of trust.

Riyanto and Jonathan [31] take an *experimental approach* (combining social network analysis with experimental economics methodology) to study the direct trust and trustworthiness in social networks. The authors consider variables such as *partners' centrality* (popularity) and *social distance* and studied how they affect trust and trustworthy behaviour and their evolution in the trust game.

As can be seen, a variety of approaches (theoretical, computational, analytical and empirical) are used to model trust and its evolution in social networks. This variety at the same time is an indication of the versatility of the problem of trust modelling and its complexity.

9.2.2.3 Trust model for IoT, MANETs and VANETs

The emergence of new distributed paradigms at the edges of the Internet such as IoT systems, mobile ad hoc networks (MANETs) and vehicular ad hoc networks (VANETs) has prompted for trust modelling in such new systems. Major challenging issues here are if a computing device such as a sensor, a camera, a mobile device, a vehicle and a UAV can be deemed as trustworthy; are data sensed from such devices trustworthy? Are data transmitted by such devices to upper levels of systems (e.g. to a Cloud) trustworthy? These and other issues are recently objective of intensive investigation by many researchers in the field. It should be noted here that in many cases, IoT devices are directly used by humans (such as a camera, a mobile device, a vehicle) and therefore the trust is directly linked to user's daily performance and activity.

Xu *et al.* [32] proposed an *autonomic agent trust model* aiming to decrease security concerns and increase reliability and credibility in dynamic IoT environments. After analysing the credibility of IoT systems, the authors provide architecture of trustable agent and agency. A similar approach, based on *mobile agent systems*, which can be useful for IoT systems as well, is presented by Shehada *et al.* [33]. The authors propose an adaptive trust and reputation model that relies on the evaluator *direct experience* and the *indirect witnesses' experience* (reputation) with *evaluate*. Weights, which are dependent on the frequency of interaction, number of interactions and honesty of witnesses, are used to combine the different evaluations.

Shabut *et al.* [34] presented a multidimensional trust management model aiming to enhance nodes' cooperation in selecting trustworthy and optimal paths between the source and destination nodes in MANETs. The trust value of wireless nodes is calculated through peer-to-peer (based on *energy* and *social trust*) and link evaluations, while link evaluation is done by computing an optimal routing path with a small number of intermediate nodes of a minimum acceptable trust value.

Features of IoT systems such as dynamics, energy-aware, variety, protocols and large-scale make trust modelling very challenging in such systems. In particular, as IoT are multi-component systems, modelling trust across all components is hard to define. Therefore the global trust can be addressed by defining various domains within the system comprising principal aspects of the trust model for each of them.

9.2.2.4 The inherent limitations of trust models

All models have their inherent limitations; therefore; trust models are not an exception. The inherent limitations of any model come from the fact that models are not able to grasp all the complexities of a real-life phenomenon aimed to be modelled. Their value is therefore measured with their usefulness. As we have seen from the above examples of trust models, such models are able to cast only partial views of the trust by defining some variables of interest. Therefore, current trust models are not able to cover cyber physical systems in their full. Thus, the heterogeneity due to coexistence of a variety of different entities in such systems (including humans, systems, systems of systems, devices) increases significantly the complexity of trust modelling because trust is differently meant for different entities and trust behaviours, interactions and relationships are different according to entities in question. In particular, trust models are not able to fully cast the trust evolution overtime, which is very complex as it is depending on many factors, of which time is the most challenging one (various models discussed here are able to rather make snapshots of trust values). The scale is yet another limitation of trust models, which makes the trust models, especially those based on empirical or analytics, questionable at very large scale of Internet-based systems.

Despite their limitations,[‡] trust models are useful and needful to understand the trust phenomenon in emerging cyberphysical systems. Their usefulness can be measured with how much they can help people, systems and devices to interact in a trusted way.

9.3 Trustworthy evaluation and prediction

Trust models aim to realistically cast the trust of different entities – trust behaviours, interactions and relationships among them in a cyberphysical system. Such models

---

[‡]George Box's aphorism: 'All models are wrong but some are useful'.

necessarily define various variables and their relationships with trust (often with non-linear relationship with the trust), which are statistically significant for the trust model. The calculation of trust values of the involved entities is therefore done as a function of such variables. Sometimes it might be useful to use weights to ponder the variables according to their importance in the model. We could speak of *entity trustworthy evaluation* of a concrete entity (a human or a device, for instance) to measure how trustworthy that entity is. When extended to the full system, we speak of *system trustworthy evaluation.*

In either case, calculation of trust values is necessary in any trust model. The validity of the model is then contrasted with real data extracted from real systems (or simulated systems) such as from social networks and IoT systems. By using the trust model, we would be able to make a trustworthy evaluation of some entity or of the whole system at any point in time. However, there are at least two limitations of using the trust model for just trustworthy evaluation: first, trustworthy evaluation would require probing/sampling the real system from time to time to calculate the updated trust values; second, it would not help in decision-making (when rare events or anomalies in trust happen as they are detected afterwards).

To overcome these limitations, trust models should enable trustworthy prediction, namely using historical values of trust and of trustworthy behaviour to predict future values of trust and of trustworthy behaviour (either of a concrete entity or of the system as a whole). Trustworthy sequences are useful in this case. An array of methods from machine learning and artificial neural network has been explored/is being explored to endow trust models with prediction capability.

For further reading, refer to Miguel *et al.* [35,36] where methodological approaches for trustworthiness assessment and prediction in mobile online collaborative learning and trustworthiness evaluation and prediction are discussed.

9.4   Blockchain and trust

Blockchain is an emerging disruptive technology in security of any kind of systems, although primarily devoted to securely record transactions with crypto-currencies. In the same way as for security, for which trust is seen as complementary to enhance system's security, given that security cannot be ensured by technological solutions alone, researchers and developers are investigating the relation between Blockchain and trust.

9.4.1   Trust-free vs. trust building

Blockchain is penetrating not only high-level transactional systems of businesses and industry but also low-level IoT systems. Current research is focusing on exploring Blockchain for building trust among entities in a cyberphysical system [37]. Research on trust models in Blockchain-based systems is just incipient. Two distant cases are identified: *Trust-free Blockchain-based systems* and *trust-building Blockchain-based systems* [38].

Trust-free Blockchain-based systems [39] are based on the premise that Blockchain-based systems enforce rules and contractual agreements without an arbitrating authority and therefore there is no need for trust (in contrast to trust in P2P systems). Obviously, a trust-free system would imply in turn a more efficient system, as it would waive the burden of building, verifying and/or predicting trust among entities in the system. Certainly, there are a number of issues with trust-free systems, among which the foremost one is how to prove that a Blockchain-based system is trust free.

Trust-building mechanisms in Blockchain-based models enable entities to calculate the level of trust. It remains therefore to establish how to use the properties of Blockchain to establish the trust. For an example refer to Litos and Zindros [40] where authors compute trust by using monetary pledges.

9.4.2   Blockchain as a factor of trust

Blockchain is seen by many researchers and developers as a key enabling technology to propel trust among actors in any cyberphysical systems. Blockchain is considered as a trustworthy alternative to traditional transaction and trust-based systems thanks to its transparent design, fully decentralised nature, data integrity and authenticity and audit trial. In addition, the consensus mechanisms of Blockchain promote trust among parties by avoiding trusted 'actors-in-the-middle'. Nevertheless, there are limits as well to the trust in Blockchain as there are underlying complex computerised and networked processes to which one may trust or not. The limitations of Blockchain in this regard are inherent to process-based trust.

9.5   Conclusions and future research

Trust has always been and is a key factor in the relationship of humans who build trust based on their perceptions and experiences with other humans. Likewise, trust is a key factor in the relationship of humans who build trust based on their perceptions and experiences with other humans through Internet-based systems. As a matter of fact, most of nowadays Internet-based applications require trust for a successful operation. Trust can therefore be established and propagated not only among humans but also among any entities being humans, systems or devices. However, with Internet-based systems arise new issues for trust, namely how to compute trust, how trust evolves over time and how to deem an entity trustworthy.

Trust modelling is a key contribution towards understanding the many issues in the trust and trust relationships. The large variety, however, of Internet-based systems as well as of computing devices and operations makes the trust modelling very challenging.

In this chapter we have surveyed some relevant concepts and models for trust, trustworthiness and trustworthy computing and have discussed their various forms in business, e-commerce, social networking, etc. Throughout the chapter, we have pointed out to complexities and challenges of trust modelling.

Future research on trust modelling will target development of fully fledged trust models comprising as many as possible features of the cyberphysical systems. Likewise, the development of joint frameworks of trust in conjunction with other security technologies such as Blockchain is important to capture current and future technological developments. Finally, the development of simulation tools for validation of trust models to account for efficiency and scalability is another research line of interest.

References

[1] Mao, C., Xu, C. and He, Q. (2019) A cost-effective algorithm for inferring the trust between two individuals in social networks. *Knowledge-Based Systems*, Vol. 164, pp. 122–138.

[2] Rahman, F.H., Au, T.-W., Newaz, S., Suhaili, W.S. and Lee, G.M. (2018) Find my trustworthy fogs: A fuzzy-based trust evaluation framework. *Future Generation Computer Systems, In Press*. https://doi.org/10.1016/j.future.2018.05.061.

[3] Alsumayt, A., Haggerty, J. and Lotfi, A. (2017) Using trust to detect denial of service attacks in the internet of things over MANETs. *International Journal of Space-Based and Situated Computing*, Vol. 7, No. 1, pp. 43–56.

[4] Habes, M.R. and Belleili-Souici, H. (2017) Towards a fairer negotiation for dynamic resource allocation in cloud by relying on trustworthiness. *International Journal of Grid and Utility Computing*, Vol. 8, No. 3, pp. 185–200.

[5] Aljazzaf, Z.M., Capretz, M.A.M and Perry, M. (2016) Trust-based service-oriented architecture. *Journal of King Saud University – Computer and Information Sciences*, Vol. 28, No. 4, pp. 470–480.

[6] Somu, N., Raman G., Kirthivasan, K. and Sriram S. (2018) A trust centric optimal service ranking approach for cloud service selection. *Future Generation Computer Systems*, Vol. 86, pp. 234–252.

[7] Tang, M., Dai, X., Liu, J. and Chen, J. (2017) Towards a trust evaluation middleware for cloud service selection. *Future Generation Computer Systems*, Vol. 74, pp. 302–312.

[8] Balakrishnan, S.M. and Sangaiah, A.K. (2017) Integrated quality of user experience and quality of service approach to service selection in internet of services. *International Journal of Grid and Utility Computing*, Vol. 8, No. 4, pp. 282–298.

[9] Chiregi, M. and Navimipour, N.J. (2016) Trusted services identification in the cloud environment using the topological metrics. *Karbala International Journal of Modern Science*, Vol. 2, No. 3, pp. 203–210.

[10] Jarratt, D. and Ceric, A. (2015) The complexity of trust in business collaborations. *Australasian Marketing Journal (AMJ)*, Vol. 23, No. 1, pp. 2–12.

[11] Bianchi, F., Casnici, N. and Squazzoni, F. (2018) Solidarity as a byproduct of professional collaboration: Social support and trust in a coworking space. *Social Networks*, Vol. 54, pp. 61–72.

[12] Choi, O.K. and Cho, E. (2019) The mechanism of trust affecting collaboration in virtual teams and the moderating roles of the culture of autonomy and task complexity. *Computers in Human Behavior*, Vol. 91, pp. 305–315.

[13] Kahar, R., Yamimi, F., Bunari, G. and Habil, H. (2012) Trusting the Social Media in Small Business. *Procedia – Social and Behavioral Sciences*, Vol. 66, pp. 564–570.

[14] Liu, L., Lee, M., Liu, R. and Chen, J. (2018) Trust transfer in social media brand communities: The role of consumer engagement. *International Journal of Information Management*, Vol. 41, pp. 1–13.

[15] Warner-Søderholm, G., Bertsch, A., Sawe, E., *et al.* (2018) Who trusts social media?. *Computers in Human Behavior*, Vol. 81, pp. 303–315.

[16] Cheng, X., Fu, S. and de Vreede, G.-J. (2017) Understanding trust influencing factors in social media communication: A qualitative study. *International Journal of Information Management*, Vol. 37, No. 2, pp. 25–35.

[17] Gilbert, E., Kaliaperumal, B., Rajsingh, E. and Lydia, M. (2018) Trust based data prediction, aggregation and reconstruction using compressed sensing for clustered wireless sensor networks. *Computers & Electrical Engineering*, Vol. 72, pp. 894–909.

[18] Yao, X., Zhang, X., Ning, H. and Li, P. (2017) Using trust model to ensure reliable data acquisition in VANETs. *Ad Hoc Networks*, Vol. 55, pp. 107–118.

[19] Cao, Q.M., Giyyarpuram, M., Farahbakhsh, R. and Crespi, N. (2018) Policy-based usage control for a trustworthy data sharing platform in smart cities. *Future Generation Computer Systems*, In Press. https://doi.org/10.1016/j.future.2017.05.039

[20] Tang, L.A. Yu, X., Kim, S., *et al.* (2013) Trustworthiness analysis of sensor data in cyber-physical systems. *Journal of Computer and System Sciences*, Vol. 79, No. 3, pp. 383–401.

[21] Lin, H., Hu, J., Xu, Ch., Ma, J. and Yu, M. (2018) DTRM: A new reputation mechanism to enhance data trustworthiness for high-performance cloud computing. *Future Generation Computer Systems*, Vol. 83, pp. 293–302.

[22] Asim, Y., Malik, A.K., Ahmad, B.R. and Shahid, R. (2019) A trust model for analysis of trust, influence and their relationship in social network communities. *Telematics and Informatics*, Vol. 36, pp. 94–116.

[23] Sherchan, W., Nepal, S. and Paris, C. (2013) A survey of trust in social networks. *ACM Computing Surveys*, Vol. 45, No. 4, 33 pages, Article 47. http://dx.doi.org/10.1145/2501654.2501661.

[24] Miguel, J., Caballé, S. and Xhafa, F. (2016) Intelligent Data Analysis for e-Learning: Enhancing Security and Trustworthiness in Online Learning Systems (1st ed.). Academic Press, Inc., Orlando, FL, USA.

[25] Ray, I. and Chakraborty, S. (2004) A Vector Model of Trust for Developing Trustworthy Systems. In: Samarati, P., Ryan, P., Gollmann, D., Molva, R. (eds.) *Computer Security – ESORICS 2004*. ESORICS 2004. Lecture Notes in Computer Science, vol. 3193. Springer, Berlin, Heidelberg.

[26] Mobasher, B, Burke, R., Bhaumik, R. and Williams, C. (2007) Toward trustworthy recommender systems: An analysis of attack models and algorithm

robustness. *ACM Transactions on Internet Technology*, Vol. 7, No. 4, Article 23. http://dx.doi.org/10.1145/1278366.1278372.

[27] Cheng, X., Macaulay, L.A. and Zarifis, A. (2013) Modeling individual trust development in computer mediated collaboration: A comparison of approaches. *Computers in Human Behavior*, Vol. 29, No. 4, pp. 1733–1741.

[28] Nolan, T., Brizland, R. and Macaulay, L. (2007) Development of individual trust within online communities. *Information Technology and People*, Vol. 20, No. 1, pp. 53–71.

[29] Jamil, I., O'Hara, K., Perry, M., Karnik, A. and Subramanian, S. (2011) The effects of interaction techniques on talk patterns in collaborative peer learning around interactive tables. In: *Proceedings of CHI 2011*, Vancouver, Canada.

[30] Zhou, L., Su, C., Sun, X., Zhao, X. and Choo, K.R. (2018) Stag hunt and trust emergence in social networks. *Future Generation Computer Systems*, Vol. 88, pp. 168–172.

[31] Riyanto, Y. and Jonathan, Y. (2018) Directed trust and trustworthiness in a social network: An experimental investigation. *Journal of Economic Behavior & Organization*, Vol. 151, pp. 234–253.

[32] Xu, X., Bessis, N. and Cao, J. (2013) An autonomic agent trust model for IoT systems. *Procedia Computer Science*. Vol. 21, pp. 107–113.

[33] Shehada, D., Yeun, C.Y., Zemerly, J.M., Al-Qutayri, M., Al-Hammadi, Y. and Hu, J. (2018) A new adaptive trust and reputation model for Mobile Agent Systems. *Journal of Network and Computer Applications*, Vol. 124, pp. 33–43.

[34] Shabut, A.M., Kaiser, M.S., Dahal, K.P. and Chen, W. (2018) A multidimensional trust evaluation model for MANETs. *Journal of Network and Computer Applications*, Vol. 123, pp. 32–41.

[35] Miguel, J., Caballé, S., Xhafa, F., Prieto, J. and Barolli, L. (2016) A methodological approach for trustworthiness assessment and prediction in mobile online collaborative learning. *Computer Standards & Interfaces*, Vol. 44, pp. 122–136.

[36] Miguel, J., Caballé, S. and Xhafa, F. (2017b) Chapter 6: Trustworthiness evaluation and prediction. In *Intelligent Data Analysis for e-Learning*, pp. 105–127, Academic Press.

[37] Hammi, M.T., Hammi, B., Bellota, P. and Serhrouchni, A. (2018) Bubbles of Trust: A decentralized blockchain-based authentication system for IoT. *Computers & Security*, Vol. 78, pp. 126–142.

[38] Hawlitschek, F., Notheisen, B. and Teubner, T. (2018) The limits of trust-free systems: A literature review on blockchain technology and trust in the sharing economy. *Electronic Commerce Research and Applications*, Vol. 29, pp. 50–63.

[39] Greiner, M. and Wang, H. (2015) Trust-free systems – A new research and design direction to handle trust issues in P2P systems?: The case of Bitcoin. In: *AMCIS 2015 Proceedings*.

[40] Litos, O.S.T. and Zindros, D. (2017) Trust Is Risk: A Decentralized Financial Trust Platform. In: Kiayias A. (ed.) *Financial Cryptography and Data Security*. Springer International Publishing, Cham, pp. 340–356.

Chapter 10
Software-defined mobile networks security
Yongfeng Qian[1] and Min Chen[2]

The future 5G wireless is triggered by the higher demand on wireless capacity. With software-defined network (SDN), the data layer can be separated from the control layer. The development of relevant studies about network function virtualization (NFV) and cloud computing has the potential of offering a quicker and more reliable network access for growing data traffic. Under such circumstances, software-defined mobile network (SDMN) is presented as a promising solution for meeting the wireless data demands. This chapter provides a survey of SDMN and its related security problems. As SDMN integrates cloud computing, SDN, and NFV and works on improving network functions, performance, flexibility, energy efficiency, and scalability, it is an important component of the next generation telecommunication networks. However, the SDMN concept also raises new security concerns. We explore relevant security threats and their corresponding countermeasures with respect to the data layer, control layer, application layer, and communication protocols. We also adopt the STRIDE method to classify various security threats to better reveal them in the context of SDMN. Finally, this chapter is concluded with a list of open security challenges in SDMN.

10.1 The evolution of software-defined mobile network

With the expected drastic increase in mobile traffic demand [1,2] and the compelling needs for provisioning of elastic service, collaborative working capability [3,4], transmission speed, and quality of service (QoS) [5,6] as well as the requirement for costly network upgrades [7,8], SDMN has been recognized as a solution to meet these challenges. SDMN is an integration of cloud computing, NFV, and SDN. In SDMN, emerging network technologies such as SDN and NFV are integrated into the mobile network architecture in order to meet its ever-changing demand. To be more specific, at the core of SDMN, the software control aims to enable dynamic traffic management and functional reconfiguration. Instead of conventional static Internet Protocol (IP)-based networking structure, the backbone network is abstracted through traffic-based NFV in SDMN. In a front haul connection, the network capability

[1]School of Computer Science, China University of Geosciences, Wuhan, China
[2]School of Computer Science and Technology, Huazhong University of Science and Technology, Wuhan, China

and QoS are improved through centralized management of wireless radio spectrum resources [9] and the implementation of software-defined radio (SDR), cognitive radio for reconfigurable networks [10].

With the development of SDMN [11], the related network security issues have drawn considerable attention [12–15]. The Open Networking Foundation Security Discussion Group is committed to security study and standardization for SDN. For example, report TR-511 proposes a set of core security principles with implementation strategies regarding SDN core protocol OpenFlow Switch Specification v1.3.4 [16]. In [17], a comprehensive survey of software-defined networking is provided, covering its context, rationale, main concepts, distinctive features, and future challenges. It also provides a detailed summary of SDN network security issues, including the point of attack, means of attack, and countermeasures. However, the security problems related to SDMN have not yet been well analyzed.

Moving from SDN to SDMN, the increased complexity, due to the hybrid infrastructure, leads to multiple security requirements that must be satisfied. To guarantee the collaborative work capability between different access technologies and SDN-enabled network nodes, pure reliance on progressive upgrading of existing 3GPP solutions cannot develop the logic part. Stringent QoS requirements that dynamic service matching should be based on light and stable basic data and protocol of cryptosystem, but security solutions currently proposed have yet to solve this problem. Even as a leading SDN technology, the application of OpenFlow in the next generation of mobile network is still a challenging problem [17].

To this end, a network security threat model is critical, as it can identify and isolate, in a systematic way, the existing drawbacks and potential attack vectors. Without such an abstraction, the improvement of safety design will become more difficult and its inherent complexity cannot be reduced. Therefore, the network security threat model has become a prerequisite for standardization and practical implementation of SDMN [18]. A preliminary attempt is made in this chapter toward this direction by the proposal of a STRIDE-based network security threat model [19,20].

Security in SDMN is a challenging issue due to the large amount of smart devices and terminals in the SDMN, which are proactive for content fetching. The main considerations of security research include the existing problems of mobile networks [21] and the security vulnerabilities of SDN. On the one hand, the virtualization mechanism is flexibly managed; on the other hand, harmful behaviors will result from an unethical malicious intent. Therefore, in addition to typical security problems of mobile networks, additional security problems caused by the introduction of SDN and NFV cannot be ignored.

10.2   SDMN architecture

The SDMN is a programmable, flexible, and flow-centric mobile network constructed by using a combination of SDN, NFV, and cloud computing. SDMN is the architecture of embodiment and application extension of the idea that the control layer in an SDN is separated from the forwarding layer in a wireless network. The traditional mobile network has distinctive differences from an SDMN. The core of the software-defined mobile packet forwarding involves the problems of matching the sending/control layer and mobile environment [22–25], the service logic of mobile communication, which is transmitted to the cloud [26] to guarantee the programmability [27] of LTC/EPC structure inside, and the combination of SDN and NFV [28]. SDMN has many advantages, such as centralized control, high flexibility, effective division, automatic network management, and reduction of the backhaul device operating cost [29,30].

SDMN is proposed as an extension of SDN, by adding the special functions of a mobile network. The SDN architecture is different from existing mobile networks with the flow-centric models [31,32], integration of inexpensive hardware, and a centralized logic controller. Like SDN, SDMN primarily consists of three parts: data plane, control plane, and application plane [33]. Furthermore, SDMN integrates SDN, cloud computing [34], and NFV. The SDMN architecture is illustrated in Figure 10.1. We introduce it in detail.

10.2.1 Network function virtualization

NFV involves decoupling the network function from the hardware application by means of IT virtualization technology, which is implemented in and operates in software. This is an innovative method that is applied in the design and deployment [35] of the network management service. Network virtualization mainly targets the aggregation of distributed resources, utilizing a shared pool of configurable computing hardware resources to realize on-demand network access.

In accordance with the NFV-based Long Term Evolution (LTE)/Evolved Packet Core (EPC) architecture as described by ETSI, Figure 10.2 shows a reduced graph of NFV members [36]. In consideration of the complexity of the virtualization program segment, the threat model can further be subdivided into threats in relation to each NFV assembly/area, such as layout and virtual management function (VMF)/virtual infrastructure management (VIM), agency and resource management program, virtual network [37], service, transport layer, and telecommunication infrastructure areas. To be more specific, avoidance of original controller/traffic management logic or disclosure of user control/data traffic is possible by attacking and concealing VMF/VIM/layout or other identities of VMF (e.g., mobility management entity (MME), serving/packet gateway (S/PG-W)) and tampering with virtual network communication traffic.

Malicious information and viruses are injected only through the address resolution protocol (ARP) plane and a replay attack is implemented (a common vector of traditional IP environment); the malicious virtual machine (VM) mechanism can destroy normal service logic [37], on the condition that NFV communication traffic exits from a virtual line of defense [38,39]. If virtualized network functions (VNFs) are operated on kernel-based VM, the threat of tampering with the integrity of the kernel will affect normal EPC status. Through kernel code and interface loopholes, the integrity of VNF will be damaged, causing denial of service (DoS) of potential NFV infrastructure (NFVI) assembly by loading loadable kernel modules (LKM), rootkit malicious software without controlled data and by attacking resource depletion [40–42].

Because the infrastructure as a service (IaaS) user group shares the same address and cannot provide an ideal VM isolation, SDMN service transport in the IaaS region will enlarge the attack level and may cause information disclosure, service denial

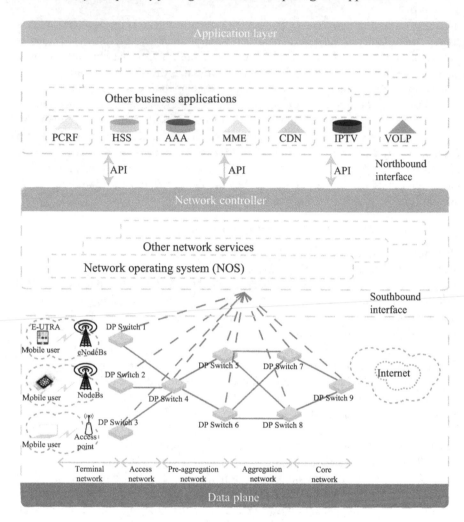

Figure 10.1   Illustration of the SDMN architecture

and privilege escalation to occur [43]. Due to the malicious use of the VM's common address and the convergence of the same resources in the NFVI region, there will be a point where malicious software can form a brief existence or VM spread, causing the depletion of hardware resources and performance degradation of the EPC running in the NFVI region. It has been proven that a side channel VM attack can acquire plaintext passwords, keys, and data memory [44,45]. It may also be used for NFVI area fingerprint technology.

The technology provides useful information for the launch of another SDMN target attack. For example, this may result in the service denial of physical infrastructure, causing the IaaS data center network to be usurped and attacked or to launch complex and continuous service denial attack [46,47]. Similarly, VIM can

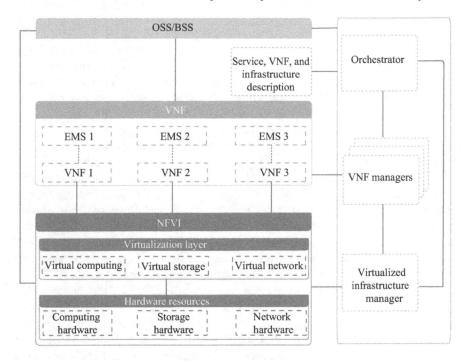

Figure 10.2 Illustration of the NFV architecture

be loaded into the module from an externally introduced transmission (end-to-end (E2E) connect SDN controller) or service (NFVSDN controller) due to the presence of the host operating system simulation program weaknesses or cross the VM attack (e.g., escape and reflection attacks) attack, and there will be a threat of privilege escalation [48]. It should be pointed out that the NFV guidelines recommend using authentication, authorization, and accounting (AAA) and reliable communication solutions throughout the virtual area. However, it is not strictly controlled by the rele-vant mechanisms, and it will make the supplier adopt an incompatible security policy (which also refers to the key management procedures) in the specific configuration of the telephone communications and IaaS architecture. Also, in the case of OpenFlow, the convergence NFV program similar to the cloud computing concept of the IaaS model posts a technical threat, which is non-characteristic for the traditional mobile core environment.

NFV proposed a virtual firewall, traffic balance, and other L4–L7 network security applications. These applications are the VNFs, which are used to meet the requirements of network communication and service management. In [49], the authors presented a framework of wireless network virtualization for 3GPP LTE mobile cellular networks, but there is no in-depth study of security issues. In [50,51], respec-tively, the authors proposed the 5G SDMN architecture that can effectively guarantee the E2E QoS and quality of experience (QoE), among which the NFV technology creates a variety of middle boxes, including the middle boxes providing security service in data encryption, firewalls, and honeypots.

10.2.2 OpenFlow

OpenFlow is a kind of open protocol, and it is proposed to standardize the communications between the data layer and control layer. In accordance with the OpenFlow threat model described in [52], Figure 10.3 shows partial, OpenFlow, simplified data flow diagrams in the SDMN architecture. In mobile networks, the assumption of using the Transport Layer Security (TLS) safety passage in the OpenFlow network and concrete cryptosecurity remains effective.

As far as threats and decoy attacks are concerned, the authors in [53] discussed the possibility of topological poison and attack or, in other words, a host address hijacking and link manufacturing attack. In consideration of the diversity of running operating servers in the NFV area of SDMN, hot delivery service (HDS) communication is made between the host hijacked SDN controller and the OpenFlow switch to provide the opportunity for the destroyed core server to hijack legitimate data and transfer information. Likewise, the LLDP protocol is used in a link manufacturing attack to inject forged internal links, and sensitive flow results in a deliberate weakening of the system processing QoS, or is used to launch attacks and cause server refusal.

Decoy attacks target the IP protocol address of the E2E/NFVSDN controller, resulting in a change/recognition of running traffic rules and avoidance of charge, safety or other mobile management policies. As network saturation and complete performance degradation is caused by the depletion of resources, the malicious host simply needs to disguise as acting SDN controller to cause partial traffic to circumvent overload control subsystem/policy and charging rules function, firewalls or other LTE/EPC control nodes, or copy/certain traffic of black holes, and thus, the legal interception mechanism may be destroyed.

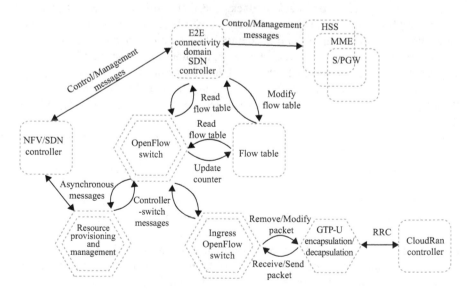

Figure 10.3   Illustration of the OpenFlow architecture

The traffic unmatched to effective rules will lead to saturation of the Open-Flow plane and overflow of the transmission plane, and distributed DoS (DDoS) is detected in the real SDN controller as a result of the transmission mechanism's failure. Moreover, the malicious OpenFlow node may tamper counter and insert false communication to some users, circumvent the charge system, and adopt incorrect rate/cost of the traffic [54]. Likewise, the entry of an OpenFlow router may become the target of the saturation attack so that the geological locations of some wireless mobile communication services can be shielded. Another tampering-related attack is a virus attack on the traffic platform or buffer memory in the controller status, which will keep the integrity of the SDMN OpenFlow topological structure.

For SDMN OpenFlow members, another information disclosure attack exists, in which the network fingerprint and controller data may be disclosed as a result of an XML external mechanism attack [55]. As mentioned above, the most convincible threat is DoS resulting from depletion of resources, link manufacturing, Hash collision attack, SDN controller overload, and OpenFlow switch circuit disconnection, as shown in [52,53,55,56]. In general, some network security viewpoints indicate that security attributes in relation to OpenFlow technology and security problems of SDN [57] itself are the major security problems of SDMN.

10.3 SDMN security issues

Due to the unique characteristics, SDMN brings about many special secure issues. We first introduce the SDN original security issues, then we give the special security issue in SDMN.

10.3.1 SDN original security issues

Since SDMN is developed on the basis of SDN, we first introduce SDN and its related security problems before discussing SDMN security issues.

10.3.1.1 SDN architecture

The SDN architecture consists of the following key planes, i.e., data plane, control plane, and application plane.

- Data plane (also known as the infrastructure layer): primarily consists of a data forwarding unit including physical switches and virtual switches for exchanging and forwarding data packets. We also categorize the physical mobile terminal as belonging in the data plane.
- Control plane: consists of a series of controllers providing centralized control. The Open API (application programming interface) enables open switches data forwarding functions to realize the state collection and centralized control of the data plane.
- Application plane (also called application layer): provides various applications to end-users, such as mobile management, security application, and network virtualization. The mobile terminal applications are categorized into this plane.

10.3.1.2   Security problems of SDN

The following security problems are inherited from SDN.

- Centralized control mode: Centralized management integrates the network configuration, network service access control, and service deployment at the control layer. Once the attacker controls the SDN successfully, it will cause the network service to be paralyzed and therefore affect the entire network.
- Programmability: The programmability of SDN has brought about new security problems. The first is traffic and resource isolation. Due to this feature, there may be additional interaction to handle different service level agreements (SLAs) and privacy issues. The second is the trust based on the third-party applications and controller. Programmability is a double-edged sword. It brings about the convenience of implementation as well as the risk of malicious applications, so it is necessary to strengthen the authentication mechanism in the communications between the application and control layers to prevent controller exposure. The last issue involves the protection for the application–controller plane interface and intermediate–controller plane interface.
- Integration with the existing protocols: When the existing protocols are applied to SDN, compatibility must be detected. At the same time, in the construction of the SDN architecture, the weakness of the existing architecture should not be repeated, or at least not inflated.
- Cross domain connection: SDN implementation requirements are infrastructures connected with different domains. This requires the establishment of trust relationship to guarantee secure channel setup.

10.3.1.3   Security principles

All the protocols, components, and interfaces in the SDN architecture should follow the following security principles [16].

- Clearly defined security dependencies and trust boundaries: security dependencies of different components should be described when these parts are constructed for the SDN network. Circular dependencies should be avoided. Based on privilege changes, information flow and data integrity and confidentiality through different domains cannot be verified. Trust boundaries of the data dependency relationship should be defined. Any external dependency should depict its trust boundary. Management of internal attacks should be considered to prevent an external environment attack.
- Assure robust identity: in order to establish effective authentication, authorization, and accounting implementation, we must establish a strong identity framework. Robust identity should be able to distinguish its owner from other entities; and robust identity should be able to generated, updated, and revoked.
- Build security based on the open standard that gives priority to use the existing mechanisms and provide the existing security mechanisms MD5 and SHA-1, which are not recommended.
- Protect the information security triad: we must consider the impact of safety control on the whole SDN architecture. Determining whether or not the effectiveness of the whole system may be reduced will be an effective method to evaluate the

new control. This control should not introduce new vulnerabilities. The method that will reduce the effectiveness of core pillars should be certified or moderated. The establishment of security control should not cause an unnecessary decrease in system performance or increase in the complexity of the system. In practice, the security requirements, cost, etc. will affect the final solution of security control.

- Protect operational reference data: incorrect information may result in the loss of confidentiality, integrity, and availability of the system. However, the lack of specific sensitive data, such as the lack of a keyword, will breach the security control.
- Make systems secure by default: when the control is unable to meet the security requirements, such as deny by default and so on, we need to establish a different security level.
- Provide accountability and traceability: based on log data, auditors cannot only identify the action of the entity but also find the correlation orders of the action.

In addition to the above seven safety guidelines, we also need to consider other control issues, such as the fact that security control must be able to be performed, maintained, and operated easily.

10.3.2 Special security issues in SDMN

Some security problems are brought about by the centralized control, resulting from the isolation between the data level and control level, and due to the specific architecture of SDMN under the cloud environment. Other than the characteristics of SDN, the combination of NFV and SDN has resulted in a series of security problems. Examples include OpenFlow, NFV, software-defined fronthaul (SDF) network security problems, terminal problems, etc. For SDF, a virtualized attack is a threat. In terms of SDF wireless programs, the threat to SDMN security is extended to the launch of the wireless medium and the recognition of attack surface [58]. Certain radio frequency interference, media access control (MAC) tampering and malicious radio frequency (RF) interference [59] can consistently adapt to the e-utran details and heterogeneous network environment, so that the radio program segment of the SDMN fronthaul can be regarded as the target of the attack [60,61].

On the other hand, the SDR awareness [60] is associated with numerous STRIDE threats, as listed in [62,63]. Considering the spectrum utilization method, the convergence of SDF program is vulnerable to be simulated by the primary user, Byzantine or spectrum sensing data operation/forgery and several DoS attacks [64–66]. Due to the development of collaborative malware attacks on smart mobile to LTERAN, the SDF program segment may provide stronghold for recursion/slow DDoS botnet attacks, considering that most of these attacks will tamper with the QoS scheduler, bandwidth requirements, and the implementation process of the nano, micro honeycomb base station [67–69].

Table 10.1 lists the main wireless network/SDN/SDMN, reviews the security issues involved, and provides the corresponding security criteria. In the table, "*" and "–" denote whether the domain specified in the column has been discussed in the survey or not. AL, CP, DP, and CL represent the application layer, control plane, data plane, and communication layer, respectively.

Table 10.1 Feature table

Existing work		Conventional security issues			SDN security issues				SDWN security issues		
		Firewall	IDS	IPS	AL	CP	DP	CL	Network architecture	Communication protocol	Mobile terminal
2015	[70]	–	–	–	–	*	*	*	*	*	–
	[17]	–	–	–	*	*	*	*	–	–	–
	[6]	–	–	–	–	*	–	–	–	–	–
	[1]	*	–	–	–	*	–	–	–	–	–
	[71]	*	*	–	*	*	*	*	–	–	–
	[72]	*	*	–	*	*	*	*	–	–	–
2014	[13]	–	–	–	–	*	*	–	–	–	–
	[73]	–	*	–	*	*	*	*	–	–	–
	[74]	*	–	–	–	–	–	–	–	–	–

10.4 SDMN security measures

We introduce the relationship between threat and security in the data layer, control layer, application layer, and communication protocols. In order to reduce SDMN attacks, there are a lot of solutions that attempt to protect the logic segment. An experiment involves SDN state processing and the use of the centralized virtualization management platform to integrate VNF and SDN logic program segments to provide a more comprehensive examination of the EPC/LTE network state and to achieve cross-domain anomaly monitoring and detection [75]. Similarly, cell-pot infrastructure coupled with intrusion/anomaly detection and protection solutions [76–79] can help one to maintain real-time security of the SDMN control channel and to provide protection for the overall mobile target. In the background of strengthening the network defense cooperation and forensic tracking [80], the network edge can provide auxiliary shielding and prevent malicious software from launching an SDMN attack which would fail the solution [81–83].

As stated in [84], current SDN defense mechanisms can only provide limited SDMN security enhancements due to the lack of structural features associated with the movement. The same conclusion can also be applied to [85]. The SDMN virtualization of security, to a large extent, is still a design direction for the computer system structure, although the concept is in the experimental stage. The fundamental differences between service and infrastructure, whether in IaaS or in the RANaaS program, are the specific trust mechanism. Resource allocation, mobility management, and the missing isolation scheme of the current virtual platform are necessary conditions. A good starting point for SDMN secure virtual direction is presented in [72], despite the fact that different schemes should be implemented to meet the different requirements of the core and fronthaul virtualization. In previous cases, the above mechanism may benefit from the guidance of safety and trust in the EPC/LTE core [84,85], while in the later cases, it may benefit from the cloud operating security policy. Liyanage *et al.,liyanage2015security* define the SDMN architecture and introduce the multitier method for SDMN. This method protects the network itself, as well as the user, based on the security question of different layers. Furthermore, he suggests to use host identity protocol (HIP) and IPSe tunneling to protect communication channels and to restrict the unwanted access by communication policy. Meanwhile, the backhaul devices are protected from the address spoofing source and DoS. Finally, SDM and data are collected to detect and prevent threats. Costa-Requena *et al.,costa2015sdn* establish the 5G network based on SDN and NFV, present the specific architecture, but do not describe about the specific implementation of methods deployed in regards to security issues.

In order to introduce the research advances in SDMN security in detail, Table 10.2 provides a comparison of the architecture of SDMN security problems addressed in the prior works. SDMN's unique security problems have been widely recognized by researchers. Figure 10.4 shows the various security aspects in the SDMN. We introduce the attacks and countermeasures at each level. The characteristics of SDN (i.e., separation of control plane and data plane, centralized management of the network through the controller, network programmability, and flow analysis are implemented via applications) can effectively resist DDoS [47]. However, these features of SDMN

Table 10.2 SDMN security framework

Work	Proposed architecture	Basic theory	Pros.	Cons.	OFN security principle
[51]	5G SDMN architecture	An end-to-end software defining architecture, which introduces a logically centralized control plane and dramatically simplifies the data plane	Give a solution to efficiently guarantee E2E QoS and QoE	No discussions on security issues	N/A
[70]	Multitier security approach with four components: SC, PBC, SMM, and Synch	Communication channel protection; limit unwanted access; threat detection by the use of SDM and data collection	Protect single-point failure of controller by the use of distributed SecGWs	No consideration of terminal devices	Assure robust identity
[50]	SDN and NFV integration for 5G network	Security issues exist from SDN controller to whole network	Analyze SDN, NFV, and 5G network, and give principles	No discussions on security	N/A
[33]	Direct the mobile network to a flow-centric model that employs hardware and a logically centralized controller	The new security challenges of the control channel of SDMNs	Address security issues in control layer	No security consideration in data layer and application layer	Properties of manageable security control

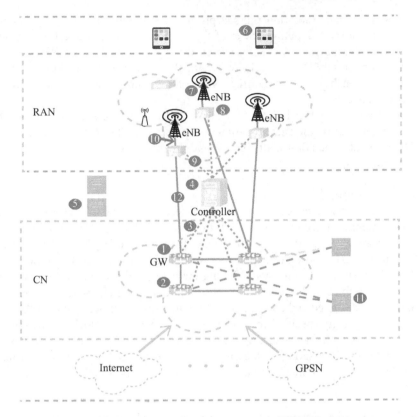

Figure 10.4 Security aspects of SDMN

are also a double-edged sword and bring a number of new vulnerabilities. Thus, we will focus on the analysis of the latter to provide better security, reliability, validity, and flexibility of the SDMN.

10.4.1 Data plane attack

10.4.1.1 Attacks aiming at the OpenFlow-enable switch

Security threats

- Attacks southbound API via false and forged flow table entries due to the intelligent lacking of APIs.
- Flow table is a hardware structure of the OF switch, and the flow entry is its basic unit. The storage capacity in the flow table is limited. A general flow table has only a few hundred flow entries [86]. The resource attack is studied in [87]. The attacker continuously sends data packets with slightly different head information to generate a disguised data stream, so that the flow table becomes overflow quickly, while the corresponding flow entry of the legitimate flows cannot be

updated on time. In addition, this sharply increased number of flow entry requests also exhaust the computing power of the controller and its applications. A new type of inference attack has also been designed by exploit the Weakness of OpenFlow-based SDN networks. When the flow table is full, the frequent operations between the data plane and the control plane are employed to regrade network performance.

- The disguised control information modifies the flow table entries due to the lack of an information authentication mechanism. Similar to the controller under DDoS attack, when flow matching with no clear rules, will lead to the forwarding overflow [86].

Countermeasures

- Improve the maintenance mechanism to ensure the flow table does not overflow.
- Add a monitoring component. Install the local security agent to each OF switch to process the application functions related to the switch [70]. This is an insertion mechanism. The most basic control protocol and user platform for communication channels are not changed. Making the network device adopt the proactive forwarding mode rather than the reactive forwarding mode, the flow entries will have been designed and configured before the network devices running [87].
- Network security mechanism synchronizing with the flow traffic: The control plane receives the latest security status of network traffic through monitoring, generates the corresponding security rules, and empties them into the flow table of the OF switch in the data plane via the issuance of flow table entries.

10.4.1.2   Attacks aiming at the terminals (i.e., client-end devices)

Security threats

- Insider threats for the mobile terminal includes misuse, downloading of application, etc. Moreover, Trojans and viruses are also the threats of the terminals. The security protection for the mobile terminal is also equipment-centered [83]. The terminal lacks effective tools, e.g., intrusion detection system (IDS), antivirus software, endpoint firewall, and spam blocking, which are very effective and common in other platforms [88], but still unworkable for mobile terminals [89].
- Due to physical access vulnerabilities, malicious code is written and injected.

Countermeasures

- Use traditional tools, but need to customize them for mobile devices and provide the security service through the cloud [21].
- Install and run lightweight safety procedures and encrypt the data of mobile devices [90]. A user-centric model named SECURED is proposed in [83], changing the status that an Internet users must provide different security profile and policies for his/her increasing number of mobile ends, like mobile phone and iPad, to simplify the device security problem.
- Monitoring the access of key ports and core programs.

10.4.2 Control plane attack

Security threats

- The limitations of the API will lead to the illegal controller access operation and counterfeit rules insertion. When a packet is not matched to the flow entries, it will be sent to the controller. As a result, an attacker detects the vulnerability of the controller by simply sending data [91].
- Attacking the eastbound API can generate Interference policies by different applications to arouse the DDoS among controller [47].
- The controller will be hijacked and compromised while the controller being made public.
- The backhaul mobile device lacks unified control of the unauthorized access to the controller, which is a loophole that can be used by the forged information to modify the entities of flow tables without authorization.
- The security issue of all kinds of database: for instance, the host location hijacking attack and link fabrication attack can exploit to poison the network topology information in OpenFlow networks. In addition, DOS attack and man-in-the-middle attack can lead to the false network routing and data packets forwarding by providing inaccurate topological information for the routing components in the controller [53].
- The controller is disguised and send harmful controlling information.
- The controller is controlled while its vulnerability is detected [91]. Recently, some vulnerabilities, which are not specific to SDN, have been practically discovered. Such as the XML eXternal entity vulnerability in OpenDay light netconfi., DDoS when deserializing malformer packets in ONOS, and the topology spoofing via host tracking. An SDN network scanning tool, called the SDN scanner [92], can easily operate the existing mobile network scanning tools (e.g., ICMP scanning and Transmission Control Protocol (TCP) synchronize sequence numbers (SYN) scanning). For the SDN networks, which do not require high performance and high bandwidth devices, these attacks will greatly reduce the network performance [47].

Countermeasures

- Rule authentication. FortNOX provides an extension of the rule-based authentication and security constraint mechanism for the OpenFlow controller of NOX. The real-time monitoring of the flow rules applies the role-based authentication to judge the legality of the rules generated by each OpenFlow application and prevent the controller from the attacks incurred by the counterfeit flow rules [93].
- Network behavior and message monitoring. As a component of the controller, SPHINX is used to detect attacks on network topology and data plane structure in SDN networks. When the behavior of the network control platform is changed, the new network behavior can be detected and a warning will be issued. It monitors and judges the legitimacy of the switches and routers. Thereby, only legitimate and harmless control messages are executed [85]. TopoGuard, a new security

extension to the OpenFlow controllers provides automatic and real-time detection of network topology poisoning attacks [13].
- Carry out an omnidirectional monitor for detecting abnormal attacks. (1) The SMM module monitors the application (APP) distributed in SDN and virtual environment through distributing virtual sensor nodes, including monitoring the network resources, network performance, flow, etc. SDM is used to manager these monitoring nodes. (2) Apply the IDS in SDN [94]. Evolving defense mechanism, a bionics-based architecture, can configure the network variations, e.g., IP address, routing, host respond, encryption algorithm, and authentication scheme, to ensure the network safety [71].
- Implement attack prevention via firewall, single-point failure recovery [70], intrusion prevention system (IPS), and authorization/authentication of valid rules and accessed objects.

10.4.3 Application plane attack

As the core equipment of the application plane, a mobile terminal is not only the source of attacks, but also the target of attacks. Therefore, the security of the mobile terminal data is even more important than that of data and control planes.

Security threats [16]
- A large number of APPs lack authentication and authorization and can be accessed by an illegal controller.
- Misusing and abusing the controller is caused by the APP containing security vulnerabilities, malicious code, and bugs.
- The harmful APP generates faulty information flow and inject rules of deceptive rules.
- Attack the northbound APIs.

Countermeasures
- Strengthen the APP management via authentication mechanism, e.g., the user authentication and the third-party certification [21].
- Assure the APP testing and debug to guarantee the correctness and reliability of APPs.
- Judge the APP unauthorized access according to the constraints of APP and its installation.

10.4.4 Attack at the communication protocols

There are also attacks at protocols for the communications between base stations and controller, controller and application services, and switches and controller.

Security threats
- The lacks of the underlying IP layer security and the authentication in the communication between backhaul devices result in IP spoofing.

- The TLS/Secure Sockets Layer (SSL) security protocol in high level is vulnerable to being attacked. For example, there exist some TCP layer attacks, such as SYN DoS and TCP reset attack [16].
- Randomness in use and complexity of configuration of TLS and communication interception [70], e.g., man-in-the-middle attack.

Countermeasures
- Improve the existing protocols: the HIP protocol and IPSec tunneling are proposed to ensure the safety of the channel between the control and data planes [70]. Prevent the threat of user authentication and communication when the user connects LTE network in the first time and the handover process is run [77].
- Detect the incorrect protocol information via IDS.
- Take advantage of the controller to guarantee the communication security between the end nodes. (1) Install the customer edge switching APP in the controller. The APP interacts with the data interaction path of the gateway and insert negotiated flow to ensure end-to-end user communication by applying the customer edge traversal protocol and extends the realm gateway function of traditional firewalls. Furthermore, the abusive, DoS, forged source addresses, and other tools can also be detected and removed. (2) Introducing the TCP-splicing mechanism to relay the user data from a host that has not been forged [50,70].
- Employ the oligarchic trust models adopting the multiple trust-anchor certification authority, e.g., one per subdomain or per controller instance [12].
- Implement the optional support for encrypted TLS communication and a certificate exchange between the switches and the controller(s) proposed in OpenFlow 1.3.0 [8].

10.4.5 *Category and analysis of STRIDE*

Furthermore, we analyze the corresponding network attacks or vulnerabilities from the point of view of computer security systems. The STRIDE method makes logical separations within the complex system security, as shown in [19,95]. STRIDE is a type of security threat method. With STRIDE, security threats are divided into six categories: spoofing of user identity (S), tampering (T), repudiation (R), information disclosure (I), e.g., privacy breach or data leak [96], DoS (D), and elevation of privilege (E).

Table 10.3 provides a study of SDMN-related attacks based on the classifications of STRIDE. The state-of-the-art of the research on the attacks of SDMN is also presented in the table. To summarize Table 10.3, a brief analysis is provided as follows:

- As shown in Table 10.3, some attacks are categorized into one layer; however, they actually may affect several layers. Therefore, corresponding strategies require the interaction and collaboration among multi-layers.
- Monitoring the network state and behavior in each layer is the common means. In addition to the traditional monitoring of network traffic, port access, and network state, one also needs to monitor the SDMN specific message and behavior between the OF switch and controller, among controllers, and between the

Table 10.3   STRIDE-based classification

Location	Category	Existing work
Data layer	S	[70]
	T	[17]
	R	[62]
	I	[62,81]
	D	[17,47]
	E	[62]
Control layer	S	[17,97]
	T	[97]
	R	[17]
	I	[97]
	D	[47,70,97]
	E	[70]
Application layer	S	[70]
	T	[97]
	R	[70]
	I	[81]
	D	[47]
	E	[70]
Communication protocol stack	S	[17,53,98]
	T	[86,87,98]
	R	[55,98]
	I	[55,98]
	D	[52,85,86]
	E	[17,98]

application layer APP and controller. However the real-time monitoring and the corresponding information preservation have brought new problems to the network traffic delay, the normal mobile terminal application running, the controller operation efficiency, the storage space of each layer, etc.

- DDoS may occur in all the layers. Once it occurs, at present, there is no better way to prevent or solve this kind of attack except isolating the related network equipment and links. Therefore, based on the network behavior and characteristics existing prior to a DDoS attack, we conclude that early detection and prevention are the most feasible measures.

10.4.6   SDMN security challenges

Although some advances are being made, there are many challenging problems in SDMN security that call for significant research efforts. Some SDMN security challenges are listed as follows:

- APP authorization and authentication mechanism.
- Security problems for multi-controller architectures.

- Security issues from multicast protocols.
- Redundant connections resulting from security guaranty mechanisms.
- Security measures of the communication with other networks.

10.5 Summary

This chapter introduces the structure of SDMN, and its special security issues. The security measures of SDMN involve three layers. First, there is the data layer, which is associated with the security threats of OpenFlow switch and terminal, and the corresponding countermeasures. Second, there is the control layer, including the security of all databases. Specific security problems of SDMN in the control layer and the corresponding measures were reviewed and discussed. In addition, the STRIDE method was used to achieve a classification of SDMN attacks, as the data layer, control layer, application layer, and communication protocol attacks. Finally, a list of security challenges of SDMN was presented that call for significant research efforts.

References

[1]   Sama MR, Contreras LM, Kaippallimalil J, *et al.* Software-defined control of the virtualized mobile packet core. IEEE Communications Magazine. 2015;53(2):107–115.

[2]   Ge X, Yang B, Ye J, *et al.* Spatial spectrum and energy efficiency of random cellular networks. IEEE Transactions on Communications. 2015;63(3): 1019–1030.

[3]   Bernardos C, La Oliva A, Serrano P, *et al.* An architecture for software defined wireless networking. IEEE Wireless Communications. 2014;21(3):52–61.

[4]   Ge X, Huang K, Wang CX, *et al.* Capacity analysis of a multi-cell multi-antenna cooperative cellular network with co-channel interference. IEEE Transactions on Wireless Communications. 2011;10(10):3298–3309.

[5]   He J, Wen Y, Huang J, *et al.* On the cost–QoE tradeoff for cloud-based video streaming under Amazon EC2's pricing models. IEEE Transactions on Circuits and Systems for Video Technology. 2014;24(4):669–680.

[6]   Chávez-Santiago R, Szydełko M, Kliks A, *et al.* 5G: The convergence of wireless communications. Wireless Personal Communications. 2015;83:1–26.

[7]   Naudts B, Kind M, Westphal FJ, *et al.* Techno-economic analysis of software defined networking as architecture for the virtualization of a mobile network. In: Software Defined Networking (EWSDN), 2012 European Workshop on. IEEE; 2012. p. 67–72.

[8]   Nunes B, Mendonca M, Nguyen XN, *et al.* A survey of software-defined networking: Past, present, and future of programmable networks. IEEE Communications Surveys & Tutorials. 2014;16(3):1617–1634.

[9]   Checko A, Christiansen HL, Yan Y, *et al.* Cloud RAN for mobile networks – A technology overview. IEEE Communications Surveys & Tutorials. 2014;17(1):405–426.

[10]   Xiao J, Hu R, Qian Y, *et al.* Expanding LTE network spectrum with cognitive radios: From concept to implementation. IEEE Wireless Communications. 2013;20(2):12–19.

[11]   Manzalini A, Saracco R, Buyukkoc C, *et al.* Software-defined networks for future networks and services: Main technical challenges and business implications. In: SDN4FNS, IEEE; 2014.

[12]   Kreutz D, Ramos F, and Verissimo P. Towards secure and dependable software-defined networks. In: Proceedings of the Second ACM SIGCOMM Workshop on Hot Topics in Software Defined Networking. ACM; 2013. p. 55–60.

[13]   Hakiri A, Gokhale A, Berthou P, *et al.* Software-defined networking: Challenges and research opportunities for Future Internet. Computer Networks. 2014;75(24):453–471.

[14]   Shin S, Porras PA, Yegneswaran V, *et al.* FRESCO: Modular composable security services for software-defined networks. In: NDSS; 2013.

[15]   Kreutz D, Bessani A, Feitosa E, *et al.* Towards secure and dependable authentication and authorization infrastructures. In: Dependable Computing (PRDC), 2014 IEEE 20th Pacific Rim International Symposium on. IEEE; 2014. p. 43–52.

[16]   Principles and Practices for Securing Software-Defined Networks; 2015. www.opennetworking.org.

[17]   Kreutz D, Ramos FM, Esteves Verissimo P, *et al.* Software-defined networking: A comprehensive survey. Proceedings of the IEEE. 2015;103(1):14–76.

[18]   Yap KK, Sherwood R, Kobayashi M, *et al.* Blueprint for introducing innovation into wireless mobile networks. In: Proceedings of the Second ACM SIG-COMM Workshop on Virtualized Infrastructure Systems and Architectures. ACM; 2010. p. 25–32.

[19]   Hernan S, Lambert S, Ostwald T, *et al.* Uncover Security Design Flaws Using The STRIDE Approach; Nov. 2006. msdn. microsoft. com.

[20]   Wikipedia. STRIDE(security)–Wikipedia, The Free Encyclopedia; 2015. [Online; accessed 20-July-2015]. Available from: https://en.wikipedia.org/wiki/STRIDE_(security).

[21]   Ali M, Khan SU, and Vasilakos AV. Security in cloud computing: Opportunities and challenges. Information Sciences. 2015;305(1):357–383.

[22]   Yazıcı V, Kozat UC, and Oguz Sunay M. A new control plane for 5G network architecture with a case study on unified handoff, mobility, and routing management. IEEE Communications Magazine. 2014;52(11):76–85.

[23]   Yang M, Li Y, Hu L, *et al.* Cross-layer software-defined 5G network. Mobile Networks and Applications. 2014;20(3):1–10.

[24]   Jin X, Li LE, Vanbever L, *et al.* Softcell: Scalable and flexible cellular core network architecture. In: Proceedings of the Ninth ACM Conference on Emerging Networking Experiments and Technologies. ACM; 2013. p. 163–174.

[25]   Costa-Requena J. SDN integration in LTE mobile backhaul networks. In: Information Networking (ICOIN), 2014 International Conference on. IEEE; 2014. p. 264–269.

[26] Kempf J, Johansson B, Pettersson S, *et al*. Moving the mobile evolved packet core to the cloud. In: Wireless and Mobile Computing, Networking and Communications (WiMob), 2012 IEEE 8th International Conference on. IEEE; 2012. p. 784–791.

[27] Sama MR, Ben Hadj Said S, Guillouard K, *et al*. Enabling network programmability in LTE/EPC architecture using OpenFlow. In: Modeling and Optimization in Mobile, Ad Hoc, and Wireless Networks (WiOpt), 2014 12th International Symposium on. IEEE; 2014. p. 389–396.

[28] Nagy M, and Kotuliak I. Utilizing OpenFlow, SDN and NFV in GPRS core network. In: Testbeds and Research Infrastructure: Development of Networks and Communities. Springer; 2014. p. 184–193.

[29] Ge X, Cheng H, Guizani M, *et al*. 5G wireless backhaul networks: Challenges and research advances. IEEE Network. 2014;28(6):6–11.

[30] He J, Xue Z, Wu D, *et al*. CBM: Online strategies on cost-aware buffer management for mobile video streaming. IEEE Transactions on Multimedia. 2014;16(1):242–252.

[31] Lei L, Zhong Z, Zheng K, *et al*. Challenges on wireless heterogeneous networks for mobile cloud computing. IEEE Wireless Communications. 2013; 20(3):34–44.

[32] Zheng K, Wang Y, Wang W, *et al*. Energy-efficient wireless in-home: the need for interference-controlled femtocells. IEEE Wireless Communications. 2011;18(6):36–44.

[33] Liyanage M, Ylianttila M, and Gurtov A. Securing the control channel of software-defined mobile networks. In: A World of Wireless, Mobile and Multimedia Networks (WoWMoM), 2014 IEEE 15th International Symposium on. IEEE; 2014. p. 1–6.

[34] Wu D, Xue Z, and He J. iCloudAccess: Cost-effective streaming of video games from the cloud with low latency. IEEE Transactions on Circuits and Systems for Video Technology. 2014;24(8):1405–1416.

[35] He J, Wu D, Zeng Y, *et al*. Toward optimal deployment of cloud-assisted video distribution services. IEEE Transactions on Circuits and Systems for Video Technology. 2013;23(10):1717–1728.

[36] Network Functions Virtualisation (NFV); 2013. Available from: https://portal.etsi.org/nfv/nfv_white_paper2.pdf.

[37] Bays LR, Oliveira RR, Barcellos MP, *et al*. Virtual network security: Threats, countermeasures, and challenges. Journal of Internet Services and Applications. 2015;6(1):1–19.

[38] Wolinsky DI, Agrawal A, Boykin PO, *et al*. On the design of virtual machine sandboxes for distributed computing in wide-area overlays of virtual workstations. In: Virtualization Technology in Distributed Computing, 2006. VTDC 2006. First International Workshop on. IEEE; 2006. p. 8–8.

[39] Wu H, Ding Y, Winer C, *et al*. Network security for virtual machine in cloud computing. In: Computer Sciences and Convergence Information Technology (ICCIT), 2010 5th International Conference on. IEEE; 2010. p. 18–21.

[40]   de Oliveira DAS, and Wu FS. Protecting kernel code and data with a virtualization-aware collaborative operating system. In: Computer Security Applications Conference, 2009. ACSAC'09. Annual. IEEE; 2009. p. 451–460.

[41]   Zhang L, Shetty S, Liu P, *et al.* RootkitDet: Practical end-to-end defense against kernel rootkits in a cloud environment. In: Computer Security-ESORICS 2014. Springer; 2014. p. 475–493.

[42]   Baliga A, Kamat P, and Iftode L. Lurking in the shadows: Identifying systemic threats to kernel data. In: Security and Privacy, 2007. SP'07. IEEE Symposium on. IEEE; 2007. p. 246–251.

[43]   Fernandes DA, Soares LF, Gomes JV, *et al.* Security issues in cloud environments: A survey. International Journal of Information Security. 2014;13(2):113–170.

[44]   Nguyen MD, Chau NT, Jung S, *et al.* A demonstration of malicious insider attacks inside cloud IaaS vendor. International Journal of Information and Education Technology. 2014;4(6):483–486.

[45]   Rocha F, and Correia M. Lucy in the sky without diamonds: Stealing confidential data in the cloud. In: Dependable Systems and Networks Workshops (DSN-W), 2011 IEEE/IFIP 41st International Conference on. IEEE; 2011. p. 129–134.

[46]   Zissis D, and Lekkas D. Addressing cloud computing security issues. Future Generation Computer Systems. 2012;28(3):583–592.

[47]   Yan Q, and Yu F. Distributed denial of service attacks in software-defined networking with cloud computing. IEEE Communications Magazine. 2015; 53(4):52–59.

[48]   Szefer J, Keller E, Lee RB, *et al.* Eliminating the hypervisor attack surface for a more secure cloud. In: Proceedings of the 18th ACM Conference on Computer and Communications Security. ACM; 2011. p. 401–412.

[49]   Liang C, and Yu FR. Wireless virtualization for next generation mobile cellular networks. IEEE Wireless Communications. 2015;22(1):61–69.

[50]   Costa-Requena J, Santos JL, Guasch VF, *et al.* SDN and NFV integration in generalized mobile network architecture. In: Networks and Communications (EuCNC), 2015 European Conference on. IEEE; 2015. p. 154–158.

[51]   Yang M, Li Y, Li B, *et al.* Service-oriented 5G network architecture: An end-to-end software defining approach. International Journal of Communication Systems. 2016;29(10):1645–1657.

[52]   Kloti R, Kotronis V, and Smith P. OpenFlow: A security analysis. In: Network Protocols (ICNP), 2013 21st IEEE International Conference on. IEEE; 2013. p. 1–6.

[53]   Hong S, Xu L, Wang H, *et al.* Poisoning network visibility in software-defined networks: New attacks and countermeasures. In: Network and Distributed System Security (NDSS) Symposium 2015. NDSS; 2015. p. 8–11.

[54]   Benton K, Camp LJ, and Small C. OpenFlow vulnerability assessment. In: Proceedings of the Second ACM SIGCOMM Workshop on Hot Topics in Software Defined Networking. ACM; 2013. p. 151–152.

[55] Shin S, and Gu G. Attacking software-defined networks: A first feasibility study. In: Proceedings of the second ACM SIGCOMM Workshop on Hot Topics in Software Defined Networking. ACM; 2013. p. 165–166.

[56] Shin S, Song Y, Lee T, *et al.* Rosemary: A robust, secure, and high-performance network operating system. In: Proceedings of the 2014 ACM SIGSAC Conference on Computer and Communications Security. ACM; 2014. p. 78–89.

[57] Schehlmann L, Abt S, and Baier H. Blessing or curse? Revisiting security aspects of software-defined networking. In: Network and Service Management (CNSM), 2014 10th International Conference on. IEEE; 2014. p. 382–387.

[58] Marinho J, Granjal J, and Monteiro E. A survey on security attacks and countermeasures with primary user detection in cognitive radio networks. EURASIP Journal on Information Security. 2015;2015(1):1–14.

[59] Naseef M. Vulnerabilities of LTE and LTE-Advanced Communication White Paper; 2014.

[60] Qi F, Sun S, Rong B, *et al.* Cognitive radio based adaptive SON for LTE-a heterogeneous networks. In: Global Communications Conference (GLOBECOM), 2014 IEEE. IEEE; 2014. p. 4412–4417.

[61] Lien SY, Chen KC, Liang YC, *et al.* Cognitive radio resource management for future cellular networks. IEEE Wireless Communications. 2014;21(1):70–79.

[62] Baldini G, Sturman T, Biswas AR, *et al.* Security aspects in software defined radio and cognitive radio networks: A survey and a way ahead. IEEE Communications Surveys & Tutorials. 2012;14(2):355–379.

[63] Park JM, Reed JH, Beex A, *et al.* Security and enforcement in spectrum sharing. Proceedings of the IEEE. 2014;102(3):270–281.

[64] Sethi A, and Brown TX. Hammer model threat assessment of cognitive radio denial of service attacks. In: New Frontiers in Dynamic Spectrum Access Networks, 2008. DySPAN 2008. 3rd IEEE Symposium on. IEEE; 2008. p. 1–12.

[65] Hlavacek D, and Chang JM. A layered approach to cognitive radio network security: A survey. Computer Networks. 2014;75(24):414–436.

[66] Zhang L, Ding G, Wu Q, *et al.* Byzantine attack and defense in cognitive radio networks: A survey. IEEE Communication Surveys & Tutorials. 2015;17(3):1342–1363.

[67] Jermyn J, Salles-Loustau G, and Zonouz S. An analysis of DoS attack strategies against the LTE RAN. Journal of Cyber Security. 2014;3(2):159–180.

[68] Golde N, Redon K, and Borgaonkar R. Weaponizing femtocells: The effect of rogue devices on mobile telecommunications. In: NDSS; 2012.

[69] Lichtman M, Reed JH, Clancy TC, *et al.* Vulnerability of LTE to hostile interference. In: Global Conference on Signal and Information Processing (GlobalSIP), 2013 IEEE. IEEE; 2013. p. 285–288.

[70] Liyanage M, Ahmad I, Ylianttila M, *et al.* Security for future software defined mobile networks. In: Next Generation Mobile Applications Services and Technologies (NGMAST), 9th International Conference on. IEEE; 2015. p. 1–9.

[71]   Zhou H, Wu C, Jiang M, *et al.* Evolving defense mechanism for future network security. IEEE Communications Magazine. 2015;53(4):45–51.

[72]   Gonzales D, Kaplan J, Saltzman E, *et al.* Cloud-trust-a security assessment model for infrastructure as a service (IaaS) clouds. IEEE Transactions on Cloud Computing. 2015;5(3):523–536.

[73]   Hu F, Hao Q, and Bao K. A survey on software-defined network and OpenFlow: From concept to implementation. IEEE Communications Surveys & Tutorials. 2014;16(4):2181–2206.

[74]   Hu H, Ahn GJ, Han W, *et al.* Towards a reliable SDN firewall. In: Presented as part of the Open Networking Summit 2014 (ONS 2014); 2014.

[75]   Matias J, Garay J, Toledo N, *et al.* Toward an SDN-enabled NFV architecture. IEEE Communications Magazine. 2015;53(4):187–193.

[76]   Alzahrani AJ, and Ghorbani AA. A multi-agent system for smartphone intrusion detection framework. In: Proceedings of the 18th Asia Pacific Symposium on Intelligent and Evolutionary Systems, Volume 1. Springer; 2015. p. 101–113.

[77]   El-Gaml EF, ElAttar H, and El-Badawy HM. Evaluation of intrusion prevention technique in LTE based network. International Journal of Scientific & Engineering Research. 2014;5:1395–1400.

[78]   Liebergeld S, Lange M, and Borgaonkar R. Cellpot: A concept for next generation cellular network honeypots. In: Workshop on Security Emergence Network Technology. NDSS; 2014.

[79]   Yan Z, Zhang P, and Vasilakos AV. A security and trust framework for virtualized networks and software-defined networking. Security and Communication Networks. 2016;9(16):3059–3069.

[80]   François J, and Festor O. Anomaly traceback using software defined networking. In: Parallel Computing Technologies (PARCOMPTECH), 2015 National Conference on. IEEE; 2015. p. 203–208.

[81]   Duan X, and Wang X. Authentication handover and privacy protection in 5G hetnets using software-defined networking. IEEE Communications Magazine. 2015;53(4):28–35.

[82]   Yang N, Wang L, Geraci G, *et al.* Safeguarding 5G wireless communication networks using physical layer security. IEEE Communications Magazine. 2015;53(4):20–27.

[83]   Montero D, Yannuzzi M, Shaw A, *et al.* Virtualized security at the network edge: A user-centric approach. IEEE Communications Magazine. 2015;53(4): 176–186.

[84]   Ding AY, Crowcroft J, Tarkoma S, *et al.* Software defined networking for security enhancement in wireless mobile networks. Computer Networks. 2014;66:94–101.

[85]   Dhawan M, Poddar R, Mahajan K, *et al.* SPHINX: Detecting security attacks in software-defined networks. In: Proceedings of the 2015 Network and Distributed System Security (NDSS) Symposium; 2015.

[86]   Leng J, Zhou Y, Zhang J, *et al.* An Inference Attack Model for Flow Table Capacity and Usage: Exploiting the Vulnerability of Flow Table Overflow in Software-Defined Network; 2015. arXiv preprint arXiv:150403095.

[87]   Tri N, Hiep T, and Kim K. Assessing the impact of resource attack in software defined network. In: Information Networking (ICOIN), 2015 International Conference on. IEEE; 2015. p. 420–425.

[88]   Dinh HT, Lee C, Niyato D, *et al.* A survey of mobile cloud computing: architecture, applications, and approaches. Wireless Communications and Mobile Computing. 2013;13(18):1587–1611.

[89]   Mobile Device Security in the Workplace: 6 Key Risks & Challenges; 2015. Available from: http://focus.forsythe.com/articles/55/Mobile-Device-Security-in-the-Workplace-6-Key-Risks-and-Challenges.

[90]   Khan AN, Kiah MM, Madani SA, *et al.* Enhanced dynamic credential generation scheme for protection of user identity in mobile-cloud computing. The Journal of Supercomputing. 2013;66(3):1687–1706.

[91]   SDN and Security; 2015. Available from: http://onosproject.org/2015/04/03/sdn-and-security-david-jorm/.

[92]   Gudipati A, Perry D, Li LE, *et al.* SoftRAN: Software defined radio access network. In: Proceedings of the Second ACM SIGCOMM Workshop on Hot Topics in Software Defined Networking. ACM; 2013. p. 25–30.

[93]   Porras P, Shin S, Yegneswaran V, *et al.* A security enforcement kernel for OpenFlow networks. In: Proceedings of the First Workshop on Hot Topics in Software Defined Networks. ACM; 2012. p. 121–126.

[94]   Giotis K, Argyropoulos C, Androulidakis G, *et al.* Combining OpenFlow and sFlow for an effective and scalable anomaly detection and mitigation mechanism on SDN environments. Computer Networks. 2014;62:122–136.

[95]   Yang M, Li Y, Jin D, *et al.* Software-defined and virtualized future mobile and wireless networks: A survey. Mobile Networks and Applications. 2014;20(1):4–18.

[96]   Li G, Wu D, Shen J, *et al.* Deciphering privacy leakage in microblogging social networks: A measurement study. Security and Communication Networks. 2015;8(17):3191–3204.

[97]   Akhunzada A, Ahmed E, Gani A, *et al.* Securing software defined networks: Taxonomy, requirements, and open issues. IEEE Communications Magazine. 2015;53(4):36–44.

[98]   Tasch M, Khondoker R, Marx R, *et al.* Security analysis of security applications for software defined networks. In: Proceedings of the AINTEC 2014 on Asian Internet Engineering Conference. ACM; 2014. p. 23–30.

Chapter 11

Dynamic public opinion evolvement modeling and supervision in social networks

Shuaishuai Zhu[1] and Xu An Wang[1]

With the booming of social networks, a large proportion of public opinion is expressed and transferred through social networks. With complex structure and varied evolving patterns, monitoring public opinion in social networks is not well solved for a long period. Motivated by the purpose of public opinion and social network evolvement rules, we developed a public opinion dynamic evolvement model and supervision mechanism in social networks. We assume our research target is a topic-based and opinion-driven social network that is the most popular one in studying public opinion. The background network of our model is a temporary social connection that we name as tornado-type social network (TTSN). In a TTSN, public opinion evolvement is decided by two basic factors: sentiment activity (SA) and opinion consistency (OC). Based on the observation of SA and OC, we have designed a model to supervise and optimize the public opinion express in social networks. Under the model, the public opinion supervision is regressed to an optimization problem. By solving the problem, both our deduction and simulation results show that public opinion in a social network tends to evolve from chaos to consistency, and SA follows approximately ideal normal distributions before a time limit T.

11.1 Introduction

Opinion social network is an online community that initiatively formed by hundreds of millions of opinion subjects who are connected with their surrounding cycles acting as opinion followers and followees. With the development of Internet technologies, online opinion is taking a dominating place in public opinion express. Many huge online social community sites, such as Facebook, Tencent Weibo, Sina Weibo, and Twitter, maintain over 5 billion active users [1]. Online social ties are becoming a necessity for Internet online users to build social connections, share resources and express opinions. Oceans of social interaction data are stored and transferred on these sites carrying their views and judgments toward user behaviors and social

[1]Electronics Department, Engineering University of the APF, Xi'an, China

topic spots. As social networks are becoming more influential in all aspects in social life, interaction data is always a hot research object in the field of ads pushing, recommendation system and potential client mining.

So far, analysis models in social networks are mainly focused on community discovery [2–7], natural language analysis [8,9], rumor spreading [10,11] and others. In the field of social network evolvement models, there are basically two types of routines: complex network evolvement at topo level [10] and sentiment tag analysis at content level [9]. These models are either biased to specially design community structures, like friend circles, or naive models to statistically analyze the word-based networks, like knowledge-sharing platforms. In this chapter, we think that the main purpose of studying evolvement of social network is to obtain the correct evaluation of opinion state and SA, so as to develop free and healthy public online environment. But so far as we know, no tactic solution is proposed to contain the evolvement process and handle risks. We extracted three difficult hard cores in the field of online public opinion research.

11.1.1 No combined analysis model for public opinion in social networks

Many excellent works emphasize on analyzing network entities and their topo structure. In this type of models, reality, rumors and noises are mixed during the message spreading, and single entity is regularly considered as probabilistic receiver and sender. The purpose is to achieve the best correctness of received information. In a typical social network, the influence of an entity is not only decided by its neighbors, but also by its historical accumulated knowledge.

In another field, models at the natural language process level can overcome the above drawbacks. Considering the semantics of information contents, the spreading flow is much more realistic to community activities. But the influence based on content exchange among users is hard to quantify, and public opinion extracted from segment of words and tags is not convincing.

The combination of the above two routines is a promising way to find a satisfying solution to modeling public opinion evolvement.

11.1.2 Dynamic challenge for public opinion sampling and inspection

Unlike real-world relative networks, online social networks are unstable, temporary, topic based and of exponential speed of evolvement. A connection occurred only on the occasion of absence of hot topic information. Novelty booms social network, while saturation indicates dying out. So the driving force of social network is accompanied by the spreading of rear information. In this process, huge amount of public opinion evolve and prevail among users, and users' attention and interests are altered under the influence of fresh opinions. Finally, a stronger feedback comes online to resonate with the original opinion, and more users get affected. Back to the purpose of studying social networks, it is hard to recognize the pattern and inspect the state of social network. The existing opinion sampling based on topics, dynamics research and interactive influences of users based on topo structure are useful tools, but we need to build a more rigid model to fully describe the process.

11.1.3 Time efficiency for public opinion supervision

In social networks, messages spread at exponential speed, and public opinions are accompanied with explosive news flood among all users. Without interference, these opinions will likely lead to radial crowd behaviors, even social turbulence. There is a strong requirement to evaluate the radical degree of public opinion and, alter the evolving direction, to avoid potentially risky social events. Until now, the methods include keywords filtering [9], network semantic analysis [12], event discovery based on community structures [6]. Although these excellent results can reveal public opinion evolvement through content mining, none of them solves the public opinion supervision problem before uncontrollable opinion flooding. A systematic opinion evolvement model is needed to accurately describe the driven forces in social networks, and necessary outside actions should be taken to gently maintain a free but controlled online opinion environment.

In this chapter, inspired by the above observations of opinion evolvement in social networks, we try to build a tactic model to define and describe the evolving process, while overcoming drawbacks of the previous models. The contributions of this chapter are as follows: we combined the social network topo analysis and content sentiment analysis and introduced a topic-based and opinion-driven social network model based on TTSN topo structure and an OC–SA supervision mechanism. In our model, we use improved hybrids of CNM [7] and Takaffoli [13] frameworks as our dynamic social network discovery modes. We simplify Takaffoli's seven subgraph events to OC and SA quantization, so as to conveniently target at monitoring the public opinion during the evolvement.

We arrange this chapter as follows: In Section 11.2, we revisited some existing works about social network evolvement. Section 11.3 introduced our dynamic public opinion evolvement model and a few conclusions about the model. In Section 11.4, evolvement algorithm is given based on the above model. Finally, a series of evaluation tests are pursued to show the performance of our model.

11.2 Related works

A lot of work has been done in terms of social network evolvement and a handful tools have been developed to make recognition, proceed analysis and extract useful knowledge from social network. A brief way to describe the evolvement process is to study the evolvement of social network topology. There are mainly three routines.

11.2.1 Evolvement based on topo discovery and graph structure change

In social networks, evolvement is accompanied with the structure change of logical topo, in which information exchange occurs among participants. So revealing the exchange somehow equals the topo discovery. Fortunato [2] and Xie [3] proposed their algorithms of community discovery, but these algorithms can only applied in simple and static social networks. On cross-community topo discovery, Palla [4] raised the first community-discovered algorithm supporting mining cross-community relationship and discussed the overlapping community evolvement. On this basis, Zhang [5,6] developed a series of approaches to identifying online social networks. On a graph structure change, Asur [14], Takaffoli [15] and Zhang [6] explored the evolvement of social networks from the angle of logical topo events. Asur [14] defined three events: maintaining, combining and splitting to describe the birth, development and decay and so on. But this model is too simple and rigorous to apply. Takaffoli [15] expended the routine and built a model to predict an event in social networks with seven basic events. But with more related events to describe and two extra controlling parameters to train, event prediction accuracy and time cost are sacrificed to some degree. Zhang [6] improved their models and proposed a community evolvement prediction method based on five types of topo event-based frameworks to construct graph production model. Takaffoli [13,15], Antonio [16], Nicholas [17], Li [18] did a lot of works in the field of dynamic community evolvement. They put their research emphasizing on event deduction and prediction through the evolvement of topology, and the absence of vertex attributes makes their evolvement models divorced from real social networks.

11.2.2　*Evolvement based on influence analysis*

The evolvement of overall network is closely influenced by a small proportion of key nodes. The complements of weight and distribution of these nodes render to the intergalactic map (IM) problem [19]. A couple of candidate algorithms are proposed to solve the problem, such as Leskovec [20], Cheng [21] and Kempe [22]. Kempe designed a greedy algorithm to reduce IM to solving a discrete optimal non-polynomial (NP) problem but restricted by scale of target social network. Leskovec [20] raised cost-effective lazy forward (CELF) strategies to enhance the executing efficiency. Cheng [21] designed the StaticGreedy algorithm to greatly improve the accuracy of key nodes. Luo [23] chose the candidate nodes by sorting influence nodes with PageRank algorithm. Goyal [24] studied the relative influence by existing user behavior information, so as to deduce the propagation strength of the overall social network. Bhagat [25] considered invest and interest as two important factors from the angle of investment to obtain maximum profit in a network. Guo [26] presented a user recommendation algorithm based on maximum individual influence computation.

11.2.3　*Evolvement based on sentiment and NLP*

Sentiment learning or known as emotion artificial intelligence (AI) [8] is a basic tool for opinion evolvement in this field. But constrained by machine learning, the analysis systems only process isolated words and classify positive and negative opinions by weights. On automatic tools [27] developed by data service providers such as Sina, Facebook and Salesforce, topic content is split into subtopics, attributes and tags. Opinions can be extracted from online content at the level of document, sentence and entity. Jiang [9] designed a method to extract ⟨Target, Opinion⟩ pairs from financial user comments, as a new approach to find user connections and express sentiment implicitly. These opinion evolvement routines are brief and fast, but the results are always tending to be fuzzy and inaccurate, unless those results come from voting scenarios.

In the field of social network research, a lot of works are done in terms of complex network analysis, relationship discovery and social network evolvement. So far, a solution to describe the inner driven forces and guide the public opinion evolvement in social networks is blank.

11.3   Dynamic public opinion evolvement modeling

In the previous models, opinion of entities is categorized with the traverse and the initiative. But for an influential event, no matter if it is a truth or a rumor, online opinion entities tend to agree and accept the first information they heard. Then with the preceding of the event, these entities are continuously influenced by a series of new information updated. During the mergence and digestion of new information, their opinions keep transferring as long as their sentiment evolves. The evolvement of public opinion is generally assumed as a sociopsychological process, and an accurate description of every dynamic entity is always a hard problem. The basic aim of our model is not to mine and control public opinion but to accurately quantify the public SA toward some major social events and to guide the public opinion to a desirable consistent degree. Still, we assume the targeting opinion entities as a graph, and in order to observe and quantify public opinion evolvement in the cluster, different kinds of sampling methods are applied. We build our model on the general graph model of social network and define our own quantifying features and characters on the graph.

11.3.1   System model and definitions

A basic social network is defined as follows. In a social network with n entities, a neighborhood entity can interact with its surrounding entities through direct links. The social network is described by a graph $G \leftarrow \langle V, E, O \rangle$, where V and E stand for the vertices and the edges of the graph, and O is a vector containing a collection of opinion attributes toward coordinate topics in G. In this chapter, we first introduced a special type of social network called TTSN as defined below to describe the spreading of opinions. In a TTSN $\in G$, a vertex contains the opinion information, and an edge carries the shared opinion from neighbor vertices. The opinions evolve in ⟨not agree(disgust), agree(favor)⟩ noted as $\langle D, F \rangle$ [9]. The sentiment that shows the opinion of an entity is a key object to evaluate, because it is the sentiment of a social network that leads the public opinion strength. The contacts among vertices can mutually influence and change each vertex's opinion with certain probability decided by graph structure, background information (e.g., common sense and original opinion) and time lapse. Then a sentiment distribution standing for the online population is formed. Basic assumptions in a social network graph are defined in the following definitions.

A couple of opinion evaluation definitions are defined.

Definition 11.1. *(TTSN) It is a directed scale-free graph TTSN ←< V =*
{leaders, fans}, E = {followees ← followers}, O_{[Topic_{i,t}]} = {O_{i,t}} >∈ G which satis-
fies |fans| ≫ |leaders| and degree_{fans} ≪ degree_{leaders}. Here the leaders not only
include those nodes with high out-degree but also those on critical paths across
subgraphs. A TTSN satisfies the following properties.

Fans of topic: In a TTSN, an edge is built by following an interesting topic from a
certain vertex and removed by declining of the topic. Almost all the connections in
the network are temporary. They only survive during the evolvement life cycle.

Expotential evolvement: The topic discussion quantity at time t is $Q \sim$
$O((\sum V)^{ut}, (\sum E)^{\delta t})$, in which V and E keep expanding during the next Δt with
the acceleration of $v\left(|leaders| \cdot \sum V^u / t\right)$, and u, δ are scale-controlling factors of
vertices and edges. Then if we simplify the structure of the TTSN as a constantly
expending network, we can evaluate the topic quantity at time t with the following
tuple expression:

$$Q = \left(\left(\sum V + \int_{\Delta t} v\left(|leaders| \cdot \frac{\sum V}{t}\right)\right)^{ut}, \left(\sum E + \int_{\Delta t} v\left(|leaders| \cdot \frac{\sum V}{t}\right)\right)^{\delta t}\right)$$

(11.1)

Definition 11.2. *(opinion evolvement model). In a TTSN at time t, the opinion of*
vertex i can be described as an iterative map $O_{i,t} \leftarrow \langle O_{i,t-1}, E_i^m, \lambda_t \rangle$, in which E_i^m is
the neighbor vertices within m jumps, and λ_t is the neighbor influence factor applied
to quantify the transferred proportion of $O_{i,t-1}$ from its neighbor vertices. The value of
a vertex is decided by the input and output opinion collections. For the convenience
of computing and without losing generality, we assume the following rules.

1. The opinions evolve in ⟨not agree(disgust), agree(favor)⟩ ← $[D, F]^n$, and
   its value is changed by average synchronous/distortion factor $\xi_{i,j} \leftarrow$
   $Distort^{-1}(\lambda_t, E) \in (-\infty, +\infty)$, which is a variable to quantify the degree of
   opinion distortion and reshaping on the basis of neighborhood opinion input.
   It is a relatively stable variable for a specified user to describe the information
   interaction between the target vertex i and its neighbor j. Then for each (i, j)
   connected with E, we have

$$\xi_{i,j} \leftarrow \begin{cases} 0, \text{ on } t = 0 \\ \dfrac{1}{O_i + O_j}, \text{ with} \dfrac{1}{D} < \xi < \dfrac{1}{F}, \text{ on } 0 < t < \infty \\ \Im, t \to \infty \end{cases}$$

(11.2)

2. Opinion of each vertex is an empty $p * q$ matrix $O_{i,0,(p*q)} \leftarrow [0]^n$ or so-called
   innocent before event information spreading in the social network, and p, q are in-
   degree and out-degree of the vertex. When $t = 0$, the public opinion evolvement

starts, and we have $\sum\limits^{N}|O| > 0$. For brief and compactness, we assume that all the matrix additive methods are a matrix combination of the coordinate position.

Then, the evolvement of $O_{i,t}$ is described by the following iterative formula:

$$
O_{i,t} \leftarrow \begin{cases} O_{i,t-1,(p,q)} + \sum\limits^{E_i} O_{E_i^1,t-1} \cdot \lambda_t, \text{if } |O_{i,t-1,(p,q)}| < |\sum\limits^{E_i} O_{E_i^1,t-1}| \\[2em] O_{i,t-1,(p,q)}, \text{if } |O_{i,t-1,(p,q)}| > |\sum\limits^{E_i} O_{E_i^1,t-1}| \end{cases} \tag{11.3}
$$

in which we can simplify the distortion function as $\lambda_t = \xi_{i,E_i} \cdot P(O_{i,t-1}|O_{E_i^1,t-1})/ P(O_{E_i^1,t-1}|O_{E_i^2,t-2})$, and $P(O_{i,t}|O_{E_i^1})$ is the probability that vertex i merges its opinion with those transferred from its neighbor vertices, and $P(O_{i,t}|O_{E_i^1}) = O_{i,t}/ (O_{E_i^1}m(t - t_0))$, which decays along with time ticks of evolvement. In a TTSN, λ_t is decided by the information flow (or the freshness of opinions) of $\langle$followee, follower$\rangle$. Then we have $\lambda_0 = 0$, $\lambda_1 = 1$ and $P(O_{follower}|O_{followee}) = 1$. By the evolvement of $\langle\lambda(\xi), m\rangle$, the supervisor of a social network can observe and control the progress of a social network.

In Definition 11.2, the opinion of a vertex is decided by its original opinion, neighbor vertices' opinions, and the vertex with more edges generates more influence in the opinion social network. These small proportions of vertices with the largest quantities of edges are called opinion leaders. In public opinion supervision, the opinion leader's opinion can be changed by supervisor's enforcement for the sake of public security.

Definition 11.3. [SA model (mild spreading model)]. *During the spreading of a mild event, for any opinion $O \in [D, F]^n$ with probability density function $F(O)$, we define two infinitude states: left wing (radical, L) and right wing (conservative, R). Then we define the map $SA \subseteq (L, R) \leftarrow sa(O)$ to evaluate the SA of a social network. Sentiment is defined to show the strength of entities holding their opinion. The public opinion distribution of two opposite states formed the SA of a social network. We define the following properties of SA.*

Addability and extension: sentiment expends with adding all the negative sentiments it accepts.

Comparability: For any $O_i, O_j \in [D, F]^n$, if $|O_i| > |O_j|$, we have $|L_i| > |L_j|$ or $|R_i| < |R_j|$.

Dynamic: During the opinion evolvement, *SA* evolves according to the definition of O.

Leader opinion reversal: In order to obtain a stable public opinion, the opinions of a minimum number of key vertices can be deliberately reversed to its opposite. The operation is described as $\{O\}_u \leftarrow \{\overline{O}\}$, in which $u \ll N$.

Left-wing public opinion is a sign leading to social turbulence, while right-wing public opinion usually causes stagnancy. An appropriate SA state is neither too radical nor too conservative. A weightful proportion of public opinion should be mild and reasonable. For the sake of computing convenience, we simplify SA in a TTSN as

$$(L, R) \leftarrow (0, +\infty) \cup (0, -\infty), \text{ and } SA = \frac{1}{\lambda_t} \exp\left\{\frac{1}{|F(O)|}\right\} \tag{11.4}$$

In this model, we are aimed to train a proper influence factor and to find the coordinate $F(O)$, so as to evaluate the strength of public opinion in a social network. The object we are working on is structure known graphics that are actually plausible to obtain from social network platform provider's database.

SA model (wild spreading model): During the spreading of a dramatic and sensitive event, we create another spreading model on the basis of Definition 11.3:

$$SA \leftarrow \frac{1}{\lambda_t} \left(\exp\left\{\frac{\sum (SA_{t-1})}{L_0}\right\} + \exp\left\{\frac{1}{|F(O)|}\right\}\right) \tag{11.5}$$

Definition 11.4. *(an ideal opinion state). For opinion distribution function F in social network G, after a limited time intervals of evolvement, the opinion distribution is stable, and the sentiment interactions are saturate. We can describe the state by the following tuple:*

$$\begin{cases} |F_O(O, t, G)| \to |\Im|, t < +\infty, \Im \text{ is the final convergence value of current topic} \\ F(SA, t, G) \subseteq \{F^{T/\Delta t}(SA, T, G), E(SA) \to 0 \text{ and } \sigma < \varepsilon\}, \varepsilon \text{ a desirable confidence} \\ \text{pre-chosen by the network supervisor} \end{cases}$$

$$(11.6)$$

In this definition, the supervision of the social network is the only response for the public opinion stability, and it seldom interferes the evolvement process. Only under the condition that the evolvement deviates far from an ideal opinion state, the supervisor moves on to opinion interference by OC–SA optimum.

Definition 11.5. *[OC and SA optimum problem (OC–SA optimum)]. It finds the optimal state of F(O) and SA by regressing the appropriate distortion function $\lambda(\xi, G)$ to obtain an ideal opinion state during the evolvement of G. So far in this chapter, the solution to OC–SA optimum does not have a mature routine. We proposed a naive method in Section 11.4 according to the following theorems to operate on a minimum set of degree serialized vertices to achieve OC and SA optimization.*

We present Lemmas 11.1 and 11.2 to show the statistical characters of public opinion in a TTSN. In Lemma 11.1, if without new topic joining in, public opinion tends to draw consistency with time expending, which is a basic rule of our evolvement model. Lemma 11.2 shows the distribution of sentiment generated by public opinion. We can find a novel angle to supervise the network by inspecting SA.

Lemma 11.1. *In a TTSN, on $t < +\infty$, $O_i \to \Im \in [D, F]$ in which $\Im$ is a constant attribute collection.*

Proof. $\varepsilon > 0$, consider a pair of neighbor vertices $\langle i, j \rangle$, we observe the opinion divergence:

$$|O_{i,t} - O_{j,t}| = \lambda_t \left| O_{i,t-1} \cdot \overset{E_i}{\Pi} P\left(O_{i,t}|O_{E_i^1,t-1}\right) - O_{j,t-1} \cdot \overset{E_i}{\Pi} P\left(O_{j,t}|O_{E_j^1,t-1}\right) \right|$$

$$= \xi_{i,E_i} \cdot P \frac{\left(O_{i,t-1}|O_{E_i^1,t-1}\right)}{P\left(O_{E_i^1,t-1}|O_{E_i^2,t-2}\right)} \left| O_{i,t-1} \cdot \overset{E_i}{\Pi} P\left(O_{i,t}|O_{E_i^1,t-1}\right) - O_{j,t-1} \cdot \overset{E_i}{\Pi} P\left(O_{j,t}|O_{E_j^1,t-1}\right) \right|$$

$$(11.7)$$

$\square$

After $t < +\infty$ intervals, according to Definition 11.2, E_i barely has any influence on i, so we have $P(O_{i,t-1}|O_{E_i^1,t-1}) \to 1$. More vertices tend to form more tactic opinion, so we have

$$P\left(O_{i,t-1}|O_{E_i^1,t-1}\right) \le P\left(O_{E_i^1,t-1}|O_{E_i^2,t-2}\right), \quad P\left(O_{E_i^1,t-1}|O_{E_i^2,t-2}\right) \to 1.$$

If $i \in follower_j$, $P\left(O_{i,t}|O_{E_i^1,t-1}\right) < P\left(O_{j,t}|O_{E_j^1,t-1}\right)$

$$|O_{i,t} - O_{j,t}| = \xi_{i,E_i}|O_{i,t-1} - O_{j,t-1}| = \xi_{i,E_i}^2|O_{i,t-2} - O_{j,t-2}| = \cdots = |\xi_{i,E_i}^{t/\Delta t+1} O_{j,1}|$$

If $j \in follower_i$, $P\left(O_{i,t}|O_{E_i^1,t-1}\right) < P\left(O_{j,t}|O_{E_j^1,t-1}\right)$

$$|O_{i,t} - O_{j,t}| = \xi_{i,E_i}|O_{i,t-1} - O_{j,t-1}| = \xi_{i,E_i}^2|O_{i,t-2} - O_{j,t-2}| = \cdots = |\xi_{i,E_i}^{t/\Delta t+1} O_{i,1}|$$

So we have

$$O_{i,t} = O_{j,t} - \xi_{i,E_i}^{t/\Delta t+1} O_{j,1} \quad \text{or} \quad \xi_{i,E_i}^{t/\Delta t+1} O_{i,1} - O_{j,t}$$

Then we consider the neighbor pair $\langle j,k \rangle$ and analyze the same relationship:

$$O_{i,t} = O_{k,t} - \xi_{j,E_j}^{t/\Delta t+1} O_{k,1} - \xi_{i,E_i}^{t/\Delta t+1} O_{j,1} \quad \text{or} \quad \xi_{j,E_j}^{t/\Delta t+1} O_{k,1} - \xi_{i,E_i}^{t/\Delta t+1} O_{j,1} - O_{k,t}$$

We iterate the above process and obtain

$$O_{i,t} \to \sum_{followees}^{N} \xi^{t/\Delta t+1} \cdot O_{followees,1} \quad \text{or} \quad O_{i,t} \to (-1) \cdot \sum_{followees}^{N} \xi^{t/\Delta t+1} \cdot O_{followees,1}$$

and

$$O_{i,t} \in [D, F].$$

According to Lemma 11.1, the opinion of any follower is ascended from the original pushing vertex, and the opinion is a constrained variable decided by the synchronous factors with neighbor vertices.

Lemma 11.2. *For an opinion social network $TTSN \in G$ with $t < +\infty$, there exists a desirable threshold $[d, f]$, makes the sampling $S_{SA} = \{O\} \subseteq [d, f]$ and $SA_{\{O\}} \in [0, 1/\lambda_t \exp \varepsilon]$ with confidence of ε.*

Proof. According to Definition 11.1, we have

$$|O_{leaders}| \ll |O_{followers}|$$

When $t < +\infty$, we have the conclusion that an opinion sample $o_{i,t} \to \Im$ with confidence $\varepsilon' \gg \varepsilon$, then there exists a T, makes $O_{i,T} < \{d, f\}_{min}$ and $|\{O_{j,T} : O_{j,T} > \{d, f\}_{min}\}| \ll |O_{i,T}| < N$ with confidence $\varepsilon' \gg \varepsilon$.   □

So we can consider that there exists an S, $|O_{leaders}| \ll |S| < N$, makes $(\varepsilon')^{|S|} \geq \varepsilon$.

Then we compute the density of SA in the wild mode evolvement according to (11.5).

$$D(SA) = \frac{D(O)}{\lambda_t} \left(\exp\left\{ \frac{\sum (SA_{t-1})}{L_0} \right\} + \exp\left\{ \frac{1}{|F(O)|} \right\} \right)$$

The sample of SA is split into two parts:

$$P_1 = \frac{D(O)}{\lambda_t} \left(\exp\left\{ \frac{\sum (SA_{t-1})}{L_0} \right\} \right) \quad \text{and} \quad P_2 = \frac{D(O)}{\lambda_t} \left(\exp\left\{ \frac{1}{|F(O)|} \right\} \right)$$

Finally, we regress them to

$$P_1 < \frac{1}{\lambda_t}(\exp \varepsilon) \text{ and } P_2 < \frac{1}{\lambda_t}(\exp \varepsilon)$$

From Lemma 11.2, we can observer SA through periodically sampling G.

11.3.2   Conditional optimization problems in dynamic public opinion evolvement

According to Definition 11.5, a desirable public opinion evolvement must satisfy a two-tuple ⟨*OC* converge, *SA* distribution⟩. If the public opinion environment evolving with sentiment over dramatic and losing its control, the administrator finds the vertex with the largest degree and let $O_{E_{max}} \leftarrow -(1/\xi_{i,E_{max}}) \cdot O_{E_{max}}$ (opinion replacement), in which $\xi_{i,E_{max}}$ can be learnt by vertices clustering. Or if the public opinion evolves with opinion splitting over a period of time, the administrator serializes the leader vertices with degree, and let $O_{E_{max}-i} \leftarrow (1/\xi_{i,E_{max}-1}) \cdot O_{E_{max}-i+1}$ (opinion combination).

Theorem 11.1. *(OC converge). For the opinion social network $G \in TTSN$ with its leader vertices $\{V\}_{Leader}^n$ and a time limit $T < +\infty$, there exists a u, $0 < u \ll |V_{leader}|$, after u times of opinion replacements, $|D(O|G, t < T)| \to 1$ holds.*

Proof. Assuming the degree density of G is

$$D(degree) \sim a \exp\{|V|\} + b$$ □

According to Lemma 11.1, when $t < T < +\infty$, $O \to \Im$ and $D(O|G) \to 1$. The coverage property of a randomly picked vertex is decided by ξ and the original opinion of the leader vertices on the path. And in a BA network, it is obvious that the changes of opinions of $\{V\}_{Leader}^n$ will influence at least $a \exp\{||V| - |V_{leader}||\} + b$ vertices by the opinion coverage operation $O_{E_{max}} \leftarrow -(1/\xi_{i,E_{max}}) \cdot O_{E_{max}}$. The density of vertex opinion shrinks at the speed of $1/\xi_{i,E_{max}}$, so for a chosen T, we have

$$1 \leftarrow D(O|G,T) > D_u(O|G, t + u\Delta t) > D_{u-1}(O|G, t$$

$$+ (u-1)\Delta t) > \cdots > D_0(O|G, t)$$

We only to prove $t + u\Delta t < T$. According to Definition 11.1, in a TTSN, $|V_{leader}| \ll N$, then $u \ll N$. So in a TTSN, the time complex of OC computing is far less than the limit T, which means $t + u\Delta t \ll T$. Here, u is a time complexity of OC converge.

Theorem 11.2. *(SA distribution). For the opinion social network $TTSN \in G$ with its leader vertices $\{V\}_{Leader}^n$ and a chosen threshold ε, there exists a u, $0 < u \ll |V_{leader}| / 2$, after u times of opinion combinations in $\{V\}_{Leader}^n$, a random sample $s \in G$ satisfies $F_s(SA, t) \propto \{F_G^{T/\Delta t}(SA, T), E(SA) \to 0$ and $\sigma < \varepsilon\}$.*

Proof. According to Definition 11.3 and Lemma 11.2, we have $F_G(SA, t) \sim N$
$\left(\frac{\Im}{\lambda_t} \exp\{-\Im\}, \frac{\lambda_t}{\sqrt{2\pi}}\right)$

$$F_G^{T/\Delta t}(SA, T) \sim \chi^2 \left(\frac{\Im}{\lambda_t} \exp\{-\Im\}, \frac{\lambda_t}{\sqrt{2\pi}}, scale\_degree = \frac{T}{\Delta t}\right)$$

$$\propto \chi^2 \left(0, \frac{\lambda_t}{\sqrt{2\pi}}, scale\_degree = \frac{T}{\Delta t}\right) \qquad \square$$

At time t, $t \to T$, the mean of s, $M_s = \Im / \Delta t \lambda_t \exp\{-\Im\} \to 0$, and the scatter degree $SD_s \to \sigma_{F_G(SA,t)}$. So we have $F_s(SA, t \to T) \propto \{F_G^{T/\Delta t}(SA, T), E(SA) \to 0$ and $\sigma < \varepsilon\}$, in which $\varepsilon = \lambda_t / \sqrt{2\pi}$.

Only to prove $t + u\Delta t < T$ before obtaining any chosen t satisfying $F_s(SA, t) \propto \{F_G^{T/\Delta t}(SA, T)\}$, which means combinations among leaders are sufficient to combine all the vertices.

Considering a BA network like TTSN, if we make combination operation by $O_{E_{max}-i} \leftarrow (1/\xi_{i,E_{max}-i}) \cdot O_{E_{max}-i+1}$ at time t, the opinions of $|V^*|$ normal vertices are combined with one of their neighbors in which $|V^*| \to N - |V_{leader}|$. And after all the u combinations, $|V^*|$ vertices have experienced almost u times of combinations, so $F_s(SA, t) \propto \{F_G^{T/\Delta t}(SA, T)\}$ holds.

In order to achieve OC–SA optimum, we abstracted the conditions of Definition 11.4 through Theorems 11.1 and 11.2. We will show how to solve the OC–SA optimum problem by vertex replacement and combination with carefully chosen parameters $(u, \lambda, \varepsilon)$ in Section 11.4.

11.4   Evolvement of public opinion and supervision

11.4.1   Preparation algorithms

In social networks, the evolvement of public opinion is usually considered as the formation and diminishes of hot spots, and the opinion environment evolves under the driven force of hot spots continuing spreading. In order to simulate and evaluate the process, we present the algorithms (Processes 0–4), see Table 11.1 to realize our model. Process 0 discovers the main structure of G and returns a vertex list containing degree and opinion information. For a given influence factor, Process 1 refreshes the public opinion in G with λ and the list generated by Process 0. For each time interval, Processes 2 and 3 test the features of OC and SA with given time bound T. After Process 0 returned, Processes 1–4 run concurrently until the OC–SA is stable enough, which means the current topic is not popular anymore.

   In Process 0, the algorithm traverses all the vertex and edges and iterates k levels with accuracy less than m. When serializing vertex, the overall network is scanned, but only key vertices are appended to List_leader_vertex. So the time complexity of Process 0 is at most $o(kmN + N^2/m)$, and storage cost is at most $o(3N + 1)$. Process 1 is only designed for our following test in Section 11.5, because in real social network, evolvement is autonomously driven by topic interest and scarce. Processes 1–4 run concurrently to set evolving value. Time and space cost of Processes 1–4 are far less than Process 0. But on one restriction, they must return a value for every time interval to keep the pace of opinion evolvement. So the time cost of Processes 1–4 must be less than Δt, and if G is too large to handle by Processes 1–4, Δt must be expended to waiting for process results, while rendering to a coarse-grained supervision.

11.4.2   Evolvement and supervision algorithms

In this section, we show how a TTSN evolves to form a crowd of public opinion in a bounded time intervals and how to trace it within a time threshold T. Two types of evolvements are given according to the number of spreading topics. The first one is a single topic algorithm, and each opinion is a one-dimensional value, see Table 11.2. For a given social network G, Algorithm 0 finds structure, trains an influence factor and traces the opinion characters for each time interval Δt.

   The second one is a multitopic algorithm, and each opinion is an n-dimensional vector, see Table 11.3. Then on $t = 1$, public opinion will be initialized as a matrix. According to Definition 11.3, on executing Processes 2 and 3, Algorithm 2 needs to check every column of the elements in $\{V\}_{Leader}^n$. But we make a trick to choose the column with the max σ to stand for all the topics, and if Process 2 or 3 returns false, Algorithm 2 keeps checking the next σ until "true" is returned.

Table 11.1 Preparation algorithms

Process	Algorithm
Process 0. Vertex serialization	Vertex_serialize(G): 1. Clustering(G, k, m) # Decide k subgraphs according to the structure of G. 2. Maximum $= m$ 3. List_leader_vertex $=$ None 4. For vertex in G: 5. For *vertex* in *vertice\List_leader_vertex*: 6. If degree(vertex) <= maximum; 7. Maximum $=$ degree(vertex); 8. Continue; 9. else if vertex is not on the path between subgraphs; 10. Continue; 11. List_leader_vertex.append(vertex); 12. End for 13. End for 14. Return *List_leader_vertex* # Generate a vertices list sorted by degree. *After successfully clustering and serializing the vertices in G, opinions exchange among all the vertices for every time interval. Go to Processes 1, 2 and 3, check by sampling vertices if OC and SA of the social network is in desirable supervision state.
Process 1. Opinion spread	Opinion_spread ($\lambda(\xi)$): 1. $\lambda = 1, P(O_{follower}\|O_{followee}) = 1$ 2. Δt_ticks() 3. $O(List\_leader\_vertex) = random([D, F]^n)$ 4. For vertex in G 5. if $len(O_{vertex}) < len(\sum O_E)$ # Update is necessary only on larger opinion space 6. $P(O_{vertex}\|O_E) = 1 - O_{vertex}/\sum O_E$ 7. Update O_{vertex} # Update opinion according to (11.3) 8. Else 9. Continue; 10. End for 11. Return Δt_ticks() $+ 1$ *The evolvement of graph in a time interval consists of opinion mergence and interactive exchange driven by Process 1.
Process 2. Convergence test of OC	OC_test($\Im, T$): 1. For each Δt_ticks() $< T$: 2. If *List_leader_vertex*(G) exists; 3. If $\|D(O\|G) - D(\Im)\|_{\Delta t} < \|D(O\|G) - D(\Im)\|_{\Delta t-1}$; 4. Return $T - \Delta t$_ticks() 5. Else return false 6. Else go to Process 0 7. End for *This process works on the opinion collections in social network G with its leader vertices list which is generated in Process 0, and test if $\|D(O\|G) - D(\Im)\|_{\Delta t} < \|D(O\|G) - D(\Im)\|_{\Delta t-1}$ holds according to Theorem 11.1.

(continued)

Table 11.1   (Continued)

Process	Algorithm
Process 3. Sentiment activity test	SA_test($T,\sigma^*,\Im$): 1. For each Δt_ticks() $< T$ 2. For each S = random_sample(G) 3. If average_cluster_coefficient(S)>average_cluster_coefficient(G); 4. If standard_deviation(S) $< \sigma^*$ and $$\text{Mean}(S) \leq \frac{\Im}{\Delta t\lambda_t} \exp\{-\Im\} \text{ in } D_t(S|G);$$ 5. Return True; 6. Else return False with SA overload; 7. Else break; # Go to try another sample. 8. End for 9. End for 10. Return Δt_ticks() $> T$ # Escape with timeout. *For each Δt, compute the character of sample $S = \{O\}$, and test the distribution of the sample S satisfy Theorem 11.2.
Process 4. Interfere	Interfere(G): 1. For each Δt_ticks() $< T$ in G 2. If SA_test(T,σ^*,ε) == False or OC_test($\Im,T$)==False 3. L=Load($List\_leader\_vertex$); 4. For element in L: 5. If SA_test(T,σ^*,ε) == False and OC_test($\Im,T$)==False # wild evolvement with replacement on the path 6. $O(L[0]) = -\lambda^*O(L[0])$; 7. $V \leftarrow$ Create_vertex($O = -\lambda^*O(L[0])$); 8. Insert(V); # mild evolvement with opinion combination on the path 9. If SA_test(T,σ^*,ε) == True and OC_test($\Im,T$)==True 10. Break; 11. Continue; 12. End for 13. End for *Realize real time supervision, and minimum interference, and return supervision time expired.

11.5   Data and results

11.5.1   Datasets and environment

In order to fully evaluate the opinion spreading model that we built in TTSN, we designed a series of comparing test including the frameworks (Asur, Takaffoli, Zhang and ours) supporting dynamic evolving networks. The main benchmarks of the tests are the activity changes including OC, SA and equivalent variables during the evolvement of opinion spreading. Our computing platform includes: Inspur NF5280M4 server with Xeon E5@2.1 GHz, 64 GB DDR4 ram, 1 T storage and 1 Gbit/s Ethernet;

Table 11.2   Algorithm 0: Evolvement (single topic)

1.	Find the structure of the input social network G with its leader vertices $\{V\}_{Leader}^n$ using CNM [7].
2.	Train the stable $\lambda(\xi)$ among neighbors for each vertex in dispersal topic serial $O \leftarrow (o_0)$. ξ can be trained as an attribute of G.
3.	On $t = 0$, for the event e^*, initiate parameters $D(O|G) = 0$, and for each vertex, let $\lambda = 0$.
4.	On $t = \Delta t$, randomly set a collection of vertices with $\{O_1, O_2, \cdots, O_n\} \leftarrow O_{iniate}$, $1 \leq n << N$, and let $\lambda = 1$.
5.	Loop: Process 0($G, T > t > \Delta t$)
6.	Loop: Process 3($G, T > t > \Delta t, \xi$)
7.	Loop: Process 2($G, T > t > \Delta t, \xi$)
8.	For($\Delta t > t^*$ and $\sigma > \sigma^*$)
9.	Call Process 4(vertices operations, $\{V\}_{Leader}^n$).
10.	End for

Table 11.3   Algorithm 1: Evolvement (multiple topic)

1.	Find the structure of the input social network G with its leader vertices $\{V\}_{Leader}^n$.
2.	Train the stable ξ among neighbors for each vertex in dispersal event serial $O \leftarrow (o_0, o_1, \cdots o_n)$. ξ can be trained as an attribute of G.
3.	On $t = 0$, for the event e^*, initiate parameters $D(O|G) = \prod_n D(o_0|G)D(o_1|G) \cdots D(o_n|G) = 0$, and for each vertex, let $\lambda = 0$.
4.	On $t = 1$, randomly set a collection of vertices with $\{O_1, O_2, \cdots, O_n\} \leftarrow O_{iniate}$, $1 \leq n << N$, and let $\lambda = 1$.
5.	Loop: Process 0($G, t > 1$)
6.	Loop: Process 3($G, t > 1, \xi$)
7.	Loop: computing all the standard variant for each object in O,
8.	For the maximum σ in O,
9.	Loop: Process 2($G, t > 1, \xi$)
10.	For($\Delta t > t^*$ and $\sigma > \sigma^*$)
11.	Call Process 4(vertices operations, $\{V\}_{Leader}^n$).
12.	Pop O with σ_{max} from List_leader_vertex
13.	End for

a controller ThinkCentre with Intel core i5@2.7 GHz, 4 GB DDR4 ram and 1 Gbit/s. Algorithms are coded with Python 3.6 running in Anaconda3(64 bit).

Our datasets include three manipulated social network datasets and three natural social networks. In the manipulated datasets (Table 11.4), random BA networks are generated as our basic structure TTSN, and the scale parameters are $\langle \mu = \delta = m = [1, 2, \ldots, upbound] \rangle$. For a different network scale and density distribution, we first choose the proper parameters through training as described in Section 11.5.2. Then we choose three typical social network samples: Epinion(trust/untrust network), Twitter(friends cycle), Tencent Weibo(friend/adversary network). After carefully filtered

Table 11.4   Basic structure of manipulated datasets

Datasets	μ for each Δt	Nodes	Edges	Cross networks	Topic list length for each node
D1	1–200	10,000	27,950	Yes	1,2
D2	1–200	1×10^5	2,887,109	Yes	1,2
D3	1–200	1×10^6	165,519,049	Yes	1,2

Table 11.5   Basic structure of collected datasets (Jan 15, 2017)

Datasets	μ for each Δt (upbound = 200)	Nodes	Edges	Cross networks	Topic list length for each node
Epinions	1–200	10,000	28,096	No	<10
Twitter	1–200	1×10^5	3,256,160	No	<10
Tencent Weibo	3–200	1×10^6	195,163,872	No	<10

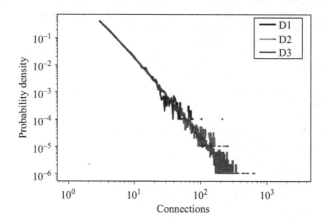

Figure 11.1   Connection density of D1–D3

content noise and kept the original opinion values, we got three datasets in Table 11.5, Figures 11.1 and 11.2 show the connection density of datasets in Tables 11.4 and 11.5.

11.5.2   Parameters $\langle \mu, \lambda, \varepsilon(t) \rangle$

In a typical social network, vertex keeps adding into current datasets carrying opinion data. So we must find the relationship between evolvement parameters and the structure of the networks by serialization and sampling according to vertex degree. Constrained from computing capability, we set structure controlling factors

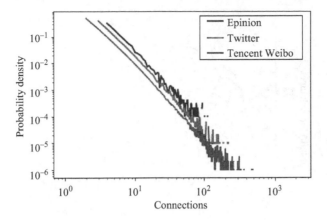

Figure 11.2   Connection density 2 of collected datasets

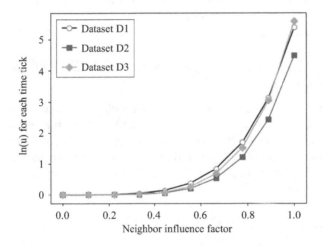

Figure 11.3   The trend of influence scale in each time ticks and neighbor influence factor and ($\mu - \lambda$)

$\mu = \delta = m$. For a target dataset, we should find the proper neighbor influence factor λ by formula (11.2) and Process 3, and then we decide the $\varepsilon(t)$ mapping onto network evolving trend according to the result of Processes 2 and 3.

According to Definition 11.2, λ of a TTSN is decided by structure and clustering degree, so we find the trend of $\mu - \lambda$ and $\mu - \varepsilon(t)$, see Figures 11.3 and 11.4. According to the result in Figure 11.1, we choose the average value and set $\lambda = [0.3, 0.8]$ in the mild sentiment model, and set $\lambda > 0.8$ in the wild sentiment model. We set $\varepsilon = 0.99$ as the confidence value of SA, and observe the trend of involved vertices scale with time intervals. In Figure 11.2, we set the time tick is 6×10^4 ms with the maximum u in Figure 11.1, and $T = 4.8 \times 10^6$ ms. After T, TTSN still can evolve without any major turbulence (Figures 11.3 and 11.4).

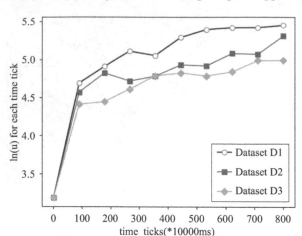

Figure 11.4   The trend of influence scale in each time ticks and time costs ($\mu - \varepsilon(t)$)

11.5.3   OC–SA optimization performance in TTSN evolvement effectiveness

In this section, we make a few tests on OC–SA with constant parameters regressed from our datasets and compare with CNM [7] and Takaffoli's frameworks. CNM and Takaffoli algorithms can decide a social network structure in a Δt. For the overall network, Takaffoli defined a *Popularity* and *Socialability* to evaluate the network activity and vertex activity. We use central activity for CNM and *Socialability* distribution for Takaffoli algorithm.

Parameters: $\lambda \leftarrow (0.34, 0.52, 0.80)$, $\varepsilon \leftarrow (0.99)$

On single topic, the results are acceptable. For any major rebounds, the TTSN will start interference immediately, so from Figure 11.5 we can see an obvious convergence of OC. The SA distribution is much more stable than Takaffoli evolvement after less than six time intervals. As we have not observed any major difference when we tried the value of λ, we omitted the rest results of OC and SA tests. Our interference method can easily obtain 5–10 time intervals ahead in OC performance and achieve approximately 40% lower in the final converged position. In Figure 11.6, SA shows central pooling distribution, because the opinions carrying the sentiment of over right and over left are ironed smooth. But on multitopics, we found that the computing burden grows dramatically using Algorithm 2, and more efficient parallel algorithm is required. So on the occasion of multitopics, we assume that all the topics on one vertex are dependent and serialize the topics to run Algorithm 1 instead of Algorithm 2. The main drawback of serializing topics is the relationship among topics is neglected.

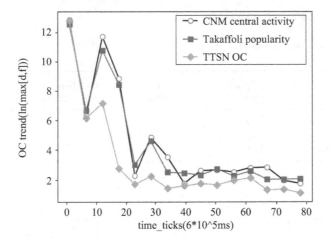

Figure 11.5   CNM, Takaffoli and TTSN topic spreading evolvement: CNM central activity, Takaffoli and Zhang Popularity and TTSN OC tendency with Dataset 3, single topic, λ =0.52, 1 ≤ u ≤ 12

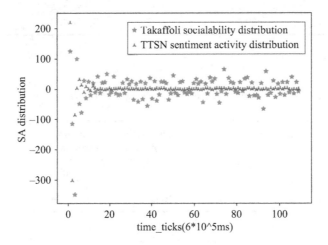

Figure 11.6   Takaffoli vs. TTSN: Socialability distribution, SA tendency with Dataset 3, single topic in mild model, ε = 0.99

11.5.3.1   Time delay/time costs

We tested our TTSN evolvement algorithms with supervision and collected the average time costs of three chosen datasets. In order to get well into the performance of two basic operations, we isolated them into two groups of tests to get accurate results. For each group, we chose three values of λ representing three types of vertices influence. Tables 11.6–11.8 demonstrate the time cost performance of replacement, and Tables 11.9–11.12 demonstrate the performance of combination.

On combination operation ($\Delta t = 60$ s):

Table 11.6   On replacement operation ($\lambda = 0.34$, $\varepsilon = 0.99$)

Datasets	μ	Replacement Ops	Time ticks ($\times 60$ s)	Ops time consumed (s)	Ram module size (MByte)
Sina Weibo	1	9	0.12	21.280	47.72
Twitter	1	32	0.79	180.914	690.90
Tencent Weibo	1	161	9.82	3,903.605	5,020.66

Table 11.7   On replacement operation ($\lambda = 0.52$, $\varepsilon = 0.99$)

Datasets	μ	Replacement Ops	Time ticks ($\times 60$ s)	Ops time consumed (s)	Ram module size (MByte)
Sina Weibo	2	10	0.19	23.409	51.79
Twitter	2	32	1.90	179.389	688.51
Tencent Weibo	2	160	22.82	3,899.460	5,009.43

Table 11.8   On replacement operation ($\lambda = 0.80$, $\varepsilon = 0.99$)

Datasets	μ	Replacement Ops	Time ticks ($\times 60$ s)	Ops time consumed (s)	Ram module size (MByte)
Sina Weibo	7	9	0.42	21.020	47.90
Twitter	7	31	7.79	177.949	673.18
Tencent Weibo	7	150	109.82	3,403.199	4,898.49

On combination operation ($\Delta t = 60$ s):

Table 11.9   On combination operation ($\lambda = 0.34$, $\varepsilon = 0.99$)

Datasets	μ	Replacement Ops	Time ticks ($\times 60$ s)	Ops time consumed (s)	Ram module size (MByte)
Sina Weibo	1	7	0.10	16.198	47.09
Twitter	1	20	0.58	114.410	678.55
Tencent Weibo	1	89	6.91	2,467.112	5,001.08

Table 11.10   On combination operation (λ = 0.52, ε = 0.99)

Datasets	μ	Replacement Ops	Time ticks (×60 s)	Ops time consumed (s)	Ram module size (MByte)
Sina Weibo	2	7	0.11	17.409	47.71
Twitter	2	21	0.96	120.002	678.98
Tencent Weibo	2	82	13.08	2,302.701	4,988.02

Table 11.11   On combination operation (λ = 0.80, ε = 0.99)

Datasets	μ	Replacement Ops	Time ticks (×60 s)	Ops time consumed (s)	Ram module size (MByte)
Sina Weibo	7	5	0.31	14.620	46.99
Twitter	7	19	5.07	117.491	677.04
Tencent Weibo	7	77	80.76	2,279.293	4,979.51

When the scale of TTSN is over 1 million, the growth of time is faster than the growth of ram cost. From the two groups of results, operation time and ram consumption are approximately proportional to the number of operations. But number of time ticks before OC–SA optimization are squared proportional to the size of TTSN. So on our platform, the analysis of TTSN with billions of users will take weeks to get a result, which is not acceptable for real-time supervision. But we also observed that time cost is closely related to the type of operations. Although combination ops are only favorable in wild evolvement such as explosive news spreading scenarios, but the time cost greatly drops than replacement. On the same datasets, only more than a half number of replacement ops are needed in combination ops with time threshold *T* drops 30%–45% but accompanied with crude interference onto the structure of subgraphs.

11.6   Discussions

With the boom of IT merging into our daily life, participating online social network is becoming an important part of our society. The purpose of monitoring public opinion is not to eliminate all the topics in social networks but to maintain a healthy evolvement state and lead to rational opinion expression. In this chapter, we extracted three main requirements from real social networks and analyzed the drawbacks of the previous solutions. Then on the basis on the existing models, we designed a TTSN scenario prototype, in which we proposed an OC–SA evolving model to achieve our goal. In this model, we demonstrated on real-time public opinion evaluation and introduced how to maintain a free and rational public opinion environment with our

OC–SA optimization. According to our tests, the model showed ideal performance in comparing with evolvement models based on topo events discovery. Also, our model obtained a novel and gentle way to alter public opinion in a social network without overinterference.

Still, many unsolved obstacles stand in our way when we extend functions of our model. On the generality, our parameters constrain only in BA-type networks, excluding knowledge sharing networks, such as wiki, Q&A forums. On the algorithm efficiency, as we combined two routines of network evolvement, time complexity grows with topo scale and time intervals of opinion evaluation. In the future work, parallel processing and opinion evaluation based on multitopic will be explored to enhance the practicability of our model.

Acknowledgments

This work was supported by the National Cryptography Development Fund of China (grant no. MMJJ20170112), Natural Science Basic Research Plan in Shaanxi Province of China (grant no. 2018JM6028), National Natural Science Foundation of China (grant no. 61772550, U1636114, and 61572521), and National Key Research and Development Program of China (grant no. 2017YFB0802000). This work is also supported by Engineering University of PAP's Funding for Scientific Research Innovation Team (grant no. KYTD201805).

References

[1] Data Center of Internet. http://www.google.com/about/datacenters/gallery/article-2219188.html.2017.4.

[2] Fortunato S. Community detection in graphs. Physics Reports, 2010, 486(3): 75–174.

[3] Xie J, Kelley S, and Szymanski B. Overlapping community detection in networks: The state-of-the-art and comparative study. ACM Computing Surveys, 2013, 45(4): 115–123.

[4] Palla G, Derenyi I, Farkas I, *et al.* Uncovering the overlapping community structure of complex networks in nature and society. Nature, 2005, 435(7043): 814–818.

[5] Zhang X, You H, Zhu W, *et al.* Overlapping community identification approach in online social networks. Physica A: Statistical Mechanics and Its Applications, 2015, 421: 233–248.

[6] Zhang X, Shen H, Zhao P, *et al.* Research on community evolution prediction based on event-based frameworks. Chinese Journal of Computers, 2017, 40(3): 729–742.

[7] Clauset A, Newman M, and Moore C. Finding community structure in very large networks. Physical Review E, Statistical, Nonlinear, and Soft Matter Physics, 2004, 70(Pt 2): 264–277.

[8] Socher R, Perelygin A, Wu J, *et al*. Sentiment Analysis. http://nlp.stanford.edu: 8080/sentiment/rntnDemo.html.2019.06.

[9] Jiang T, Wan C, and Liu D. Extracting target-opinion Paris based on semantic analysis. Chinese Journal of Computers, 2017, 40(3): 617–633.

[10] Wang J, Zhao L, and Huang R. SIRaRu rumor spreading model in complex networks. Physica A: Statistical Mechanics and its Applications, 2014, 398(15): 43–55.

[11] Han Q, Wen H, and Wu J. Rumor Spreading and Security Monitoring in Complex Networks. International Conference on Computational Social Networks. Springer, Cham. Lecture Notes in Computer Science, vol 9197: 48–59. Springer, July 2015.

[12] Kar A, and Mandal DP. Finding opinion strength using fuzzy logic on web reviews. International Journal of Engineering and Industries, 2011, 2(1): 37–43.

[13] Takaffoli M, Rabbany R, and Zaiane R. Community evolution prediction in dynamic social networks. Proceedings of the 2014 ACM International Conference on Advances in Social Networks Analysis and Mining. Istanbul, Turkey, 2014: 9–16.

[14] Asur S, Parthasarathy S, and Ucar D. An event-based framework for characterizing the evolutionary behavior of interaction graphs. ACM Transactions on Knowledge Discovery from Data, 2009, 3(4): 913–921.

[15] Takaffoli M, Sangi F, Fagnan J, *et al*. Community evolution mining in dynamic social networks. Procedia—Social and Behavioral Sciences, 2011, 22(2): 49–58.

[16] Antonio M, Boris P, and Sergey V. Spontaneous recovery in dynamical networks. Nature Physics 2014, 10: 34–38.

[17] Nicholas A, and James H. Social contagion theory: examining dynamic social networks and human behavior. Statistic in Medicine. 2013; 32: 556–577.

[18] Li Y, Charu A, and Wang H. Community Search in Dynamic Social Networks. Microsoft Community Research Publications. TechReport, MSR-TR-2013-14, 2013.

[19] Domingos P, and Richardson M. Mining the network value of customers. Proceedings of the 7th ACM SIGKDD International Conference on Knowledge Discovery and Data Mining. San Francisco, USA, 2001: 57–66.

[20] Leskovec J, Krause A, Guestrin C, *et al*. Cost-effective outbreak detection in networks. Proceedings of the 13th ACM SIGKDD International Conference on Knowledge Discovery and Data Mining. San Jose, USA, 2007: 420–429.

[21] Cheng S, Shen H, Huang J, *et al*. Static greedy: Solving the apparent scalability-accuracy dilemma in influence maximization. Proceedings of the 22nd ACM International Conference on Conference on Information & Knowledge Management. San Francisco, USA, 2013: 509–518.

[22] Kempe D, Kleinberg J, and Tardos E. Maximizing the spread of influence through a social network. Proceedings of the 9th ACM SIGKDD International Conference on Knowledge Discovery and Data Mining. Washington, USA, 2003: 137–146.

[23]   Luo Z, Cai W, and Li Y. A *PageRank*-based heuristic algorithm for influence maximization in the social network. Recent Progress in Data Engineering and Internet Technology. Berlin Heidelberg, Germany, 2012: 485–490.

[24]   Goyal A, Lu W, and Lakshmanan L. CELF++: Optimizing the greedy algorithm for influence maximization in social networks. In Proceedings of the 20th International Conference Companion on World Wide Web. Hyderabad, India, 2011: 47–48.

[25]   Bhagat S, Goyal A, and Lakshmanan L. Maximizing product adoption in social networks. Proceedings of the 5th ACM International Conference on Web Search and Data Mining. Seattle, USA, 2012: 603–612.

[26]   Guo J, Zhang P, and Zhou C. Personalized influence maximization on social networks. Proceedings of the 22nd ACM International Conference on Information and Knowledge Management. San Francisco, USA, 2013: 199–208.

[27]   Twitter and web based analysis tools. Online application. https://werfamous.com/sentimentanalyzer/dataset-sentiment-analysis.2017.04.

Chapter 12

Privacy verification of PhotoDNA based on machine learning

Muhammad Shahroz Nadeem[1], Virginia N.L. Franqueira[1], and Xiaojun Zhai[2]

PhotoDNA is a perceptual fuzzy hash technology designed and developed by Microsoft. It is deployed by all major big data service providers to detect Indecent Images of Children (IIOC). Protecting the privacy of individuals is of paramount importance in such images. Microsoft claims that a PhotoDNA hash cannot be reverse engineered into the original image; therefore, it is not possible to identify individuals or objects depicted in the image.

In this chapter, we evaluate the privacy protection capability of PhotoDNA by testing it against machine learning. Specifically, our aim is to detect the presence of any structural information that might be utilized to compromise the privacy of the individuals via classification. Due to the widespread usage of PhotoDNA as a deterrent to IIOC by big data companies, ensuring its ability to protect privacy would be crucial. In our experimentation, we achieved a classification accuracy of 57.20%. This result indicates that PhotoDNA is resistant to machine-learning-based classification attacks.

12.1 Introduction

Protecting the privacy of people in the current digital world is of paramount importance. PhotoDNA is one of these technologies that ensure the privacy of IIOC cases by converting the images to hash values. This makes the search easy without exposing the contents of the images. PhotoDNA is widely accepted as a reliable tool, due to which it has been adopted by many big data companies to fight IIOC. Any breach of privacy in PhotoDNA technology could have catastrophic consequences. It is estimated that around 1.8 billion unique images are uploaded on the internet every single day [1]. Naturally, this means that generation and distribution of IIOC is also increasing annually which puts children at risk [2]. To secure such images and to protect the identities of children involved, law enforcement maintains a centralized database

---

[1]College of Engineering and Technology, University of Derby, Derby, UK
[2]School of Computer Science and Electronic Engineering, University of Essex, Colchester, UK

called the child abuse image database. Recent reports indicate that around 10 million such known images exist [3]. Microsoft has made very strong claims with regards to PhotoDNA technology. According to them, PhotoDNA hash cannot be used to identify any object or individual, neither it can be used to recreate the source image [1]. However, it is a known fact that even the most secure systems have been compromised or simply broken down, in the past.

In this data-driven age, machine-learning-based methods have seen tremendous success. They can extract hidden patterns and learn features that can be used to perform certain tasks. Recently, privacy-preserving (PP)-based machine learning (PPML) methods are gaining a lot of recognition. PPML methods use some form of encrypted data to train the model. Moreover, this training can be done simultaneously or iteratively by more than one individual or entity. The advantage of using PPML is that the privacy of the data is preserved without sharing it with all the stakeholders. Instead of using the raw data, it either encrypts or transforms the original data to different feature space. In distributed face-recognition systems, the facial feature vectors are extracted and sent to the centralized server instead of the images. Thus, in case of a privacy breach, only these facial features would be compromised instead of the images of individuals. According to Al-Rubaie *et al.* [4], when training PP machine-learning methods, two main transformation approaches can be applied: cryptographic or perturbation. Based on these transformations, many deep-learning solutions have also been proposed which perform image classification, retrieval and searching using encrypted data. To facilitate the development of such methods, new deep frameworks have also been produced. These frameworks can facilitate quick processing of encrypted data preserving privacy and saving computational power which is beneficial to big data service providers. However, an increasing concern is that this technology could also be used to compromise privacy. Recently, Hitaj *et al.* [5] have shown how deep-learning-based methods can be utilized to attack such PP methods. In their work, they designed a generative-adversarial-network-based attack that compromised a collaborative PP method. Their work highlights the significance of such specialized attacks that can expose many vulnerabilities in PPML. What if the machine-learning-based approach could be utilized to breach the privacy of PhotoDNA?

The mentioned characteristics and concerns of machine learning motivated us to test the PP capability of PhotoDNA against machine-learning-based classification attacks. Our aim was to evaluate if machine-learning-based classification attack could be employed to extract any features that could compromise privacy protection capability of PhotoDNAs. For this, we experimented with traditional and recent algorithms, presented and evaluated their performance on a dataset of nonsensitive images. The dataset was provided by Microsoft which contained PhotoDNA hash values for images of bird, fish and invertebrates, taken from ImageNet [6]. We experimented with tree-based, distance-based and function-based classifiers. Our results show that PhotoDNA is resistant to machine-learning-based classification attacks. In our experiment, the best performing machine-learning algorithm achieved an accuracy of 57.20%. Even though according to the claims of Microsoft, Machine Learning method should have completely failed, still some gains in performance were observed. However, these performance gains were not sufficient enough to claim that privacy-protection of PhotoDNA has been compromised. Furthermore, we discuss what could be the potential reasons for the accuracy scores achieved by the top classifiers.

12.2 Hash functions

A hash function should have the ability to map any given input to fixed-size output. Different hash functions have been proposed with different properties for different purposes. Steinebach *et al.* [7] explain in their work the difference between such hash functions. According to them, the major classes of hash functions include cryptographic, robust and piecewise hashing. Cryptographic hashes are extremely sensitive to changes in data, even a small change of 1 bit can affect this hash, whereas robust hashing techniques are built for multimedia files. They use perceptual features to generate hash values thus called perceptual hash. Piecewise hashes are a combination of cryptographic hash and data segmentation; hash values for each data segment, which are calculated and then combined, are also called fuzzy hashes.

Fuzzy hashes are formally known as context triggered piecewise hashes which are used to detect similar or slightly modified data, by comparing the order of identical bytes. Fuzzy hashes are known to be robust and are very good at detecting similar content. Initial fuzzy hash-based tools include ssdeep [8] and sdhash [9] for which NIST has given reference hash sets. These tools split the data into chunks, hash these chuck and then concatenate them together. According to Roussev [10], sdhash tool is much better at detection over smaller block of similar bytes.

12.3 PhotoDNA

PhotoDNA is also categorized as a fuzzy hash-based tool which specializes in IIOC detection and lies in the perceptual-based similarity category of approximate hash based matching (AHBM) [11]. PhotoDNA works by converting images to gray scale and then dividing the images into smaller chunks. From these chucks, intensity derivatives are calculated and a histogram is build, after which the hash values are generated [1]. Typical PhotoDNA hash value consists of 144 numeric values that are used to detect the presence of IIOC images from repositories of already known images. Its primary advantages include generation of hash values that are resistant to minor changes in color, resizing and format and its ability to avoid false positives while remaining computationally efficient. PhotoDNA's popularity can be estimated by the fact that it is now used by many on-line service providers like Google, Facebook, Adobe systems and most importantly National Center for Missing and Exploited Children [1]. PhotoDNA is now a de-facto tool for the detection of known images of IIOC by investigative authorities.

12.4 Content-based image classification

Content-based classification and detection of images is a relatively mature task of computer vision. Traditionally, methods which relied on hand crafted features were used to discover keypoints. Recently, convolutional neural network (CNN)-based methods have emerged that replace these traditional methods for feature selection. The most important characteristic of these methods is the fact they learn features automatically from the data, which are robust and performed far better than traditional handcrafted-based methods. CNN-based methods have outperformed humans in many tasks such as object detection. Here we discuss these two categories of classifiers in detail.

12.4.1   Feature-descriptor-based image classification

Traditionally, image classification was done using handcrafted feature descriptors. These descriptors were difficult to design and required domain knowledge of the problem underhand. Due to this fact, these features were as good as the number scenarios that were put under consideration, while designing these methods. Naturally, they were not very reliable and robust which affected their performance especially under real-world conditions. The most notable of such method is the SIFT [12]. SIFT features as reported are invariant to scaling and rotation while they are also moderately invariant to view point and illumination. According, to Lowe [12], SIFT features are calculated through a four-stage process which include (1) scale-space extrema detection, (2) keypoint localization, (3) orientation assignment and (4) keypoint descriptor. Calculating SIFT features is a computationally expensive task due to which they are not an attractive option for real-time systems. To tackle this limitation, a variant of SIFT called speeded up robust features (SURF) [13] was designed. SURF uses Gaussian second derivative mask as feature detector, while local Haar wavelet is used for feature description. SURF features are far better in terms of speed in comparison to SIFT. However, the performance is somewhat similar. Binary Robust Independent Elementary Features (BRIEF) [14] also aim at reducing the complexity of feature descriptor by calculating binary string directly from the image. It therefore takes less computation and memory to store these feature descriptors. However, BRIEF descriptors are not invariant to in-place rotation. Moreover, binary strings are matched using hamming distance which makes BRIEF faster than SIFT. This property of BRIEF has caused it to be adapted as a feature descriptor in oriented FAST and rotated BRIEF (ORB) [15]. ORB is a modified combination of FAST detector [16] and BRIEF descriptor. According to Karami *et al.* [17], ORB is the fastest algorithm in comparison to SIFT and SURF. However, SIFT still is the most robust amongst them and performs better in most cases.

12.4.2   CNN-based image classification

Image classification has seen tremendous success through CNN-based methods. The most basic element of these methods is the convolution operation. Such operations allow Deep CNN networks to learn generic representation of the underlying data, as long as a large volume of data is provided as input. This data hungry nature has to be coupled with high computational power which enables CNN to learn robust features automatically without requiring domain knowledge. The high computational power is available due to graphical processing units (GPUs). GPUs play a huge role in the training of a CNN network. Due to this reason, CNN-based methods have given state-of-the-art performance for many vision tasks such as image segmentation [18], contour detection [19], face recognition [20,21] and pose estimation [22]. This shows that CNNs are very powerful feature extractors. However, it all started with image classification.

The famous challenge for image classification ImageNet Large Scale Visual Recognition Challenge (ILSVRC) [6] also known as ImageNet has given birth to many such deep CNN models some of which have even beaten humans. The first method to win the ImageNet 2012 for object classification was the AlexNet [23]. AlexNet was seven layers deep, out of which the first five were convolutional layers followed by two fully connected layers. Afterwards, many other CNN networks that designed the notable deep architectures include ZFNet [24], VGGNet [25], GoogLeNet [26], ResNet [27] and DenseNet [28]. Initially, Zeiler *et al.* [24] produced a novel visualization approach to better understand how these CNN models were able to learn features and perform so well for image classification task. In the pursuit of understanding the internal working of CNN, they proposed a new CNN method that outperformed AlexNet which was later called the ZFNet.

These networks even though were considered deep looked shallow in front of CNN networks such as the GoogLeNet [26], VGGNet [25] and ResNet [27]. GoogleNet [22] was 22 layers deep and used a novel inception module that not only increased the depth but also made the network wider. GoogLeNet [26] was not only deeper than the AlexNet [23] rather it has fewer number of trainable parameters, which meant that it had a smaller memory footprint then the AlexNet [23]. Their network won the 2014 ImageNet competition. The runners up during this year also produced a deep CNN model which is called the VGGNet [25]. It had two variants, the first variant was 16 and the second variant was 19 layers deep. Each variant consisted of only (3×3) convolutional filters. However, they had a staggering number of 138 and 144 million trainable parameters, respectively. Increasing the depth was very desirable; however, training a deep network had its own challenges. The most important challenge was the gradient vanishing problem. ResNet [27] took the depth to extreme levels by overcoming the gradient vanishing problem through the addition of residual connections also called skip connections. ResNet had an enormous depth of 152 layers. ResNet had an error rate of 3.57% beating the human performance on image classification on the ImageNet 2015. Recently, another deep network has been proposed by Huang *et al.* [28] which is called DenseNet. DenseNet takes the concept of skip connections to a newer level by adding them to every layer in a feed forward manner. Image classification is said to have matured. However, the next challenge naturally is building such networks that can classify more categories easily with less data just like humans. This is now the ultimate goal in image classifications.

12.5 Encryption-based image classification

Data privacy has become a very concerning matter not only for corporations but individuals as well. Commercial corporations in particular benefit largely from data collection from their users. This data may be related to entertainment, medical or banking transactions, some of which might be categorized as sensitive. Such corporations deploy big data services to benefit from this gathering of data. However, if compromised, they can put customers at risk. This provides an opportunity for PP techniques to be deployed in big data.

One possible solution is to encrypt data. However, this approach becomes computationally expensive especially when the service provided requires frequent access to data, due to which PP methods are gaining more significance. Such methods have been successfully deployed for encrypted face recognition [29] and image retrieval [30,31]. This section discusses encryption-based PP methods to protect user information that are deployed in big data servers.

Each classification system requires features that are extracted and could represent the underlining data. A PP variant of SIFT has been proposed by Hsu *et al.* [30]. They call their method PP-SIFT which is based on homomorphic encryption. In their approach, they calculated the difference-of-gradient under the Paillier cryptosystem to generate secure features that can be utilized for different tasks. Similar SIFT-based method for privacy preservation is SecSIFT proposed by Qin *et al.* [32]. Their methods aim at removing the limitation of relying on homomorphic encryption by enabling the outsourcing of computational complexity to cloud servers without compromising on privacy. The system architecture of SecSIFT consists of five stages: (1) image encryption, (2) scale-space cube generation, (3) interesting point localization, (4) descriptor generation and (5) descriptor decryption. This system is two order of magnitude faster than its predecessors.

Liu *et al.* [31] proposed another method that classifies images over the network by keeping privacy in mind. Their classification model uses the bag of feature representation. The images that are present over the network are not collected in a central repository. Rather, their feature representation is transmitted, thus preserving privacy of images. They have proposed a four-step process which includes (1) using bag-of-feature framework as feature extractor, (2) training weak learners on local machines, (3) using these weak learners for classification and (4) an ensemble of classification results is used for final decision. Instead of training on powerful classification model, they train many weak learners on the local machine over the networks. These weak learners once trained pass the bag-of-feature representation over the network instead of the image. Every weak learner then outputs its classification scores and sends back to a decision making (aggregation) machine.

According to Samanthula *et al.* [33], performing certain data mining operations on encrypted data is very challenging. Especially, encryption-based classification is a very difficult task and often results are poor. Decrypting the data multiple times put computational strain on the cloud servers. For this, they have proposed PP K-nearest neighbor (KNN) method that classifies semantically encrypted data based on Paillier cryptosystem. Once the encrypted data has been transmitted to the cloud, no decryption is needed. Their method protects the encrypted data, any access patters and search queries of the user.

In contrast to these traditional methods, deep-learning solutions to protect the privacy have also been in the limelight recently. Wang *et al.* [34] have proposed a multilayer extreme learning-machine-based classification system for encrypted images.

The images were encrypted using Data Encryption Standard (DES) and Advanced Encryption Standard (AES) algorithms. The datasets used to generate the encrypted images were Modified NIST (MNIST) database* of handwritten digits and National Institute of Standards and Technology (NIST) Special Database.† DES-based datasets had better accuracies then AES-based datasets.

Another method that uses CNN is proposed by Gilad-Bachrach *et al.* [35]. This method is coupled with homomorphic encryption and is called CryptoNets. They demonstrate the ability of CryptoNets by applying them on MNIST dataset on which they have achieved 99% classification accuracy. They claim that CryptoNet can help make encrypted prediction. For this, they utilize homomorphic encryption that preserves structure after transformation.

Similarly CryptoDL is another deep framework which works on PP deep-learning solutions [36] without revealing sensitive data. They performed their experimentation on MNIST and CIFAR-10, while achieving accuracy scores of 99.52% and 91.5%, respectively. A recent deep-learning framework "DeepSecure" has been proposed by Rouhan *et al.* [37]. This framework uses garbled circuit instead of homomorphic encryption and enables execution of many popular deep-learning architectures. They claim to be better than CryptoNet in terms of security and accuracy. They empirically evaluated their framework across different benchmarks which include image and audio benchmarks.

12.6 Experiments

In Section 12.6.1, we present our experimental approach, tools and libraries used for experimentation purpose. In Section 12.6.2, we describe the Microsoft provided PhotoDNA dataset.

12.6.1 Experimental framework

For classification of PhotoDNA generated hash values, we have used two Python-based libraries: Scikit-Learn [38] and Keras with Google's TensorFlow [39] as backend, to deploy machine-learning algorithms. Other Python libraries are NumPy [40], Pandas [41] and Matplotlib [42].

Scikit-learn [38] is an open source robust python-based library for machine-learning algorithms, with paid sponsorships from Google, INRIA and Python Software Foundation. To train CNN models for classification, we used Keras API which uses Google's TensorFlow [39]. Initially, we made a list of supervised machine-learning algorithms for classification of PhotoDNA hash; some of the most commonly used algorithms from tree-base, distance-based and function-based classifiers were selected. The selected algorithms were support vector machine (SVM), KNN, decision tree (DL), random forest (RF), artificial neural network (ANN) and CNN.

---

*http://yann.lecun.com/exdb/mnist.
†http://www.nist.gov/srd/nistsd19.cfm.

Specifically, while training CNN models, we used Adam optimizers [43], with a batch size of 128. The loss function used was cross-entropy and the base learning rate was set to 0.001. We trained networks with different levels of depth. However, as the number of examples were not enough to train a deeper network, we used a CNN model that consisted of 3 convolution layers with kernel sizes of 3×3 followed by 2 fully connected layer, trained for 200 epochs.

All the optimizations, evaluations and hyper-parameter selection were done using the built-in functionalities provided by these libraries. Here, we want to emphasize that our goal was not to develop a new algorithm. It is worth noting that our goal was not to develop a new algorithm but rather to see if PhotoDNA hash values could be classified or not. We experimented with the abovementioned algorithms on PhotoDNA hash dataset. Here our goal was to see if the classification of images based on PhotoDNA hash is possible or not, evaluate these classifiers and report their performance, and judge that which category is being better classified then other.

12.6.2 PhotoDNA hash values dataset

We received this dataset for nonsensitive PhotoDNA hash values from Microsoft. According to Microsoft, images used to generate the hash values were taken from ImageNET [6]. The categories of images selected for hash value generation are birds, fish and invertebrates. This dataset contained a total of 3,496 examples, out of which 1,288, 789 and 1,410 images belonged to birds, fish and invertebrate, respectively. The sample images used to generate the hash values are shown in Figure 12.1. The number of examples used for the three categories was kept constant to keep the classes balanced in our experimentation. The dataset was divided into 80% training and 20% testing set.

Training a CNN for classification required that the one-dimensional hash values were transformed to two-dimensional matrices. Naturally, each 144 numeric hash value was reshaped to an image of dimension $(12 \times 12 \times 1)$. The images were reshaped

*Figure 12.1   Sample images taken from ImageNET [6] which were used by
Microsoft to generate the PhotoDNA dataset explained in
Section 12.6.2*

in both row and column major formats for experimentation purposes. These newly transformed hash values are shown in Figure 12.2. Upon close inspection, we can see that these images mirror or appear to be noisy and showed very least amount of structural information. These fact shows that classifying PhotoDNA hash is a difficult and complex problem.

To better understand the dataset, we performed exploratory data analysis (EDA) on it. We performed certain preprocessing steps, which included min–max normalization, finding correlation between PhotoDNA hash values and generating graphs to get a better visual view of the data. The most meaningful graph which revealed many interesting facts about the PhotoDNA hash values was the histogram. Figure 12.3 illustrates the graphs which show the frequency distribution of PhotoDNA hash values for the three categories. In this figure, we can see that the frequency distribution

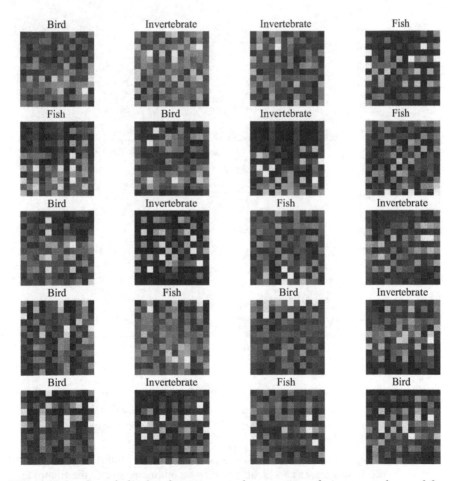

Figure 12.2   Sample hash values converted into gray scale images to be used for training our three layer CNN model. Dimension of each image is (12 × 12 × 1)

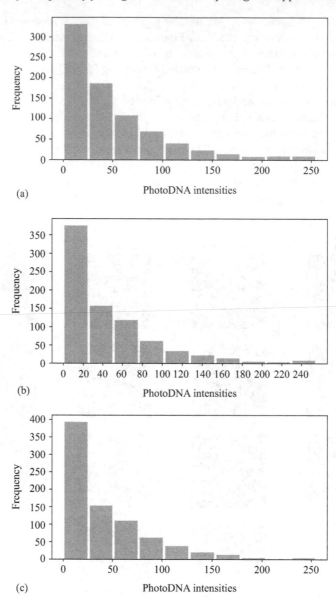

*Figure 12.3   Frequency distribution graphs for the categories: (a) bird, (b) fish,
and (c) invertebrates of the PhotoDNA hash value dataset. We can
observe that there is a right skewness for all the categories*

for all three category is positively skewed. Generation of PhotoDNA values that
mostly lie in the first quartile can be attributed as a characteristic of the PhotoDNA
technology. This shows on average for a PhotoDNA hash value that its mean would
be higher than its median. The second observation in Figure 12.3 displays that the

Table 12.1   *Evaluation of the PhotoDNA dataset. We have compared the accuracies of the selected algorithms in Section 12.7, and the best ones (RF and CNN) are highlighted in bold*

Classifier type	Classifier	Accuracy
Distance based	KNN	47.50
Tree based	Decision tree (DT)	42.32
	Random forest (RF)	**57.20**
Function based	SVM	34.23
	ANN	40.47
	CNN	**53.40**

highest frequency is for the first bin in the histogram. After further analysis of the data, it was revealed that the number with the highest frequency was "0" across all the categories followed by "1." The third spike was for the value "255." This also further explained the noise-like nature of the transformed PhotoDNA hash values in Figure 12.2 where most of the pixels are dark.

12.7 Results

All the selected algorithms were trained on the dataset and the accuracies were recorded. The highest accuracies achieved by each classifier are mentioned in Table 12.1. Based upon our work, the best classifier turned out to be: RF with an accuracy of 57.2%. Second highest accuracy of 53.40% was achieved by CNN. All the other classifiers had very poor performance, DT, ANN and KNN achieved accuracies of 42.32%, 40.47% and 47.50%, respectively. SVM on the other hand completely failed to classify PhotoDNA hash values. The base accuracy of any classification system can be calculated using (12.1). According to this formula, in this case, we can achieve an accuracy of 33%. SVM reported an accuracy of 34.23%.

Definition 12.1 (Base accuracy). *The minimum accuracy that is achieved irrespective of the performance of the classifier:*

$$Base\ Accuracy = \frac{1}{n} \times 100 \qquad (12.1)$$

The learning behavior of CNN model on training and validation set is shown in Figure 12.4. We can see that on training set, the accuracy is around 99%, while on the validation set, the performance just reached over 50%. This behavior is generally exhibited when the model over-fits on the dataset. To avoid this, we added L_2 regularization and dropout layer [44]; however, the results did not improve. Usually, as a rule of thumb, if a CNN is able to over-fit, generalization is possible over a larger dataset.

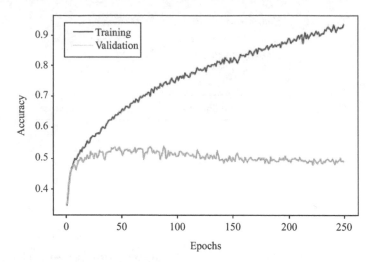

Figure 12.4   Plot of training and validation accuracy over 250 epochs of our CNN model on the PhotoDNA dataset

Thus, one possible venue to explore would be to train CNN over a larger PhotoDNA hash value dataset.

In order to understand the poor performance of the best accuracies obtained, we generated the confusion matrices to gain insights about which classes caused most uncertainty for the classifiers. For this purpose, we generated the confusion matrices for the top two classifiers, i.e., RF and CNN. Their confusion matrices are shown in Figures 12.5 and 12.6, respectively. If we observe these two matrices, we can quickly see that both classifiers are comparatively more confused in the fish category. Therefore, the hashes for fish images are more heavily misclassified than for birds and invertebrates.

A total of 144 test examples for each category are present in their confusion matrices. For the confusion matrix of RF: 92 bird, 51 fish and 81 invertebrates examples were correctly classified. A number of 33 and 19 bird examples were incorrectly classified as fish and invertebrates and 51 and 42 fish examples were incorrectly classified as birds and invertebrates. The number of misclassified invertebrates was quite low in comparisons to other categories, as 35 and 28 invertebrate examples were incorrectly classified as birds and fish (Figure 12.5).

Similar behavior is observed in the confusion matrix of CNN; in the bird category, 72 examples were correctly classified as birds, while 37 and 35 were wrongly classified as fish and invertebrates. In the fish category, 54 examples were correctly classified as fish, while 51 and 39 were wrongly classified as birds and invertebrates. In the invertebrate category, 85 examples were correctly classified as invertebrate, while 30 and 29 were wrongly classified as bird and fish (Figure 12.6).

There were some similarities between the confusion matrices of both classifiers. First, both the classifiers had difficulty while classifying fish category. RF had misclassified the same number of fish examples as bird which it correctly classified as

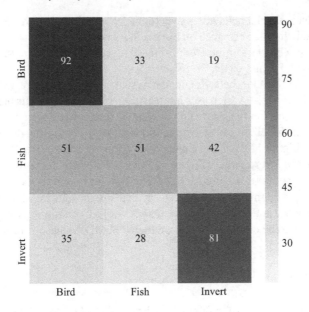

Figure 12.5 Confusion matrix for RF classifier

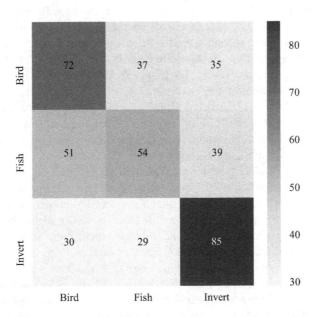

Figure 12.6 Confusion matrix of our CNN model

fish, i.e., 51. Near similar behavior is seen for CNN's confusion matrix. However, both classifiers had better performance on birds and invertebrates categories as compared to fish category, while less number of misclassification exists only for the invertebrate category for both RF and CNN.

We can attribute this behavior to the visual artifacts that are utilized for the generation of PhotoDNA, which uses intensity derivatives to calculate hash value. The shape of invertebrates in the images gives more discontinuations in its gradient flow. The evidence for this claim can also be found by closely comparing the histograms of each category (Figure 12.3). Upon close observation, we can see that the intensities in the first bin of the invertebrates (Figure 12.3(a)) are slightly higher compared to fish (Figure 12.3(b)) and bird (Figure 12.3(c)). The histograms for the last two categories are very similar. With this in mind, we can say that any image which has higher degree of gradient flow disruption compared to images with less disruptions to gradient flow is perhaps easier to be classified based on their PhotoDNA hash values.

12.8 Discussion

These classification results for PhotoDNA hash values (Table 12.1) show that some accuracy gains were achieved. However, based on the claims by Microsoft, these accuracy scores were surprising. In this section, we will discuss the reasons that might explain the achieved accuracy. First, as per Microsoft, PhotoDNA uses edge information or rather intensity gradients [1] in the generation of the digital signature for each image (Section 12.3). According to the available documentation of PhotoDNA [1], the images are divided into segments. However, the specific implementation is not public information. The experiment shows that images that have high gradient disruptions in the divided segments tend to be easily distinguished. In support of this argument, we can see that invertebrates are classified much more easily as compared to birds and fishes (Section 12.7). This trend can also be seen by close observation of the frequency distribution graphs of the categories (Figure 12.3). The histogram of invertebrates (Figure 12.3(c)) has slightly higher intensities for the first bin in comparison to the histograms of bird (Figure 12.3(a)) and fish (Figure 12.3(b)). As compared to bird and fish, invertebrates might have more gradient disruption due to their shape (as shown in Figure 12.1).

Second, the PhotoDNA hash value itself does not provide enough structural information or features that machine-learning algorithms can exploit to attack successfully through classification. With a total number of 144 numeric feature columns, with high frequency of zeros as explained in Section 12.6.2. Even the transformed hash values (Figure 12.2) look like randomly generated noise images. The digital signatures produced through PhotoDNA have an inherent right skewness in them. Due to these factors and properties of the PhotoDNA, the data is difficult to classify inherently. This establishes the structural integrity of PhotoDNA as a very secure hash function. One possible avenue to explore in the future could be projecting the hash values into higher dimensions and apply feature engineering techniques. However, the experiments suggest that leakage of information is not possible through PhotoDNA.

Third, we believe the number of examples in the dataset provided to us by Microsoft was not enough to train bigger deep CNN networks. We can clearly see that our CNN model has over-fitted [45] on this dataset (Figure 12.4). We used L_2 regularization, cross validation and dropout [44] to improve generalization. The next logical step would be to provide more data thus training deeper networks and verifying PhotoDNA's resistance.

12.9 Conclusion

In this chapter, we tested the PP capability of PhotoDNA hash values through machine-learning-based classification attacks. The dataset was provided by Microsoft and contained hash values of nonsensitive images taken from ImageNet. We performed EDA for this dataset in order to better understand the PhotoDNA hash values. We experimented with different supervised machine-learning algorithms which include tree-based, distance-based and function-based classifiers. We reported the performance of the selected classifiers and, based on our results, RF achieved the best accuracy score of 57.20%, followed by CNN of 53.40%, while SVM failed at classification with a score of 34.23%. These results indicate that PhotoDNA is resistant to machine-learning-based classification attacks. Our experimentation suggests that images with high gradient intensity disruptions are easy to classify compared to images with less gradient intensity disruption. This most probably explains the classification scores achieved. However, such scores are not sufficient enough to claim that PhotoDNA's PP capability has been compromised. Therefore, based on the dataset used, PhotoDNA can still be considered as a secure hashing technology.

References

[1] Microsoft Corporation. PhotoDNA and PhotoDNA Cloud Service: Fact Sheet. 2016. Available from: https://news.microsoft.com/uploads/2016/03/photo DNACloudServiceFS.pdf.

[2] BBC. Sex Offences Against Children Increase; 2018. Available from: https://www.bbc.co.uk/news/uk-scotland-43116257.

[3] Dodd V. Internet Firms are Failing to Tackle Child Abuse Images, Police Chief Says; 2018. Available from: https://www.theguardian.com/society/2018/jun/21/internet-companies-can-should-screen-out-child-abuse-images.

[4] Al-Rubaie M. and Chang JM. Privacy-Preserving Machine Learning: Threats and Solutions. IEEE Security & Privacy, 2019;17(2):49–58.

[5] Hitaj B, Ateniese G, and Perez-Cruz F. Deep models under the GAN: Information leakage from collaborative deep learning. In: Proceedings of the 2017 ACM SIGSAC Conference on Computer and Communications Security. ACM; 2017. p. 603–618.

[6] Russakovsky O, Deng J, Su H, *et al.* ImageNet Large Scale Visual Recognition Challenge. International Journal of Computer Vision. 2015;115(3):211–252.

[7]   Steinebach M, Klöckner P, Reimers N, *et al.* Robust hash algorithms for text. In: IFIP International Conference on Communications and Multimedia Security. Springer; 2013. p. 135–144.

[8]   Kornblum J. Identifying Almost Identical Files Using Context Triggered Piecewise Hashing. Digital Investigation. 2006;3:S91–S97.

[9]   Roussev V. Data fingerprinting with similarity digests. In: Proceedings of the Sixth IFIP WG 11.9 International Conference on Digital Forensics. Springer; 2010. p. 207–226.

[10]   Roussev V. An Evaluation of Forensic Similarity Hashes. Digital Investigation. 2011;8:S34–S41.

[11]   Bjelland PC, Franke K, and Årnes A. Practical Use of Approximate Hash Based Matching in Digital Investigations. Digital Investigation. 2014;11: S18–S26.

[12]   Lowe DG. Distinctive Image Features from Scale-Invariant Keypoints. International Journal of Computer Vision. 2004;60(2):91–110.

[13]   Bay H, Tuytelaars T, and Van Gool L. SURF: Speeded up robust features. In: European Conference on Computer Vision. Springer; 2006. p. 404–417.

[14]   Calonder M, Lepetit V, Strecha C, *et al.* BRIEF: Binary robust independent elementary features. In: European Conference on Computer Vision. Springer; 2010. p. 778–792.

[15]   Rublee E, Rabaud V, Konolige K, Bradski G. ORB: An efficient alternative to SIFT or SURF. 2011 International Conference on Computer Vision, Barcelona; 2011, p. 2564–2571.

[16]   Rosten E, and Drummond T. Machine learning for high-speed corner detection. In: European Conference on Computer Vision. Springer; 2006. p. 430–443.

[17]   Karami E, Prasad S, and Shehata M. Image matching using SIFT, SURF, BRIEF and ORB: Performance comparison for distorted images. arXiv preprint arXiv:171002726. 2017.

[18]   Girshick R, Donahue J, Darrell T, *et al.* Rich feature hierarchies for accurate object detection and semantic segmentation. In: Proceedings of the 2014 IEEE Conference on Computer Vision and Pattern Recognition (CVPR'14). IEEE; 2014. p. 580–587.

[19]   Shen W, Wang X, Wang Y, *et al.* DeepContour: A deep convolutional feature learned by positive-sharing loss for contour detection. In: Proceedings of the 2015 IEEE Conference on Computer Vision and Pattern Recognition (CVPR'15). IEEE; 2015. p. 3982–3991.

[20]   Parkhi OM, Vedaldi A, Zisserman A, *et al.* Deep face recognition. In: Proceedings of the British Machine Vision Conference (BMVC). BMVA Press; 2015. p. 41.1–41.12.

[21]   Sun Y, Liang D, Wang X, *et al.* DeepID3: Face Recognition with Very Deep Neural Networks. Clinical Orthopaedics and Related Research. 2015;abs/1502.00873. Available from: http://arxiv.org/abs/1502.00873.

[22]   Toshev A, and Szegedy C. DeepPose: Human pose estimation via deep neural networks. In: Proceedings of the 2014 IEEE Conference on Computer Vision and Pattern Recognition (CVPR'14). IEEE; 2014. p. 1653–1660.

[23] Krizhevsky A, Sutskever I, and Hinton GE. ImageNet classification with deep convolutional neural networks. In: Proceedings of the 25th International Conference on Neural Information Processing Systems (NIPS'12). Curran Associates Inc.; 2012. p. 1097–1105.

[24] Zeiler MD, and Fergus R. Visualizing and understanding convolutional networks. In: Proceedings of the European Conference on Computer Vision (ECCV 2014). Springer; 2014. p. 818–833.

[25] Simonyan K, and Zisserman A. Very Deep Convolutional Networks for Large-scale Image Recognition. Clinical Orthopaedics and Related Research. 2014;abs/1409.1556. Available from: http://arxiv.org/abs/1409.1556.

[26] Szegedy C, Liu W, Jia Y, *et al.* Going deeper with convolutions. In: Proceedings of the 2015 IEEE Conference on Computer Vision and Pattern Recognition (CVPR); 2015. p. 1–9.

[27] He K, Zhang X, Ren S, *et al.* Deep residual learning for image recognition. In: Proceedings of the 2016 IEEE Conference on Computer Vision and Pattern Recognition (CVPR). IEEE; 2016. p. 770–778.

[28] Huang G, Liu Z, Van Der Maaten L, *et al.* Densely connected convolutional networks. In: Proceedings of the IEEE Conference on Computer Vision and Pattern Recognition; 2017. p. 4700–4708.

[29] Lu H, Martin K, Bui F, *et al.* Face recognition with biometric encryption for privacy-enhancing self-exclusion. In: Digital Signal Processing, 2009 16th International Conference on. IEEE; 2009. p. 1–8.

[30] Hsu CY, Lu CS, and Pei SC; IEEE. Image Feature Extraction in Encrypted Domain with Privacy-Preserving SIFT. IEEE Transactions on Image Processing. 2012;21(11):4593–4607.

[31] Liu C, Shang Z, and Tang YY. An Image Classification Method that Considers Privacy-Preservation. Neurocomputing. 2016;208:80–98.

[32] Qin Z, Yan J, Ren K, *et al.* Towards efficient privacy-preserving image feature extraction in cloud computing. In: Proceedings of the 22nd ACM International Conference on Multimedia (MM'14). ACM; 2014. p. 497–506.

[33] Samanthula BK, Elmehdwi Y, and Jiang W. K-nearest neighbor classification over semantically secure encrypted relational data. IEEE Transactions on Knowledge and Data Engineering. 2015;27(5):1261–1273.

[34] Wang W, Vong CM, Yang Y, *et al.* Encrypted Image Classification Based on Multilayer Extreme Learning Machine. Multidimensional Systems and Signal Processing. 2017;28(3):851–865.

[35] Gilad-Bachrach R, Dowlin N, Laine K, *et al.* CryptoNets: Applying neural networks to encrypted data with high throughput and accuracy. In: International Conference on Machine Learning; 2016. p. 201–210.

[36] Hesamifard E, Takabi H, and Ghasemi M. CryptoDL: Deep neural networks over encrypted data. arXiv preprint arXiv:171105189. 2017.

[37] Rouhani BD, Riazi MS, and Koushanfar F. DeepSecure: Scalable provably-secure deep learning. In: Proceedings of the 55th Annual Design Automation Conference. ACM; 2018. p. 2.

[38]   Varoquaux G, Buitinck L, Louppe G, *et al.* Scikit-Learn: Machine Learning Without Learning the Machinery. GetMobile: Mobile Computing and Communications. 2015;19(1):29–33.

[39]   Abadi M, Barham P, Chen J, *et al.* TensorFlow: A system for large-scale machine learning. In: OSDI. vol. 16; 2016. p. 265–283.

[40]   Oliphant TE. A Guide to NumPy. Trelgol Publishing, USA, 2006.

[41]   McKinney W. Data Structures for Statistical Computing in Python. Proceedings of the 9th Python in Science Conference, Austin, TX, 2010, p. 51–56.

[42]   Hunter JD. Matplotlib: A 2D Graphics Environment. Computing in Science & Engineering. 2007;9(3):90–95.

[43]   Kingma DP, and Ba J. Adam: A Method for Stochastic Optimization. Clinical Orthopaedics and Related Research. 2014;abs/1412.6980. Available from: http://arxiv.org/abs/1412.6980.

[44]   Srivastava N, Hinton G, Krizhevsky A, *et al.* JMLR.org. Dropout: A Simple Way to Prevent Neural Networks from Overfitting. The Journal of Machine Learning Research. 2014;15(1):1929–1958.

[45]   Hawkins DM. The Problem of Overfitting. Journal of Chemical Information and Computer Sciences. 2004;44(1):1–12.

Chapter 13

Chaos-based communication systems

Xiaojing Gao[1]

With the rapid development of optical communications and the increasing amount of data exchanged, it has become utterly important to provide effective architecture to protect sensitive data. The use of chaotic optoelectronic devices has already demonstrated great potential in terms of additional computational security at the physical layer of the optical network. Chaotic signals have been proposed as broadband information carriers with the potential of providing a high level of robustness and privacy in data transmission. An emerging discipline, chaos-based communication has been an important research topic in the past two decades. In this chapter, some several typical continuous chaotic systems for chaos are introduced, and optical chaos secure communication systems are discussed.

13.1 Cryptography and chaos

Since Poincaré first studied the relationship between *three-body motion* and *chaos* in the early twentieth century, the theoretical study of chaotic systems has been developed rapidly. In 1979, *Lorenz butterfly effect* was famous all over the world, that is, the *chaos* phenomenon: a small wind can cause a tornado-like shock effect. *Chaos* means that in a dynamic system, small changes in initial conditions will bring unpredictability to the evolution of the system. This sensitivity of initial values can be described as *millimeter difference, thousands of miles fallacy*. When the atmospheric thermal convection was studied, *Lorentz* proposed a simple weather model [1]. This nonlinear meteorological model only has three state variables interacting with each other. However, such a simple model can produce chaos phenomena, which is also the first chaotic attractor described as *Lorentz attractor*. With the advent of Lorenz chaotic system, researchers began to pay attention to the chaotic systems and the wide application of chaos in various fields. Chaos phenomena are no longer regarded as uncontrollable harmful behavior. At the same time, with the development of control theory, how to enter the desired chaotic state of anti-control system has been abundantly studied. In 1976, Rössle chaotic system was proposed. Subsequently, Chen's system was proposed in

[1]School of Computer Science, China University of Geosciences, Wuhan, China

1999 by using chaotic anti-control strategy. Chen's system is not the same as Lorenz system. It has more than two attraction centers [2]. Compared with Lorenz system, the dynamic behavior and phase-space structure of Chen's system are more complex. In 2002, Lu Jinhu and Chen Guanrong also discovered the Lü system. These three systems mentioned above are called Lorenz system family.

Up to now, there is no unified standard definition of chaos. In 1975, Li Tianyan and his mentor J. Yorke published the article *Period 3 Meaning Chaos* in the *American Mathematics Monthly* magazine and gave the mathematical definition of *chaos* for the first time, that is, *Li-Yorke theorem*. In 1989, R.L. Devaney gave a more intuitive definition, that is, *Devaney definition*. More often, chaotic systems are described by the following characteristics:

1. *Initial sensitivity*: Any chaotic system, starting from two initial values that are infinitely close to each other, will have different orbits over time.
2. *Boundedness*: Any chaotic system, no matter how its parameters are chosen, will converge to the same bounded region over time, that is, chaotic attraction region.
3. *Random*: Even if the chaotic system is always confined to a limited area, its motion is unpredictable and its trajectory is never repeated.
4. *Ergodicity*: The boundedness of chaotic system and its inherent randomness determine the ergodicity of chaotic system. The system trajectory traverses every state point in the chaotic region.
5. *Fractal dimension*: The geometric form of chaotic system in phase space has a multilayered self-similar structure, that is, *strange attractor*.
6. *Positive Lyapunov exponent*: Describes the degree of orbital separation of a system as it evolves over time from arbitrarily approaching different initial values.

Since the discovery of chaotic systems, researchers have found that there is an astonishing consistency between the complex dynamic characteristics of chaotic systems and cryptography. For this reason, chaotic systems are widely used in the field of information security. Secure communication technology based on chaotic systems has become an international research hotspot in the field of information security. There are two main applications of chaotic systems in the field of information security: chaos cryptography, which uses chaotic maps to construct ciphers to encrypt information; secure communication based on chaos synchronization, which uses continuous chaotic carriers to hide information.

13.2   Continuous chaotic systems

In the section, several typical continuous chaotic systems will be introduced.

13.2.1   Chua's chaotic system

Chua's circuit has been one of the first analog circuits found, which exhibits nonlinear dynamics. It was developed by Leon O. Chua and gained popularity as a model for chaos [3]. Figure 13.1 shows the circuit diagram of Chua's circuit.

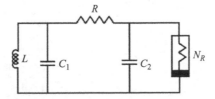

Figure 13.1 Chua's circuit diagram

Chua's circuit contains an inductor L, a linear resistor R, two capacitors C_1 and C_2, and a single voltage controlled nonlinear resistor N_R. The nonlinear resistor N_R can be realized in the form of an operational amplifier, diodes, transistors, and operational transconductance amplifiers [4].

A mathematical model of Chua's circuit, developed by using basic Kirchhoff's voltage and current law [5], is given below:

$$\begin{cases} \dfrac{dV_2}{dt} = \dfrac{I}{C_2} - \dfrac{G}{C_2}(V_2 - V_1) \\[2ex] \dfrac{dV_1}{dt} = \dfrac{G}{C_1}(V_2 - V_1) - \dfrac{1}{C_1}f(V_1) \\[2ex] \dfrac{dI}{dt} = -V_2/L \end{cases} \qquad (13.1)$$

In [4], nonlinear dynamics analysis of Chua's circuit has been done by varying parameter $f(V_1)$.

The normalization equation of Chua's chaotic system can be expressed as

$$\begin{cases} \dot{x}_1(t) = a(x_2(t) - m_1 x_1(t)) + f(x_1(t)) \\[1ex] \dot{x}_2(t) = x_1(t) - x_2(t) + x_3(t) \\[1ex] \dot{x}_3(t) = -b x_2(t) \end{cases} \qquad (13.2)$$

with the nonlinear characteristics

$$f(x_1(t)) = \frac{1}{2}(m_1 - m_0)(|x_1(t) + 1| - |x_1(t) + 1|) \qquad (13.3)$$

which belongs to sector [0,1]. Parameters $a = 9$, $m_1 = 2/7$, $m_0 = -1/7$, and $b = 14.286$ [6]. The initial conditions of the system are $x(t) = [0.2, 0.3, 0.2]^T$. System (13.2) can have the chaotic attractors as shown in Figure 13.2.

13.2.2 Lorentz chaotic system

Mathematical meteorologist, E.N. Lorenz, in 1963, introduced a system of three nonlinear differential equations that showed chaotic dynamics.

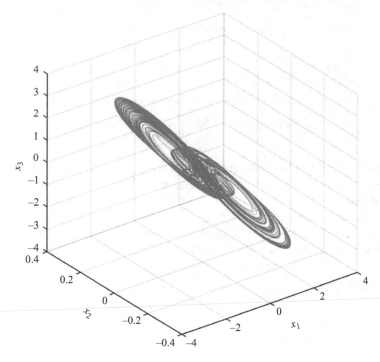

Figure 13.2   Chaotic behaviors of Chua's chaotic system with parameters $a = 9$,
$m_1 = 2/7$, $m_2 = -1/7$, and $b = 14.286$

The electronic circuit equivalent equations of Lorentz as derived in [4] are given as follows:

$$
\begin{cases}
\dot{u} = \left(\dfrac{1}{R_5 C_1}\right)\left[\left(\dfrac{R_4}{R_1}\right)v - \dfrac{R_3}{R_2 + R_3}\left(1 + \dfrac{R_4}{R_1}\right)u\right] \\[2ex]
\dot{v} = \left(\dfrac{1}{R_{15} C_2}\right)\left[\dfrac{R_{11}}{R_{10} + R_{11}}\left(1 + \dfrac{R_{12}}{R_8} + \dfrac{R_{12}}{R_9}\right)\left(1 + \dfrac{R_7}{R_6}\right)u - \dfrac{R_{12}}{R_8}\right. \\[2ex]
\qquad \left. \times\, v - \dfrac{R_{12}}{R_9} \times uw\right] \\[2ex]
\dot{w} = \dfrac{1}{R_{20} C_3}\left[\dfrac{R_{19}}{R_{16}} \times uv - \dfrac{R_{18}}{R_{17} + R_{18}}\left(1 + \dfrac{R_{19}}{R_{16}}\right)w\right]
\end{cases}
\tag{13.4}
$$

The corresponding circuit implementation of Lorentz equations, as done in [4], is shown in Figure 13.3.

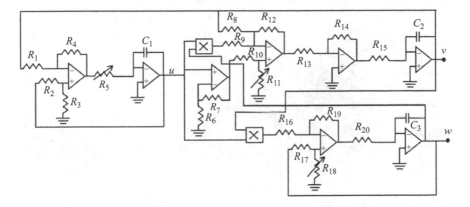

Figure 13.3 Lorentz circuit diagram

The normalization equation of Lorentz chaotic system can be expressed as

$$\begin{cases} \dot{x}_1(t) = a(x_2(t) - x_1(t)) \\ \dot{x}_2(t) = cx_1(t) - x_2(t) - x_1(t)x_3(t) \\ \dot{x}_3(t) = x_1(t)x_2(t) - bx_3(t) \end{cases} \tag{13.5}$$

Parameters $a = 10$, $b = 8/3$, and $c = 28$. The initial conditions of the system are $x(t) = [0, 1, 0]^T$. System (13.5) can have the chaotic attractors as shown in Figure 13.4.

13.2.3 Chen's chaotic system

Chen's chaotic system was proposed by Chen Guanrong in 1999, which can be expressed as

$$\begin{cases} \dot{x}_1(t) = a(x_2(t) - x_1(t)) \\ \dot{x}_2(t) = (c - a)x_1(t) + cx_2(t) - x_1(t)x_3(t) \\ \dot{x}_3(t) = x_1(t)x_2(t) - bx_3(t) \end{cases} \tag{13.6}$$

Parameters $a = 35$, $b = 3$, and $c = 28$. The initial conditions of the system are $x(t) = [0, 1, 0]^T$. System (13.6) can have the chaotic attractors as shown in Figure 13.5.

13.2.4 Lü chaotic system

Lü chaotic system was proposed by Lü Jinghu in 2002, which can be expressed as

$$\begin{cases} \dot{x}_1(t) = a(x_2(t) - x_1(t)) \\ \dot{x}_2(t) = cx_2(t) - x_1(t)x_3(t) \\ \dot{x}_3(t) = x_1(t)x_2(t) - bx_3(t) \end{cases} \tag{13.7}$$

Parameters $a = 36$, $b = 3$, and $c = 20$. The initial conditions of the system are $x(t) = [0, 1, 0]^T$. System (13.7) can have the chaotic attractors as shown in Figure 13.6.

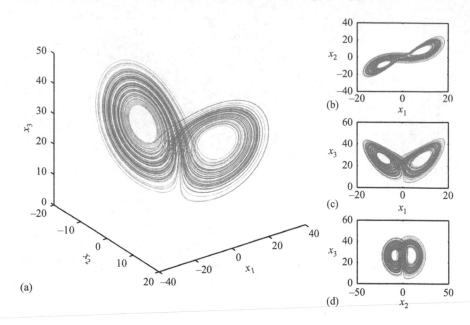

Figure 13.4   *Chaotic behaviors of Lorentz chaotic system with parameters a = 10,*
b = 8/3, and c = 28. (a) Phase portraits in x₁−x₂−x₃ plane; (b) Phase
portraits in x₁−x₂ plane; (c) Phase portraits in x₁−x₃ plane;
(d) Phase portraits in x₂−x₃ plane

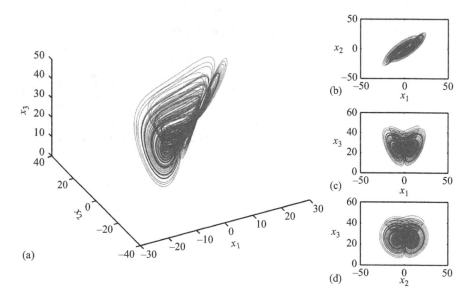

Figure 13.5   *Chaotic behaviors of Chen's chaotic system with parameters a = 10,*
b = 8/3, and c = 28. (a) Phase portraits in x₁−x₂−x₃ plane; (b) Phase
portraits in x₁−x₂ plane; (c) Phase portraits in x₁−x₃ plane;
(d) Phase portraits in x₂−x₃ plane

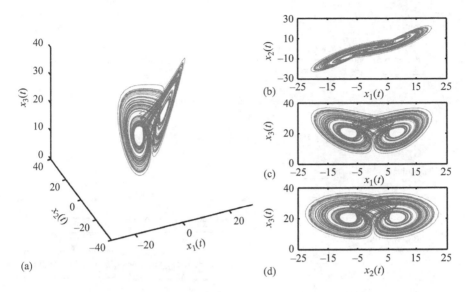

Figure 13.6 *Chaotic behaviors of Lü chaotic system with parameters a = 36,*
b = 3, and c = 20. (a) Phase portraits in $x_1−x_2−x_3$ plane; (b) Phase
portraits in $x_1−x_2$ plane; (c) Phase portraits in $x_1−x_3$ plane;
(d) Phase portraits in $x_2−x_3$ plane

13.3 Chaotic secure communication and its application in optical communication

Since Pecora *et al.* used a circuit to realize chaotic synchronization [7], secure communication based on chaotic synchronization has become a hot research topic in the field of information security. Chaos has unique advantages: high sensitivity to initial values, ergodicity, non-periodicity, continuous broadband spectrum, noise-like, and so on, which can guarantee the security of message signals. At the same time, the existence of chaotic synchronization can also guarantee the secure communication based on chaotic synchronization.

13.3.1 The design of chaotic secure communication

In chaotic communication systems the masking of the message is performed at the physical layer by embedding the signal within a chaotic carrier in the emitter. The recovery of the message is based on the synchronization phenomenon by which a receiver, quite similar to the transmitter, is able to reproduce the chaotic part of the transmitted signal [8]. At present, there are three kinds of secure communication technologies based on chaotic synchronization: *chaos masking, chaos shift keying,* and *chaos modulation.*

13.3.1.1 Chaos masking

In 1991, *chaos masking* was first proposed by Oppenheim and Kocarev *et al.* Its principle is shown in Figure 13.7 [9].

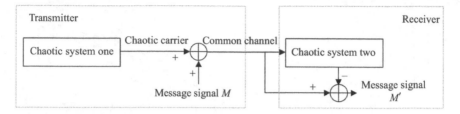

Figure 13.7   Chaotic masking communication

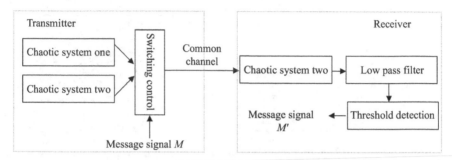

Figure 13.8   Chaos shift keying communication

At the transmitter, the information signal S is directly modulated by the chaotic carrier X to generate message signal M, such as $M = S + X$. The message signal is sent to the receiver through the common channel. At the receiver, the same chaotic carrier signal is obtained by using chaotic synchronization technology for demodulation to obtain the message signal M', $M' \rightarrow M$. In the chaotic masking communication model, it is required that the transmitted message signal has a small amplitude. If the amplitude energy is too large, the attacker can obtain the characteristics of the transmitted message by analyzing the spectrum of the intercepted signal.

13.3.1.2   Chaos shift keying

Chaos shift keying was first proposed by Hasler [10]. Its principle is shown in Figure 13.8.

According to the input of information signal, the emitter switches between several different chaotic systems. In a certain time window, the chaotic sequence output from one system is transmitted through a common channel, and in the next time window, the chaotic sequence output from another different chaotic system is transmitted through a common channel. Receiver demodulates the information signal by synchronization error detection based on chaotic synchronization technology.

13.3.1.3   Chaos modulation

Chaos modulation was first proposed by A.R. Volkovskii. Its principle is shown in Figure 13.9 [11].

At the transmitter, the information signal is directly injects into the chaotic generator. The chaotic outputs contain information signal, which are transmitted through the

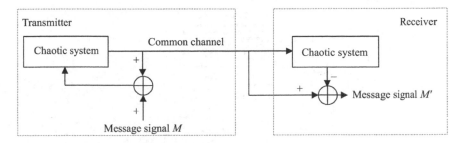

Figure 13.9 Chaos modulation communication

common channel. The receiver demodulates the information signal based on chaotic synchronization technology.

13.4 Optic chaotic communication

With the rapid development of information society and the increasing demand for broadband rate, optical communication has become the main means of communication. Optical chaotic secure communication has many excellent characteristics, such as large bandwidth, large capacity, low attenuation, and high speed. It can satisfy the speed requirement of high-speed optical communication and ensure its security.

Time-delay (TD) systems have attracted considerable attention in the field of optical secure communication due to their unique advantages [12,13]. These systems have simple structures and can provide high-dimensional attractors for a higher level of computational security to/against embedding techniques [14,15]. Recently, laser systems with TD feedback have been proposed and gained much research attention in the area of chaos secure communication [16,17].

Besides the popular external cavity laser diode setups, we focus in this book on another experimental realization involving electro-optic (EO) feedback loops, with delay.

13.4.1 Ikeda-delayed chaotic system

The schematic of the Ikeda-delayed chaotic system is illustrated in Figure 13.10. A continuous-wave (CW) semiconductor laser (SL) seeds a CW light into a Mach–Zehnder modulator (MZM) whose direct-current (dc) half-wave voltage is V_{dc}. After the TD part, the delayed optical signal is converted to an electrical voltage by a photodiode (PD). Then, the electrical voltage is amplified and sent into the MZM by a radio-frequency (RF) amplifier [18].

The mathematical modeling of the Ikeda-delayed chaotic system can be expressed as [19]:

$$x + \tau \frac{dx}{dt} + \frac{1}{\theta} \int_{0}^{t} x(s)ds = \beta \cos^2(x(t-T) + \Phi) \tag{13.8}$$

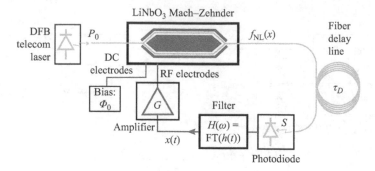

Figure 13.10   Experimental setup of the Ikeda optical chaotic system. LD, laser diode; MZM, Mach–Zehnder modulator; PD, photodiode; RF, radio-frequency amplifier; FDL, fiber delay line

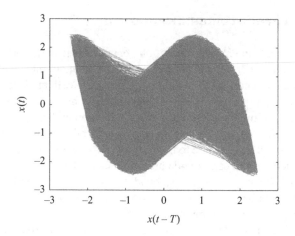

Figure 13.11   Chaotic behaviors of Ikeda-delayed chaotic system with parameters $\tau = 25$ ps, $\theta = 5$ μs, $\beta = 5$, $\Phi = -\pi/4$, and $T = 30$ ns

where τ, θ, β, and Φ are system parameters, T is the TD parameter. The parameters of the system are given as $\tau = 25$ ps, $\theta = 5$ μs, $\beta = 5$, $\Phi = -\pi/4$, and $T = 30$ ns. System (13.8) can have the chaotic attractors as shown in Figure 13.11.

13.4.2   A chaotic system with suppressed time-delay signature based on multiple electro-optic nonlinear loops

In [19], Apostolos *et al.* demonstrated high-speed long-distance communication based on chaos synchronization over a commercial fiber-optic channel. An optical carrier wave generated by a chaotic laser is used to encode a message for transmission over 120 km of optical fiber in the metropolitan area network of Athens, Greece. The message is decoded using an appropriate second laser which, by synchronizing with the chaotic carrier, allows for the separation of the carrier and the message. Transmission rates in the gigabit per second range are achieved, with corresponding bit-error rates below 10^{-7}.

Although the initial Ikeda DDE model already features rich and highly complex dynamics, there are some problems when the delayed chaotic system meets communication application. For the security of Ikeda chaotic optical system, the key issue is the TD concealment. However, TD can be vulnerable since it can be identified by using the autocorrelation function (ACF) [20,21], delayed mutual information (DMI) [22], extrema statistics [23,24], and filling factor [25]. On the other hand, the key space dimension is relatively low compared to algorithmic cryptography [20], and this fact may cause some security vulnerabilities under the brute-force attack.

To overcome these two main deficiencies, many approaches have been proposed, for example, a semiconductor ring laser with a cross-feedback configuration [22], adjusting the TD close to the laser relaxation period [26], mutual couple of three EO chains [27], combining all-optical and EO systems [28].

13.4.3 System model

In the remaining sections, we will focus more on a TD chaotic system by adopting multiple EO nonlinear loops [29]. The mathematical modeling of the TD chaotic system can be expressed as

$$
\begin{cases}
x_1 + \tau_1 \dfrac{dx_1}{dt} + \dfrac{1}{\theta_1} \displaystyle\int_0^t x_1(s)ds = b_1 \cos^2(x_2(t - T_1) + x_3(t - T_1) + \Phi_1) \\[4mm]
x_2 + \tau_2 \dfrac{dx_2}{dt} + \dfrac{1}{\theta_2} \displaystyle\int_0^t x_2(s)ds = b_2 \cos^2(x_1(t - T_2) + x_3(t - T_2) + \Phi_2) \\[4mm]
x_3 + \tau_3 \dfrac{dx_3}{dt} + \dfrac{1}{\theta_3} \displaystyle\int_0^t x_3(s)ds = b_3 \cos^2(x_2(t - T_3) + x_1(t - T_3) + \Phi_3)
\end{cases}
\tag{13.9}
$$

where b_j is called the bifurcate parameter, assuming that $b_i = b$, $\Phi_i = \Phi$, $\tau_j = \tau$, $\theta_j = \theta$, and x_j is the state variable, constant T_j is the TD, $j = 1, 2, 3$.

To realize system (13.9), some off-the-shelf fiber-optic telecommunication devices are adopted. The schematic of the system is illustrated in Figure 13.12. It is composed of a CW SL diode (LD_j), where the light is modulated by a Mach–Zehnder modulator (MZ_j). The optical signal is then detected by a photodetector (PD_j). The resulting electrical signal is filtered by a band-pass filter (BPF_j) with low- and high-cutoff frequencies f_L and f_H and then amplified by a radio-frequency (RF_j) driver.

In what follows, the simulations are conducted by using the MATLAB® software. The integrations of system (13.9) were done with a fourth-order Runge-Kutta algorithm at a sampling rate of 5 ps. The bifurcation diagram and dynamic complexity

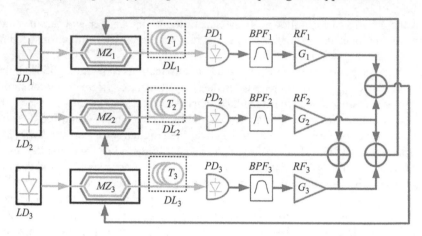

Figure 13.12   *The schematic of the proposed chaos system. LD_j, laser diode; MZ_j,*
Mach–Zehnder modulator; DL_j, optical delay line; T_j, time-delay;
PD_j, photodetector; BPF_j, band-pass filter; RF_j, band-pass
amplifier; $j = 1, 2, 3$

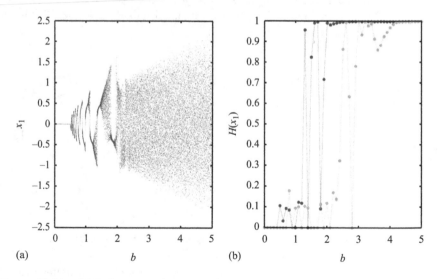

Figure 13.13   *(a) Bifurcation diagram of system (13.9) in the range of $b = 0$–5. (b)*
The PE as a function of the bifurcate parameter b for $L = 6$, $D = 2$.
A 3×10^2 ns time series x_1 with 6×10^4 data points is used for PE

of system (13.9) are shown in Figure 13.13 for $\Phi = -\pi/4$, $\tau = 25$ ps, $\theta = 5$ μs,
$T_1 = 22$ ns, $T_2 = 28$ ns, and $T_3 = 34$ ns.

From Figure 13.13(a), we know that system (13.9) is chaotic in the range of $b = 2.07$–5. The dynamic complexity of system (13.9) is mapped by using permutation entropy (PE) [25,26]. PE is defined as $H(x_1)$ and is calculated for the ordinal pattern length $L = 6$ and embedding delay $D = 2$ (data points). We choose the length N of the measured time series x_1, $N = 6 \times 10^4$, which is large enough to allow for a reasonable distribution of possible ordinal patterns ($L!$), yet low enough for practical computation time [26]. In Figure 13.13(b), the curve of $H(x_1)$ (darker line) verifies these results from Figure 13.13(a). In the range of $b = 2.07$–5, system (13.9) can generate the most complex time series [$H(x_1) \approx 0.99$]. Compared with the original system with single TD (light color line), the complexity curves are similar in trends. However, the proposed system can enter chaotic zone with a small value of b.

13.4.4 Time-delay signature suppression

We study the performance of TD signature (TDS) suppression in this section. We define $T = (T_1, T_2, T_3)$ then investigate the security performance of system (13.9) by using $ACF(x_1)$, $DMI(x_1)$, and $H(x_1)$ for $T = (22, 22, 22)$ ns, and $T = (22, 28, 34)$ ns, respectively, when $b = 4.5$. As shown in Figure 13.14, there are obvious peaks in $ACF(x_1)$, $DMI(x_1)$, and $H(x_1)$ at the relevant TD $S = 22$ ns or its multiples for $T = (22, 22, 22)$ ns.

And when $T = (22, 28, 34)$ ns, no significant peak appears under the three different attack methods. These results show the effectiveness of our strategy preliminarily under the condition that $T_i \neq T_j$, $i \neq j$, $i,j = 1, 2, 3$, and $b = 4.5$. According to our simulation, to study the detailed conditions of the TDS suppression, two factors should be considered, the bifurcation parameter b and the minimum interval between different TDs δ ($\delta = \min\{T_i - T_j\}$, $i \neq j$, $i,j = 1, 2, 3$).

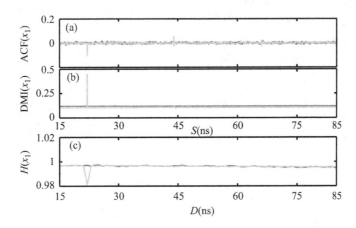

Figure 13.14 *(a) The ACF and (b) the DMI of the chaotic signal x_1, a 1.25×10^3 ns time series with 2.5×10^5 data points is used. (c) The PE $H(x_1)$ as a function of embedding delay D for $L = 6$, a 3×10^2 ns time series with 6×10^4 data points is used. The parameters are given as $b = 4.5$, $\Phi = -\pi/4$, $\tau = 25$ ps, $\theta = 5$ μs, and $T = (22, 22, 22)$ ns (light color line), $T = (22, 28, 34)$ ns (darker line)*

First, we focus on the influence of the bifurcate parameters b at the level of security for TDS suppression. Figures 13.15–13.17 show the size of the peaks found in $ACF(x_1)$, $DMI(x_1)$, and $H(x_1)$ at relevant TDs ($T_1, T_2, T_3, T_1 + T_2, T_1 + T_3, T_2 + T_3$, and $T_1 + T_2 + T_3$) as a function of the bifurcate parameter b. As shown in Figure 13.15, the peaks are distinguishable in $ACF(x_1)$ when b is small. When b grows to a threshold of about 3.5, the peaks are unapparent from the background, that is, the TDS is suppressed. Similar results can be obtained by using DMI, the thresholds of b for TDS suppression is 2.5, as shown in Figure 13.16.

The background Q_{ACF}, and Q_{DMI} in the $ACF(x_1)$ and $DMI(x_1)$ are defined as

$$
\begin{cases}
Q_{ACF} = \left[\underline{p}_{ACF}(b), \overline{p}_{ACF}(b) \right] \\[2mm]
\underline{p}_{ACF}(b) = \mathrm{mean}\{ACF(x_b) - SD(ACF(x_b))\} \\[2mm]
\overline{p}_{ACF}(b) = \mathrm{mean}\{ACF(x_b) + SD(ACF(x_b))\} \\[2mm]
Q_{DMI} = \left[\underline{p}_{DMI}(b), \overline{p}_{DMI}(b) \right] \\[2mm]
\underline{p}_{DMI}(b) = \mathrm{mean}\{DMI(x_b) - SD(DMI(x_b))\} \\[2mm]
\overline{p}_{DMI}(b) = \mathrm{mean}\{DMI(x_b) + SD(DMI(x_b))\}
\end{cases}
\tag{13.10}
$$

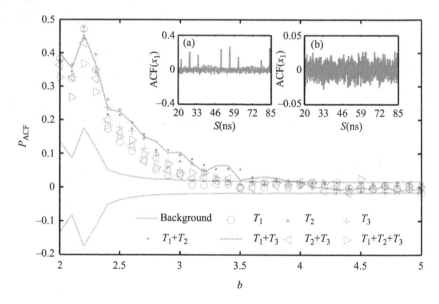

Figure 13.15   *Value of the peak in $ACF(x_1)$ at $S = T_1, T_2, T_3, T_1 + T_2, T_1 + T_3$, $T_2 + T_3$, and $T_1 + T_2 + T_3$ for increasing the bifurcate parameter b, $\Phi = -\pi/4$, $\tau = 25$ ps, $\theta = 5$ μs. A 1.25×10^3 ns time series with 2.5×10^5 data points is used. Insets (a) and (b), the $ACF(x_1)$ for $b = 2.6$ and $b = 4.5$*

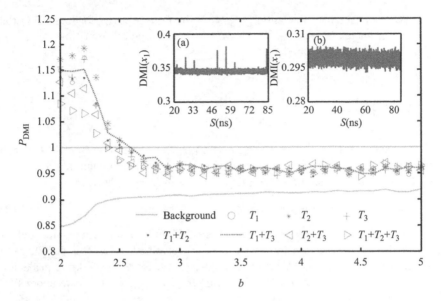

Figure 13.16   *Value of the peak in DMI(x_1) at S = $T_1, T_2, T_3, T_1 + T_2$, b,*
Φ = −π/4, τ = 25 ps, θ = 5 μs. A 1.25 × 10³ ns time series with
2.5 × 10⁵ data points is used. Insets (a) and (b), the ACF(x_1) for
b = 2.6 and b = 4.5

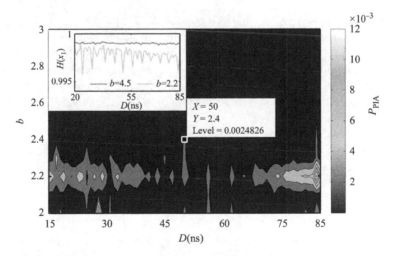

Figure 13.17   *Peak value under PIA for increasing the bifurcate parameter b,*
Φ = −π/4, τ = 25 ps, θ = 5 μs. A 3 × 10² ns time series with
6 × 10⁴ data points is used. Inset, the PE H(x_1) for b = 2.2 (light
color line) and b = 4.5 (darker line)

where *SD* is the standard deviation [17]. x_b is the time series x_1 for increasing the bifurcate parameter *b*. $ACF(x_b)$ and $DMI(x_b)$ are computed from time series x_b. And the peaks size are defined as

$$\begin{cases} P_{ACF}(b) = ACF(x_b) \\ P_{DMI}(b) = \dfrac{DMI(x_b)}{DMI(x_b) - SD(DMI(x_b))} \end{cases} \tag{13.11}$$

at the relevant TDs $(T_1, T_2, T_3, T_1 + T_2, T_1 + T_3, T_2 + T_3$ and $T_1 + T_2 + T_3)$ for each *b*. The detailed conditions for TDS concealment against the permutation information analysis (PIA) are also studied. And the peaks size in $H(x_1)$ is defined as

$$P_{PIA}(b) = |H(x_b, D) - \text{mean}(H(x_b))| \tag{13.12}$$

where $\text{mean}(H(x_b))$ is the mean value of the PE for different embedding delays $(D = 15\text{–}85)$, x_b denotes the time series x_1 for a given *b*, $H(x_b, D)$ is the PE for a given embedding delay *D*. As shown in Figure 13.17, for $b = 2\text{–}2.4$, the peaks are distinguishable (red line for $b = 2.2$ in the inset). For larger *b*, it is safe under PIA (blue line for $b = 4.5$ in the inset).

Then we consider the influence of the minimum interval δ between different delays. If δ is too small, the differences between different delays can be seen as a minor perturbation to the same delay value, which will certainly cause the leak of the TDS. The results are similar to the phenomenon shown in Figure 13.14 when three TDs are the same.

Here we set $T_2 = 22$ ns, T_1 and T_3 are set as $T_1 = T_2 - \delta$, $T_3 = T_2 + \delta$, respectively. Then we increase δ from 0 to 45 ps, and the largest peak sizes near the relevant TD T_2 in ACF, DMI, and PIA are calculated. As shown in Figure 13.18, the threshold of δ for TDS suppression in ACF is 15 ps, which means there is no peak in the range of T_1–T_3 when $\delta > 15$ ps. As for the DMI and PIA, the threshold of δ is much smaller, even a difference of $\delta = 5$ ps will cause the failure of the attack strategy, as shown in Figure 13.18(b) and (c).

Therefore, we can draw the conclusion that if the bifurcate parameter $b \geq 3.6$, $T_i \neq T_j$, $i \neq j$, $i, j = 1, 2, 3$, and $\delta \geq 15$ ps, the TDS will be completely suppressed under ACF, DMI, and PIA. Similar results (not plotted here) can be obtained from the time series x_2 and x_3.

13.4.5 Synchronization scheme

With the TDS suppressed, the proposed chaotic system could be used in secure communication. Here we give a chaotic synchronization scheme by adopting wave division multiplex technology.

The schematic of the synchronization system is shown in Figure 13.19. The system components are similar to those in Figure 13.12. At the transmitter side, two message signals $m_1(t)$ and $m_2(t)$ are injected into the first and the second EO chain, respectively. The two messages are masked by the chaotic carriers with different wavelengths and sent into the same optical fiber channel by using a wavelength division

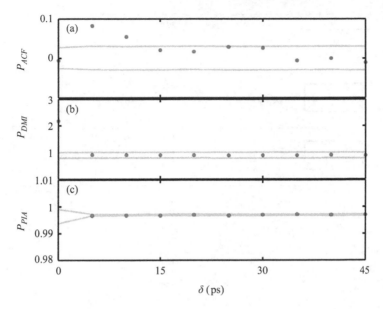

Figure 13.18 *Value of the largest peak size in (a) ACF(x₁), (b) DMI(x₁), and*
(c) H(x₁) in the range T₁–T₃ for increasing δ, Φ = −π/4, τ = 25 ps,
θ = 5 μs. A 1.25 × 10³ ns time series with 2.5 × 10⁵ data points is
used

multiplexer. At the receiver side, an open loop system is designed according to the
emitter. The two encrypted signals are separated by a demultiplexer and injected into
the loop. The original messages $m_1(t)$ and $m_2(t)$ are then recovered with a propagation
delay T_C. The corresponding mathematical model of Figure 13.19 can be written as
follows.

Transmitter side:

$$
\begin{cases}
x_1 + \tau_1 \dfrac{dx_1}{dt} + \dfrac{1}{\theta_1} \displaystyle\int_0^t x_1(s)\,ds \\[2mm]
\quad = b_1 \cos^2(x_2(t - T_1) + x_3(t - T_1) + \Phi_1) + m_1(t - T_1) \\[4mm]
x_2 + \tau_2 \dfrac{dx_2}{dt} + \dfrac{1}{\theta_2} \displaystyle\int_0^t x_2(s)\,ds \\[2mm]
\quad = b_2 \cos^2(x_1(t - T_2) + x_3(t - T_2) + \Phi_2) + m_2(t - T_2) \\[4mm]
x_3 + \tau_3 \dfrac{dx_3}{dt} + \dfrac{1}{\theta_3} \displaystyle\int_0^t x_3(s)\,ds \\[2mm]
\quad = b_3 \cos^2(x_2(t - T_3) + x_1(t - T_3) + \Phi_3)
\end{cases}
\tag{13.13}
$$

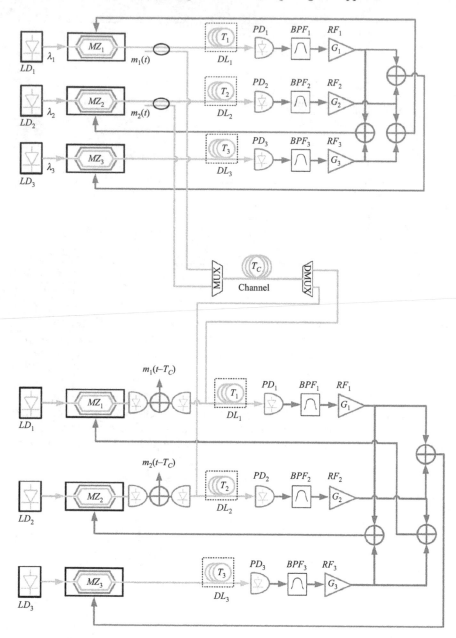

Figure 13.19   The schematic of the secure communication system on the basis of the proposed chaos system. The devices are similar to those used in Figure 13.12

Receiver side:

$$
\left\{
\begin{aligned}
& y_1 + \tau_1 \frac{dy_1}{dt} + \frac{1}{\theta_1} \int_0^t y_1(s)ds \\
& = b_1 \cos^2(x_2(t - T_1 - T_c) + x_3(t - T_1 - T_c) + \Phi_1) + m_1(t - T_1 - T_c) \\
& y_2 + \tau_2 \frac{dy_2}{dt} + \frac{1}{\theta_2} \int_0^t y_2(s)ds \\
& = b_2 \cos^2(x_1(t - T_2 - T_c) + x_3(t - T_2 - T_c) + \Phi_2) + m_2(t - T_2 - T_c) \\
& y_3 + \tau_3 \frac{dy_3}{dt} + \frac{1}{\theta_3} \int_0^t y_3(s)ds \\
& = b_3 \cos^2(y_2(t - T_3) + y_1(t - T_3) + \Phi_3)
\end{aligned}
\right.
\tag{13.14}
$$

According to (13.13) and (13.14), the synchronization manifold $y_i \rightarrow x_i(t - T_C)$, $i = 1, 2, 3$ can be obtained. From the schematic of the system, the decrypted messages $m_{R1}(t)$ and $m_{R2}(t)$ can be written as

$$
\left\{
\begin{aligned}
m_{R1}(t) & = b_1 \cos^2(x_2(t - T_c) + x_3(t - T_c) + \Phi_1) + m_1(t - T_c) \\
& \quad - b_1 \cos^2 y_2(t) + y_3(t) + \Phi_{(1)} \\
m_{R2}(t) & = b_2 \cos^2(x_1(t - T_c) + x_3(t - T_c) + \Phi_1) + m_2(t - T_c) \\
& \quad - b_2 \cos^2 y_1(t) + y_3(t) + \Phi_{(2)}
\end{aligned}
\right.
\tag{13.15}
$$

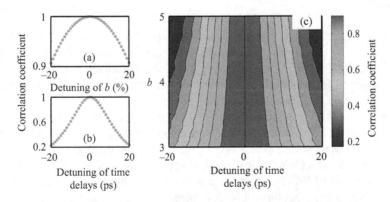

Figure 13.20   (a) Influence of the feedback strength detuning on the synchronization. (b) Influence of the time-delays detuning on the synchronization. (c) Influence of the feedback strength b on the sensitivity of the time-delays

Considering the synchronization manifold and (13.15), we can obtain

$$m_{R1}(t) \rightarrow m_1(t - T_c), m_{R2}(t) \rightarrow m_2(t - T_c) \tag{13.16}$$

Thus means the original messages can be recovered with a constant delay T_C.

From the secure communication point of view, the robustness of the synchronization and the sensitive dependence on the secret key are both significant issues. The secret key (parameter) should be sensitive enough to resist the attack. However, the need for synchronization allows for a certain degree of parameter detuning. Figure 13.20 presents the correlation coefficient of $x_1(t - T_C)$ and $y_1(t)$ as a function of the detuning of feedback strength and TDs. Without losing generality, we assume that the three TDs are detuned simultaneously. As shown in Figure 13.20(a), when the detuning of b grows to 20%, high-quality synchronization (correlation coefficient > 0.9) can still be achieved. As for the detuning of TDs, even a mismatch of 20 ps will cause the synchronization quality degrade seriously (correlation coefficient $= 0.2$), as shown in Figure 13.20(b).

These results indicate that the synchronization is very robust to feedback strength detuning, but very sensitive to TD. According to the literature [27], the detuning of the feedback strength is mainly caused by environmental changes of the channel that is basically uncontrollable. However, the mismatch of the T can be maintained at a very low degree due to the technology of variable optical delay line (the precision of a commercial use tunable optical delay line product could be up to several femtoseconds). Moreover, the sensitivity of TDs is slightly affected by the feedback strength. A larger b results in a higher sensitiveness to the TDs, as shown in Figure 13.20(c). Therefore, the synchronization scheme is both secure and feasible in real world applications.

References

[1]   Capeáns R, Sabuco J, Sanjuán MA, *et al.* Partially controlling transient chaos in the Lorenz equations. Philosophical Transactions. 2017;375(2088):20160211.

[2]   Tang WKS, and Danca M. Emulating "chaos + chaos = order" in Chen's circuit of fractional order by parameter switching. International Journal of Bifurcation & Chaos. 2016;26(06):1650096.

[3]   Kennedy MP. Three steps to chaos. I. Evolution. IEEE Transactions on Circuits & Systems I: Fundamental Theory & Applications. 1993;40(10):640–656.

[4]   Thukral MK, Sherpa KS, and Garg K. Application of Analog Electronic Circuits in Secure Communication: A Review. In: Janyani V, Tiwari M, Singh G, and Minzioni P. (eds.), Optical and Wireless Technologies. Lecture Notes in Electrical Engineering, vol. 472. Singapore: Springer; 2018.

[5]   Chow TWS, Feng JC, and Ng KT. An adaptive demodulator for the chaotic modulation communication system with RBF neural network. IEEE Transactions on Circuits & Systems I Fundamental Theory & Applications. 2002;47(6): 902–909.

[6] Wang T, Zhao S, Zhou W, *et al.* Finite-time master-slave synchronization and parameter identification for uncertain Lurie systems. ISA Transactions. 2014;53(4):1184–1190.

[7] Pecora LM, and Carroll TL. Synchronization in chaotic systems. Controlling Chaos. 1996;6(08):142–145.

[8] Banerjee S. Chaos Synchronization and Cryptography for Secure Communications: Applications for Encryption. Hershey PA: IGI Global; 2011.

[9] Sushchik M, Tsimring LS, and Volkovskii AR. Performance analysis of correlation-based communication schemes utilizing chaos. IEEE Transactions on Circuits & Systems I: Fundamental Theory & Applications. 2000; 47(12):1684–1691.

[10] Dedieu H, Kennedy MP, and Hasler M. Chaos shift keying: Modulation and demodulation of chaotic carrier using self-synchronizing Chua's circuits. IEEE Transactions on Circuits & Systems II: Analog & Digital Signal Processing. 2002;40(10):634–642.

[11] Puebla H, and Alvarez-Ramirez J. Stability of inverse-system approaches in coherent chaotic communication. IEEE Transactions on Circuits & Systems I: Fundamental Theory & Applications. 2001;48(12):1413–1423.

[12] Zhao Q, and Yin H. Performance analysis of orthogonal optical chaotic division multiplexing utilizing semiconductor lasers. Optics & Laser Technology. 2013;47(4):208–213.

[13] Sun J, Shen Y, Yin Q, *et al.* Compound synchronization of four memristor chaotic oscillator systems and secure communication. Chaos. 2013;23(1): 821–12.

[14] Vicente R, Dauden J, Colet P, *et al.* Analysis and characterization of the hyperchaos generated by a semiconductor laser subject to a delay feedback loop. IEEE Journal of Quantum Electronics. 2005;41(4):541–548.

[15] Farmer JD. Chaotic attractors of an infinite-dimensional dynamical system. Physica D: Nonlinear Phenomena. 1982;4(3):366–393.

[16] Erueux T, Larger L, Lee MW, and Goedgebuer, J-P. Ikeda Hopf bifurcation revisited. Physica D: Nonlinear Phenomena. 2004;194(1):49–64.

[17] Cohen AB, Bhargava R, Murphy TE, *et al.* Using synchronization for prediction of high-dimensional chaotic dynamics. Physical Review Letters. 2008;101(15):154102.

[18] Larger L. Complexity in electro-optic delay dynamics: Modelling, design and applications. Philosophical Transactions. Series A, Mathematical, Physical, and Engineering. 2013;371(1999):20120464.

[19] Apostolos A, Dimitris S, Laurent L, *et al.* Chaos-based communications at high bit rates using commercial fibre-optic links. Nature. 2005;438(7066):343–6.

[20] Romain Modeste N, Pere C, Laurent L, *et al.* Digital key for chaos communication performing time delay concealment. Physical Review Letters. 2011;107(3):034103.

[21] Mengfan C, Lei D, Hao L, *et al.* Enhanced secure strategy for electro-optic chaotic systems with delayed dynamics by using fractional Fourier transformation. Optics Express. 2014;22(5):5241–5251.

[22]   Romain Modeste N, Guy V, Jan D, *et al.* Loss of time-delay signature in chaotic semiconductor ring lasers. Optics Letters. 2012;37(13):2541–2543.

[23]   Udaltsov VS, Goedgebuer JP, Larger L, *et al.* Cracking chaos-based encryption systems ruled by nonlinear time delay differential equations. Physics Letters A. 2003;308(1):54–60.

[24]   Prokhorov MD, Ponomarenko VI, Karavaev AS, *et al.* Reconstruction of time-delayed feedback systems from time series. Physica D: Nonlinear Phenomena. 2005;203(3):209–223.

[25]   Bünner MJ, Meyer T, Kittel A, *et al.* Recovery of the time-evolution equation of time-delay systems from time series. Physical Review E, Statistical Physics Plasmas Fluids & Related Interdisciplinary Topics. 1997;56(5):5083–5089.

[26]   Rontani D, Locquet A, Sciamanna M, *et al.* Time-delay identification in a chaotic semiconductor laser with optical feedback: A dynamical point of view. IEEE Journal of Quantum Electronics. 2009;45(7):879–1891.

[27]   Cheng M, Gao X, Lei D, *et al.* Time-delay concealment in a three-dimensional electro-optic chaos system. IEEE Photonics Technology Letters. 2015;27(9):1030–1033.

[28]   Hizanidis J, Deligiannidis S, Bogris A, *et al.* Enhancement of chaos encryption potential by combining all-optical and electrooptical chaos generators. IEEE Journal of Quantum Electronics. 2010;46(11):1642–1649.

[29]   Gao X, Cheng M, Deng L, *et al.* A novel chaotic system with suppressed time-delay signature based on multiple electro-optic nonlinear loops. Nonlinear Dynamics. 2015;82(1):1–7.

Index

Printed in the USA
CPSIA information can be obtained
at www.ICGtesting.com
JSHW011509221024
72173JS00005B/1247